W9-BNP-871

Global Powers in the 21st Century

A WASHINGTON QUARTERLY READER

Global Powers in the 21st Century

STRATEGIES AND RELATIONS

EDITED BY

ALEXANDER T. J. LENNON
AND AMANDA KOZLOWSKI

The contents of this book were first published in *The Washington Quarterly* (ISSN 0163-660X), a publication of The MIT Press under the sponsorship of The Center for Strategic and International Studies (CSIS). Except as otherwise noted, copyright in each article is owned jointly by the Massachusetts Institute of Technology and CSIS. No article may be reproduced in whole or in part except with the express written permission of The MIT Press.

George Perkovich "Is India a Major Power?" *TWQ* 27, no. 1 (Winter 2004); C. Raja Mohan, "Balancing Interests and Values: India's Struggle with Democracy Promotion," *TWQ* 30, no. 3 (Summer 2007); Teresita C. Schaffer, "Building a New Partnership with India," *TWQ* 25, no. 2 (Spring 2002); Xenia Dormandy, "Is India, or Will It Be, a Responsible International Stakeholder?" *TWQ* 30, no. 3 (Summer 2007); Robert Sutter, "Why Does China Matter?" *TWQ* 27, no. 1 (Winter 2004); Evan A. Feigenbaum, "China's Challenge to *Pax Americana*," *TWQ* 24, no. 3 (Summer 2001); Yong Deng and Thomas G. Moore, "China Views Globalization: Toward a New Great-Power Politics?" *TWQ* 27, no. 3 (Summer 2004); Wu Xinbo, "The Promise and Limitations of a Sino-U.S. Partnership," *TWQ* 27, no. 4 (Autumn 2004); David Shambaugh, "The New Strategic Triangle: U.S. and European Reactions to China's Rise," *TWQ* 28, no. 3 (Summer 2005); Zbigniew Brzezinski, "Putin's Choice," *TWQ* 31, no. 2 (Spring 2008); Clifford G. Gaddy and Andrew C. Kuchins, "Putin's Plan," *TWQ* 31, no. 2 (Spring 2008); Celeste A. Wallander, "Russian Transimperialism and Its Implications," *TWQ* 30, no. 2 (Spring 2007); Dmitri Trenin, "Russia Redefines Itself and Its Relations with the West," *TWQ* 30, no. 2 (Spring 2007); Sarah E. Mendelson and Theodore P. Gerber, "Us and Them: Anti-American Views of the Putin Generation," *TWQ* 31, no. 2 (Spring 2008); Robert E. Hunter, "Europe's Leverage," *TWQ* 27, no. 1 (Winter 2004); Timothy M. Savage, "Europe and Islam: Crescent Waxing, Cultures Clashing," *TWQ* 27, no. 3 (Summer 2004); Gideon Rachman, "The Death of Enlargement," *TWQ* 29, no. 3 (Summer 2006); Robin Niblett, "Europe Inside Out," *TWQ* 29, no. 1 (Winter 2006); Franco Algieri, "A Weakened EU's Prospects for Global Leadership," *TWQ* 30, no. 1 (Winter 2007); Edward J. Lincoln, "Japan: Using Power Narrowly," *TWQ* 27, no. 1 (Winter 2004); Richard J. Samuels, "Japan's Goldilocks Strategy," *TWQ* 29, no. 4 (Autumn 2006); Akio Watanabe, "A Continuum of Change," *TWQ* 27, no. 4 (Autumn 2004); Michael J. Green, "U.S.-Japanese Relations: Convergence or Cooling?" *TWQ* 29, no. 4 (Autumn 2006).

Selection and introduction, copyright © 2008 by The Center for Strategic and International Studies and the Massachusetts Institute of Technology.

MIT Press books may be purchased at special quantity discounts for business or sales promotional use. For information, please email special_sales@mitpress.mit.edu or write to Special Sales Department, The MIT Press, 55 Hayward Street, Cambridge, MA 02142.

This book was set in Goudy Old Style BT and Humanist 521 BT by MHz Editorial Services and was printed and bound in the United States of America.

Library of Congress Cataloging-in-Publication Data

Global powers in the 21st century : strategies and relations / edited by Alexander T.J. Lennon and Amanda Kozlowski.
    p.   cm. — (A Washington quarterly reader)
    Includes bibliographical references.
    ISBN 978-0-262-62218-9 (pbk. : alk. paper)
    1. Balance of power—Forecasting. 2. World Politics. I. Lennon, Alexander T.J., 1969– II. Kozlowski, Amanda, 1985–

JZ1313.G56 2008
327.1'12—dc22

2008019735

CONTENTS

Alexander T. J. Lennon and Amanda Kozlowski

Introduction: Concert or Clash of Global Powers in the 21st Century?

Unlike previous eras, the contemporary international system contains no major contests of territory or ideology among the major powers. At the same time, new threats such as terrorism, disease, climate change, and the spread of weapons of mass destruction gives all of the major powers a stake in maintaining stability and spreading peace and security.[1] Global cooperation under these conditions is both a unique opportunity and an imperative.

Even before the war in Iraq, among other events, undermined visions of a unipolar world, the 2002 National Security Strategy defined two priorities for the United States: "pursuing American interests within cooperative relationships," and "preventing the reemergence of the great power rivalries that divided the world in previous eras."[2] As this document notes, the absence of fundamental conflict between the great powers is unusual in historical terms, presenting an opportunity for strategic planners and policymakers.

Although the United States remains unchallenged in many elements of its power, particularly military and economic, a post–Iraq war emphasis on multilateralism in foreign affairs has grown in the United States and

---

Alexander T. J. Lennon is editor-in-chief of *The Washington Quarterly* and a research fellow in international security policy at the Center for Strategic and International Studies (CSIS). He is also an adjunct professor in security studies at Georgetown University. Amanda Kozlowski is the associate editor of *The Washington Quarterly*.

---

throughout the world. Through the 2008 campaign, presidential candidates on both sides of the aisle emphasized the necessity of alliances, partnerships, and institutions.[3] Meanwhile, Prime Minister Gordon Brown of the United Kingdom advocates "hard-headed internationalism" to jointly achieve concrete results to global problems.[4]

The rise of new global powers has created a dynamic geopolitical landscape. How China and India rise, how Russia reemerges, how Europe consolidates its experiment in shared sovereignty, how Japan chooses to define its international identity—and how the United States reacts to these developments—will shape the international system and the nature of international relations in the coming years. The newcomers and established players will naturally view one another with suspicion, but will also need to work together to address common threats and challenges more effectively.

Given this blend of competition and cooperation, can the world avoid a return to great-power politics? This feat is not without precedent. In the nineteenth century, the Concert of Europe successfully achieved a balance of power and avoided major war for several decades. More recently, the United States and the Soviet Union used implied understandings on the avoidance of nuclear conflict or direct armed intervention to steer clear of a major clash.

A twenty-first century concert of the great powers would be fundamental to maintaining peace and spreading security, but how feasible is it? Beginning to find the answer to that question lies in understanding the domestic politics within other contemporary major countries, the sources of their national power, changes after 9/11, their relations with the United States, adjustments to globalization, their vision for the world, and the ends that they seek with their growing power. By analyzing India, China, Russia, the European Union, and Japan in today's world, this book hopes to shed light on these key issues.

In Part One, experts evaluate whether India is already a contemporary great power, assessing New Delhi's key interests, values, and relationships which will affect its global rise. George Perkovich of the Carnegie Endowment for International Peace reasons that India has just enough power to resist the influence of others, but must still make great strides before it can attain significant power over other states and thus in the international system at large. Looking forward, C. Raja Mohan asks whether promoting democracy abroad will become a more important natural component of Indian foreign policy as many in the West hope. Considering its capabilities, will, interests, and values, India would seem to make an ideal U.S. partner in Asia and even globally. Yet, according to Ambassador Teresita C. Schaffer, the future of the U.S.-Indian relationship is not a comprehensive alliance, but a selective partnership based on specific, common goals. Finally, Harvard's Xenia Dormandy, former director for South Asia at the National Security Council, gauges whether India will live up to the U.S. definition of a "responsible stakeholder" in the international system.

Part Two looks at the rise of China, and the increasingly complex U.S.-Chinese relationship, with an emphasis on nationalism, Japan, military relations, energy, and strategic hedging. Based on its size, strategic location, and rising economic and military power, China already exerts worldwide economic influence and is the leading regional military and political power in Asia. Yet, Georgetown University professor Robert Sutter argues that Chinese leaders are not inclined to assert influence in world affairs more forcefully. The next two chapters present contrasting visions of China's role in the world. Evan A. Feigenbaum looks back to the 1996 missile exercise in the Taiwan Strait. Since then, Chinese leaders have begun to articulate a decidedly alternative vision of the underlying principles of international relations that could continue to create tensions with the United States. According to Yong Deng and Thomas G. Moore, however, China's strategic choices increasingly seek to use globalization as a way to make China rich and strong, reduce international fears of its rising material power, and transform great-power politics to a more cooperative form of interstate competition that increases prospects for China's peaceful rise.

The final two pieces assess China's relationship with the West. Fudan University's Wu Xinbo reasons that terrorism has introduced a new focus to Chinese foreign policy and an opportunity to improve relations with the United States. The subsequent orientation and narrow focus of U.S. foreign policy, including Iraq, however, has aroused strong Chinese concern, constraining the emerging partnership. David Shambaugh, director of George Washington University's China Policy Program, concludes the section by expanding the discussion from bilateral relations to a new strategic triangle. He argues that, although the United States and Europe share similar views on many aspects of China's place in the international community, they differ over their perceptions of global order, China's rise, and the resources devoted to analyzing China. Greater dialogue and coordination among all three are overdue.

As if the rise of India and China were not complicated enough, the Kremlin has recently reasserted its global significance with a vengeance. Part Three presents international perspectives on Moscow's emerging strategy and how the West should respond. Zbigniew Brzezinski considers how history will judge Vladimir Putin. He argues that Putin's decisions, despite their apparent short-term success, are likely to have negative long-term effects on the Russian political system, economy, and geopolitical prospects. The Brookings Institution's Clifford G. Gaddy and CSIS's Andrew C. Kuchins then delve into the roots of Putin's plan for Russia, finding that the roots of the strategy lie not in Marxism-Leninism, but in Western business theory. True to these roots, in March 2008 Putin orchestrated the election of a new president, Dmitry Medvedev, to succeed him as strategic planner, or the CEO of "Russia Inc.," who will continue to seek domestic and international stability.

Next, Georgetown University professor Celeste A. Wallander looks beyond the debate over whether Russia is a postimperial power that seeks global cooperation or a neoimperial one that seeks to control weaker countries. Rather, Russian strategy is shaped by modern, or transnational, and imperialist causes. In other words, she argues it is a new, transimperialist power requiring new strategies. Deputy Director of the Carnegie Moscow Center Dmitri Trenin, furthermore, contends that Russia does not crave world domination and that its leaders do not dream of restoring the Soviet Union, but they do plan to rebuild Russia as a great power with global reach, organized as a supercorporation. From Moscow's perspective, Russian-Western relations are competitive but not antagonistic. To conclude, Sarah E. Mendelson and Theodore P. Gerber look beyond the focus on Putin the individual to discover an important political and social development inside Russia: a new, young generation that now reflects his values, favoring to restore a hypersovereign Russia and to resist or reject international legal norms.

Part Four considers Europe's evolving power, beginning with the 2005 French and Dutch rejections of the EU constitution, apparently at least temporarily ending European enlargement. Can it stabilize its periphery without the carrot of enlargement? Robert E. Hunter, a senior adviser at RAND and former ambassador to NATO, argues that much of what the United States seeks to do elsewhere in the world will depend on its ability to gain the support and active engagement of European power—and European powers—politically, economically, and militarily. Delving into Europe's internal politics, career U.S. foreign service officer Timothy M. Savage warns that if Europe and its Muslim communities fail to reach an accommodation, increased social strife, national retrenchment, and potentially significant civil conflict are likely to overwhelm the vision of a continent that is whole, free, and united.

The potential death of the EU enlargement process, however, is a huge blow to the goals of spreading prosperity and democracy in Europe, concludes the *Financial Times'* Gideon Rachman. Despite the French and Dutch votes, he argues that the prospect of membership has still not completely lost its potency to spur reform, but the risk is that all parties involved might suffer a bitter disillusionment in the end. On the other hand, Chatham House director Robin Niblett contends that the constitutional crisis may actually strengthen the EU and increase its global engagement over the next decade by recalibrating the drivers of European integration from economics to the search for common foreign policies and closer cooperation on issues of domestic security. Finally, on the international stage, Franco Algieri asserts that, although the EU is still a world champion in trade policy and development aid, it is in danger of becoming an irrelevant power in light of the French and Dutch rejections of the constitution.

Part Five considers the other major power that is a U.S. treaty ally: Japan and its strategic challenges in its quest to once again become a normal nation. Analyst Edward J. Lincoln finds that Tokyo has used economic and other nonmilitary sources of power at its disposal to meet Japan's immediate needs. Yet, Japan does not have its own seat at the table of international policymaking, so its interests have remained more limited.

MIT professor Richard J. Samuels delves into the emerging debate he sees within Japan between those who would construct a national identity for it as a great or middle power, defining its role in regional or global terms, and those who would seek to emphasize balancing Japan's relations neither too close to nor too far from Beijing and Washington. Will any of them gain consensus support in Tokyo? Continuing the domestic debate, Research Institute for Peace and Security president Akio Watanabe presents the viewpoint that, outside the United States, among the most significant effects of the September 11 terrorist attacks are the realignment of today's major powers and a larger global international security role for Japan, including a transformed military posture.

Finally, focusing on the U.S.-Japanese relationship, former National Security Council senior director Michael J. Green asks if personal connections between Bush and recent Japanese leaders mask underlying areas of divergence between the two nations. His look at bilateral relations between these leaders, Japan's external threat environment, common values, and economic relations gives some insight into relations ahead.

How these major powers continue to evolve, redefining themselves and their role in the world, and how the next U.S. administration treats the dynamic changes within and among these great powers will have a major bearing on the shape of the international system to come. By presenting U.S. and international perspectives on each major power's domestic politics, sources of national power, changes after 9/11, relations with the United States, adjustments to globalization, and vision for the world, *Global Powers in the 21st Century* gives readers an in-depth look at how that world might develop.

Notes

1. See Richard Haass, *The Opportunity: America's Moment to Alter History's Course* (New York: PublicAffairs, 2005), p. 21.

2. "National Security Strategy of the United States of America," September 2002, http://www.whitehouse.gov/nsc/nss.pdf.

3. Hillary Clinton, "Security and Opportunity for the 21st Century," *Foreign Affairs* 86, no. 6 (November/December 2007): 2–18; John Edwards, "Reengaging With the World," *Foreign Affairs* 86, no. 5 (September/October 2007): 19–36; Rudolph W. Giuliani, "Toward a Realistic Peace," *Foreign Affairs* 86, no. 5 (September/October 2007): 2–18; John McCain, "An Enduring Peace Built on Freedom," *Foreign Affairs*

86, no. 6 (November/December 2007): 19–35; Barack Obama, "Renewing American Leadership," *Foreign Affairs* 86, no. 4 (July/August 2007): 2–16; Mitt Romney, "Rising to a New Generation of Global Challenges," *Foreign Affairs* 86, no. 4 (July/August 2007): 17–32.

4. Gordon Brown, "Lord Mayor's Banquet Speech," November 12, 2007, http://www.number-10.gov.uk/output/Page13736.asp.

Part I:
Does India Belong?

George Perkovich

Is India a Major Power?

Kenneth Waltz provided a useful, colloquial definition of power as the "extent that [one] affects others more than they affect [oneself]." A state's power can thus be understood as a combination of its capacity to influence others to behave as it wants them to and, conversely, to resist the unwelcome influence of others.[1] India today lacks great power in that, for the most part, it cannot make other important states comply with Indian demands. Nor can India obtain all that it desires in the international arena. It cannot compel or persuade technology suppliers to ignore nonproliferation strictures and supply new power reactors to the country, nor can it alone win preferred trade terms in World Trade Organization (WTO) negotiations. India cannot persuade others to isolate Pakistan and probably cannot gain a permanent seat on the United Nations Security Council in the foreseeable future. Yet, India does have the capacity to resist most if not all demands placed upon it by other states, including the recognized major powers.

Like any state, India's capacity to affect others and to resist undesired influence results from the country's various forms of hard and soft power. These forms of power include military strength, social cohesion and mobilization, economic resources, technological capacity, qual-

---

George Perkovich is vice president for studies at the Carnegie Endowment for International Peace, in Washington, D.C., and author of *India's Nuclear Bomb*.

Copyright © 2003 by The Center for Strategic and International Studies and the Massachusetts Institute of Technology
The Washington Quarterly • 27:1 pp. 129–144.

ity of governance, and diplomatic and intelligence acumen. A careful analysis of India in each of these realms confirms that the country has just enough power to resist the influence of others but must still make great strides before it can attain significant power over other states and thus in the international system at large. Yet, India is home to so many people that achieving socioeconomic development and internal peace through democratic means would be a great global triumph. India is more populous and diverse than the United States, Canada, Mexico, Central America, South America, France, Germany, and the United Kingdom combined. Getting India "right" would be a manifestation of great global power; failing to meet the aspirations of India's citizenry would consign India to the world's middle ranks.

Socioeconomic Indicators

The material well-being and productivity of a society sets the conditions for its international power. A poor, conflicted society will lack global muscle or respect. A prospering one will command resources and authority to make others pay it heed.

A country's per capita gross domestic product (GDP) is a useful indicator of its socioeconomic health and prospects. A relatively low GDP for a country typically indicates that its citizens have many unfulfilled longings and aspirations for basic socioeconomic goods, which in turn establishes priorities and major challenges for its government. The governments of poor countries must scramble for resources to meet basic needs and stem social discontent that can threaten internal order. Such governments are pleaders for international assistance more than positive influencers of global affairs. Simply put, states with low per capita GDP struggle to translate their aggregate productivity into effective international power. Ranking near the bottom of per capita GDP comparisons of regional and global powers, India's estimated 2002 per capita GDP was $2,540, measured in purchasing power parity (PPP) (the value of goods and services that could be bought in the United States with the dollar equivalent of the Indian per capita GDP). In 2002, China's per capita GDP was $4,600, and Brazil's was $7,600. The

Indian government, therefore, still faces the great challenge of mobilizing the Indian population to achieve significant domestic objectives. This is a precondition for wielding economic, political, or military power in shaping the direction of the international system.

Other measures help evaluate states' socioeconomic health and prospects. The UN Human Development Index (HDI) provides an additional means for evaluating states' socioeconomic status by assessing how states meet their citizens' basic needs, which in turn affects current and potential economic productivity. The HDI is composed of four variables: life expectancy at birth, adult literacy rate, school enrollment, and GDP per capita (PPP in U.S. dollars). India ranks 115 out of 162 countries for which data were available. In comparison, India's National Security Council Secretariat uses a variant of this index called the Population Index, which takes a country's population and multiplies it by its HDI coefficient, with the aim of adjusting the ranking of a state's population to take into account the development (including life expectancy, literacy, and education) of that population. By this index, India ranks second, behind China and two positions ahead of the United States. Despite its low per capita GDP, India has enjoyed a sound growth rate over the last decade, with an average 5.9 percent increase in annual GDP growth since 1992–1993. The rate of poverty alleviation, however, has been only a bit more than 1 percent per year.

A 2002 study by World Bank economist Martin Ravallion explains that India's economic growth, which has largely been driven by services, has not significantly helped alleviate poverty because the bulk of India's poor live in rural villages that depend on agriculture, which lags behind the overall level of economic growth.[2] India's decade of improved economic growth has occurred chiefly in regions that are already better off, while the poorest parts of the country have experienced the least growth and development. Yet even within the rural sector, some regions utilize what little economic growth there is to lower poverty while others do not.

To achieve the level of economic development that can raise the quality of life of all Indians, especially the poor, the nation must average at least 7–8 percent annual growth during the next decade.[3] Attaining such desired levels of growth requires the Indian government, at the national and state levels, to provide the infrastructural, health, and educational resources necessary to improve the capacities of the 25 percent of Indians who remain impoverished. Indian states with programs that effectively promote literacy and health care, especially for women, reportedly experience higher rates of economic growth. States with higher-quality rural roads, irrigation, and other infrastructure also have higher rates of per capita GDP. Unfortunately, according to Ravallion, no state in India has developed good rural infrastructure and human resource programs.[4] Few challenges, therefore, are as important to India's power potential as rural development.

Education should also improve a society's prospects for increasing economic productivity. Here, India seems bifurcated. It possesses world-class scientific and technological education institutions but still has a vast undereducated population. The Indian Institutes of Technology graduate a large number of engineers, programmers, and technicians who drive India's and, through emigration, the world's information technology sectors. The Indian Institute of Sciences and other higher education institutions have produced thousands of top-class scientists, earning India recognition as a world-class player in at least three vitally important sectors of the twenty-first-century global economy: information technology, biotechnology, and space. At the same time, however, India is miserably deficient at providing primary education to its large population. Much of India's workforce lacks the basic knowledge and skills required to be effective in a modern industrial and service economy.[5] With 60 percent of the population tied to agriculture, the lack of adequate rural schooling, especially for girls, imposes a major handicap on India's prospects.

India is thus caught in a vicious cycle. With the aggregate central and state government deficit running at a debilitating 10 percent of GDP since 1998, interest payments on this debt comprise the single-largest government expense. Fiscal debt servicing combines with defense spending and subsidies to total 60 percent of the budget. Insufficient funds remain for necessary investments in health, primary education, and infrastructure. Economists have identified several methods to reduce the fiscal deficit, but in a democracy, interest groups mobilize to block each of these pathways to fiscal solvency.[6] India's emergence as a major global power will depend significantly on whether state and society can simultaneously mobilize investment to improve the capacities of its poor and reduce the country's fiscal deficit.

International Trade

Greater participation in international trade, particularly increased exporting, can boost national income significantly as well as enhance a state's power by making others depend on it, either as a buyer or provider of key desired goods and services. On the other hand, trading partners can subject an internationally engaged state to influences. Still, theory and history suggest that trade heightens efficiency and wealth production, suggesting a correlation between share of world trade and power potential. India's small share, accounting for less than 1 percent of world trade in goods and services, has not prevented recent healthy levels of economic growth, but it does impede India's acquisition of international power as a major importer and/or exporter.[7]

Nevertheless, certain Indian corporations, largely in the information and biotechnology sectors, have become global leaders. Outstandingly managed Indian information technology firms account for much of the growth in India's foreign trade; exports grew at an 11 percent annual average from 1993 through 2001.[8] These private firms, which arose without government control or subsidy, also can be a model for other Indian entrepreneurs and object lessons for politicians about the relative virtue of private over state-owned or -managed enterprise. As Yasheng Huang and Tarun Khanna recently concluded, the success of Indian companies may indicate that India's long-term economic prospects are greater than China's.[9] According to Huang and Khanna's analysis, China's receipt of large amounts of foreign direct investment reflects a relative absence of domestic entrepreneurship and therefore signifies weakness as well as strength. Unlike China, India has only recently encouraged nonresident nationals to invest in "the motherland." If investment in existing firms grows, India will benefit much more than if investment were directed, as in China, to manufacturing platforms of nonindigenous corporations.

The fact that India and China are neighbors, competitors, and global colossi makes comparisons inevitable. Yet, economic comparisons overlook the vital qualitative distinction of India's democracy. Although political evolution may (or may not) bring unforeseeable destabilizing changes to China, India's economic progress is likely to be more sustainable for having been democratically produced. Most importantly, though, the political freedom and justice available in India are profoundly valuable in their own right. The ultimate measure of a state and society is the quality of life enjoyed by its members, not calories consumed, television hours watched, or automobile rides enjoyed. Simply put, power is ultimately a means, not an end; improving the quality of life for India's citizens is the goal.

State Capacity and Political Cohesion

A second category of state power, beyond economics, is governmental capacity and political cohesion. This category includes variables such as what one study called a state's "capacity to set goals," the "extent of elite cohesion," "relative power of social groups," the capacity of the state to collect higher levels of taxes from direct levies versus taxes on trade, and so on.[10] A state with a disgruntled or dissident citizenry will divert precious resources to impose order and will not be able to mobilize the full creativity and energy of its people. India's vibrant representative democracy allows its diverse citizenry to mobilize and pursue their interests through constitutionally regulated politics. At the same time, however, the incomprehensible caste, economic, religious, ideological, and geographic tensions among this citizenry make it extremely difficult to mobilize the nation as a whole in a decisive direction. The recent rise of militant and intolerant majoritarian demands by Hindu chauvinists, which often seem directed at the country's 150 million Muslims, highlights the challenge.

As a functioning democratic political system, India has performed with mixed results. The polity's forward direction has been handicapped by communal violence, secessionism, corruption, and myriad conflicting interests. This record should not be underestimated, however, for no state in history has been as populous, diverse, stratified, poor, and at the same time democratic as India. The attempt to resolve all of India's internal conflicts through democratically representative government, almost by definition, leads to middling outcomes.[11] Specifically, India's representative institutions often preserve rough order by canceling out competing factional interests, resulting in lowest-common-denominator policies that deprive the nation of clear direction, as in economic reforms.

The particular conflicts India confronts today include the mobilization of historically disadvantaged groups within electoral politics; politically organized lower castes and *dalits* competing with each other and opposing upper castes; entrenched criminals in politics in several high-population states; fragmented national political parties; violence between Hindus and Muslims; and the emergence of Hindutva, or Hindu nationalism, as the most important ideological challenge to the secular constitutional vision of the liberal state.[12] Each of these phenomena involves competition to acquire the power and patronage of government offices. The practical aim is less to stimulate economic growth or pursue the common good than to acquire government jobs and to distribute state resources to allies.

Meanwhile, the imperatives of economic liberalization and globalization require diminishing the role of government in overall national activity, setting up a dilemma for New Delhi. On one hand, an active, representative democracy gives long-disadvantaged groups opportunities to mobilize and compete for control of government and, therefore, patronage. On the other hand, unregulated private markets do not provide such clear avenues for the disadvantaged to advance, potentially intensifying political conflict. Yet, it is private enterprises that offer the greatest potential to create jobs and growth and to meet the demands of global investors and liberalization, potentially improving the size of the overall economy along the way.

India's current central government reveals conflicting attempts to do both. While national economic reformers seek to increase the size of the overall economy, the Hindu chauvinist base of the ruling Bharatiya Janata Party (BJP) and other regional and caste-based parties emphasize issues related more to the allocation of resources among groups. In other words, powerful Hindu-nationalist groups such as the Rashtriya Swayamesevak Sangh (RSS) and the Vishwa Hindu Parishad (VHP) seek to overcome what they perceive as the self-denying effects of diversity by imposing a dominant character and direction in Indian politics. Others feel that the militant Hindu agenda will disadvantage them. Caste-based parties compete to protect and provide benefits to their members. The definition of a clear and widely accepted common good remains elusive.

The carnage in Gujarat last year dramatizes the stakes at hand in the conflict over the identity of the Indian nation and state. Although exact details remain disputed, perhaps as many as 2,000 Muslims were killed in a pogrom following the burning of 58 Hindu campaigners on a train that stopped in the town of Godhra. The BJP-led state authorities in Gujarat failed to stop the violence for several days, a failure that many allege was purposeful. India's manifold diversity precludes easy conclusions about the likely outcome of the campaign for Hindu majoritarian direction of India's polity and the clashes this stimulates. The BJP aspires for sustained national leadership. This ambition requires it to temper its social agenda to attract diverse political partners into the coalition it needs to rule the central government. Among the BJP's 22 current coalition partners, many do not subscribe to Hindutva. Geographically, the Hindutva movement draws its strength primarily from northern Indian states and is anathema to many in the south, adding a geographic fault line to the communal one.

Achin Vanaik, an eminent social observer, has argued that a campaign for cultural nationalism of any kind contravenes the very essence of India's democratic nationalism, which seeks to "try and build a sense of Indianness which recognizes and respects the fact that there are different ways of being and feeling Indian, and that it is precisely these plural and diverse sources of a potential nationalism that constitute India's strength."[13] Thus, at the same time that India is generating the material economic and military resources to become a major global power, the Indian political system struggles to clarify the nation's essential identity. The very character and conduct of this struggle will profoundly affect India's cohesion and stability. India's stability and particularly the relations between the Hindu majority and enormous Muslim minority also will affect the way the rest of the world regards India. In a world looking for models of harmony between Muslims and non-Muslims and seeking secure, predictably governed markets for investment, India's management of its internal tensions will affect its attractiveness to the international community.

Will India gain greater global respect as a decidedly Hindu nation in a twenty-first-century world defined in terms of civilizations?[14] Or, as the writer Raja Mohan has suggested, will India win global power and respect as a carrier of the Enlightenment project of scientific rationalism, individual liberty, and constitutional protection of rights into Asia? Either course is possible. Yet, if analysts of international power are correct, then the most empowering course will be the one that provides the greatest mass of the Indian populace with the education, infrastructure, and political-economic liberty and security necessary to lead productive lives. The most successful course will be the one that strengthens the cohesion and allegiance of the greatest number of India's diverse citizens and groups. In an inherently pluralistic society, pluralism, not cultural nationalism, offers the only viable model to release the creative energies of a vast population. The alternative is civil conflict and disorder that make other major powers chary of investing economic or political capital in ties with India. Moreover, as the international community struggles to redress the increasingly violent alienation of Muslims, an India that successfully integrates its enormous Muslim population will gain major soft power as an exemplar.

Military-Security Indicators

Measuring military power is more complicated than it might seem. First, for the measurement to be meaningful, a requirement must exist against which to measure the state's military power. What are the threats the military is to deter or defeat? Second, measuring effectiveness itself is difficult. War provides a true empirical test, but states would like to know the effectiveness of their military before they enter war. Expenditures can be measured easily but do not necessarily indicate military effectiveness, and numbers of men under arms and numbers of tanks, aircraft, and ships do not necessarily connote fighting effectiveness. Although all states might naturally desire absolute security—confidence that no adversary or combination of adversaries could do one any harm—in the real world, states settle for relative security. In addition, the degree of security a state practically seeks depends largely on its basic capabilities at a given time. In other words, a state's security ambitions can grow as its power potential grows.

India's military security challenges begin at home, with internal security against insurgents and terrorists. The next and most dramatic ring of the threat circle encompasses Pakistan. India seeks to deter or defeat Pakistani support of subversion within India, including most prominently in the state of Jammu and Kashmir. India also must deter or defeat Pakistani attempts to escalate the conflict between the two countries. India strives to retain a free hand to punish Pakistani violence by imposing greater losses on Pakistan than Pakistan imposes on India. This amounts to a battle for dominance of the potential escalatory process. India also requires the capacity to deter or physically deny China from coercively blackmailing India into an unacceptable resolution of their border dispute. Next, India seeks to protect its sea lines of communication to the east toward Indochina and to the west through the Arabian Sea and the Indian Ocean. Importantly, India's aims are not to acquire additional territory or, with the possible exception of Pakistan, to coerce others to meet Indian demands. Rather, India wishes to preserve India's autonomy and to receive the prestige and political influence that come with military capacity.

India recently has increased significantly its expenditure on and accumulation of military instruments. Its budget for fiscal year 2003–2004 raises defense spending by 17 percent, the fourth consecutive year of annual defense budget increases greater than 12 percent. In the last three years, India has signed at least $4 billion worth of contracts with Russia to purchase advanced military equipment. These purchases reflect India's accretion of foreign reserves, its government's desire to manifest muscle, and the legacy of the 1999 Kargil war with Pakistan and subsequent war scares following terrorist attacks on India.

When Indian leaders tested nuclear weapons in May 1998, many Indians felt that their country finally had entered the ranks of the major powers. Indian scientists and engineers have continued to increase the state's stockpile of nuclear materials and weapons, and the country is currently estimated to possess 40 or more nuclear weapons. The technical composition of India's nuclear arsenal remains publicly unclear, including how many, if any, of these weapons are thermonuclear, boosted-fission, or fission. India's capacity to deliver nuclear weapons also continues to expand; fighter-bomber aircraft remain the principal means of delivery. India is also developing and deploying at least three models of mobile ballistic missiles, the short-range Prithvi and the Agni I and Agni II, with longer-range Agni IIIs and IVs on the drawing board.

Yet, nuclear weapons are not sufficient to make a major power. Otherwise, Pakistan too would qualify as a major power, as would Israel and perhaps North Korea. In today's world, nuclear weapons are illegitimate, and thus ineffective, tools for coercing non–nuclear-weapon states. Nuclear weapons could not help France achieve its aims in Algeria, nor the United States in Korea or Vietnam, nor the Soviet Union in Afghanistan, nor China vis-à-vis Taiwan. The sole effective use of nuclear weapons is to deter other states from using nuclear weapons, but this deterrent, although important, does not alone make a great power. Nuclear weapons cannot grow an economy, gain international market share, or win political support for a nation's demands to shape the political-economic order. Israel, India, Pakistan, and North Korea may possess nuclear weapons, but their political-economic problems and inability to transcend local conflicts and become net producers of international security prevent them from being major powers.

Neither nuclear weapons nor a recent dramatic increase in conventional military procurement, largely from Russia, has freed India from Pakistani security threats. India's growing military and economic strength heightens the nation's frustrated desire to "teach Pakistan a lesson once and for all," but Indian statesmen also recognize that Pakistan's nuclear weapons make decisive military intervention to punish Pakistan enormously risky. Consequently, India must accept relatively manageable insecurity regarding Pakistan.

India passionately seeks to decouple, or de-hyphenate, Pakistan from India. The world's usual treatment of the two states as twins diminishes India. Indians (and many others) believe that India is superior to Pakistan in every category except one: nuclear weapons. Unfortunately for India and the world, however, nuclear weapons are great deterrent equalizers. The world fears the humanitarian horror that nuclear weapons could unleash in South Asia as well as the potential disorder it could bring to the international system. Thus, when Pakistan, or terrorist groups affiliated with it, instigate a crisis in Kashmir and India responds by threatening military retaliation, the world worries that the escalatory process could result in nuclear war. This fearful reaction might very well play into Pakistan's interest. Pakistan traditionally has wanted the United States to fear the potential for nuclear war over Kashmir so that Washington would intervene to compel India to offer better terms for an Indo-Pakistani settlement than Pakistan could obtain by itself through diplomacy with India. India recognizes this and refuses to play into the Pakistani strategy, insisting instead that India can and will retaliate heavily against any Pakistani aggression. The problem is that Pakistan's refusal to be deterred makes it difficult for the United States and others to discount the likelihood of nuclear warfare resulting from a military crisis. Nuclear weapons thus give Pakistan the capacity to stay in the game, to continue to pop up and grab India by the *dhoti*. Neither the United States nor India has the power to compel Pakistan to do otherwise. Nor can the United States or India take over Pakistan, and neither would benefit from economically strangulating Pakistan. Thus, neither country can escape from the reality that it has to deal with Pakistan.

Finally, the prominence and power of the Pakistani army, intelligence services, and jihadists arguably will not diminish as long as the prominence and power of Hindu militants continues to rise in India. Fundamentally opposed, the internal dynamics of Islamic extremism and Hindu chauvinism feed on each other. Pakistanis cite the menacing rhetoric and occasional violence of the RSS and VHP as proof that Hindus are out to destroy Muslims and, of course, Pakistan. The RSS and VHP, in turn, use the prominence of Islamist parties and terrorist organizations in Pakistan as proof that Muslims are evil. Pursuit of the Hindutva agenda only tightens the handcuffs, or the infamous hyphen, connecting Pakistan and India. Thus, pluralist liberalism, not cultural nationalism, provides the path toward growing India's power, not only by improving India's internal stability and cohesion but also by negating the Pakistani argument that Hindu-majority India is inveterately hostile to Muslims. This is necessary, but not sufficient, to liberate India from Pakistan.

Regarding China, India finds itself on a more positive trajectory. India's growing economic, military, and diplomatic strength, combined with China's desire to concentrate on internal political-economic development, induces Beijing to improve relations with New Delhi. India's rather astute cultivation of better ties with the United States and China has encouraged Beijing to seek better relations with India so that India should not align closely with the United States against China. New Delhi and Beijing thus augment their national military capabilities while simultaneously engaging in mutual diplomatic reassurance.

The June 2003 visit of Indian prime minister Atal Bihari Vajpayee to China highlighted the positive profile of Sino-Indian relations. Only the fourth-ever Indian prime minister to visit China and the first since Narasimha Rao in 1993, Vajpayee and the Chinese leaders he met evinced increased will to negotiate a resolution of the Sino-Indian border dispute and heralded the growing priority of economics in the bilateral relationship. They pledged to double bilateral trade within two years and to act in concert in WTO negotiations. The two states may be in a process of recognizing that their real priorities are internal development, influencing neighbors other than each other, and managing hegemonic U.S. power. Both would gain time, calm, and resources to attend to these priorities if they received assurances that their bilateral relationship was stable. Hence, India and China are steadily building each other's confidence. Both countries' international power will increase to the extent that they divert fewer resources and less political energy to standing up to each other and concentrate more on growing their economies, reforming their troubled states, and helping to meet global challenges such as AIDS, terrorism, and climate change.

Strategic Diplomacy

Statecraft can increase or decrease a country's influence relative to its material capabilities. The combination of leadership, strategic vision and tactics, moral example and suasion, and diplomatic acumen can earn a state great international influence. So, too, a state's power grows to the extent that it has authority in international institutions that set rules for state behavior—military, economic, political—and shape international responses to threats to peace and security. The UN Security Council is the most obvious such institution, along with the WTO and the international financial institutions.

The potency of India's statecraft has ebbed and flowed in decades-long tides. The currently rising tide follows decades of trough after the years of Prime Minister Jawaharlal Nehru. The overt demonstration of India's nuclear-weapon capabilities seems to have heightened Indian leaders' confidence in developing and prosecuting an international diplomatic strategy. Since 1998, under the leadership of Vajpayee and Foreign Minister Jaswant Singh, India has displayed new vigor and imagination in its interactions with the United States, China, Pakistan, Russia, the European Union, and other counterparts.[15]

In early 2003, Indian leaders showed how far their strategic and diplomatic acumen has evolved since the days of knee-jerk moralistic denunciations of U.S. power. India did not support the decision of President George W. Bush to intervene militarily in Iraq. Indians have felt to a large extent that the United States displays disingenuousness or even hypocrisy in waging war against Saddam Hussein as a terrorist while supporting Pakistani president Gen. Pervez Musharraf. In Indian eyes, Pakistan is a greater source of terrorism than Iraq. Whereas Indian leaders in decades past would have blasted the United States in morally laden denunciations, New Delhi in 2003 displayed diplomatic savoir faire by keeping a low profile on the issue. "India has not been happy with the United States because of its inability to pressure Pakistan on cross-border terrorism and lifting of sanctions," an Indian official declared, "but the government did not go beyond saying that it was 'disappointed' over the move. The government was not going by the sentiment; national interest weighed supreme in the minds of decisionmakers."[16] Vajpayee summed up the new statesmanship tellingly: "We have to take the totality of the situation into consideration and craft an approach which is consistent with both our principles and our long-term national interest. Our words, actions, and diplomatic efforts should be aimed at trying to achieve pragmatic goals, rather than creating rhetorical effect. Quiet diplomacy is far more effective than public posturing."[17] This insight, if applied regularly, could greatly increase India's influence in the halls of global power.

Yet, democracy makes such dispassionate diplomacy difficult. As the United States encountered unexpected difficulties securing Iraq, Washington quietly beseeched India to supply an army division to work with U.S. forces in the country. The Indian army has proved adept at such missions, and the Vajpayee government, recognizing the goodwill such a contribution would earn in Washington, indicated its desire to supply the force Washington sought. Nevertheless, Indian politics ultimately prevented the government from joining with the Bush administration. The Indian public and especially many political parties resented the rhetoric and intentions of a Bush administration that was widely perceived as arrogant, unilateral, and militaristic. Worse, Indians felt that the administration was hypocritically self-centered to India's disadvantage: if the United States was leading a war against terrorism, why did it coddle Pakistan—a great source of terror not only against India but also against the United States? Faced with a looming year of elections, the Indian government did not want to join with such an unpopular U.S. leadership and cause.

India's complicated interests and attitudes also limit the government's effectiveness in international institutions and regimes. India has displayed an ambivalent attitude toward negotiations to liberalize global trade, a position that reflects diverse economic interests.

The Indian service sector would benefit from freer global markets for its exports. Indian agriculture, in which 60 percent of the population toils, mainly on small plots, and with almost no safety nets to protect displaced farmers, could be harmed by surges of subsidized imports. As agriculture and old-styled manufacturing industries express their interests through the political process, Indian trade diplomats must tread cautiously. In the November 2001 WTO negotiations at Doha, India appeared the primary impediment to a stronger international consensus favoring liberalization. Fairly or not, the richer countries, particularly the United States, felt that the chief Indian negotiator, Murasoli Maran, typified an old, unwelcome, and counterproductive Indian style of moralism and doggedness. In contrast, in the September 2003 WTO negotiations in Cancun, India worked closely with China and Brazil to lead a 21-country bloc to press the United States, the EU, and Japan to accommodate developing country interests more fully in the supposed Development Round of trade talks. If India can help maintain cohesion and constructive direction in this bloc, its international power will grow as the richest states in the system will have to be more forthcoming in dealing with this new bloc that represents half the world's population.

The international nonproliferation regime represents another arena for Indian diplomacy. Here, India has conflicting interests. It opposes the further spread of nuclear weapons and other weapons of mass destruction. It also wants to be recognized as a nuclear-weapon state and to be freed of export denials and other limitations related to India's nonmembership in the Nuclear Non-Proliferation Treaty (NPT). Indian leaders exhort the United States and others to remove bars to nuclear and other technology transfers to India. The United States, Japan, and others resist, arguing that removing limitations on India would reward proliferation and undermine the interests of the 180-plus states that have forsworn nuclear weapons through adherence to the NPT. Current evidence does not allow a sound prediction of how India and the world will fare on this matter.

Finally, India, similar to other states, regards a permanent seat on the UN Security Council as a measure of major power. Yet, India would be unlikely to win a vote to award it such a seat, either from the current

Security Council members or the General Assembly. The greatest realpolitik problem is that China, if forced to choose, would likely vote against an Indian bid in the interest of maintaining its own advantage and blocking a gain by its greatest long-term rival for power status in Asia. Beijing also likely would be sympathetic to Pakistan's pleas to prevent India from being elevated. Pakistan might also be able to rally other Muslim majority states to block India in the General Assembly. More broadly, India's long position as a moralistic, contrarian loner in the international community has not excited others about the prospect of working with India at the apex of the UN system. Furthermore, the Security Council is the ultimate enforcer of the NPT; India's nonmembership in this treaty puts it in an awkward position, say, to vote on sanctions or use of force against actors newly seeking to acquire nuclear weapons. One measure of Indian diplomacy in the future will be how it either lowers the value of a seat on the Security Council or alternatively how it attains a seat.

Is India a Major Power?

From the standpoint of the United States, India has neither the interest nor the power to contest Washington across the board. Nor does India have the interest or power to augment U.S. interests in many areas. Yet, India is too big and too important in the overall global community to measure in terms of its alignment with any particular U.S. interest at any given time. It matters to the entire world whether India is at war or peace with its neighbors, is producing increasing prosperity or poverty for its citizens, stemming or incubating the spread of infectious diseases, or mimicking or leapfrogging climate-warming technologies. Democratically managing a society as big, populous, diverse, and culturally dynamic as India is a world historical challenge. If India can democratically lift all of its citizens to a decent quality of life without trampling on basic liberties and harming its neighbors, the Indian people will have accomplished perhaps the greatest success in human history.

India will struggle to do this largely on its own, disabused of notions that the United States or others might help without asking anything in return. This capacity to do things on one's own is autonomy, a form of power that India has achieved to its great credit. To go further and make others do what one wants them to do through payment, coercion, or persuasion is a more demanding measure of power. Iraq raises questions whether even the United States has this power. India, to be great, has more urgent things to do.

Notes

1. Kenneth Waltz, *Theory of International Politics* (Reading, Penn.: Addison-Wesley, 1979), pp. 191–192.

2. Martin Ravallion, presentation to the Brookings Institution-Carnegie Endowment for International Peace conference "Making Globalization Work," December 2, 2002, pp. 7–8 (transcript of panel 1) (hereinafter Ravallion presentation). See Martin Ravallion and Gaurav Datt, "Why Has Economic Growth Been More Pro-Poor in Some States of India than Others?" *Journal of Development Economics* 68 (2002): 381–400, http://poverty.worldbank.org/files/13995_JDE2002.pdf (accessed October 28, 2003).

3. Sanjaya Baru, "The Strategic Consequences of India's Economic Performance," in *India's National Security Annual Review 2002*, ed. Satish Kumar (New Delhi: India Research Press, 2003), p. 177.

4. Ravallion presentation.

5. Pradeep Agarwal et al., *Policy Regimes and Industrial Competitiveness: A Comparative Study of East Asia and India* (Houndmills, UK: Macmillan, 2000), p. 272.

6. Leading debt-reduction options are to reduce the size of government by cutting payrolls and privatizing state enterprises or, alternatively, increase the productivity of government workers and enterprises; attract foreign investment, particularly in infrastructure; or increase tax collections, not necessarily tax rates.

7. Baru, "Strategic Consequences of India's Economic Performance," p. 191.

8. T. N. Srinivasan and Suresh D. Tendulkar, *Reintegrating India with the World Economy* (Washington, D.C.: Institute for International Economics, 2003), p. 28.

9. Yasheng Huang and Tarun Khanna, "Can India Overtake China?" *Foreign Policy* (July–August 2003): 74–81.

10. Ashley J. Tellis et al., *Measuring National Power in the Postindustrial Age* (RAND, 2000), pp. 22–27.

11. B. R. Nayar and T. V. Paul, *India in the World Order: Searching for Major-Power Status* (New York: Cambridge University Press, 2003), p. 60; Francine

Frankel, "Contextual Democracy: Intersections of Society, Culture and Politics in India," in *Transforming India*, eds. Francine Frankel et al. (New Delhi: Oxford University Press, 2000), p. 20.

12. Frankel, "Contextual Democracy," p. 5.

13. Achin Vanaik, "Interface between Democracy, Diversity and Stability," in *Democracy, Diversity, Stability*, eds. D. D. Khanna, L. L. Mehrotra, and Gert W. Kueck (New Delhi: MacMillan India Ltd., 1998), p. 301.

14. Using Samuel Huntington's controversial categories, the world can be seen as divided along the following civilizational lines: Western, Latin American, African, Islamic, Sinic, Hindu, Orthodox, Buddhist, and Japanese. Samuel Huntington, *The Clash of Civilizations and the Remaking of World Order* (New York: Simon and Schuster, 1996).

15. For a more thorough discussion of these developments, see George Perkovich, *India's Nuclear Bomb: The Impact on Global Proliferation* (Berkeley, Calif.: University of California Press, 2001), pp. 495–501 (paperback ed.).

16. Sanjay Singh, "Thin Red Line: New Delhi's Balancing Act," *Pioneer*, March 23, 2003.

17. Ibid.

C. Raja Mohan

Balancing Interests and Values: India's Struggle with Democracy Promotion

In 2005, early in his tenure as prime minister of India, Manmohan Singh underlined the importance of Indian democracy to the world:

> If there is an 'idea of India' by which India should be defined, it is the idea of an inclusive, open, multi-cultural, multi-ethnic, multi-lingual society. … [W]e have an obligation to history and mankind to show that pluralism works. … Liberal democracy is the natural order of political organization in today's world. All alternate systems, authoritarian and majoritarian in varying degrees, are an aberration.[1]

Coming from the leader of the world's largest democracy, Singh's remarks seem relatively unexceptional. Viewed in the context of the Indian foreign policy tradition, however, he was making a major departure in unabashedly praising liberal democracy and relating India's own democratic system to the current problems of the world.

As India celebrates the 60th anniversary of its independence, a paradox stands out. Much of the world sees a profound commitment to democracy amidst bewildering diversity as the defining feature of modern India. Yet, democracy as a political priority has largely been absent from India's foreign policy. New Delhi's conspicuous lack of emphasis on

C. Raja Mohan is a professor at the S. Rajaratnam School of International Studies of Nanyang Technological University in Singapore and a member of the editorial board of *The Washington Quarterly*. He can be reached at iscrmohan@ntu.edu.sg.

Copyright © 2007 by The Center for Strategic and International Studies and the Massachusetts Institute of Technology
The Washington Quarterly • 30:3 pp. 99–115.

democracy in its engagement with the world is largely a consequence of the Cold War's impact on South Asia and India's nonaligned impulses in the early years of its independence. It attached more weight to solidarity with fellow developing countries and the defense of its own national security interests without a reference to ideology at the operational level.

Since the end of the Cold War, however, supporting democracy abroad as an objective has begun to factor into India's policymaking. This priority has been triggered by intensive engagement with the United States since the early 1990s. In the final days of the Clinton administration and through subsequent terms of the Bush administration, Washington has emphasized the importance of India as the world's largest democracy, underlined the role of shared political values in transforming bilateral relations, and explored options for working with New Delhi on the promotion of democracy worldwide. India has in turn confronted new challenges, such as potential failed states in the region; managing consequences of internal conflicts within its smaller neighbors; and if possible, nudging these countries toward democratic evolution. As an emerging great power in its own right, India has also been increasingly called on to contribute to international peace and security, which in the contemporary world increasingly focuses on conflicts within states.

Among these external impulses, the question of India's political values and their role in the conduct of India's international relations are bound to figure more prominently in the future policy discourse in New Delhi. Yet, the question remains: Will democracy become a more important natural component of future Indian foreign policy as many in the West hope?

Cold War Priorities: Nonalignment over Democracy

During the Cold War, external and internal factors combined to prevent India from highlighting the relevance of its own democracy to the rest of the world. The impact of the Cold War on the subcontinent resulted, to put it simply, in the U.S. democracy aligning with military-ruled Pakistan and Communist-led People's Republic of China. India in turn found itself in the arms of the Soviet Union.

Once this regional balance of power system acquired a measure of rigidity, India and the United States could not build on their shared political values. Although the governments of the two nations often paid lip service to the notion of political pluralism, which was also at the center of the East-West ideological divide, there was no escaping the fact that India was not merely closer to the Soviet Union but also the only democracy that stood outside the system of U.S. alliances and in political opposition to the West on most international issues. Inevitably then, "estranged democracies" became the defining metaphor of Indian-U.S. relations.[2]

Liberal U.S. rhetoric on democracy often drew cynical jeers from the Indian intelligentsia, who pointed to the U.S. military alliance with military-ruled Pakistan. The U.S. policy of supporting military dictatorships and conservative religious forces within the developing world, as part of its effort to contain the influence of communism, created deep anxieties within the Indian establishment. As it watched military coups undermine many nationalist regimes and nascent democracies in the newly decolonized states, India was anxious that its own democracy might be targeted by the West.

The internal anticolonial strain in the newly independent India morphed into sustained anti-imperialist posturing within the political discourse on world affairs. India's first prime minister, Jawaharlal Nehru, certainly did not define nonalignment as a conscious anti-Western orientation. For him, India's nonalignment was a means to protect India's newly won freedom to conduct its own independent foreign policy and to maximize India's relative gains in the bipolar system. Nehru was never enthusiastic about creating a third bloc of nonaligned countries.

The injection of anti-imperialism into nonalignment and the identification of the Soviet Union as a natural ally of the developing world came after Nehru. As India drifted toward economic populism and a leftist orientation at home starting in the late 1960s, India's foreign policy articulation increasingly acquired a strident anti-Western tone. As the Non-Aligned Movement (NAM) became radicalized in the 1970s, the vision of a declining capitalist West and a rising socialist East gripped the imagination of Third World leaders. As the North-South ideological battles dominated the UN fora, India saw itself leading the charge in restructuring the global order against the West.

Equally consequential in undermining the liberalism of India was the extraordinary fascination with socialism among the founders of the Indian republic. Having grown up amidst the crises in Western capitalism in the 1920s and the impressive economic performance of the Soviet Union, many nationalists saw Indian socialism as the fastest means to transform the lives of their people. Although most of them were not willing to abandon freedom for the sake of socialism, they were indeed convinced that a third way, tilted toward state-led economic growth, existed between the models offered by Western capitalism and Eastern communism.

This article of faith for the political class was reflected in the decision by the Indira Gandhi government to convert India into a socialist republic in the late 1970s through a constitutional amendment. Although this was done during the brief emergency rule that suspended Indian democracy from 1975 to 1977, the political establishment did not even attempt to reverse it after that period.

India's collective faith in socialism crumbled only when its state-led economic model went bankrupt at the turn of the 1990s. It took Indian leaders 15 years of cautious economic liberalization and globalization to discover the virtues of liberal orthodoxy. It was not entirely accidental that Singh, who launched India's economic reforms in 1991, was also the first Indian leader to begin to underline India's relevance as an "an open society and an open economy."[3]

Unlearning the Cold War Experience

The end of the Cold War made it possible for India and the United States to consider anew the prospect of building on their shared democratic values. Whereas the Western world celebrated the triumph of liberal democracy over authoritarian forms of governance at the turn of the 1990s, the world's largest democracy had very little reason to cheer the collapse of the Soviet Union. Having developed a huge stake in the strategic alliance with Moscow, New Delhi was in deep mourning. It was more concerned about the loss of a reliable strategic partner than the far-reaching systemic implications of the Soviet Union's collapse. New Delhi did not envision itself as a leading democracy in the world. As it coped with an uncertain world after 1991, India was more fearful of U.S. dominance in a unipolar world than enthusiastic for the triumph of democratic principles. Indian intelligentsia, although highly sensitive to any violation of democratic principles within the nation, seemed utterly insensitive to the international value of political pluralism.

In the United States, foreign policy efforts on deepening democracy throughout the 1990s focused sharply on eastern and central Europe, which saw many new democracies emerge in the wake of the collapse of the Warsaw Pact. In South Asia, however, the initial years of the Clinton administration saw U.S. energies devoted almost entirely to nuclear nonproliferation. In fact, the instincts of the Clinton administration at its beginning and more broadly of the liberal U.S. establishment to emphasize democracy as part of a neo-Wilsonian internationalism did not lead to U.S. recognition of the strategic value of Indian democracy. It ironically led to an emphasis on the shortcomings of the Indian democratic experiment. Single-issue groups in the United States focusing, for example, on human rights abuses or the practice of religious freedom or those seeking a linkage between trade and child labor tended to focus intensely on India's difficulties in these areas.

When issues relating to democracy did come up, they arose as U.S. criticism of India for the human rights situation in Kashmir, which New Delhi viewed as part of the traditional U.S. tilt toward Pakistan. Sikh Khalistani groups and the Kashmiri separatists backed by Pakistan also actively campaigned in the U.S. Congress to pass resolutions against the Indian state's human rights violations in the Punjab and Kashmir. (India did eventually beat back these efforts by its own intensive lobbying.) Washington's 1993 questioning of the legality of the accession of the state of Jammu and Kashmir to India stoked all the visceral Indian suspicions of U.S. ulterior motives in the region. The enduring U.S. alliance with Pakistan and the U.S. tilt toward Islamabad in its dispute with New Delhi on Kashmir convinced many in India that Washington had little consideration for its unity and territorial integrity and was fundamentally opposed to the emergence of a powerful Indian state. The newly triumphal post–Cold War U.S. liberalism seemed to have no empathy for an India that was fighting its own demons. At the extreme, many U.S. internationalists were quite happy to berate Indian democracy as an "illiberal" one.

At the global level, the Clinton administration's focus on assertive multilateralism and empowering the United Nations with the right to intervene in the internal affairs of developing nations raised alarm bells in India about potential U.S. plans to meddle in Kashmir. India subsequently opposed the new international interventionist agenda of President Bill Clinton and UN Secretary General Kofi Annan. At annual voting sessions of the UN Human Rights Commission in Geneva, India voted against or occasionally abstained on Western resolutions throughout the 1990s and beyond. In affirming its conventional nonaligned stand on human rights issues, India gained support from many Third World countries, including China and Iran, in beating back Pakistani resolutions on the political situation in Kashmir. Internationally, India saw defending the sovereignty of the Third World against the new interventionists as more important than defending the values of democracy.

The Turning Point: India and the Community of Democracies

It took the first U.S. presidential visit to India in 22 years, by Clinton in the spring of 2000, for Washington to recognize the importance of Indian democracy. Clinton's sensitivity to the extraordinary diversity of the country and his celebration of India's multicultural tradition put democracy back at the center of Indian-U.S. relations. Clinton's support of India in the 1999 Kargil war against Pakistan and his publicly expressed view that the United States has no interest in balkanizing India eased, if not erased, the traditional Indian perceptions about U.S. hostility.

Although Clinton brought new warmth to Indian-U.S. relations and successfully removed much of the poison that had accumulated during the Cold War, India's struggle to adapt to the changes in world order continued. In the first-ever substantive and sustained political and security dialogue between Washington and New Delhi from 1998 to 2000, the Clinton administration sought Indian support for an initiative to promote democracy worldwide.[4] India was aware that being part of an international club built around the idea of political pluralism would help to differentiate it from two of its principal adversaries, China and Pakistan. Yet, the Indian establishment was skeptical whether the new connection with Washington on promoting democracy would in any way change the fundamentals of U.S. policy toward India. They wanted to see U.S. support in changing India's nuclear status, U.S. neutrality in the conflict with Pakistan over Jammu and Kashmir, and U.S. treatment as an equal to Beijing.

As the United States sought India's help on democracy promotion, New Delhi by sheer force of inertia tended to hold on to its traditional foreign policy position on nonintervention in the internal affairs of developing nations. During Clinton's visit to India, for example, the United States proposed setting up a Center for Asian Democracy, with natural overtones against China, and sounded out India on its willingness to vote against Beijing or at least abstain on China's human rights record at the UN Commission on Human Rights. India was in both cases unwilling to lend itself to a potential campaign against Beijing. Afraid of a U.S. intervention in Kashmir at one of the weaker moments of the Indian state, New Delhi still found it more convenient to align with China and the nonaligned bloc in defending the principle of nonintervention rather than with the West on human rights issues.

Yet, India would not reject out of hand the Clinton administration's proposal on working together on democracy promotion. At a minimum, decisionmakers in New Delhi were compelled to review for the first time what the nature of its internal politics meant for the rest of the world. Washington's idea was to form a small core group of democracies representing different regions that would meet regularly to address the challenges to the rule of law and democracy. In considering the implications of joining what clearly was an ideological project, India had to take into account the potential weakening of its established diplomatic equities in the UN and other multilateral forums as a leading NAM member.

The multilateralists in the Indian foreign policy establishment, reflecting an entrenched Third World perspective, were opposed to letting a new political fashion replace the familiar ways of doing business at the UN. Yet, the political leadership of the center-right Bharatiya Janata Party, which was trying to reorient Indian foreign policy, chose to go along cautiously with Clinton's proposal. In 1999, India became one of the 10 founding members of the Community of Democracies initiative. The 10 countries, meeting at the ministerial level, issued a concept paper declaring that the first-ever platform of nations sharing the same political values "provide[s] an unprecedented opportunity for exchanging experiences, identifying best practices, and formulating an agenda for international cooperation in order to realize democracy's full potential."[5]

At the first meeting of the Community of Democracies in Warsaw in June 2000, in which foreign ministers and officials from 106 countries participated, India was given a prominent role as a founding member and was chosen to lead one of the ministerial panels. Despite real U.S. diplomatic enthusiasm for presenting India in a lead role in the new initiative, a tentative India was unwilling to step too far out. New Delhi had not yet resolved the fundamental tension in its own worldview between the notions of sovereignty and intervention. Its own national experience had tended to emphasize the argument that, to be successful, democracy must have a strong internal basis and cannot be enforced from abroad.

To be sure, India recognized the value of sharing experiences and best practices but was not willing to inject more into the notion of democracy promotion. More immediately, New Delhi was not convinced that Washington itself was ready to insulate democracy promotion from the larger dynamics of its foreign policy. The skepticism of the Indian conservatives was reflected in an assessment on the eve of the Warsaw conference:

> There is no harm in India participating in the forthcoming Warsaw conference on the Community of Democracies ... [but] [o]ver-enthusiasm and wishful-thinking that India is now an equal partner of the US in a new jehad for democracy would be unwise. ... We should avoid letting ourselves be used by Washington in this venture to advance its interests unless there is a genuine convergence of the interests of the [United States] and India.[6]

Thus, India went along with the United States on the Community of Democracy initiative, but it was not prepared to invest significant political or diplomatic energies into it. After the Warsaw conference, the United States sounded out India on leading the Caucus of the Community of Democracies at the UN, to coordinate the positions of caucus members on various issues. India, weighed down by its past association with the developing world's Group of 77 and NAM, large numbers of which are nondemocratic states, was reluctant to give up traditional ways of mobilizing support for Indian positions at the UN.

The Indian decision to turn down the U.S. request to lead the UN Democracy Caucus reportedly left Washington "puzzled." As journalist Malini Parthasarathy remarked, "On the one hand, India is seen as seeking international support for its initiatives against terrorism and has been canvassing vigorously its claims to a Security Council seat, but on the other hand it seems to have passed up an opportunity to take on a high-profile role in the context of the United Nations."[7]

Two factors defined India's ambivalence toward the Clinton administration's agenda on democracy promotion. The first was the unsurprising lag between the prospect of India emerging as a great power and the evolution of New Delhi's attitudes from that of a vulnerable Third World state to those of a nation capable of shaping the international system. India's self-confidence as a rising force on the global stage has been building, with its May 1998 nuclear tests in defiance of the United States and the nonproliferation system as well as its subsequent capacity to withstand international sanctions, its success in creating a niche for itself in the information technology area, and above all an acceleration of its economic growth.

The immediate post-1998 years were marked by an extraordinary diplomatic dynamism in New Delhi and a political leadership that was willing to break the inherited ideological mold. Multilateralism was not the highest priority for New Delhi at a moment when it was reconfiguring its relations with the great powers, reestablishing its relevance in a resurgent Asia, and reordering its ties with two of its most important neighbors, China and Pakistan. The new realists running India's foreign policy had little reverence for the grandstanding in multilateral forums of the past.

Focused as they were on rebuilding India's power, they had no time for fanciful multilateral projects, thus reducing India's emphasis on NAM and activism in the UN, the sole exception being its campaign for a permanent seat on the UN Security Council. This lack of interest in the UN at the highest level meant, paradoxically, some autonomy for the multilateralists in the Indian system who were happy to plod along the beaten path.

The second and perhaps more consequential reason for India's disinterest in a global campaign for democracy was the difficulty of engineering a new convergence of strategic interests with the United States. Despite Clinton's eventual empathy toward India, his administration was rigid in its opposition to accommodating India on the nuclear question. After its nuclear tests, the new center-right government in India, which was so different from the left-liberal governments that had dominated India for decades, was pitching for a genuine strategic partnership with the United States. The new approach was highlighted by Prime Minister Atal Bihari Vajpayee, who departed from the conventional wisdom in New Delhi in proclaiming India and the United States to be "natural allies."[8]

The Clinton administration, with its commitment to neo-Wilsonian internationalism, was polite in noting the new Indian enthusiasm but had no interest in building new alliances or pursuing geopolitical goals in Asia. Conventional U.S. liberal internationalism was not willing to look at India as a potential ally. President George W. Bush, however, who had a very different view of the world and of India, was ready to make amends.

Simplifying Democracy Promotion

Unlike Clinton and the liberal Democrats in the United States, Bush was prepared to take a simpler but strategic view on the importance of Indian democracy. Senior Bush aides have underlined his strong admiration for Indian democracy. As one adviser said, "When I asked … Bush in early 1999 about the reasons for his obvious and special interest in India, he immediately responded, 'a billion people in a functioning democracy. Isn't that something? Isn't that something?'"[9]

Bush's personal enthusiasm translated into policy initiatives toward India that departed from the traditional approach to the region. Unlike his predecessors, who saw India through the limiting prism of Pakistan and the subcontinent, Bush was prepared to rank New Delhi as a potential major power with global significance. This addressed India's long-standing complaints that Washington had little regard for New Delhi's global aspirations.

After the September 11 attacks, the war on terrorism produced greater empathy from the United States for India's concerns about terrorism emanating from Islamic militant groups based in Pakistan. Despite its renewed reliance on Pakistan in the war on terrorism, Washington was not prepared to sacrifice its incipient partnership with New Delhi. Determined not to let U.S. policy drift back to a zero-sum game between India and Pakistan as it was during the Cold War, Washington successfully expanded relations with both states. Unlike the Clinton administration, which was unwilling to hold Pakistan responsible for these attacks and underlined India's shortcomings in Kashmir, the Bush administration began to mount political pressure on Pakistan to stop cross-border terrorism after the September 11 attacks. Although Bush has not been able to make Pakistan completely stop such support, India saw the value of the positive change in Washington's approach.

Above all, Bush managed to correct the perspective in New Delhi about a U.S. tilt toward Pakistan on Kashmir. By shedding the activist approach of Clinton in pushing India toward substantive negotiations on Kashmir with Pakistan, resisting the temptation to mediate, and endorsing the internationally observed elections to the provincial assembly of Jammu and Kashmir as free and fair, Bush removed New Delhi's entrenched suspicions about U.S. intentions in Kashmir. Somewhat counterintuitively, Washington's reduced activity on Kashmir opened the space for India to initiate the first purposeful negotiation in decades on the long-standing conflict with Pakistan.

Furthermore, the Bush administration's willingness in its first term to sidestep disputes with India on nonproliferation allowed New Delhi to warm up to Washington on a range of international political issues. India was eager to assist the United States in its war on terrorism after the September 11 attacks. Despite the U.S. decision to rely on Pakistan, India was fully aware of the big opportunity for transforming Indian-U.S. relations in the Bush years and seriously considered Bush's request to send a division of troops to Iraq in the summer of 2003. Although the Vajpayee government held back in the end for the fear of a domestic backlash, its readiness for a new framework of political cooperation with the United States was unmistakable.

Finally, Bush's controversial agreement with Singh in July 2005 to initiate civilian nuclear energy cooperation with India and modify the global nonproliferation regime instilled a new confidence in the prospects for a genuine partnership and generated a readiness to take political risks on aligning with U.S. policy on such ideological issues as promoting democracy. In the global nuclear order built around the Nuclear Non-Proliferation Treaty of 1970 (NPT), India had had an anomalous standing. India was in possession of nuclear weapons but could not be accepted as a nuclear-weapon state under the NPT. Moreover, India would not give up its nuclear weapons and join the treaty as a non–nuclear-weapon state. For 35 years, finding a way to keep its nuclear weapons and to regain the benefits of international nuclear commerce have been among the highest national security objectives for New Delhi. This priority, however, ran headlong into the solid U.S. domestic consensus on ensuring strict adherence to the NPT. Bush was the first U.S. president since the mid-1960s to seek a new domestic consensus to let India have both nuclear weapons and access to the global nuclear energy market.

The July 2005 White House summit between Bush and Singh went beyond the nuclear question to announce a joint global democracy initiative. India and the United States declared that they "have an obligation to the global community to strengthen values, ideals, and practices of freedom, pluralism, and rule of law" and agreed to assist states seeking to become more open and democratic.[10] Bush and Singh committed to support the new UN Democracy Fund, which had the relatively modest objective of funding projects for strengthening democratic institutions and promoting human rights around the world. Recognizing the special personal importance attached by Bush, Singh disregarded advice not to appear with Bush at its launch in the fall of 2005. Speaking at the occasion, Singh expanded on the virtues of Indian democracy and its universal relevance: "For us, the democratic ideal is a common heritage of mankind. Those fortunate to enjoy its fruits have a responsibility to share its benefits with others."[11]

Singh also dropped the traditional Indian defensiveness in the debate on democracy versus development.

> Poverty, illiteracy, or socio-economic backwardness do not hinder the exercise of democracy. Quite the contrary, our experience of more than 50 years of democratic rule demonstrates how democracy is a most powerful tool to successfully overcome the challenge of development. But most of all, democracy alone gives the assurance that the developmental aspirations of the poorest citizens of our society will be taken into consideration.[12]

Unlike in the Community of Democracies initiative, in which India chose to take the back seat, New Delhi was now more enthusiastic in the context of the big changes that Bush was prepared to take toward the transformation of bilateral relations. The Indian government's willingness to do this amidst the known visceral opposition from the Communist allies of the ruling coalition to any political cooperation with the United States, let alone on democracy promotion,[13] was a signal that the Indian establishment had acquired an unprecedented political comfort level with the United States. Yet, there was still considerable resistance within the Indian foreign policy establishment to supporting the UN Democracy Fund. The multilateralists in the foreign affairs office were particularly concerned that joining the United States on the democracy issue would cost India its traditional NAM allies at the UN.[14]

The criticism was not merely from the Indian side. The skepticism was considerable within the United States, increasingly polarized in the Bush years, over India's decision to warm up to Bush and his ideological agenda. The growing sense that the Bush intervention in Iraq had failed generated a new skepticism among both liberals and conservatives about the prospects for democracy promotion around the world. Furthermore, there is no shortage of U.S. critics who question India's credentials as a democracy.[15]

The waxing and waning of support for democracy promotion in the United States, however, is part of a familiar and unending cycle in which the pendulum swings from an emphasis on realism, caution, and the primacy of self-interest to a vigorous focus on spreading U.S. values abroad. In any case, Clinton placed the question of supporting democracy abroad on the Indian-U.S. agenda, and Bush has enthusiastically built on it. Pragmatists in Washington and New Delhi are aware that initiatives such as the Community of Democracies and the UN Democracy Fund are unlikely to set the world on fire. These kind of multilateral forums become routinized over time and lose policy relevance sooner than later. The real question that underlines the political engagement between India and the United States on democracy promotion is whether they can cooperate in specific circumstances to achieve political outcomes in favor of freedom around the world.

Indian-U.S. Convergences and Divergences

Evidence from the ground offers some interesting insights into the potential as well as the limits of future Indian-U.S. political cooperation on democracy promotion. The democratic transition in Nepal, which saw a peaceful movement forcing an ambitious monarch to surrender his absolute powers and accept far-reaching constitutional changes, is a favorable sign. Throughout the crisis, which began with a spectacular regicide in the summer of 2001 and ended five years later when popular protests forced King Gyanendra to cede power to the people, New Delhi and Washington engaged in unprecedented diplomatic coordination. By cooperating with each other and with other major powers such as the European Union in coercing the Nepalese and by cautioning China not to break the arms embargo imposed by the Western powers and India, New Delhi and Washington successfully prevented the monarchy from dividing the great powers to its advantage.

To be sure, there were many tactical differences between India and the United States in managing this transition, especially in the final stages. Whereas India was prepared to countenance a political role for the Maoists, the United States was more apprehensive of being taken in by the promises of the rebels, who were branded as terrorists by Washington and New Delhi. The U.S. view of treating Maoists purely from the perspective of terrorism was indeed a view that was shared strongly by sections of the Indian establishment. New Delhi was torn between those who sought to deal with the Maoists simply as terrorists and others who sought to put the question in the larger context of the struggle for democratic and social change in Nepal. As the crisis unfolded rapidly in the spring of 2006, the latter won the day. The assessment that Maoists in Nepal were not different from the many insurgent groups in India that were ultimately brought into the mainstream through political accommodation has been borne out, at least for the moment.

The Nepal experience could be seen as heralding a new phase of substantive political cooperation between India and the United States in supporting the region's positive evolution. For decades, India was deeply suspicious of the U.S. role in its neighborhood, insisting that other great powers keep out of its backyard on principle.[16] In turn, the United States had offered a sympathetic ear to smaller South Asian nations' complaints of Indian hegemony. This began to change with the decision of the Bush administration to establish a regional security dialogue with India in 2002.

The new framework allowed the two wary governments to begin to understand each other's concerns and explore the prospects for diplomatic and political cooperation. The dialogue has certainly been productive, with greater recognition of shared interests in the region, including ending the Sri Lankan civil war on the principles of federalism and protecting minority rights as well as encouraging political responsibility amidst the anarchy in Bangladesh. The convergence of Indian and U.S. interests was also strong in promoting the reconstruction of Afghanistan after the ouster of the Taliban. India has emerged as one of the top donors to Afghanistan, and the United States has warmly welcomed the substantive Indian contribution. The frequent interaction between the two foreign policy establishments also helped to remove historically accumulated mutual distrust.

Despite the positive evolution of Indian-U.S. cooperation on promoting democracy, the limits are evident. The Bush administration, which has endorsed India's high-profile economic diplomacy in Afghanistan, has been hesitant to seek New Delhi's participation in bolstering the military capabilities of the Karzai government. Dependent as Washington is on the Pakistani army's pivotal role in stabilizing its lawless border with Afghanistan, it is especially sensitive to Islamabad's concerns about New Delhi gaining a strong political position in Kabul. The Bush administration also feels that Afghanistan must be insulated from a potentially harmful Indian-Pakistani rivalry.

The United States is also unwilling to discuss democracy in Pakistan in its dialogue on shared political values with India. Indian-U.S. cooperation is arguably essential to engineer a significant political evolution in Pakistan toward modernization and democratization. Yet, the immediate U.S. stakes in Pakistan are so high that it cannot afford to antagonize Islamabad by being seen as engaging India on internal Pakistani matters. Although the United States has been willing to defer to India's leadership in dealing with the internal crises in the smaller neighbors of the subcontinent, Washington finds it necessary to deal with Pakistan in an entirely different manner.

India also finds it difficult to agree with the U.S. approach to promoting democracy in Burma by isolating it and tightening the sanctions against the military regime. India's own policy toward Burma, with which it shares a long land border and the expansive Bay of Bengal, has evolved over a period of time. In the wake of the 1988 coup by the Burmese army, India was a strong and perhaps the only supporter of the democracy movement. Aung San Suu Kyi, the interned leader of the movement for restoration of democracy, had studied in New Delhi and had a huge number of admirers in India, often at the very highest levels of government.

Yet, as New Delhi saw Beijing rapidly expand its political and strategic influence in the 1990s, India reversed its policy of hostility to the Burmese government and began what it called a policy of constructive engagement. Although there were other factors, such as the security of India's restive northeastern provinces, that impelled India to renew engagement with Burma, the competitive dynamic with China has steadily deepened India's relations with Burma to include even defense cooperation.

Former Bush administration officials who see the shared commitment to spreading democracy as one of the "pillars of the United States' transformed strategic relationship with India" are dismayed by the "hard-edged realist mentality" that India has demonstrated in its approach to the democracy question in Burma.[17] Just as the United States finds it impossible to elevate the objective of democracy promotion above all other interests all the time, India's own calculus on the balance between spreading democracy and defending its other interests are naturally not always consistent, varying from situation to situation. Although an Indian-U.S. dialogue on the first principles of democracy promotion has value, political cooperation on a case-by-case basis could ultimately lend substance to the agreed agenda of promoting democracy around the world in a more practical manner.

Resolving India's Dilemmas

The divergence between India and the United States on Burma is perhaps emblematic of a potentially larger divide between India and the West on the questions of sovereignty and nonintervention. As India, a rising power, begins to define its own interests in more expansive terms and seeks to protect its regional primacy from Chinese encroachment, its impulse to compete with Beijing is only bound to intensify in the coming years. Whether it is in the search for equity oil, securing raw materials, or developing international political influence, India is already locked into competition, if not rivalry, with China. This will inevitably often compel India to ignore the internal orientation of the regimes it is engaging in many parts of the developing world, putting it at odds with the West, just as China finds itself regarding Sudan.

Although India's stand on the situations in Sudan and Burma might mirror that of China, an important distinction must be made between the approaches of New Delhi and Beijing. Despite sounding the same when opposing intervention in internal affairs and defending the notion of absolute sovereignty, India's diplomatic practice tells a very different story from that of China. Within the subcontinent and its environs, India's presumed sphere of influence, New Delhi has not hesitated either to support democratic movements or occasionally use military force beyond its borders to defend what it considers to be universal values. Long before humanitarian intervention became the international fashion, India chose to intervene in East Pakistan in 1971 to end genocide committed there by the Pakistani army. India's successful creation of Bangladesh occurred in the face of UN and U.S. opposition. India also used force, although unsuccessfully, in Sri Lanka in the late 1980s to defend the territorial integrity of Sri Lanka and to protect the rights of the Tamil minority there.

India's traditional attitude toward nonintervention had two distinctive elements. At the global level, it sought to oppose interventions by the great powers that could set the precedent for potential interventions against itself. Within its own neighborhood, however, India's policy mirrored those of great powers choosing to intervene when its interests or principles demanded so. These attitudes of a weak nation fearful of other powers undermining its territorial integrity have given way to a more open consideration of the responsibilities that come with being a great power. As India faces up to the threats arising from potential failed states in its region and must find ways to generate positive internal change within those societies, it is coming to terms with the many accompanying conceptual and policy dilemmas.

In an important speech in February 2005, Indian foreign secretary Shyam Saran laid out some broad markers on New Delhi's attitude toward democracy in the region and hinted at the inherent sets of tensions between encouraging democratic change and exporting it; between national proximate and long-term interests; and between rival conceptions of order and justice. On the first set of issues, Saran argued that, "[a]s a flourishing democracy, India would certainly welcome more democracy in our neighborhood, but that too is something that we may encourage and promote; it is not something that we can impose upon others." Saran also warned against the temptations of seeking short-term advantage in the neighborhood by supporting nondemocratic forces: "We believe that democracy would provide a more enduring and broad-based foundation for an edifice of peace and cooperation in our subcontinent. ...

[W]hile expediency may yield short-term advantage, it also leads to a harmful corrosion of our core values of respect for pluralism and human rights." Although he recognized the importance of a democratic foundation in relations with neighbors, Saran also emphasized that India cannot afford to suspend engagement with undemocratic regimes, saying that although "democracy remains India's abiding conviction, the importance of our neighborhood requires that we remain engaged with whichever government is exercising authority in any country." To resolve the tension between the necessity of engaging regimes and seeking to change their orientation, Saran focused on the need to engage civil societies: "We will promote people-to-people interaction and build upon the obvious cultural affinities that bind our peoples together. We need to go beyond governments and engage the peoples of South Asia to create a compact of peace and harmony throughout our region."[18]

The bad news from Saran, from the perspective of democracy promotion, was that India was not going to elevate the spread of freedom as an overriding national objective. India will take a long time to resolve the fundamental dilemmas of when and where to intervene in defense of higher universal values. Even the world's most powerful nation ever, the United States, has found it difficult to answer these questions. As the United States recoils from the failed intervention in Iraq, democracy promotion could well become a less salient objective in its deepening relationship with India. The good news is that India, which will soon have the capacity to influence regions other than its own, has begun to wrestle with these questions. It is equally welcome that New Delhi is shedding some of its past burdens of Third World ideology; is prepared to often, if not always, cooperate with other democratic powers to promote freedom; and is coming to terms with the complex relationship between democratic values and the use of diplomacy as well as force to promote them beyond its borders.

Notes

1. "PM's Speech at India Today Conclave," New Delhi, February 25, 2005, http://www.pmindia.nic.in/speech/content.asp?id=78 (speech by Manmohan Singh).

2. Dennis Kux, *India and the United States: Estranged Democracies, 1941–1991* (Washington, D.C.: National Defense University Press, 1992).

3. "PM's Speech at India Today Conclave"; "PM's Address at 'The Economist' Round Table on India," New Delhi, March 13, 2007, http://www.pmindia.nic.in/speech/content.asp?id=510 (speech by Manmohan Singh).

4. See Strobe Talbott, *Engaging India: Diplomacy, Democracy and the Bomb* (Washington, D.C.: Brookings Institution Press, 2004).

5. U.S. Department of State, "Toward a Community of Democracies" (paper, February 7, 2000), http://www.state.gov/www/global/human_rights/democracy/000207_democracies.html.

6. B. Raman, "Community of Democracies," *South Asia Analysis Group Papers*, no. 119 (April 20, 2000), http://www.saag.org/papers2/paper119.html.

7. Malini Parthasarathy, "India Declines U.S. Proposal to Head Caucus of Democracies," *Hindu*, September 21, 2000, http://www.hinduonnet.com/thehindu/2000/09/21/stories/01210002.htm.

8. Atal Bihari Vajpayee, "India, U.S.A. and the World" (speech, New York, September 28, 1998), in *Foreign Relations of India: Select Statements, May 1998–March 2000* (New Delhi: Ministry of External Affairs, 2000), pp. 57–69.

9. Robert D. Blackwill, "A New Deal for New Delhi," *Wall Street Journal*, March 21, 2005, http://bcsia.ksg.harvard.edu/publication.cfm?program=CORE&ctype=article&item_id=1169.

10. U.S. Department of State, "U.S. India Global Democracy Initiative," July 18, 2005, http://www.state.gov/p/sca/rls/fs/2005/49722.htm.

11. "PM's Remarks at the Launching of UN Democracy Fund," New York, September 14, 2005, http://www.pmindia.nic.in/speech/content.asp?id=193 (speech by Manmohan Singh).

12. Ibid.

13. See Prakash Karat, "Community of Democracies: India Joins American Ideological Enterprise," *Marxist* 16, no. 1 (January–March 2000), http://www.cpim.org/marxist/200001_marxist_us_india.htm; Kuldip Nayar, "Democracy Talk," *Indian Express*, July 19, 2005, http://www.indianexpress.com/res/web/pIe/columnists/full_column.php?content_id=74667.

14. C. Raja Mohan, "PM Steps Out of Third World Shadow," *Indian Express*, September 15, 2005, http://www.indianexpress.com/res/web/pIe/archive_full_story.php?content_id=78166.

15. Barbara Crosette, "Think Again: India," *Foreign Policy*, January 2007, http://www.foreignpolicy.com/story/cms.php?story_id=3693.

16. See Devin Hagerty, "India's Regional Security Doctrine," *Asian Survey* 31, no. 4 (April 1991): 351–363.

17. Michael J. Green, "The Strategic Implications of the Burma Problem," testimony before the U.S. Senate Foreign Relations Committee, Subcommittee on Asia Pacific Affairs, March 29, 2006, http://www.senate.gov/~foreign/testimony/2006/GreenTestimony060329.pdf.

18. Shyam Saran, "India and Its Neighbours" (speech, New Delhi, February 14, 2005), http://www.mea.gov.in.

Teresita C. Schaffer

Building a New Partnership with India

India watchers these days are suffering from a bad case of whiplash. The "buzz" of President Bill Clinton's last year in office—with his dramatic trip to India and Indian prime minister Atal Bihari Vajpayee's return engagement in Washington—has been followed since September 11 by an intense U.S. reengagement with Pakistan. At the same time, the rapid pace of high-level contacts that was established early in President George W. Bush's administration has, if anything, accelerated. High-level Indian visitors to Washington in the last quarter of 2001 included Vajpayee, Foreign Minister Jaswant Singh, and National Security Adviser Brajesh Mishra. Senior U.S. government officials who spent time in New Delhi include Secretary of State Colin Powell, Defense Secretary Donald Rumsfeld, and Admiral Dennis Blair, commander in chief of U.S. forces in the Pacific. Expectations are high for a Bush trip to New Delhi in 2002. Longtime students of Indo-U.S. relations marvel at the change of pace and the shift in attitude compared with most of the past 50 years but wonder how this development will mesh with the intensified U.S. interest in Pakistan.

Washington's increased interest in India since the late 1990s reflects India's economic expansion and position as Asia's newest rising power.

Teresita C. Schaffer is the director of the South Asia Program at CSIS and a retired U.S. ambassador.

Copyright © 2002 by The Center for Strategic and International Studies and the Massachusetts Institute of Technology
The Washington Quarterly • 25:2 pp. 31–44.

New Delhi, for its part, is adjusting to the end of the Cold War. As a result, both giant democracies see that they can benefit by closer cooperation. For Washington, the advantages include a wider network of friends in Asia at a time when the region is changing rapidly, as well as a stronger position from which to help calm possible future nuclear tensions in the region. Enhanced trade and investment benefit both countries and are a prerequisite for improved U.S. relations with India. For India, the country's ambition to assume a stronger leadership role in the world and to maintain an economy that lifts its people out of poverty depends critically on good relations with the United States.

For all their increased interest in each other, however, India and the United States still view the world differently. The United States, already very conscious of its standing as the world's sole remaining superpower, has a newly heightened sense of mission about world leadership since September 11. India remains uncomfortable with the very high profile of the United States as the arbiter of world security and hopes to see a more multipolar world emerge, with India recognized as one of the poles.

The model for the emerging relationship is not an alliance, virtual or otherwise, but a selective partnership based on specific, common goals and an expansion of the U.S. network of strong, friendly relations in Asia. Both countries need to approach their dialogue with candor, imagination, steady nerves, and—above all—realism.

A Changing India and a Changing Asia

The current U.S. focus on New Delhi emerges against a background of four major transformations in India. The first, and the one that has driven the change in U.S.-Indo relations the most thus far, is economic. The first stage of market-oriented reforms in 1991 brought about a marked increase in both domestic and foreign investment. Since then, the annual growth in India's gross domestic product (GDP) has averaged 6.4 percent, one of the highest rates in the world. In addition, during the same period, the services sector expanded from 6 percent to 8 percent of the economy. The dramatic development of the information technology industry has made India a power in a sector that is transforming the world economy; indeed, the large, prosperous, and prominent Indian-American community is now joined at the hip with "Silicon Valleys" in the United States and in India. Despite its low per capita income, India's economy—with a GDP of $442 billion in 1999—ranks eleventh in the world. On the basis of purchasing power parity, India has the world's fourth-largest economy.[1]

At the same time, India's political system has been moving away from its traditional domination by the Congress Party. By the end of the 1990s, two parties had emerged as national competitors: the Congress Party and the Hindu nationalist Bharatiya Janata Party (BJP). Both have gained votes at the expense of third parties, but neither is strong enough to govern by itself. Today, as never before, coalition building brings into the national political game the sensitivities, demands, and personalities of regional parties, some of them limited to only one of India's 29 states. At the same time, the former untouchables and other so-called backward castes that make up the majority of India's poor rural population—once solid members of the Congress Party's "vote banks"—are disappointed at the Congress Party's inability to address their economic and social needs and have formed their own increasingly powerful parties. These developments have brought new voices into the national political debate, but they have also made the country's politics more volatile and created a tremendous need for leadership.

India has long been South Asia's predominant military power, but in 1998 it also became an overtly nuclear power. India possesses the fourth largest army in the world. Its navy, with the largest submarine fleet and the only aircraft carriers among the Indian Ocean's littoral states, plans a sharp increase in its long-range projection capability. During much of the Cold War, India was a small factor in U.S. thoughts on international security issues, except for India's chronic dispute with Pakistan, which was an ally of the United States throughout that period. India's nuclear testing made its conflict with Pakistan more dangerous but also focused U.S. attention on India's importance as the largest military power between two major centers of U.S. military presence, in the Persian Gulf and in East Asia. The result is heightened U.S. interest in serious dialogue with India and the potential for more cooperative security policies in the future.

Meanwhile, India's foreign policy has adjusted to the end of the Cold War. Although Russia remains India's most important military supplier and a valued political contact, it can no longer deliver the kind of international support to which India had become accustomed for its policies. India is now actively cultivating a broader range of relationships, focusing on countries to which it had previously paid little attention. One example is increased attention to its ties in Southeast Asia, not just in the cultural and economic arenas but also in military contact with nations in the area—a new dimension in India's relations with its eastern neighbors.

As part of this reorientation, the United States is emerging as India's key external relationship. Indian leaders all acknowledge the importance of Indo-U.S. economic ties. Many recognize that India's security interests are not harmed, and may even be bolstered, by the U.S. security presence in the Persian Gulf and East Asia. This situation represents a much more solid base for cooperation on foreign policy issues than the two countries have had in decades.

The outlook in the United States has evolved as well. U.S. interest in strengthening its ties on the subcontinent also reflects the changes that have occurred in East Asia in the late 1990s: the financial crisis in the area, the opening of talks between the two Koreas, and the prolonged economic slump in Japan. These developments argue strongly for expanding the U.S. network of important Asian friendships. Today's high-level exchanges between the U.S. and Indian governments clearly indicate that the United States wants to develop cooperation on economic issues and on security and foreign policy issues as well.

The change in the U.S. perspective on Asia's and India's economic growth represents the promise of a new Indo-U.S. relationship, although the traditional concerns that drove U.S. policy on South Asia during the past decade are problems that still need to be overcome. The dispute between India and Pakistan, with its nuclear dimension, and the destabilizing impact of weak states in Afghanistan and Pakistan remain and indeed have intensified as a result of the events of September 11.

The sudden reestablishment of close relations between Islamabad and Washington came as a jarring surprise to New Delhi. In Indian eyes, the supreme irony is that antiterrorism is the basis for the new U.S. involvement in Pakistan. India was one of the first countries to support the antiterrorism campaign; moreover, India sees Pakistan as the source of India's own problems with terrorism, not the solution. The military buildup between India and Pakistan that followed the bombing of the Indian parliament in December 2001 put the problem in sharp relief. For India, U.S. willingness to force Pakistan to break with the militant groups accused of that incident was a critical test of whether the United States took India's terrorism problem seriously. For Pakistan, the crisis placed two of its highest priorities—its Kashmir policy and its new relationship with the United States—in conflict. The U.S. reaction satisfied neither country. Steps to counter terrorism had already been the subject of a pragmatic and productive Indo-U.S. dialogue before September 11, and the issue will probably constitute a long-term bond between the two countries. In the short term, however, periodic India-Pakistan crises are likely to place great stress on this feature of the bilateral relationship.

India's Future and the New Indo-U.S. Relationship

India's rising power provided the foundation for a changing relationship with the United States, but sustaining new Indo-U.S. ties will depend on India's evolution during the next 10 years. The first requirement is continued economic growth. An optimistic forecaster would estimate India's economic growth at 8 percent per year, a pace that would double the country's gross national product (GNP) in 10 years and bring it on par with present-day Japan and China and would raise India's per capita GDP almost level with present-day Peru. This scenario would involve a sharp increase in international trade. In the past decade, the value of India's exports has more than doubled, from $18 billion to $38 billion. With accelerated growth, a more rapid expansion of exports—perhaps as much as fourfold—could be expected. Given the continued vibrancy of India's software development sector, an increase of exports to the

United States on at least that scale is entirely possible, bringing the total to $36 billion or more.

This scenario is by no means out of reach, but it would require a more focused and determined approach to economic reform than the Vajpayee government has shown thus far. In particular, this projected state of affairs would require a major reform of the troubled electric power sector, faster liberalization in such key sectors as telecommunications, and an intense and widespread effort to improve the effectiveness of the government's economic institutions. As a result of these measures, today's Indian economy would advance substantially. A comparison with China's economy is both interesting and sobering because China is the benchmark against which Indians often measure their own international profile. According to the World Bank's World Development Indicators, China's GDP in 1999 was about 2.25 times the size of India's; China's exports totaled $194.9 billion, about 5.5 times as large as India; and its exports to the United States, at $81 billion, were nine times those of India.[2] According to this optimistic scenario, India would narrow those gaps. Barring an economic disaster in China, however, India will still be far from parity with its eastern neighbor.

Sustaining today's 5–6 percent growth rate is probably the minimum requirement for India to retain enough economic heft for a spot on the U.S. radar screen. This expectation is reasonable, despite the downturn reflected in the most recent economic statistics, but both the difficult political decisions involved in continued economic reform in India and the spreading recession in the United States and India's other trading partners will tend to pull growth down from the level it achieved in the 1990s.

Mediocre growth will extract a high price in terms of political and foreign policies. Without reforms, India's economy will sag, leading to competitive subsidization and spiraling fiscal deficits. A more worrisome issue for the United States, however, is that this situation could tempt India's government to take an unusually strident line toward Pakistan and its other neighbors, which, in turn, would increase the risk of some kind of miscalculation or desperate move by Pakistan.

If ineffective economic policy extracts high political and security costs, economic success has a political price as well: growing inequality, especially between the prosperous and backward states within India. During the 1990s, the economy of India's fastest-growing state, Gujarat, expanded by 8 percent per year, while Bihar, the slowest performer, grew by less than 3 percent.[3] Two of India's three largest states—Uttar Pradesh and Bihar—are also the slowest economic performers, but their populations are growing at well above the national average, leaving a smaller piece of a meager pie to distribute. If, as seems likely, these states continue to be excluded from the rest of India's prosperity, their large parliamentary delegations will surely try to compensate by means of subsidies or other forms of income redistribution. The prosperous states, moreover, are making a strong bid for greater devolution of power and resources to the state level. The argument for decentralization is strong, especially in a country as large and complex as India. Reducing the resources the poorer states receive from the central government to achieve this decentralization, however, is bound to prompt resistance to the government's efforts. Managing the political repercussions will fall squarely on the prime minister's shoulders. Whether the government is managing the problems of successful or of mediocre performance, the need to maintain a strong coalition at the national level will make the leadership vulnerable to distractions in the states.

A more substantial role for India globally will also require reasonable political stability and a high level of political leadership in the country. The Vajpayee government has demonstrated its ability to make bold decisions on issues involving economic and foreign policies, but these decisions have too often languished without the vigorous follow-up required. Today's coalitions are more difficult to manage than yesterday's Congress Party–dominated politics. A political leadership that governs by avoiding risks will not be able to pursue economic reforms.

Both major parties are likely to undergo a leadership transition in the next 5–10 years. The BJP has a relatively large pool of potential leaders, but most of them have a reputation for taking a harder line than Vajpayee on foreign policy and on domestic issues relating to the BJP's agenda for cultural nationalism. Unless they move to the center, they will have trouble assembling a governing coalition. The shift will not be easy for them. On the Congress Party side, second-tier leaders outside the Nehru-Gandhi family have been reluctant to challenge Sonia Gandhi's leadership; the alternative is Sonia Gandhi's daughter, Priyanka. The prospects for a real infusion of new blood are not encouraging. Apart from the two major parties, the regional parties, especially those in southern India, could be a source of attractive new leadership. Established state leaders, however, have thus far been reluctant to allow someone else to run their state power bases while they make their bids for national leadership positions. The transition, in short, is likely to be messy.

In addition, the pragmatic thrust in India's foreign policy during the past decade needs to continue if the new Indo-U.S. relationship is to bear fruit. The end of the Congress Party's political domination may have made this approach easier to sustain. The Congress Party is the traditional home of India's "Nehruvian internationalists," who shaped India's foreign policy during the country's first 40 years, emphasizing a high moral tone (thereby often annoying their U.S. interlocutors), exhibiting their devotion to the Non-Aligned Movement, and leaving a strong legacy of suspicion toward the United States. The BJP is the natural cradle of India's "hypernationalists," who favor a hawkish foreign policy, especially toward their neighbors, and look to military strength as the most effective way of realizing India's international ambitions.

In practice, India's foreign policy—particularly as it relates to issues outside the neighborhood—has reflected a third, pragmatic approach, especially since the country's 1998 nuclear testing program began. Pragmatists see trade and investment as the tools for reaching India's international aspirations and have been eager to establish a cooperative relationship with the United States. Vajpayee, having achieved his party's long-standing goal of taking India into the nuclear age, has been the prime spokesperson for this approach, as have most of his recent predecessors from various parties. The pragmatists are not based in any real political party, but their approach has a strong attraction for the party in power.[4]

If India's government stays on the pragmatic track, relations with the United States can be expected to deepen during the next decade. A more serious Indian dialogue with Japan as well as Southeast Asia is also likely, as is a continuing effort to improve relations with China, despite Indians' strong consensus that China is their most serious strategic rival.

From the U.S. point of view, a pragmatic foreign policy will produce mixed results for India's approach to the Middle East. India only established diplomatic relations with Israel in 1992, but Israel has already proven to be a significant source for security consultations and an attractive "niche supplier" of military equipment. A common interest in restraining Islamic fundamentalism will undergird continuing development of India's relations with Israel.

On the other hand, India's sensitivity to relations with its major energy suppliers will remain strong throughout the coming decade. Even if India's government makes substantial improvements in the management of its energy sector, the country's energy requirements will rise, and the increased supply will need to come from imports. Points of potential friction between India and the United States include Iran, from which India currently buys about nine percent of its imported oil and with which it hopes to expand trade; Iraq, traditionally India's closest Arab friend; and the Central Asian countries, already an arena for fierce rivalry with Pakistan, particularly as a great deal of overheated speculation has emerged about possible pipeline routes through Pakistan into India.

The U.S. Role in Sustaining the New Partnership

Whereas India must sustain its new relationship with the United States through economic growth, political leadership, and a creative and pragmatic foreign policy, the United States needs to contribute a steady dose of political attention as well as to foster a sensitive and candid dialogue with India's leadership. The U.S. government's priorities regarding nuclear nonproliferation and India's role in it are ripe for reevaluation.

The security dialogue could well emerge as the most dynamic aspect of Indo-U.S. relations in the next decade. The Vajpayee government's positive reaction to Bush's announcement of a strategic policy centered on missile defense brought cheers from Washington (and groans from some of India's traditional foreign policy elites), but U.S. and Indian strategic approaches remain some distance apart. The most fundamental difference is seldom explicitly discussed: the United States sees itself as the sole remaining superpower, whereas India is still uncomfortable with unipolarity and considers itself one of the logical shapers of a multipolar international order. Consequently, India is likely to continue cultivating close ties with countries that see themselves as counterweights to U.S. dominance. The most important among them is Russia, from which India still buys much of its imported military equipment. If Russia's internal situation revives enough to sustain a more active diplomatic posture, developing a common agenda with India will be a very attractive option and one that, despite the end of the Cold War, could occasionally prove awkward for the United States. Yet, this quest for multipolarity will coexist with India's efforts to develop closer relations with the United States.

When it comes to nuclear proliferation—the thorniest issue on the security agenda—strategic thinkers in India consider the Bush administration's strategic approach a significant move away from the treaty architecture that has been the basis of U.S. nonproliferation and arms control policy for decades. India foresees the possibility of entering into selective, de facto agreements with the United States in areas where divergent policies toward the Non-Proliferation Treaty (NPT) and the Comprehensive Test Ban Treaty made agreement impossible in the past. Despite the Bush administration's significant shift in tone and emphasis, bridging this gap will not be easy. Nevertheless, India shares some of the most important goals in this area with the United States, notably the policy of not exporting nuclear know-how or material to countries that have not yet "gone nuclear." The continued participation of the United States in the NPT precludes recognizing India as a nuclear weapons state as defined in the treaty. In practice, the United States has decided that it can accept the existence of nuclear weapons under Indian control, but it still needs to enlist India as one of the leaders of the global effort to limit the further spread of nuclear danger. With a little imagination, restructuring the international institutions that deal with nuclear export controls so that India can become one of the managers of that part of the nonproliferation regime, rather than simply the object of its controls, should be possible.

India will consider technology transfer as a key indicator of a real shift in U.S. policy. The U.S. administration has lifted the sanctions imposed after India's nuclear testing began in 1998 and has restored the normal procedure under which the U.S. government reviews each proposed export license for India case by case, assessing the impact of each on a list of policy criteria, including human rights, regional security, and protection of sensitive technology. In past years, proposed sales of sensitive equipment and technology to India could languish for months or even years in the approval process, and many were ultimately rejected. If India and the United States are indeed developing a broader range of common security interests, simply restoring the old pattern will not suffice. The Indian government and the key commercial participants in this process will need to understand the new rules of the game. The two governments have discussed these issues, but the real test will come as actual applications work their way through the system.

Even with the lifting of the post-1998 sanctions, however, U.S. law goes well beyond NPT requirements and all but bans cooperation with India on issues related to nuclear weapons. The White House and the U.S. Congress need to make this legislation more flexible. A strong argument can be made for permitting U.S.-Indo cooperation related to reducing the risk of nuclear conflict between India and Pakistan. India will probably be anticipating establishing more far-reaching nuclear trade, however, particularly given the Bush administration's energy policy, which puts new emphasis on developing nuclear energy in the United States. This area could be a bone of contention between the two governments.

Two candidates for a productive dialogue between India and the United States about security issues are especially promising. The first involves the Indian Ocean. Both India and the United States are increasingly conscious of the importance of the sea-lanes that will carry Persian Gulf oil east to the world's most rapidly growing energy markets, and both countries have begun limited cooperative naval activities in the Indian Ocean. The military as well as political dimensions of this dialogue need to be deepened. Beyond that, the United States should support India's efforts to strengthen its ties in East Asia, including eventual membership in the Asia-Pacific Economic Cooperation (APEC) forum. Drawing India into this Asian network will strengthen the forces in India attempting to achieve economic reform and establish a pragmatic foreign policy.

The second promising topic is counterterrorism. A productive joint working group in this area was established in 2000, but U.S. reengagement with Pakistan following the September 11 attacks has complicated the situation. In the long term, India and the United States share fundamental interests in this policy area. Some time may pass, however, before disentangling the issue of terrorism from the question of India-Pakistan relations and forging cooperation that extends to the multilateral arena becomes possible.

The alliance model that the United States has used to build ties in Europe and East Asia will not fit its relationship with India. Recognizing this disparity is another contribution the United States must make to the sustainability of the new relationship. U.S. and Indian views on the architecture of international politics are too different to fit comfortably into an all-encompassing structure of cooperation. Instead, aiming at a selective partnership, starting with common interests that both sides can pursue without too much strain and expanding as both countries develop the habit of working together, is more sensible.

Some on the U.S. political right see in India a natural counterweight to an increasingly hostile China, and these individuals have found common ground with some of India's nuclear hawks. China is already high on the list of topics that India and the United States discuss in depth. The reality, however, is likely to be subtler and less dramatic than this kind of anti-China stance. Neither India nor the United States wishes to see a single power dominating Asia. India anticipates an enduring rivalry between itself and China but has taken great pains to make whatever improvements are possible in the relationship. India has no interest in contributing to China's fear of encirclement. For its part, China is less preoccupied with India, largely because it sees Indian power as not great enough or close enough to key Chinese vulnerabilities to pose a major threat.

In fact, strong Indo-U.S. relations do not imply hostility toward China, and an effective U.S.-China relationship does not suggest animosity toward India. In the past year, the increasing attention that high-level U.S. officials have directed toward India has encouraged China to respond with high-level visits to India and occasional overtures toward the United States. U.S. policy should try to encourage this kind of "virtuous cycle." A good relationship with the United States is likely to enhance China's willingness to play a constructive role in South Asia, for example, by encouraging Pakistan's leaders to lay a foundation for peace. In contrast, ineffective or stormy relations between the United States and China could tempt Beijing to look to South Asia for ways to make life more difficult for the United States, as China has done in the past.

The Pakistan Factor

Particularly striking about the building blocks for the new Indo-U.S. relationship is how little Pakistan figures in them. Yet, the long-standing dispute between India and Pakistan remains the greatest obstacle to the role India wants to play in the world, and the possibility of unintended Indo-Pakistani conflict is still the single greatest potential danger the United States perceives in South Asia. Leaving Pakistan out of a discussion of Indo-U.S. ties would be disingenuous, particularly in the aftermath of September 11.

India's unresolved problems with Pakistan start with Kashmir, the subject of conflicting claims by India and Pakistan and the object of two wars between them as well as a continuing insurgency, supported by Pakistan, in the Indian-held parts of the state. The list of problems between the two countries also includes a group of secondary issues related to Kashmir, such as the status of the world's most desolate, disputed military installation on the Siachen Glacier in the high Himalayas, as well as a number of other "normalization" issues, including trade and visa regulations.

Since September 11, the level and frequency of violence has increased within Kashmir and across the "Line of Control" that separates

India and Pakistan. Statements coming from both governments provide no encouragement that the leadership of either country is close to a sustainable formula for resuming talks about the situation. India's most recent initiative for beginning talks with Kashmiri political leaders also seems to be going nowhere.

Even worse, high-profile terrorist incidents, including suicide bombings of the State Assembly building in Srinagar (capital of the part of Kashmir administered by India) and more recently at the Indian parliament in New Delhi, have raised tensions between India and Pakistan dramatically. The most likely culprits in both cases are militant organizations that also appear on the U.S. government's list of terrorist organizations, active in Kashmir but headquartered in Pakistan. U.S. actions since that latest incident have made clear that the freedom of action these groups have enjoyed in Pakistan is incompatible with the relationship Pakistan is now trying to establish with the United States. The regional military buildup that followed the bombing demonstrates how easily such incidents can provoke a cataclysmic set of reactions and how vulnerable regional peace is to another violent incident.

Resolving these problems will require a high level of Indian and Pakistani leadership. Both countries, as well as Kashmiri representatives, urgently need to start a process that will eventually lead to an arrangement that is comfortable for all three parties and that addresses the issue of the Indo-Pakistani relationship and the problems of governance within Kashmir. Any such process would be slow and crisis-ridden; finding a solution is a marathon effort, not a quick fix.

The obstacles to the success of such an endeavor are daunting. In India, coalition politics and broad popular resentment against Pakistan make it difficult for a leader to push even in the best of times for a reasonable settlement of India's problems with Pakistan. If India's economic performance is mediocre, this task will become more difficult. For Pakistan, Kashmir has powerful popular appeal. The political compromise required for a settlement would be very painful, and the strength Pakistan's government has gained by confronting militant groups over their activities in Afghanistan will not easily carry over to Kashmir. Without such an effort, however, the likelihood of new and dangerous confrontations over Kashmir is unacceptably high. Despite the new is-sues that unite India and the United States, this all-too-familiar one remains at the top of U.S. foreign priorities and cries out for a sustained and sophisticated U.S. diplomatic strategy.

Moving Ahead: Policy and Process

The policy agenda for the United States to sustain this shift in its rela-tions with India is clear. India's own economic progress is one of the key drivers of the new relationship. U.S. policy should recognize its stake in India's growth and select its economic reform agenda based chiefly on the broad economic impact of proposed reform measures. The U.S. government will need to manage its remaining differences with India with sensitivity, candor, and sophistication. Increased economic ties will be accompanied by inevitable trade problems, which will need to be addressed in the same way. The White House must devise a formula for bringing India into a position of greater leadership in international arrangements to stem the onward spread of nuclear proliferation. As the United States leaves sanctions behind, the government should es-tablish a more user-friendly system for dealing with transfers of sensitive technology and ensure that export license approvals reflect the broader array of common interests that the two countries are developing. A seri-ous dialogue on the security of the Indian Ocean should be an instruc-tive and fruitful exercise for both sides.

Both the long-term health of U.S. relations with India and short-term concerns about maintaining peace in South Asia argue for a more active U.S. diplomatic engagement on the issue of relations between India and Pakistan, including Kashmir. Reengagement with Pakistan and the build-up of ties with India has produced the strongest simultaneous set of bilat-eral U.S. relations with both countries in many decades. A sophisticated but persistent effort to press the participants to develop a peace process is needed. Neither side will greet these attempts with unalloyed enthusiasm. Pakistan traditionally welcomes international involvement, but its gov-ernment will have to acknowledge that the first U.S. demand is likely to be a real crackdown on violent militant groups. India's long-standing preference is for a purely bilateral approach, but a quiet diplomatic effort will almost certainly be accepted if the United States can build up the trust it has begun to establish with India. The stakes are too high for all parties concerned to ignore the issue.

In some ways, the key for the United States is the process itself. Presidential telephone calls in times of crisis and regular political-level discussions that go well beyond the usual South Asian topics have already become part of the United States' modus operandi with India. The next steps involve giving this process roots, as both governments develop the habit of having political leaders and senior-level officials consult on a wide range of issues. Moving from dialogue to cooperative action, the two governments should work together on a smaller agenda of bilateral issues. Because the multilateral setting raises India's interest in demonstrating its autonomy and independence of action, multilateral cooperation will be more difficult, but, as the relationship deepens, coordination should be possible here too on a selected yet expanding agenda.

A significant omission, now being actively addressed, has been dialogue between the two countries on military issues. Another surprising occurrence is the very thin expertise on India that exists in the U.S. government and expertise on the United States within the Indian government. Exchanges, training assignments, and other devices for building greater expertise among officials in both governments can give the new relationship stability and depth; signs indicate that this evolution is beginning. Both countries should take advantage of the bonds created by the Indian-American community and the wealth of organizations that are active in the private sectors of both countries. Above all, the U.S. and Indian governments should accept, with good grace if possible, that the two countries will continue to hold different views on many subjects, even as they develop their new partnership.

Notes

1. Gross domestic product (GDP) statistics from the World Bank (World Development Report). Economic growth as estimated in the Economic Survey of India, 2000–2001, Ministry of Finance, Government of India.

2. Figures from World Bank, World Development Indicators.

3. Montek Singh Ahluwalia, "State Level Performance under Economic Reforms in India," paper presented at the conference on Indian Economic Prospects: Advancing Policy Reform, Stanford, Calif., May 2000.

4. A more extensive discussion of these three schools of thought can be found in Kanti Bajpai's forthcoming book on India's Grand Strategy.

Xenia Dormandy

Is India, or Will It Be, a Responsible International Stakeholder?

It has become a cliché that the key strategic challenges facing Washington and the wider international community, such as energy, water, terrorism, economic development, and nonproliferation, cannot be solved by the United States alone. Although the United States unarguably retains its post–Cold War preeminent position, events since the September 11 attacks have shown the limitations of Washington's hard and soft power. Meanwhile, the power of Europe and Japan are waning as they face internal distractions that limit their influence, while China's is rising globally and in Asia, arguably the most important region to the United States strategically. China's increasingly high military spending has built strong and capable armed forces, and its economic power is developing swiftly, with annual growth averaging nearly 10 percent over the past 20 years.[1] From a low following Beijing's crackdown on the 1989 Tiananmen Square protests, China's influence is growing as well.[2] These power fluctuations compel the United States to seek out like-minded allies that will proactively help to resolve global as well as Asian challenges.

In September 2005, Deputy Secretary of State Robert Zoellick asked whether China would rise peacefully to become a "responsible stake-

Xenia Dormandy is executive director for research at the Belfer Center for Science and International Affairs at Harvard University and former director for South Asia at the National Security Council. She may be reached at xenia_dormandy@harvard.edu.

Copyright © 2007 by The Center for Strategic and International Studies and the Massachusetts Institute of Technology
The Washington Quarterly • 30:3 pp. 117–130.

Global Powers in the 21st Century: Strategies and Relations

holder" that "recognize[s] that the international system sustains their peaceful prosperity, so [that] they work to sustain that system."[3] He went on in the speech to solicit China's cooperation on a number of global issues, including North Korea, nonproliferation, and terrorism. Considering India's significant rise over the past few years, the same question could be asked of India.

Largely unnoticed by the global community, India has ascended to the world stage over the past 15 years, building on its economic reforms of the early 1990s and nuclear tests in 1998. In addition to an economic growth rate second only to China's, at 8 percent annually over the past three years, New Delhi continues to retain its position as leader and cofounder of the Non-Aligned Movement (NAM) and unofficial head of the developing world. India has the third-largest army, fourth-largest air force, and seventh-largest navy worldwide and is eagerly lobbying to be considered a global player, actively seeking a permanent seat on the UN Security Council.

Both President George W. Bush and then–Prime Minister Atal Bihari Vajpayee have described the bilateral relationship as that of "natural partners."[4] The United States has made India one of its central foreign policy foci and a powerful success story, especially since President Bill Clinton's triumphal five-day visit in 2000. Considering its capabilities, will, interests, and values, India would seem to make an ideal partner in the region and even globally. Will India live up to the U.S. definition of an "international stakeholder"? What might be the constraints on its desire or ability to do so?

As Zoellick stated, international stakeholders help to defend or create an international system. Such an international system could be defined as a norm-sharing mechanism that establishes and enforces behavioral standards while sharing information to support those ends. In this case, stakeholders are less focused on who brings what resources to the table and more on identifying and prioritizing geopolitical issues, as is the case in the Shanghai Cooperation Organization (SCO) and the South Asian Association for Regional Cooperation (SAARC), organizations that focus on issues such as security, terrorism, economic development, and energy exchange. Alternatively, an international system could be a burden-sharing mechanism in which stakeholders are states willing to shoulder responsibility and make sacrifices to meet mutual goals, such as the response group to the 2004 Asian tsunami or the coalition of the willing in Afghanistan.

Whether India qualifies as a global stakeholder, either as a partner to help set international norms or to bear resource burdens, is a valid question. As a norm-setting partner, New Delhi is already valuable. India is a multiethnic and multireligious democracy with a strong military; great diplomatic influence, particularly within the developing world; and rising soft power. Its interests are not dissimilar to those of the United States. Its principal foreign policy concerns include terrorism, energy, nonproliferation, narcotics, and managing China as well as Pakistan. As Prime Minister Manmohan Singh has stated, "Our goal should be to ensure a prosperous, secure and dignified future for our people and to participate actively in contributing to the evolution of a just world order."[5] Can the United States look to India as a burden-sharing partner on the international stage?

Breaking Out of Its Nonaligned Shell

India's recent emergence as a norm-setting partner of the United States should not be taken for granted. Historically, India has not been a strong supporter of U.S. interests. Its founding and subsequent leadership of the NAM, which came from a desire to avoid the East-West ideological confrontation of the Cold War, led it to pursue alternative interests that strictly avoided any perceived tilt in either direction. As Prime Minister Jawaharlal Nehru asserted in his speech before the 1955 Asian-African Conference, marking NAM's founding, "Every pact has brought insecurity and not security to the countries which have entered into them."[6]

Although India has been much more evenhanded in its foreign policies and its friends since 1991, many in the Indian government still see the United States as Pakistan's ally, an untrustworthy partner, and a nation that spent significant diplomatic resources on keeping India out of the global power structure, particularly in the area of nonproliferation as India declined to sign the Nuclear Non-Proliferation Treaty (NPT). Nevertheless, as the United States distanced itself from Pakistan after the Soviet Union pulled out of Afghanistan in 1989, India also separated itself from the Soviet Union and subsequently from Russia.

Over the past decade, India has embraced development while retaining its leadership of the developing world. As it moves into the group of more developed nations, its interests will change to reflect this. India is already rejecting foreign aid, recognizing the value of being a provider, as demonstrated most notably during the 2004 Asian tsunami and the 2005 Pakistani earthquake. As India becomes more industrialized, its need to protect its agricultural base will diminish, and it will thus open up to more global trade and investment. India now has a significant and growing middle class, by some counts larger than the entire U.S. population, and the resources to invest overseas. New Delhi continues to improve its relations with its neighbors big and small, building a more benign reputation that allows it more flexibility of action.

India's relationship with China has improved notably since 2002, although both sides remain cautious and continue to compete for influence in Asia and beyond. Despite ongoing border disputes, the two countries started a strategic dialogue and conducted their first joint military exercises together in 2005. President Hu Jintao visited India in November 2006, making him the first Chinese head of state to travel to India in a decade.

The Indian-Pakistani relationship has weathered several recent storms. The 1999 Kargil incursion, during which the Pakistani military, dressed as freedom fighters, crossed into India in the state of Kashmir, severely strained relations. The Indian government responded by mobilizing approximately 200,000 troops. Without the actions of the international community, this incident would likely have led to a nuclear war. Bilateral relations were further stressed by a terrorist attack on the Indian parliament in December 2001, which is believed to have been undertaken by Pakistan-based militants.

Perhaps in reaction to the stark consequences of a collapse in relations, the subsequent Composite Dialogue has built trust between the governments and particularly between the two peoples. The dialogue has resulted in small but meaningful successes, including cross-border bus and train routes, military-to-military communication, and cricket competitions. Many in India believe that the time is ripe for real progress in 2007, particularly on some of the more controversial border issues of Kashmir, Sir Creek, and the Siachen Glacier.

India is also responsibly engaging smaller countries in the region. In conjunction with the United States and the United Kingdom, India played a vital role in pressuring King Gyanendra of Nepal to reinstate democracy after he dismissed the government in February 2005. Although India has resisted playing a central role in Sri Lanka since Prime Minister Rajiv Gandhi's 1991 assassination by a Sri Lankan secessionist, New Delhi is more recently bringing resources and pressure to bear to promote peace. Additionally, New Delhi has invested about $750 million in building infrastructure and training security forces in Afghanistan.[7] Finally, India was one of the five countries that came together as the core response group within 24 hours of the Asian tsunami in December 2004, eventually contributing more resources than any other country besides the United States, and is now leading an effort to develop a regional disaster alert system.

New Delhi is also beginning to take more interest in Asian regional architecture in conjunction with its "look east" policy. Many Southeast Asian nations urged India's involvement in the East Asia Summit (EAS), launched in December 2005, despite China's and Malaysia's clear desire to exclude them to ensure Chinese leadership of the organization. India is already a member of the SAARC as well as the Bay of Bengal Initiative for Multi-Sectoral Technical and Economic Cooperation and is pushing for membership in the Asia-Pacific Economic Cooperation (APEC) forum and the Association of Southeast Asian Nations. They are an observer in the SCO, which includes China and Russia but notably not the United States. In 2005 this organization proposed that the United States provide a timetable for withdrawal of its troops from its member nations. India's engagement with these organizations would have been unthinkable under Nehru's nonaligned foreign policy, but the country's contemporary goal of building economic growth encourages such alignments.

India's activities as a norm builder should not be overlooked. As a nation with similar objectives and values to those of the United States, its leadership in such organizations, particularly those in which the United States does not participate, can be extremely valuable. India's role in the EAS as a counterweight to China will likely ensure that this organization does not promote policies antithetical to U.S. aims and will not replace APEC as the leading Asian regional organization. Likewise, if India were to become a full member of the SCO, this organization would not likely take actions such as voting to remove all U.S. troops from Central Asia.

Stepping Up to the Global Stage

India's support for norm-building mechanisms is already evident in its quest for membership in regional organizations. In norm-building terms, it is on the cusp of becoming a responsible stakeholder globally. Whether India is ready to take on a burden-sharing role is another question, but Singh has at least articulated the need to strengthen global norm-setting institutions and multilateral arrangements, particularly for issues such as nonproliferation, the environment, and global and regional security.[8]

NONPROLIFERATION

The Indian government has long described the nation as having "an exemplary nonproliferation record" and as one that supports the highest "nonproliferation standards and goals,"[9] despite not being a member of the treaties and agreements that constitute the nonproliferation regime. India regularly expresses its concordance with such agreements as the Missile Technology Control Regime and, as the Congressional Research Service reports, it has been very good at controlling the spread of sensitive nuclear technologies.[10] With the signing of the U.S.-Indian Peaceful Atomic Energy Cooperation Act on December 18, 2006, which allows the United States to conduct civilian nuclear cooperation with India, and the ongoing efforts by both countries to persuade the Nuclear Suppliers Group to pass similar rules, India is no longer entirely outside the international nonproliferation architecture. Crossing a long-standing redline, this deal would be the first legitimate exchange of nuclear technology with an NPT nonsignatory since its creation in 1968. This provides an opportunity where India has or could show both norm-setting and burden-sharing leadership.

For norm setting, India declared in the 2005 U.S.-Indian Joint Statement that it would work with the United States for the "conclusion" of a multilateral fissile material cutoff treaty to ban the production of weapons-grade uranium and plutonium that could be used in nuclear bombs.[11] Being apprehensive of letting any nation have insight into its civil or military nuclear programs as verification of any treaty would require, the United States has shown some reticence toward this treaty. India, however, could and should take more action to move this agreement forward.

On the burden-sharing side, India has not yet taken steps to contribute to the international system. The potential certainly exists. Although India's atomic scientists and many in the political sphere reject outright any proposal that might limit India's self-sufficiency in this area, India could help create an agreement on enrichment and reprocessing by agreeing to forgo such activities on its own soil and signing up instead to the international fuel bank proposed by the International Atomic Energy Agency (IAEA), thereby setting an example for other countries, such as Iran.

At a minimum, India should join the Proliferation Security Initiative (PSI), an effort launched in 2003 to enhance interdiction capabilities worldwide that now has more than 70 participants. India has significant resources to bring to bear, not least its navy and its geographic location, both of which would make valuable additions to the PSI and any interdiction activity. India also has great influence with the nonaligned and developing countries; its actions could lead others to follow. Gaining India's leadership or, at a minimum, active involvement would be a significant boon to the nonproliferation community. In so doing, India would at little cost show its willingness to be a contributor to this community.

ENERGY AND ENVIRONMENT

Given its rate of development and gross domestic product (GDP) growth, India is becoming an increasingly important player in the global energy market. It is the fifth-largest consumer of energy worldwide,[12] and with anticipated annual GDP growth of 8 to 10 percent over the next decade, its energy demands will increase significantly. By 2030 it will likely be the world's third-largest energy consumer, after the United States and China.[13] As of 2006, approximately 70 percent of India's electricity needs are met by domestic (and dirty) coal resources, with electricity demand expected to double by 2015. Although the country produces a lot of electricity, 30 to 50 percent is lost along the delivery chain.[14]

India's increased energy demand will tighten the worldwide energy market, raising prices, and will have a growing environmental impact. Slowing or stopping India's burgeoning demand is not an option, so encouraging India to become a responsible energy consumer is paramount. To date, New Delhi's actions on this issue have been unimpressive. It has joined the Asia Pacific Partnership on Clean Development and Climate, a group that boasts many of the largest consumers, including Australia, China, Japan, South Korea, and the United States, but that has not yet taken any action.

India has significant potential for efficiency improvements. Given its relatively basic level of infrastructure, it could choose more environmentally friendly technologies from the start rather than incurring the additional costs of converting infrastructure as must many other countries. India could agree to adhere to short-term environmental targets as laid out in the Kyoto Protocol or another paradigm at relatively low cost and sacrifice. Such a step would set an example for other developing nations and demonstrate to the United States and other major powers its willingness to bear global burdens. Moreover, it would enjoy domestic support, as 51 percent of Indians considers global warming to be a critical threat.[15]

India also has a role to play in supporting global energy security. One-half of the world's oil is transported through the Malacca Straits, a route highly susceptible to terrorism and piracy that lies to India's southeast across the Bay of Bengal. India has had some part in ensuring the stable movement of shipping in this area despite the resistance of some of its Southeast Asian neighbors, notably Indonesia, Malaysia, and Singapore, who are wary of India's navy encroaching on their sovereignty and projecting Indian power into the region.[16] India's resources, namely its navy and proximity to the straits, make it a vital player to protect this channel in partnership with other countries in the region.

India currently reasons that attention to environmental concerns will diminish economic growth. As a developing nation, it believes that it should not be held to certain environmental standards until it reaches consumption levels similar to those of the United States. As Thomas Friedman recently pointed out, however, nations and companies that include "green" considerations in their planning will see economic returns over time as others have to catch up later on.[17] Despite much evidence to support this argument, it would take significant political capital for the government to sell this to India's population. Nevertheless, given the bilateral U.S.-Indian agreement to start a new "green revolution," the U.S. government and business sector can do much to support these efforts toward greater efficiency and alternative technologies that can be catalysts for this process.

REGIONAL AND INTERNATIONAL SECURITY

Because India prioritizes internal economic development, it requires external stability and security. India's military is exceptionally capable and well trained to support these ends. Its competence was proven clearly when it bested the U.S. military in joint air exercises in February 2004.[18] India continues to modernize its military, spending more than $19 billion in 2005[19] and increasing the budget by almost 11 percent from 2001 to 2006.[20]

Perhaps most significant to the United States, India has the potential to play a vital role with Iran. As a longtime friend of Iran, India has the influence that the United States is lacking, but it must be willing to see its relationship with Iran in a larger perspective that looks beyond its own personal bilateral history and energy concerns to the greater global challenge that a nuclear Iran might become. It has voted in the IAEA to condemn Tehran's deceit over its nuclear program, but it now needs to do more to apply real pressure. Although expecting India to forgo cooperation in the area of energy is unrealistic—an Iran-Pakistan-India pipeline is currently on the table—making it clear that, like many in the international community, India does not trust Iran with a nuclear capability will go a long way toward convincing Tehran that it has little foreign support for their intransigent position, even from old friends.

New Delhi also has a direct and vital role in ensuring regional stability vis-à-vis Pakistan and in promoting the development of China as a responsible partner. Although the United States does not "have a policy that would build up a relationship with India to contain China,"[21] Washington and New Delhi are watching Beijing carefully and pursuing policies that will induce China to move in a positive direction. India has made clear that it will not be a pawn against China, and like the United States, it is increasingly engaging in political, diplomatic, and military exchanges with China. Given the commonality of U.S. and Indian concerns and hopes about China, this is an issue on which they can and must closely collaborate.

Given its impressive economic growth and location, India could support trade with Central Asia through Afghanistan and Pakistan. India is beginning, like China, to reach out to Africa, another region of the world where it has interests. Its increasing need for energy sources makes Africa and Latin America two particular foci of attention,[22] but unlike China, it does not pursue this policy to the detriment of democracy or human rights. Activity in Africa is also a sign of its wider efforts to become a global power and the realization of the importance of the African grouping in the United Nations, as India needs Africa's support in a bid for permanent membership on the Security Council.

Having experienced terrorist attacks for decades, India is a central player in the war on terrorism. New Delhi has stepped forward in some areas, providing training and significant infrastructural support in Afghanistan. Given their focus on domestic terrorism, however, particularly in Kashmir, they have been less active in helping to create an international definition of terrorism or even a local regional norm. India has worked with Pakistan and others in South Asia to sign the Regional Convention on Suppression of Terrorism, but this has not resulted in any action.[23] Given their multiethnic and religious heritage and as the country with the second-largest Muslim population in the world, their contributions in resources, training, and norm setting would be meaningful.

As the world's largest democracy, India has enormous soft power and influence that it could use to support democracy promotion more actively in other countries of the region and world. To date, India has only been willing to promote democracy passively or as part of a larger group, such as cofounding the UN Democracy Fund, but they have shown some reticence in taking leadership.[24]

Finally, in the economic field, India has already taken a positive role in the international community through its leadership of the Group of 77 developing countries in the World Trade Organization (WTO). For the Doha round to succeed, however, the Indian government needs to do more than insist that the United States and the European Union compromise. They too will need to find a middle ground with developed nations.

The Critical Test: Will India Take On Burden Sharing?

Aside from its role in the tsunami response group and in UN peacekeeping operations, the government has been less enthusiastic about participating in burden-sharing mechanisms. Although both norm-setting and burden-sharing systems are important, the Bush administration has clearly favored the burden-sharing construct. Its treatment of the UN, Secretary of State Condoleezza Rice's absence from the 2005 APEC summit, and its dismissal of the Kyoto Protocol exemplify its disregard for organizations or agreements that only promote ideas or are unverifiable or ineffective in addressing particular problems. Although the United States has some responsibility to create space in the international community for India, New Delhi must show that it is willing to bear the burdens that come with being a global power, including navigating significant domestic and international constraints.

India's colonial history and NAM leadership have built a strong domestic consensus to retain its autonomy. The perception of independence has factored into its UN vote on Iran, the decision regarding troops in Iraq, and most recently the furor over the U.S.-Indian nuclear deal. In these cases, the domestic political dialogue revolved around the primacy of India's sovereignty and ensuring that decisions were made to promote national, not international, goals. As Singh stated during the parliamentary debate on the nuclear deal, "[N]othing will be done that will compromise, dilute, or cast a shadow on India's full autonomy in the management of its security and national interests."[25]

India will also be constrained by a political and practical necessity to focus on reducing rural poverty. The economic and social gap between the rich and poor within India is growing.[26] With 25 percent of the population, more than a quarter of a billion people, living in poverty,[27] the government is focused on lifting them up. The previous Bharatiya Janata Party–led government lost the May 2004 national elections due to a significant vote from the rural population expressing their dissatisfaction over their standard of living and lack of growth. New Delhi will inevitably need to make compromises for the sake of stability, growth, and integration into the global economy,[28] but it will be less willing to devote attention and resources to foreign policies that are not directly relevant to promoting the welfare of its poverty-stricken population.

India's willingness to devote resources to international objectives that do not directly benefit its people in clear and concrete ways is therefore in doubt. Officials in the prime minister's office have privately stated the priority that domestic interests have over foreign ones and their intent to avoid the costs associated with taking a leading role in international burden-sharing mechanisms.[29] Leading pundits in India agree, expressing no great need for India to take on wider public responsibilities, considering the costs they involve and the possibility of being perceived as a U.S. pawn.

New Delhi has stepped up to the plate when its domestic and foreign priorities require, such as its role in the tsunami response or its condemnation of Iran through the IAEA. In these cases, India's actions have supported its broader goals of being a global provider or maintaining its security—India wants a nuclear Iran as little as the United States does. Otherwise, it is less proactive, focusing on a general norm-setting role. The lack of strategic perspective of many of India's elites reinforces this tendency. Too many still think in transactional terms, looking for a direct quid pro quo rather than appreciating broader or more long-term benefits, a policy that has long been reinforced by the lack of trust between the Indian and U.S. governments. Although certainly not the case among the very top of India's foreign policy community, elsewhere it is widespread, if changing slowly. Moreover, the increasing fractionalization and regionalization of Indian politics makes creating and implementing substantive policies ever more difficult for the administration. The necessity of building and ruling by coalition in India often requires the government to reduce policy to the lowest common denominator.

The nation is not yet willing to forgo immediate domestic interests for longer-term international objectives. To become a major international player, however, India will at times have to put its own requirements second. Until it shows an ability to do so more regularly and on more vital issues, India's reputation as a responsible stakeholder will be tenuous.

How Can Washington Ease the Transition?

Beyond its domestic priorities and opposition, if India were to assume greater global leadership roles, other states will often be antagonized. The United States has ways to make it easier. Although in the fall of 2005 the U.S. government resisted declaring explicit support for an Indian seat on the UN Security Council, expressing the need for reform before expansion, it should now do so. Washington should also overcome its inherent resistance to expansion and historical bureaucratic concerns regarding India and support its entrance into international regimes such as the APEC forum and the Group of Eight.

Perhaps as important as support for India's ambitions and membership in these organizations, the United States should not expect a quid pro quo. Such expectations would play into India's fear that it would compromise its own independence and would add enormous political tension to the already significant sacrifices asked of Singh as he tries to reform long-held views of perceived U.S. imperialism. Not asking for something in return may run afoul of some current or former U.S. policymakers, who already feel that Washington has given India enough without reciprocation. They have argued that India's politicians have not shown gratitude for U.S. nuclear recognition, instead maintaining that they were entitled to it and resenting the strings, however few and loose, that the U.S. Congress attached to the deal.[30]

The United States should also do what it can to help India's economic development. Although India's success is currently restrained by problems in areas such as business regulations, enforcement, labor laws, and intellectual property rights, as India reforms Washington should support investment; consider increasing visas for highly skilled workers; and resist any backlashes against outsourcing, which will be particularly vocal in the run-up to the 2008 U.S. presidential elections.

Finally, the United States should not automatically assume that India, as a responsible international stakeholder, is always going to act in the U.S. interest. They are not always going to be aligned. In the WTO negotiations, for example, even if India finds a compromise position, it is unlikely to be where the United States would like it. A good faith effort should be enough. At the end of the day, India's interests will be parallel to those of the United States more often than not, but they will not be identical. Regardless, this should not be the test of a responsible international stakeholder.

A Work in Progress

The Indian and U.S. bureaucracies have long been wary of one another, sometimes with good reason. India has voted against the United States in the UN more times than Cuba has. Trust must be built in the coming years for a strong partnership to flourish. The pending U.S.-Indian civilian nuclear deal is a good start, but only a start. For its part, in time India will need to assume more burden-sharing responsibilities globally if it wants the United States to recognize its membership in the top tier of the international community.

In time, India's reticence will likely diminish. The civilian nuclear agreement, when it is completed, will finally remove the concrete barrier that has long kept India out of the nuclear nonproliferation regime. It will also remove the more intangible intellectual barrier that has stopped Indian governments and its people from playing a more assertive role in the international community.

Even now, however, the United States should not overlook that India is already acting as a responsible stakeholder, setting the norms and pursuing the values that are such an important part of what the United States represents. Like the United States, India is synonymous with democracy, development, equality, freedom, liberty, and other such fundamental beliefs. As former defense minister Pranab Mukherjee stated, "[The U.S.-Indian] partnership will ... help shape global norms and institutions that are universally accepted and democratic."[31] As India gradually becomes a wealthy nation able to meet the basic needs of its population, it will take on those additional burdens with capabilities it is already beginning to develop. For that day, the United States needs to have patience for a powerful friend and eventual partner to continue to emerge.

Notes

1. International Monetary Fund, "World Economic Outlook Database," September 2006; Public Affairs Division, Public Affairs and Communications Directorate, Organization for Economic Cooperation and Development, "Economic Survey of China 2005," *OECD Policy Brief*, September 2005, http://www.oecd.org/dataoecd/10/25/35294862.pdf.

2. Joshua Kurlantzick, "China's Charm: Implications of Chinese Soft Power," *Policy Brief*, no. 47 (June 2006), http://www.carnegieendowment.org/files/PB_47_FINAL.pdf.

3. Robert Zoellick, "Whither China: From Membership to Responsibility?" (speech, New York, September 21, 2005), http://www.ncuscr.org/articlesandspeeches/Zoellick.htm.

4. Office of the Press Secretary, The White House, "President Signs U.S.-India Peaceful Atomic Energy Cooperation Act," Washington, D.C., December 18, 2006, http://www.whitehouse.gov/news/releases/2006/12/20061218-1.html; Stanley A. Weiss, "America and India Are Getting Together, and It's About Time," *International Herald Tribune*, February 9, 2001, http://www.iht.com/articles/2001/02/09/edstan.t.php.

5. Manmohan Singh, "India: The Next Global Superpower?" (speech, New Delhi, November 17, 2006), http://pmindia.nic.in/speeches.htm.

6. "Speech to Bandung Conference Political Committee, 1955," Bandung, Indonesia, April 1955, http://www.fordham.edu/halsall/mod/1955nehru-bandung2.html (speech by Jawaharlal Nehru).

7. "India Increases Aid to Afghanistan," *Hindu*, January 19, 2007, http://www.app.com.pk/en/index.php?option=com_content&task=view&id=2276&Itemid=2.

8. Manmohan Singh, "Making Globalization Work: An Indian Perspective" (speech, New Delhi, December 17, 2006), http://www.ficci.com/media-room/speeches-presentations/2006/dec/dec18-pm.htm.

9. Shyam Saran, "Indo-U.S. Relations: An Agenda for the Future" (speech, Washington, D.C., March 30, 2006), http://www.indianembassy.org/newsite/press_release/2006/Mar/43.asp.

10. Sharon Squassoni, "U.S. Nuclear Cooperation With India: Issues for Congress," *CRS Report for Congress*, RL33016, July 29, 2005, p. 7, http://www.fas.org/sgp/crs/row/RL33016.pdf.

11. Office of the Press Secretary, The White House, "Joint Statement Between President George W. Bush and Prime Minister Manmohan Singh," Washington, D.C., July 18, 2005, http://www.whitehouse.gov/news/releases/2005/07/20050718-6.html.

12. Energy Information Administration, U.S. Department of Energy, "International Energy Annual 2004," May–July 2006, http://www.eia.doe.gov/iea/overview.html.

13. Carin Zissis, "India's Energy Crunch," *Council on Foreign Relations Backgrounder*, December 8, 2006, http://www.cfr.org/publication/12200/indias_energy_crunch.html?breadcrumb=%2Fissue%2F426%2Fenergy.

14. Paul Maidment, "Energy Outlook 2007: India's Powerful Dilemma," *Forbes*, November 28, 2006, http://www.forbes.com/business/2006/11/28/india-energy-environment-biz-cx_pm_1128indiaenergy.html.

15. Chicago Council on Global Affairs, "The United States and the Rise of China and India: Results of a 2006 Multination Survey of Public Opinion," 2006, http://www.thechicagocouncil.org/UserFiles/File/GlobalViews06Final.pdf.

16. "Singapore on Saturday Welcomed India's Offer to Help Safeguard the Malacca Strait," *IndiaDaily*, June 3, 2006, http://www.indiadaily.com/editorial/9380.asp.

17. Thomas L. Friedman, "The Power of Green," *New York Times Magazine*, April 15, 2007, http://www.nytimes.com/2007/04/15/magazine/15green.t.html?em&ex=1176782400&en=821b6cf046e2c6ed&ei=5087%0A.

18. Hampton Stephens, "USAF: Indian Exercises Showed Need For F/A-22, Changes in Training," *Inside the Air Force*, June 4, 2004, http://vayu-sena.tripod.com/exercise-iaf-usaf-su30-f15-article01.html.

19. "India's Defence Imports to Touch $35 bn by 2026: Antony," *India PRwire*, January 15, 2007, http://news.indiamart.com/news-analysis/india-s-defence-impo-14556.html.

20. Pramit Mitra and John Ryan, "Gathering Steam: India and the U.S. Extend Military Ties," *CSIS South Asia Monitor*, no. 99 (October 2, 2006), http://www.csis.org/media/csis/pubs/sam99.pdf.

21. Office of the Press Secretary, The White House, "Transcript: White House Press Briefing by Tony Snow and State's Burns," Washington, D.C., December 18, 2006, http://newdelhi.usembassy.gov/uploads/images/xiQWRyxHN-MI0B9Qa2MDA9w/snowburnsprbrief121806.pdf.

22. "Africa, Latin America Have Remained on Indian Radar," *Deccan Herald*, November 6, 2006, http://meaindia.nic.in/interview/2006/06/11in01.htm.

23. "SAARC Regional Convention on Suppression of Terrorism," http://untreaty.un.org/English/Terrorism/Conv18.pdf.

24. See C. Raja Mohan, "Balancing Interests and Values: India's Struggle with Democracy Promotion," *The Washington Quarterly* 30, no. 3 (Summer 2007): pp. 99–116.

25. "Statement of PM in Rajya Sabha on the India-U.S. Nuclear Agreement," New Delhi, August 17, 2006, http://pmindia.nic.in/parl/pcontent.asp?id=30.

26. Pranab Bardhan, "India Must Reduce Inequality to Usher in Reform," *Financial Times*, August 8, 2006, Asian edition, p. 11; Gurcharan Das, "The India Model," *Foreign Affairs* 85, no. 4 (July 2006): 2–16.

27. CIA, "World Factbook: India," https://www.cia.gov/cia/publications/factbook/geos/in.html.

28. Pranab Mukherjee, "India's Strategic Perspective" (speech, Boston, September 25, 2006), http://www.indianembassy.org/newsite/press_release/2006/Sept/8.asp.

29. Indian officials, interviews with author, New Delhi, January 2007.

30. Ashton Carter, "How Washington Learned to Stop Worrying and Love India's Bomb," January 10, 2007, http://www.foreignaffairs.org/20070110faupdate86175/ashton-b-carter/how-washington-learned-to-stop-worrying-and-love-india-s-bomb.html.

31. Mukherjee, "India's Strategic Perspective."

Part II:
The Rise of China

Robert Sutter

Why Does China Matter?

U.S. misperceptions, exaggerations, and sharp swings in thinking about China's significance in world affairs[1] date as far back as U.S. expectations in the nineteenth and early twentieth centuries about profits to be made in the Chinese market. In the half century since the end of World War II, such misperceptions have abounded, beginning with President Franklin D. Roosevelt's postwar push for an international order in Asia based on the power of a resurgent China, when in reality the nation was divided by a corrupt and crumbling regime under nationalist leader Chiang Kai-Shek. Although British prime minister Winston Churchill was more hardheaded about China's weaknesses, he failed to dissuade the United States from granting Chiang's government elite status as one of the Big Five war victors with a permanent seat on the United Nations Security Council.[2] U.S. leaders made a similar mistake following President Richard Nixon's historic trip to China in 1972 when they widely believed that, as a great power, China could force the Soviet Union to abandon its expansionist policies and accommodate the West. At the time, China was actually a weak state with a stagnating economy and an obsolete military enmeshed in a wrenching leadership struggle.

Robert Sutter is a visiting professor of Asian studies at the School of Foreign Service at Georgetown University.

Copyright © 2003 by The Center for Strategic and International Studies and the Massachusetts Institute of Technology
The Washington Quarterly • 27:1 pp. 75–89.

On the other hand, the United States grossly underestimated Chinese resolve when thousands of China's Soviet-backed "volunteers" first entered the Korean War in 1950 and then misjudged the fighting endurance of those volunteers, who would engage U.S. soldiers for three years of hard combat.

The 1989 crackdown in Tiananmen Square quickly replaced the 1980s U.S. perception of an economically alluring and reforming China with one of an oppressive Communist dictatorship likely to collapse just as East Germany had, only for China's rapid economic expansion in the 1990s to belie such expectations as well as modernize China's military. Aggressive Chinese military behavior toward Taiwan and the dispute over Taiwan's independence along with other Chinese territorial disputes prompted U.S. concern about China as a long-term strategic threat capable of contesting U.S. power in the not-so-distant future. More recently, the Chinese government's cooperation with the Bush administration, following the 2001 terrorist attacks against the United States, markedly reduced the U.S. focus on the Chinese threat, as Beijing worked closely with U.S. leaders as a partner in the war on terrorism and in addressing North Korea's nuclear weapons program.

History suggests, therefore, that, in times of significant U.S. attention toward China, U.S. assessments of China's global role have tended toward exaggerations and extremes, collectively resulting in a steady pendulum swing in perceptions of China as friend or foe that neglects careful analysis of China's various attributes and weaknesses. With U.S. priorities being its strategic commitments in Southwest Asia, wide-ranging contingencies in the war on terrorism, and international hot spots such as North Korea, an opportune moment has now emerged for a more balanced, dispassionate, and accurate appraisal of China's global power and influence.

Current Importance and Outlook

China's present international significance rests heavily on its rapidly growing economy and its increasing integration with the world economy. China's military and coercive power is more limited, though it is growing faster than any other Asian nation and poses major concerns particularly for Taiwan, Japan, and India, among other Chinese neighbors, and for their supporters, notably the United States. China's political role and influence in Asia has grown substantially in recent years, reflecting a more adroit Chinese approach to the region that effectively uses Chinese economic, military, and other strengths to expand Chinese influence, especially in areas where the United States, Japan, and other powers have been less active and attentive. Further, although Chinese ideology, culture, and other aspects of soft power have had limited international appeal, they reinforce Chinese efforts to win friends and influence opinion in nearby Asia.[3]

Looking forward, specialists often disagree sharply about China's future direction.[4] A balanced projection falling between those of disagreeing specialists sees China advancing the following policy priorities: shoring up Communist rule in China; pursuing the integration and integrity of Chinese territories, notably Taiwan; modernizing the Chinese economy and military; achieving greater regional preeminence; and enhancing China's global influence. Chinese leaders currently tend to believe that China is making progress toward these objectives but is far from having achieved them, particularly the regional and global goals.

Chinese leaders hold that their country is in no position to challenge the United States seriously. The more accommodating posture they have taken toward the Bush administration since 2001 is based in part on judgments that confrontation with the dominant and aroused U.S. superpower would be contrary to Chinese policy priorities. It would risk the stability so important to Chinese and Asian economic modernization, force Asian states to choose between the United States and China, and alienate the majority of Asian leaders who seek to avoid instability as well as choosing between Washington and Beijing.

Economic Assets

The Chinese economy remains the main bright spot in Asia and a major source of international economic dynamism. Difficulties caused by Severe Acute Respiratory Syndrome (SARS) in the first half of 2003 have passed, at least for now. China's economy expanded by more than 9 percent in the first quarter, and although the SARS episode reduced growth in the second quarter, the economy is on track to grow more than 7 percent, and possibly more than 8 percent, for the year. Some specialists may question the accuracy of such high growth figures, but the overall direction of the Chinese economy seems indisputable. Foreign direct investment (FDI) (China was the largest recipient in 2002), membership in the World Trade Organization (WTO), and hundreds of millions of Chinese consumers drive the economy's growth.

The Chinese economy now exerts important and growing influence on world trade.[5] China's WTO accession caused a slight increase in overall world trade that benefits many, but China's share of foreign trade last year accounted for almost 5 percent of world trade, or about $620 billion. The share of world trade in 2002 was almost double the 2.7 percent of world trade China carried just seven years earlier.[6] This trend is neither new, with annual foreign trade growth having roughly doubled the annual growth of the Chinese economy for many years, nor is it likely to decline, with total trade in the fiscal year ending in May 2003 up 40 percent more than the previous year.[7]

At the same time, the impact of the rising Chinese economy and its growing international integration on countries with resource, labor, and export structures similar to China has been negative. Southeast Asian exporters and labor-intensive export platforms in Mexico and elsewhere appear to be losing out to Chinese competitors. At the beginning of the 1990s, Southeast Asia took 61 percent of the FDI flows to developing Asian countries, while China received 18 percent. By the end of the decade, the situation had reversed.[8]

As its fourth-largest trading partner and the source of the largest U.S. trade deficit (more than $100 billion in 2002), China's economy is important even for the United States. U.S. importers are increasingly reliant on China, with almost 11 percent of U.S. imports coming from China. In 2002, Chinese imports grew faster than overall U.S. imports, at a growth rate of 22 percent.[9] Data for the first few months of 2003 show a large increase in U.S.-China trade, with the trade deficit forecast at $130 billion for the year. China's trade position—the relative importance of Chinese imports and exports for a given country or group of countries—is even higher with the European Union, while in Asia it is the number one trading partner for Hong Kong, Taiwan, South Korea, and Japan. Advanced economies increasingly seek advantageous investments and enterprises on the Chinese mainland. According to data provided by the Chinese government, foreign-funded enterprises conducted about half of China's trade in 2002; a large share of these enterprises is owned by entrepreneurs from Hong Kong and other parts of Asia who have shifted manufacturing to China to take advantage of lower costs for their exports and to gain greater access to the burgeoning mainland Chinese market.[10]

FDI in China in 2002 grew by nearly 13 percent, an impressive figure considering that worldwide FDI in developing countries at the same time fell more than 25 percent. Pledged FDI to China was up 42 percent in the first five months of 2003. The Chinese government predicts that FDI will reach an annual utilized rate of $100 billion in 2005. Along with other foreign investors, large U.S. corporations, including Motorola, Atlantic Richfield, Coca Cola, BP Amoco, United Technologies, Pepsi Cola, Lucent Technologies, General Electric, General Motors, and Ford Motor, have all increased their foreign investment in China.[11]

China's economy affects key world production and commodities, which in turn affect world supplies and prices. In steel, Chinese producers are developing so quickly that China is likely to surpass Japan as the world's largest importer of iron ore in this decade and is forecast to be among the most competitive exporters of steel in the next decade because of strong investment in state-of-the-art production facilities. Automobile sales in China jumped 56 percent in 2002 to more than 1.13 million vehicles sold. China's ports are now some of the world's most active, with Shanghai the world's fourth-largest port and Shenzhen outside Hong Kong the world's fifth-largest container port.[12]

China is a fast-growing U.S. export market ($22 billion in U.S. exports in 2002). U.S. exporters foresee important gains in China based on the spending power of more than 200 million middle-income consumers (those earning $1,000 or more annually), a broader population with a savings rate of more than 40 percent, and massive infrastructure needs. For example, China has the world's largest market for mobile phone networks, with 145 million current cellular phone users, and the potential for significant growth as only 13 percent of the population now uses mobile phones. Boeing predicts that China will be the largest market for commercial air travel outside the United States for the next 20 years, forecasting Chinese purchases of 1,912 aircraft valued at $165 billion. In 2002, China replaced Japan as the world's second-largest market for personal computers and will soon be the third-largest market for autos, with China's demand predicted to grow 20–30 percent annually over the next decade. China also continues to be the top destination for U.S. soybean exports, at a value amounting to more than $1 billion annually.

China now has the ability to affect world currency values and related trade flows. Impressive savings rates and large trade surpluses support China's foreign exchange holdings in excess of $346 billion, second only to Japan. Moreover, Chinese holdings of U.S. Treasuries impact the U.S. economy. Given large U.S. government spending deficits, Chinese creditors are estimated to possess about 9 percent of U.S. federal government holdings, such as U.S. Treasury bonds, owned by foreign creditors in 2003. Overall Chinese holdings of U.S. government (national, state, local) debt instruments amount to $150 billion.[13]

China maintains what it refers to as a "managed float" exchange rate system that is more or less pegged to the U.S. dollar. Some U.S. and foreign business representatives have charged for years that China's currency is significantly undervalued vis-à-vis the dollar. Government and business leaders in Japan, the EU, the United States, and elsewhere are pushing for a change in China's currency peg. Since the decline in the value of the dollar relative to other world currencies during the past year, the pressure for China to appreciate its currency has grown. Seeking to preserve the trading advantage and wary of instability that could flow from a currency appreciation, Chinese leaders resist this pressure. Many fear that the decline in the U.S. (and Chinese) currency value relative to other major currencies will give Chinese exporters an added and unfair trading advantage at a time of burgeoning Chinese exports and large trade surpluses with European, North American, and other markets.

Leading U.S. government commentators on this issue have included the secretaries of treasury and commerce as well as the chairman of the

Federal Reserve. Presumably mindful of strong U.S. interest in working with China on issues such as North Korea, President George W. Bush has said little specifically critical of China's unwillingness to strengthen its currency. Vocal advocates of Chinese revaluation have included Japanese, South Korea, Canadian, and European officials and representatives of industries in developing countries hard hit by burgeoning Chinese competition. Groups in the U.S. Congress have sent letters, promoted legislation, and organized themselves to counter China's actions.[14]

Not all U.S. commentators think a higher value for the Chinese currency would be good for the United States. China's determination to maintain the peg to the dollar requires it to buy huge amounts of dollars to prevent the Chinese currency from appreciating. This money is used to purchase U.S. government bonds, meaning that China is partly responsible for lowering long-term U.S. interest rates that in turn spur U.S. economic growth. The reduction in the cost of capital may well be more important to U.S. manufacturers than the gains that would flow from a higher value of the Chinese currency.[15]

Military Power

Although dwarfed by the U.S. defense budget of more than $300 billion in recent years as well as by advanced U.S. military technologies and power, Chinese military capabilities are rapidly growing. Official defense spending has increased markedly, often at double-digit annual rates since the early 1990s. Foreign estimates of Chinese defense spending usually are a few times larger than the stated official Chinese defense budget and place China second or third in the world in overall defense spending. A July 2003 report by the U.S. Department of Defense stated that China's defense spending amounted to "as much as $65 billion" a year.[16]

Chinese impatience to modernize prompted Beijing in the early 1990s to depart from its previous emphasis on self-reliance and purchase large numbers of advanced Russian equipment and technology needed to improve China's lagging power-projection abilities, particularly in air and sea power. During each of the last four years, China has purchased $2 billion worth of Russian military equipment, roughly double the annual level of such purchases in the 1990s.[17] Even though Western manufacturers have maintained an embargo on military sales to China since the crackdown in Tiananmen Square in 1989, Russian suppliers are ready to meet most Chinese requests. Sales have included naval surface combatants; submarines; fighter aircraft; and surface-to-air, air-to-air, and surface-to-surface missiles. The Russian equipment, along with China's own impressive development of shorter-range ballistic missiles, has been deployed to prevent Taiwanese moves toward greater separateness and to warn the United States not to intervene.

Assessments of the dangers posed by the Chinese buildup vary. The Defense Department warns of the implications for Taiwan of the buildup of China's short-range ballistic missiles (450 in 2003), the modernization of air and naval assets, and the shift in the People's Liberation Army's (PLA) planning to focus on a surprise attack that would bring Taiwan to terms before U.S. forces could intervene.[18] More moderate analyses such as that of a Council on Foreign Relations (CFR) task force in 2003 also make for sober reading.[19] It predicts that China probably will overtake Japan in the next decade or two to become Asia's "major regional military power" and suggests that the Chinese buildup in air and sea power will require "a continued robust U.S. naval and air presence that can likely offset the ability of Beijing to leverage future military capabilities into a real advantage against U.S. and allied interests in the Asia-Pacific region over the next twenty years."[20] It warns that "the Taiwan Strait is an area of near-term military concern."[21]

The CFR task force warns that Beijing may choose to use force even if the balance appeared to favor the United States and Taiwan, and the PLA has the ability now to undertake intensive, short-duration air, missile, and naval attacks on Taiwan, as well as more prolonged air and naval attacks. Although the report judges that U.S. forces would ultimately prevail in a military conflict over Taiwan, the report notes that PLA naval surface combatants, submarines, and missiles and torpedoes could slow a U.S. intervention.[22]

The United States can have some degree of confidence in its ability to offset China's rising military power, but China's neighbors are much less certain. Taiwan, Japan, and India have complained about China's military advances, while others have seen their interests better served by a low-key approach that avoids antagonizing the emerging Asian strategic leader.

Other sources of Chinese military power involve Chinese nuclear weapons and Chinese proliferation of weapons of mass destruction (WMD). Although the CFR report notes that "the United States will continue to possess overwhelming dominance over China's nuclear forces for the foreseeable future,"[23] China is improving the number and sophistication of its several hundred nuclear weapons. As new road-mobile, solid-fueled, long-range missiles are deployed during the next several years, they will pose an improved Chinese second-strike capability in the event of a U.S. nuclear attack on China, even if the United States deploys a ballistic missile defense.[24] During the longer term, as U.S. and Russian nuclear forces decline in numbers as a result of post–Cold War negotiations, the salience of China's several hundred improved nuclear weapons is sure to grow.

Chinese proliferation of WMD and related technologies continues to loom large in world affairs. The scope of Chinese WMD proliferation has narrowed to focus on such long-standing partners as Pakistan, Iran, and North Korea, although egregious Chinese transfers of nuclear warhead designs and materials appear to be a thing of the past. The consequences of China's earlier transfer of nuclear weapons designs and materials to Pakistan appeared much more serious when it was reported this year that Pakistan in turn had transferred its nuclear weapons know-how to North Korea in exchange for ballistic missiles.[25] Concerns that Iran may benefit from such indirect (such as via North Korea) or direct Chinese transfers in its reported efforts to develop nuclear weapons provided a context for the U.S. government this year to sanction several Chinese entities along with other international companies for alleged WMD transfers to Iran.[26]

Foreign Policy Influence

Based on its size, strategic location, and rising economic and military power, China has become the leading regional power in Asia; and factors of geography and interest have made Asia the main international arena where the Chinese government has always exerted influence. China's focus on Asia was blurred for decades, however, as Chinese leaders couched their Asian policy in often controversial and unappealing terms of broader international efforts to foster armed struggle and revolution against imperialism and its Asian and other supporters. Former president Jiang Zemin and his contemporaries, backed by current president Hu Jintao and the recently installed new generation of Chinese leaders, have changed this pattern and are following a focused policy in Asia involving enhanced diplomatic, economic, and military exchanges; increased Chinese participation in Asian multilateral organizations; and greater Chinese flexibility on territorial disputes that, on the whole, has served Chinese interests well.

In broad terms, the Chinese leadership has worked pragmatically to sustain regional stability and has sought greater economic advantage and political influence without compromising core Chinese territorial, security, or other interests. Its efforts encountered difficulties, notably in the early 1990s, when China's assertiveness regarding disputed territories along its eastern and southern flanks and its bellicose posture during the Taiwan Strait crisis of 1995–1996 alarmed its neighbors. Subsequently, China unveiled in 1997 the "New Security Concept,"[27] which emphasized the Five Principles of Peaceful Coexistence, mutually beneficial economic contacts, and greater dialogue promoting trust and the peaceful settlement of disputes. Chinese leaders also sought to establish "partnerships" or "strategic partnerships" with most of the powers along China's periphery (e.g., Russia, the Association of Southeast Asian Nations [ASEAN], Japan, and South Korea) as well as with other world powers. These partnerships emphasized putting aside differences and seeking common goals.[28]

Chinese political and military leaders have also actively interacted with visitors from other Asian countries and traveled extensively throughout the region to foster closer economic, political, and military cooperation. In 2000, Chinese officials were instrumental in establishing the Shanghai Cooperation Organization (SCO), which includes Russia, Kazakhstan, Kyrgyzstan, Tajikistan, and Uzbekistan; and they have worked carefully to improve China's relations with ASEAN, proposing an ASEAN-China Free Trade Agreement and a China-ASEAN security pact. China also worked closely with ASEAN, Japan, and South Korea in the so-called ASEAN Plus Three dialogue that emerged around the time of the Asian economic crisis of 1997–1998. Backed by growing Chinese economic and military power, China's increased high-level attention to Asia has been well received throughout the region and has opened the way to expanding Chinese influence in Asia.

Chinese authorities have been less condescending and have shown more genuine respect even for smaller neighbors such as Cambodia and Burma than they did during the Maoist period. Presumably reflecting greater assuredness in dealing with Asia, Chinese leaders have been less prone than in the past to seize on differences and react in jarring and assertive ways that would add to Asian nervousness about Chinese intentions. For example, they were notably discreet in dealing with the anti-Chinese riots in Indonesia in the late 1990s.[29] Chinese leaders have been more open to Asian multilateral arrangements, reflecting less concern than in the past that such regimes could be used against Chinese interests. They have become active participants in the regional security dialogue, the ASEAN Regional Forum, and have agreed to a code of conduct with other claimants to islands in the South China Sea. Chinese officials seem to see multilateral arrangements in Asia and elsewhere as useful in trying to constrain U.S. policy and isolate Taiwan from other Asian players.[30]

Current Chinese efforts seem to have multiple long-term objectives:
- to help secure China's foreign policy environment at a time when the Chinese government is focused on sustaining economic development and political stability;
- to promote economic exchange that assists China's economic development;
- to calm regional fears and reassure Asian neighbors about how China will use its rising power and influence;
- to boost China's regional and global power and influence;
- to isolate Taiwan internationally; and
- to secure the flow of advanced arms and military technology to China despite a continuing Western embargo on such transfers.

Although wary of the U.S. superpower and other important regional states, Chinese leaders seem increasingly confident of China's power and influence. Aware that most Asian governments do not want to choose between China and the United States, the Chinese government generally avoids explicit competition with the United States or its allies, notably Japan. Yet, Chinese leaders seem gratified that China's relations with all neighboring powers, with the possible exceptions of Taiwan and Japan, have improved in recent years in ways that bolster China's influence at a time when U.S. leaders are largely preoccupied and distracted by other pressing issues. Beijing's influence in Southeast Asia and Korea has grown markedly, and the Sino-Russian strategic partnership has served the interests of each side despite obvious limitations.

Those limitations were displayed when Russian president Vladimir Putin's forthcoming approach to Washington following the September 11 attacks set back Chinese efforts to use improved ties with Russia as a counterweight to the United States. Meanwhile, other trends contrary to Chinese interests saw the U.S.-led war against terrorism in Afghanistan markedly increase the U.S. military presence and influence throughout Central and South Asia and appear to upset Chinese efforts to use the SCO and other means to check the spread of U.S. influence along China's western flank.[31] The antiterrorism campaign also lowered the priority that China and India have given to their slow but steady efforts to improve relations in recent years. Nonetheless, during the past year Chinese officials have persisted with efforts to strengthen ties with Russia, the SCO, and India, achieving incremental improvements in China's relations in these areas.[32]

Reflecting its rising stature and influence in Asia, China has become a key player in dealing with regional hot spots. China more than any other power will ultimately decide whether war or peace prevails in the Taiwan Strait, arguably the only area in the world that risks a war among great powers involving the United States. China's salience in dealing with the North Korean nuclear controversy has grown markedly in 2003, with senior Chinese officials playing the central role in sustaining diplomatic efforts to deal with the crisis. As Pakistan's main international ally, China has played an important role in supporting peace and antiterrorist efforts in South Asia by cooperating with the United States, India, and others in ensuring that South Asian tensions do not lead to major conflict. China is the only power among the territorial claimants that could turn the territorial disputes in the South China Sea into a serious military controversy.

Beyond Asia, Chinese leaders have adopted a low-risk approach to most international issues. They greatly value China's status as a permanent member of the UN Security Council. In recent years, they have sought to use the power and prerogatives of the UN as a means to check U.S. initiatives contrary to Chinese interests, though they rarely take the lead in the global body except to protect core Chinese concerns, notably involving Taiwan.

In 1999, Chinese officials had an unusually high profile in strongly supporting Russia against the U.S.-led intervention in Yugoslavia but were left in the lurch as NATO proceeded without endorsement by the UN and Russia compromised with the West. More recently, the Chinese have backed away from strident efforts to foster an international "antihegemony" front that targeted U.S.-led policies concerning the Kosovo crisis, NATO expansion, ballistic missile defense, U.S.-Japanese security cooperation, and Iraq. Straddling the fence in the UN Security Council regarding the 2003 war in Iraq, Chinese officials stayed in the shadow of France and Russia while they privately promised not to block U.S.-led military action. China's passive approach means that it can be taken for granted that China will follow the majority on most issues. Nevertheless, China's veto power needs to be taken into account when countries lobby for specific outcomes.

Constraining Taiwan still drives Chinese leaders to extraordinary efforts to exert influence in often small and otherwise inconsequential countries and international organizations. Exerting diplomatic pressure to isolate Taiwan and force it to come to terms on reunification with China remains among the very top Chinese foreign policy priorities. Few countries are willing to counter Chinese wishes by establishing contacts with Taiwan that would meet with the serious disapproval of Beijing. Beijing has scuttled UN peacekeeping and other plans that were indirectly related to Taiwan's international standing. During the past year, it wooed Nauru (population 12,000) away from

Taiwan and made strenuous efforts to keep Taiwan out of the World Health Organization (WHO) despite the massive controversy over China's handling of the SARS crisis, including Chinese officials repeatedly lying to WHO officials over the scope of the disease.

Beyond the Taiwan issue, China has selectively sought membership in major multilateral organizations if they serve the core foreign policy objectives previously listed. For example, China sought membership in the WTO to help set international trade rules affecting China's economy and to use those rules to drive Chinese economic reform. By contrast, the G-8 is so dominated by the United States and the Western-aligned countries that Chinese leaders, who fear being co-opted or marginalized, approach the organization cautiously, carefully calculating the pros and cons when invitations are extended, as they were most recently by France in 2003.

Struggling with Soft Power

China has only limited amounts of what social scientists call normative power and influence. Following the collapse of international communism, the world appeal of Chinese ideology has continued to decline as observers try to discern the relevance of the many Chinese treatises extolling Jiang's theories. In 2003 the government's initial handling of the SARS epidemic and the massive demonstration in Hong Kong in July 2003 against government policies seen as too accommodating to the Communist regime in Beijing underlined international skepticism about official Chinese values.

Nevertheless, China's bland new security concept receives high marks in nearby Asia. Its noncontroversial precepts find acceptance among Asian leaders anxious to get along with one another, avoiding conflict and confrontation, and also appeal to influential ethnic Chinese in Southeast Asia who seek opportunities in the Chinese market. For a while in the 1990s, China's leaders endeavored to make common cause with conservative leaders in the region, supporting Asian values as opposed to more liberal values in the West. This approach declined, however, with the collapse of many Asian economies based on these values in the 1997–1998 regional economic crisis.

Chinese leaders receive positive feedback from many international leaders who are relieved that China, unlike Russia and other weakened states, does not seek continued handouts and increasingly pays its own way in world affairs. The care that China takes not to be perceived as a "spoiler" or "rogue" nation, seeking to disrupt important elements of international affairs, is also appreciated. In this regard, increasing efforts by China's leaders to conform more to international norms on sensitive issues regarding economic practices, WMD proliferation, and even environmental standards are well received internationally. Many continue to roundly criticize the Chinese government's human rights practices. This has continued to tarnish China's international influence and reputation but has appeared to have only a small impact on Chinese practices.

First Asia, Then ... ?

China exerts worldwide economic influence and is the leading military and political power in Asia, but its importance and influence would be much greater if Chinese leaders were inclined to assert Chinese influence in world affairs more forcefully. Post–Mao Zedong leaders generally eschew such a global approach. Preoccupied with a long list of domestic economic, political, and social priorities, China's leaders focus on maintaining the internal stability and economic prosperity essential to the Chinese Communist Party's monopoly of power. In sharp contrast to Mao's messianic vision and provocative behavior, Chinese reformer Deng Xiaoping and succeeding leaders have been prepared more to deal with the world as it is, seeking out opportunities that help the massive Chinese task of nation building and over time build greater comprehensive national power.

As China's power grows, Chinese leaders presumably will become more confident in exerting influence in world affairs. The Chinese party and government congresses during the past year reported that China seeks a 20-year period to focus primarily on internal development.[33] Chinese leaders intend to continue trying to stabilize China's international environment to preserve good conditions for Chinese economic development. Few specialists outside China would hazard a 20-year forecast of Chinese leadership behavior, but recent behavior and trends suggest a continued comparatively cooperative and accommodating Chinese approach to most world issues for now. Based on rising Chinese economic and military power and expanding Chinese diplomatic and political interchange abroad, the overall power and importance of an accommodating China will continue to grow in world affairs. There likely will come a point well before 2020 when Chinese leaders will develop sufficient power to choose a different and more assertive approach to international affairs. Unfortunately, the evidence is insufficient to determine if that approach will support or oppose U.S. and other interests in the prevailing world order. Prudence seems to argue for a middle course in U.S. policy that works for cooperation but is prepared for difficulty and challenge.

Notes

1. See Michael Schaller, *The United States and China* (Oxford: Oxford University Press, 2002); Warren I. Cohen, *America's Response to China* (New York: Columbia University Press, 1990).

2. Nancy Bernkopf Tucker, *Taiwan, Hong Kong and the United States* (New York: Twayne, 1994), p. 16.

3. For quarterly treatment of Chinese political, economic, military, and foreign policy developments and trends, see the *China Leadership Monitor*, located at www.chinaleadershipmonitor.org.

4. See *Journal of Democracy* 14, no. 1 (January 2003), http://muse.jhu.edu/journals/journal_of_democracy/toc/jod14.1.html (accessed October 7, 2003).

5. "On a Roll," *Economist Global Agenda*, June 27, 2003; David Murphy, "Roaring Ahead," *Far Eastern Economic Review*, June 17, 2003.

6. "On a Roll."

7. Murphy, "Roaring Ahead."

8. Catherin Dalpino and Juo-yu Lin, "China and Southeast Asia" in *Brookings Northeast Asia Survey 2002–2003*, eds. Richard Bush and Catherin Dalpino (Washington, D.C.: Brookings Institution, 2003), p. 83.

9. Wayne M. Morrison, "China-U.S. Trade Issues," *CRS Issue Brief for Congress*, IB91121, updated July 2, 2003, p. 3, www.house.gov/htbin/crsprodget?/ib/IB91121 (accessed August 20, 2003).

10. Ibid., pp. 1–2.

11. Wayne M. Morrison, "China's Economic Conditions," *CRS Issue Brief for Congress*, IB98014, updated July 7, 2003, p. 3, www.house.gov/htbin/crsprodget?/ib/IB98014 (accessed August 21, 2003); Morrison, "China-U.S. Trade Issues," p. 4.

12. "On a Roll."

13. Briefing, Paris, France, June 27, 2003.

14. "What to Do About the Yuan," *Wall Street Journal*, July 17, 2003; "Trade With China Is Heating Up as a Business and Political Issue," *Wall Street Journal*, July 30, 2003, p. 1; Steven Pearlstein, "Facing Up to the China Challenge," *Washington Post*, August 1, 2003, p. E1; Geoffrey York, "China in World Spotlight Over Currency Controversy," *Toronto Globe and Mail*, August 4, 2003.

15. Hugo Restall, "Why China Is a Paper Tiger," *Asian Wall Street Journal*, August 1, 2003.

16. U.S. Department of Defense, *Annual Report on the Military Power of the People's Republic of China: Report to Congress Pursuant to the FY2000 National Defense Authorization Act*, July 28 2003, p. 41, www.defenselink.mil/pubs/20030730chinaex.pdf (accessed August 15, 2003) (hereinafter 2003 annual report on Chinese military power).

17. Ibid, p. 5.

18. 2003 annual report on Chinese military power.

19. *Chinese Military Power* (New York: Council on Foreign Relations, 2003), http://cfr.org/pdf/China_TF.pdf (accessed October 3, 2003) (report of an independent task force).

20. Ibid., p. 2.

21. Ibid., p. 3.

22. Ibid.

23. Ibid., p. 4.

24. See Michael Swaine, "Ballistic Missile Development," in *Strategic Asia: Power and Purpose 2001–02*, eds. Richard J. Ellings and Aaron L. Freidberg (Seattle: National Bureau of Asian Research, 2002), pp. 302–308.

25. Husain Haqqani, "The Pakistan-North Korea Connection," *International Herald Tribune*, October 26, 2002; Peter Brookes, "The Nuclear Cosa Nostra," *New York Post*, August 11, 2003.

26. Campion Walsh and Murray Hiebert, "U.S. Sanctions China Firms for Iranian Arms Sales," *Wall Street Journal*, July 7, 2003; Murray Hiebert and Kathy Chen, "Tackling China on Arms Sales," *Far Eastern Economic Review*, August 7, 2003.

27. David Finkelstein, *China's New Security Concept: Reading Between the Lines* (Alexandria, Va.: CNA Corp., 1999).

28. For more discussion, see Robert Sutter, "China's Recent Approach to Asia," *NBR Analysis* 13, no. 1 (March 2002): 13–38.

29. "Chinese Media Asked to Play Down Indonesia Riots," *Ming Pao*, May 16, 1998, p. A15.

30. Dalpino and Lin, "China and Southeast Asia," pp. 83–84.

31. Martha Britt Olcott, "Central Asia," in *Strategic Asia 2002–03: Asian After-shocks*, eds. Richard J. Ellings and Aaron L. Friedberg (Seattle: National Bureau of Asian Research, 2003), p. 251.

32. Quarterly assessments of Chinese relations with neighboring governments are provided by *Comparative Connections*, www.csis.org/pacfor/ccejournal.html.

33. "Hu Jintao Addresses CPC's Study Session on Global New Military Changes," Xinhua, May 24, 2003, translated by Foreign Broadcast Information Service.

Evan A. Feigenbaum

China's Challenge to *Pax Americana*

China has been a largely reactive international power for most of the period beginning in 1949 with the formation of the Communist state, willingly—and often skillfully—playing the pivot in the strategic competition of other states. In the 1960s and 1970s, its leaders briefly promoted a model of international order that stressed national revolution and proletarian solidarity. Yet, with that exception, the country has offered no real alternative vision of the international system for most of the past five decades. Beneath the rhetorical veneer, Chinese leaders have conducted their own foreign policy largely on the basis of the same calculations of balance of power and relative national advantage that drove the behavior of other major powers during the Cold War. Thus, Chinese foreign policy evolved during the first 50 years of the People's Republic in a context set almost entirely by others.

In the years since Beijing's 1996 missile exercise in the Taiwan Strait, however, Chinese leaders have begun to articulate a decidedly alternative vision of the underlying principles of international relations. This clarification has emerged gradually, in an ad hoc fashion, and has yet to cohere into a neatly bundled grand strategic vision. The concept is still evolving. Most importantly, it has emerged inadvertently—as a consequence of China's narrow concern with the issue of Taiwan.

Evan A. Feigenbaum is executive director of the Asia-Pacific Security Initiative at Harvard University's John F. Kennedy School of Government.

Copyright © 2001 by The Center for Strategic and International Studies and the Massachusetts Institute of Technology
The Washington Quarterly • 24:3 pp. 31–43.

U.S. strategists in particular should note just how much Chinese and U.S. views have diverged on the most fundamental organizing principles of international politics, not simply on specific issues of peace and security in Asia. Although tracing its origin to a comparatively narrow concern—Taiwan—this new, more comprehensive Chinese strategic vision touches the most essential bread-and-butter issues of international relations: How should the international system be organized? Who should make decisions about global security? What is the appropriate role of military force? Who should decide international law? What is the meaning of globalization? What should be the role of the United Nations (UN)? Are alliances legitimate?

In nearly every significant aspect, China's emerging approach to world order is opposed to the prevailing U.S. view of international statecraft, and in nearly all cases, China's narrow preoccupation with the question of national reunification shapes its approach to the big questions of the international system. The longer the Taiwan problem persists, therefore, the more likely it is that these strategic ideas will become more systematic—and, thus, institutionalized—in Chinese foreign policy.

The Taiwan issue seems unlikely to be resolved soon. Over time, this single issue may give birth to a consistent and deeply embedded set of Chinese strategic preferences that will challenge the predominant U.S. approach to the foundation of international politics.

Two Roads Diverging

Chinese and U.S. worldviews increasingly diverge on six fundamental questions.

ON WHAT DOMINANT PRINCIPLE SHOULD THE INTERNATIONAL SYSTEM BE ORGANIZED?

Although China was a latecomer to Westphalian nation-state diplomacy, Chinese leaders have anchored their security and diplomatic practice for the past five decades in what has been evocatively termed "hyper-sovereignty values."[1] Throughout the 1990s, as U.S. foreign policy gradually discarded the notion that sovereignty is inviolable (the interventions in Panama, Haiti, and Kosovo provide three examples), China's stance on sovereignty remained rigid in rhetoric and almost always inflexible in practice. Indeed, only one case of significant compromise on principles of territorial sovereignty occurred in the history of the Chinese Communist state—a side deal to the Sino–Soviet alliance through which China grudgingly agreed to recognize Mongolian independence.

Even as China has become uncharacteristically flexible in recent years on certain aspects of political sovereignty—especially those issues tied to trade prerogatives and the World Trade Organization (WTO) regime, several areas of human rights, and issues regarding international peacekeeping—these subtleties are utterly lacking on topics concerning Taiwan.[2] Taiwan remains the single issue to which China continues to subjugate any broad conceptions of grand strategy and, indeed, virtually its entire national security strategy.

Some of this rhetorical rigidity reflects a deepening conviction—shared, in many cases, with Russia, India, and perhaps even some European states such as France—that a principled stand against certain core U.S. strategic concepts will allow them to claim the moral "high ground" against the United States.[3] This comparatively rigid approach to sovereignty is by no means inconsistent with the largely security-oriented approach that has defined Chinese foreign policy for five decades. The United States denied Beijing the opportunity to veto Kosovo military operations by circumventing the UN entirely and conducting the operation through North Atlantic Treaty Organization (NATO) structures. Thus, at a time when U.S. and European leaders increasingly stress the interdependencies that have eroded political and economic sovereignty, Chinese leaders stubbornly cling to orthodox principles of sovereignty that many U.S. and European observers view as antique.

Chinese leaders argue, first, that concern for human rights, even genocide, can never override inviolable principles of sovereignty. Nevertheless, China may be rethinking this position in the most extreme cases of genocide; Rwanda has become a subject of ex post facto debate among some Chinese strategists. Yet the issues of precisely how to define "genocide" and how neutrally to evaluate accusations of genocide remain uncharted territory in Chinese statecraft.

This comparative inflexibility on sovereignty questions derives from two longtime articles of Chinese diplomatic faith. First, Chinese strategists premise their analysis on the fact that the world comprises both big and small states, developed and developing countries. Because weak countries generally lack the confidence and ability to interfere in the affairs of the strong, Chinese diplomats argue that sovereignty must remain an inviolable principle to protect the weak. Second, the orthodox Chinese approach presumes that sovereignty is the last defense of developing countries. Thus, China routinely condemns the implicit (and sometimes explicit) challenges to sovereignty embedded in what its diplomats term the "Clinton/Blair doctrine" of intervention, as well as any NATO effort to formulate a new strategy that is no longer exclusively defensive. Both are viewed in Beijing as a creeping challenge to the inviolability of state sovereignty.

Undoubtedly, the United States and Europe debate rancorously about the premises of Kosovo-style interventions. The U.S. political spectrum, however, will concede the unilateral right to violate the sovereignty of another country if it has been determined that to do so is in the U.S. national interest.

In mid-1999, the UN experience in East Timor signaled that China's orthodox view of sovereignty might be less intractable than Beijing's rhetoric would otherwise indicate. China sent observers, for example, to participate in a UN peace enforcement operation that violated what was still sovereign Indonesian territory.

Chinese strategists have since offered two critical distinctions to justify Chinese support for the Timor operation; both preserve the orthodoxy intact. Ultimately, these strategists argue, a sovereign state— Indonesia—invited the UN force into East Timor; moreover, the operation had UN legal authorization. Thus, because the Timor operation did not violate China's mostly nonnegotiable principles of sovereignty, China could set aside its usual call for noninterference in the internal affairs of another state. Indeed, some argue, as long as the two conditions (invitation and UN authorization) are met, China can support and perhaps even participate in such operations.

For the most part, however, China continues to regard political sovereignty as inviolable, as opposed to more broadly construed economic sovereignty, exemplified in the WTO regime. Thus, U.S. and Chinese views of sovereignty seem unlikely to converge in the period ahead, particularly if new forms of peacekeeping and peace enforcement gain impetus over the next decade.

WHAT RULES OF BEHAVIOR SHOULD GOVERN STATE ACTION IN INTERNATIONAL RELATIONS?

Chinese and U.S. approaches to world order also diverge on the rules of behavior that should govern state action. China has continued to cling to long- and often-repeated principles of nonintervention and territorial self-defense, even as the post–Cold War *Pax Americana* has rewritten those rules by promoting new rationales for intervention and the use of force.

Chinese diplomats and strategists routinely argue that the only truly "vital" interest is territorial self-defense. In this formulation, an "unprovoked" use of force against Taiwan that most Americans would, no doubt, view as aggressive is justified as a strictly defensive action involving territorial integrity. The more encompassing U.S. definition of vital interests, by contrast, ranges beyond the mere defense of homeland. Chinese strategists, therefore, argue that U.S. statements of the national interest tend to enshrine a "law of the jungle" in international politics that violates legal norms and is conceptually distinct from questions of peacekeeping.

A recurrent theme in Chinese strategic journals is dissection of the U.S. concept of "shape, respond, and prepare," the national military strategy that calls for the United States to "shape the international environment" and "respond to the full spectrum of crises" while it "prepares for an uncertain future."[4] To a growing number of Chinese analysts, the phrase is important because the notion of "shaping" suggests an aggressive effort to extend U.S. interests beyond the homeland and thereby preserve U.S. hegemony.

Chinese analysts will readily concede that military means can be necessary to defend sovereignty and territorial integrity. China, therefore, can "legitimately" brandish military instruments in the Taiwan Strait or the South China Sea. Unilateral actions that go beyond the defense of sovereignty, however, even under a claim that vital interests are at stake, are tantamount to aggression.

On the one hand, this view suggests that China will be loath to use force beyond the borders that it presently claims. This argument is important conceptually, given the frequency with which some analysts charge that China has the potential to develop into an "aggressive" power. It also suggests that China regards nearly every U.S. use of force as illegitimate under international law, which lays important groundwork for a widening gulf between U.S. and Chinese perceptions of the national interest, of the distinction between vital and other interests, and of the legitimacy of military action in strategic contingencies.

HOW SHOULD STATES ORGANIZE THEIR RELATIONS WITH ONE ANOTHER?

China was an early enthusiast of alliance diplomacy. In 1950, it entered into a treaty of mutual defense with the Soviet Union. Later in the Cold War, when China feared both an active threat from its former Soviet ally and latent Japanese militarism, U.S. transatlantic and Asian alliances continued to serve the strategic purpose of checking Soviet expansionism and "corking the bottle" of Japanese militarism.

This enthusiasm has waned over the past three years, and Chinese analysts increasingly view alliance structures as a threat to peace and intrinsically aggressive in nature. No longer are the U.S.–Japan and NATO alliances viewed in China primarily as a means to cooperative defense. Indeed, a growing number of Chinese strategists appear willing for China to compete with Japan without the U.S. presence as a restraint. This shift can only be understood in context. Chinese foreign policy has come to view the alliance as a possible obstacle to a potential use of force against Taiwan and as "cover" for rearmament by an increasingly assertive Japan.

Four sets of events triggered this gradual shift in the Chinese perception of U.S.–Asian alliances. First, the 1995 Nye initiative proposed new guidelines for security-related aspects of the U.S.–Japan relationship. Although the United States insists that military cooperation should be viewed as just one component flowing from the broader political and economic relationships that it maintains with its strategic partners, Chinese diplomacy has come to stress the military aspects of such alliances, particularly the U.S.–Japan alliance, almost exclusively. As such, the Nye initiative inadvertently created new ambiguities about Japanese involvement in U.S. military operations, while feeding Chinese fears of Japanese logistical support for U.S. forces in a Taiwan contingency. Indeed, the entire Japanese security debate of the last half of the 1990s has been viewed in Beijing largely as an effort to lift Japan's gaze from a strictly minimalist strategy of homeland defense to broader roles and responsibilities in regional security.

Second, the review and promulgation of the Nye initiative's guidelines coincidentally preceded Lee Teng-hui's post-1996 administration of Taiwan. Directly elected in 1996 by voters in the first free presidential election of Taiwan's tumultuous new democracy, Lee spent much of the 1996–1999 period laying the groundwork for an increasingly aggressive assertion of Taiwan's de facto independence. Inevitably, this action fed Chinese suspicion of U.S. alliances: Lee's efforts took place against the backdrop of the 1996 deployment of two U.S. carrier battle groups to the area around Taiwan and the considerable ambiguity about Japanese roles and missions under the revised guidelines.

Third, escalating tensions between North Korea and the United States and its Asian allies further exacerbated Chinese concerns. Japan's approach toward North Korea became even more confrontational than Washington's or Seoul's after the August 1998 test launch of a North Korean Taep'odong long-range missile over northern Japan.[5] From Beijing's perspective, subsequent close U.S.–South Korean coordination with Japan on North Korea policy indicates clearly that the United States is prepared to carry out "theater war" in joint operations with South Korean and Japanese forces.

Finally, the eastward expansion of NATO's membership was followed by the shift in NATO strategy away from purely defensive and deterrent concepts and subsequently by the Kosovo operation, launched without the backing of a UN resolution. Indeed, the shift in NATO strategy in particular reinforced Chinese perceptions that U.S. alliances in both Europe and Asia have evolved away from original concepts of cooperative defense toward more expansive definitions of alliance roles and missions. Kosovo thereby demonstrated to Chinese strategists that the United States and its allies were prepared to circumvent the UN process and norms of international law that China views as inflexible.

China's increasing preoccupation with the evolving structure of U.S. alliances has, for this reason, centered around the view that a set of partnerships that once promoted peace by deterring Soviet expansion now contributes to strategic instability. As a military matter, Chinese analysts routinely contend that alliances, by their very nature, exist primarily to deter specific and identifiable threats. Yet if alliances require targets, then they must exist primarily to ensure the security of their members at the expense of another. Against the backdrop of the U.S.–Japan guidelines review and evolving Taiwan separatism, Chinese strategists have argued with increasing emphasis that the target of allied deterrence in the Asia–Pacific region must inevitably become China itself.

As an alternative to alliances, therefore, China has argued aggressively for "peaceful coexistence;" confidence-building measures; and, increasingly, various forms of cooperative security. This course flies squarely in the face of a U.S. strategy for the Pacific that continues to enshrine U.S.–Asian alliances as the centerpiece of a continuing U.S. military presence as well as the backbone of regional peace and stability. The United States will not willingly give up its Asian alliances. Ironically, then, the harder China has pushed against enhanced roles and missions for Japan's Self-Defense Forces, the more ambivalent Japanese views of Chinese intentions have become.

Chinese and U.S. perspectives on the role and utility of alliances continue to diverge. This difference has rapidly become a dominant feature of China's strategic debate at precisely the moment when U.S. commitment to Asian alliances has reached a new peak. As China's attitude toward alliances has grown more hostile, U.S. strategy has sought to shore up the alliance structure as the basis of U.S. policy in Asia.

THROUGH WHAT INTERNATIONAL STRUCTURES CAN STATES LEGITIMATELY TAKE MILITARY ACTION?

Much of China's negative reaction to the Kosovo operation stemmed from the ease and speed with which the United States decided to bypass the UN Security Council to avoid Russian and Chinese opposition. Since the war, Chinese foreign policy has placed renewed stress on the need to revitalize UN structures, particularly Permanent-5 (P-5) coordination within the Security Council. Kosovo set a dangerous precedent for Chinese interests by sidelining the one international organization in which Beijing has sought to make its voice heard on global security issues that transcend China's immediate strategic environment in Asia.

China's argument for increased reliance on Security Council mechanisms rests, in large part, on the view that peace and hegemony, no matter how benign, are incompatible. One nation or a handful of countries acting alone, Chinese diplomats argue, cannot preserve the peace.

In fact, China has voted in favor of many international peacekeeping efforts or, at a minimum, has chosen not to impede them. Chinese diplomats stress the need to adhere to rules of procedure, thus establishing P-5 consensus as essential to China's view of how to manage the global security environment.

This new emphasis on UN structures contains no small degree of irony. Despite China's long-standing preference for bilateral diplomacy, Chinese foreign policy in the past year has increasingly stressed the multilateralization of global decisionmaking, particularly on issues involving the use of force. Beijing argues that any intervention must be based on P-5 consensus and not on unilateral action, as in Kosovo, or through alliance structures that lack UN legal sanction. In keeping with the principles of inviolable political sovereignty and noninterference, peacekeeping, say the Chinese, and not peace enforcement should be the main focus of multinational intervention. China has also explicitly rejected most forms of "preventive diplomacy," arguing that they most often obscure the hidden hand of great-power interests.

WHAT IS THE PROPER RELATIONSHIP BETWEEN OFFENSIVE, DEFENSIVE, AND DETERRENT WEAPONS AND STRATEGIES?

The U.S. debate about the role of nuclear weapons has increasingly focused on the future of deterrence and the prospects for missile defense. China's voice has been among the most strident in urging a return to more conventional principles of deterrence as the basis for strategic stability. China has cast its stance largely as an effort to defend three decades of arms control, while preventing a new arms race as well as the militarization of outer space.

The specific number of national missile defense interceptors the United States ultimately seeks to deploy will, no doubt, affect the pace and tenor of a two-decade-long force modernization program that has sought to give China a more robust, solid-propelled strategic deterrent.[6] In public, however, Beijing has chosen to emphasize its political and symbolic, rather than narrowly technical, concerns. China has argued, for example, that the U.S. missile defense debate reflects a "Cold War mentality" premised on the belief that military superiority lies at the root of security. On the contrary, Chinese strategists argue, defense does not always produce security. Instead, Marxist dialectics suggest that every action produces a reaction. A stronger shield, therefore, will meet with the response of a sharpened sword. Any U.S. move to abrogate the Anti-Ballistic Missile (ABM) Treaty, China has argued, would only trigger a chain reaction that would destroy decades of arms control and disarmament efforts.

Chinese debates have sought especially to tie missile defenses to the prospect for arms race behavior among some countries that the United States brands as "rogue" states. The United States, China has suggested, will succeed only in creating the very conditions against which it has sought so strenuously to defend. Offense is technically simpler than defense. Thus, more countries will succeed in developing offensive platforms and effective countermeasure technology before the United States is able to deploy defenses between 2005 and 2010.

China's objection to theater missile defense (TMD) systems has been particularly strenuous, in large part because Beijing explicitly links

TMD to the possibility of dramatically enhanced U.S.–Taiwan defense cooperation, as well as to new forms of Japanese power projection. Joint U.S.–Japan TMD development, especially of naval theater-wide systems deployable to ocean-going ships, speaks directly to China's argument that the U.S.–Japan alliance has become a cover for an increasingly independent Japanese force projection capability. In addition to its narrowly technical role as a potential force multiplier, TMD threatens to revive a formal U.S.–Taiwan defense relationship that Beijing had insisted be abrogated as one of the main preconditions to the normalization of diplomatic relations with the United States in 1979. Politically, rather than purely technically, China views the prospect of Taiwan participation in TMD development as symbolic evidence of the de facto reestablishment of a U.S.–Taiwan military alliance.

Last, China has sought to reject the notion that defense is purely benign in nature—a form of "deterrence plus." Instead, a growing number of Chinese strategists have argued that missile defense, in most variants, has strong offensive implications. Some in Beijing have largely accepted the view that lower-tier antimissile systems are purely defensive in nature. Yet they have argued with growing conviction that upper-tier interceptors may violate the convention on the nonmilitarization of outer space.

HAS GLOBALIZATION FUNDAMENTALLY REMADE THE ROLE OF THE STATE?

Chinese strategists who argue that U.S. security policy reflects the vestiges of a "Cold War mentality" obscure the degree to which U.S. economic policy increasingly seeks to lower borders. On one level, free trade and globalization are thoroughly inconsistent with the orthodox conceptions of sovereignty and noninterference to which China continues to cling in the security realm. With its sweeping commitment to the requirements of economic restructuring under the WTO regime, however, China has reversed several decades of industrial policy that depended heavily on the very state-centric, import-substitution mechanisms that U.S. trade policy has sought so assiduously to tear down.

Chinese economic policy embraces technology and capital penetration from abroad, as well as the compromises of sovereignty that accompany entry into the WTO regime. Yet not all Chinese policymakers are so comfortable with the mantra of globalism that has become closely associated with U.S. policy during the 1990s. Like many voices of protest in Seattle and Washington, some Chinese foreign policy makers publicly fret that globalization may only leave the developing world behind. Still other Chinese policymakers have sought to preserve important pillars of the developmental and industrial policy state, especially in China's high-technology sectors, where arbitrary state regulation remains pervasive and the government continues to nurture a deep commitment to the development of indigenous industries in software, new and special materials, and space technology.[7]

In fact, the outcome of China's struggle to remake its economic structure will intersect with the preceding five areas of its national security strategy in complex ways. A China that breaks decisively with its economic past will become a nation more deeply embedded in the global economy than at any time in its modern history. China would also shed important structural impediments that have hindered indigenous technical innovation. Even as it anchored the country in the global economy, such a shift would gradually reduce Chinese dependence on foreign technology transfers. It would also provide a stronger foundation for defense modernization than currently exists.

By contrast, a China that clings to past aspects of its industrial policy will, among other problems, remain burdened by an inefficient high-technology sector capable only of limited indigenous breakthroughs, leaving intact much of the system that has made China so dependent on foreign technology transfers. It would, in some ways, also represent a China that continues to look askance at its trade partners and at the process of globalization itself—viewing it largely in instrumental terms, as a means to acquire from abroad what Chinese industry cannot itself provide.

Issue Delinkage

Ultimately, all six of these points of divergence—the bread-and-butter of how to shape and maintain world order—trace their roots to China's growing obsession with the lingering problem of Taiwan. Reunification has become the root of China's defense planning and, in some ways, of its entire national security strategy. Thus, China insists on an orthodox approach to sovereignty on a global scale for fear of the precedent any change would set with respect to Taiwan. Most Chinese defense planners now assume U.S. military intervention will occur during a Taiwan crisis. Yet, principles of noninterference remain pivotal to Chinese policy, which insists that Taiwan's status must ultimately be determined by Chinese on both sides of the strait. China argues that the U.S.–Japan alliance has shifted its focus beyond homeland defense; any Taiwan contingency would place enormous pressure on U.S. forces forward deployed to the region, while firming up U.S. reliance on the alliance network. China's renewed emphasis on the UN Security Council stems, in part, from the deeply unsettling demonstration of unilateralism that China observed in the United States and its allies during the Kosovo crisis. TMD is intrinsically linked to the offense–defense balance in the Taiwan Strait and speaks to the evolving nature of the U.S. military commitment to Taiwan. Although China's lingering attachment to industrial policy is less clearly related to the Taiwan issue, the course China chooses as it enters the WTO will affect its technological capability, defense planning, and weapons acquisition, as well as, at a higher level, China's continuing dependence on infusions of capital and technology from across the Taiwan Strait. The Taiwan problem has no simple solution. Yet the dominant U.S. policy toward Taiwan is to call for patience, especially from the Chinese side, postponing to a still-distant future the question of Taiwan's status vis-à-vis the Chinese mainland. Clearly, such an approach has merit within the narrow context of U.S.–China relations and East Asian strategic stability.

The Taiwan problem, however, seems unlikely to be resolved soon. If this forecast is accurate, it will have important and deeper consequences for issues that lie far beyond East Asian security. Foremost among these problems is the gradual institutionalization of a Chinese strategic vision that could hamstring U.S.–China relations on a variety of important questions in international politics that will appear, at first glance, to be only marginally related to the U.S.–China relationship.

The Taiwan issue increasingly shapes China's entire approach to the big questions of international relations. The United States, therefore, should prepare for such a confrontational future. At its very best, continued divergence of core strategic concepts will produce a mixed pattern of cooperation and rivalry over the next 5–10 years in which Chinese and U.S. leaders work feverishly, and amid considerable tension, to separate issues and prevent problems from infecting points of cooperation. Rarely have Chinese and U.S. leaders shown the necessary skill in managing their bilateral relationship, particularly in recent years.

More importantly, divergent U.S. and Chinese views of the international order could produce firmly institutionalized patterns of diplomacy in which China and the United States find themselves disagreeing on issues that are simply fundamental to great-power cooperation. On some issues of importance, China and the United States might even seek to obstruct one another's policies.

This situation requires a U.S. approach that explicitly stresses issue delinkage—a painstaking and skillful effort to work through the big international issues with a Chinese leadership that views nearly every question in international relations through the prism of Taiwan. Paradoxically, U.S. policy toward China throughout the 1990s has revolved around a debate about the merits of linkage. The Clinton administration opted for linkage between trade and human rights policies in 1993, then reversed its approach in 1994–1995. Powerful constituencies in Congress and the U.S. public continue to support a linkage-based approach to China policy.

The problem, of course, is not that issue linkage is never appropriate, merely that it can have inadvertent—and adverse—consequences when used as a method for conducting foreign policy. China routinely links Taiwan's status to a wide variety of issues that may seem, at first glance, to have little relevance to U.S.–China relations or even to East Asia. What Europeanist in the State Department would have predicted a Chinese veto of a peacekeeping force for Macedonia?

Yet with Chinese and U.S. perspectives diverging so sharply on the fundamentals of the international system, skillful management of the relationship will require more meaningful efforts to delink the Taiwan question from issues around the globe that are of vital interest to the United States. Many such issues will seem to have little intrinsic connection to the relationship between the United States and China. To be sure, the United States can afford for the foreseeable future to ignore Chinese perspectives. Although assuaging Chinese concerns should not become the standard by which U.S. policy elsewhere is judged—in Kosovo, for example, the United States pursued its declared strategic interest over strenuous Chinese objections—such an approach will produce longer-term adverse consequences. The United States has already begun to feel some of these consequences because of the Kosovo experience, as well as through the missile defense debate. Initially, both issues were regarded in U.S. policy discussions as only weakly connected to U.S.–China relations.

U.S. strategists have since learned otherwise, especially with respect to missile defense. China must still mature as a truly global power. Without stronger efforts to delink Taiwan from other issues, U.S. and Chinese perspectives will move further apart on the important fundamentals of international politics.

In various ways, this divergence could hamstring all aspects of the U.S.–China relationship. Chinese, Russian, and Indian perspectives on world affairs will surely move closer together. China could more aggressively employ its veto in the UN Security Council. The United States might in turn further decrease its reliance on UN mechanisms of peacemaking and peace enforcement. Ultimately, preserving U.S. flexibility might require expanded roles for alliances, and perhaps even greater U.S. unilateralism. For the United States and its allies, this would be a heavy price to pay for more aggressive coordination with China on problems in international politics that transcend U.S.–China relations and the immediate East Asian strategic environment.

Notes

1. Alastair Iain Johnston, "China's Militarized Interstate Dispute Behavior, 1949–1992: A First Cut at the Data," *China Quarterly* 153 (March 1998): 2.

2. See, for example, Bates Gill and James Reilly, "Sovereignty, Intervention, and Peacekeeping: The View from Beijing," *Survival* 42, no. 3 (Autumn 2000): 41–59.

3. "China, India Are Our Ideological Allies, Says Russia," *Hindu*, July 15, 2000.

4. U.S. Joint Chiefs of Staff, "Shape, Respond, Prepare Now–A Military Strategy for a New Era," 1997 National Military Strategy.

5. Michael J. Green, "The Forgotten Player," *National Interest* (Summer 2000): 46.

6. China's solid propellant program, for example, began to receive renewed emphasis from force planners as early as 1983. Xing Qiuheng, "Zili gengsheng fazhan wo guo de guti huojian shiye [Develop our country's solid propellant rocketry through self-reliance]," in Nie Li and Huai Guomo, eds., *Huigu yu Zhanwang: Xin Zhongguo de Guofang Keji Gongye* [Retrospect and prospect: New China's defense science and technology industry] (Beijing: National Defense Industry Press, 1989), 282.

7. Evan A. Feigenbaum, "Who's Behind China's High-Technology 'Revolution': How Bomb Makers Remade Beijing's Priorities, Policies, and Institutions," *International Security* 24, no. 1 (Summer 1999): 95–126.

Yong Deng and Thomas G. Moore

China Views Globalization: Toward a New Great-Power Politics?

China is rising in the age of globalization. Although China initially accepted greater interdependence largely out of economic necessity early in the reform era, Beijing has since come to embrace interdependence and globalization with increasing enthusiasm. Yet, the country's political elites recognize that economic globalization is a double-edged sword for China. Although undoubtedly an engine of national economic growth, if mishandled, this transformative force could very well derail China's quest for great-power status. Globalization introduces powerful new sources of economic vulnerability. Similarly, the growth of nontraditional threats, such as terrorism and the spread of infectious disease, presents serious global challenges to China's security. Thus, although Beijing has embraced globalization overall, the Chinese government has also sought to manage the process by reconfiguring its thinking about security and taking bold steps such as domestic banking reforms and active trade diplomacy to defend the country's economic interests. The fact that Chinese political elites today perceive issues as diverse as capital flows, weapons proliferation, epidemics, terrorism, and cybercrime in terms of globalization suggests that the country's views on globalization

Yong Deng is an associate professor of political science at the United States Naval Academy. Thomas G. Moore is an associate professor of political science at the University of Cincinnati.

The Washington Quarterly • 27:3 pp. 117–136.

113

have evolved in tandem with its tumultuous quest for development, security, and status during the past decade.

To the extent that globalization is perceived to be the distinguishing feature of contemporary U.S. hegemony, China's views on globalization reflect its evaluation of the world order and shape its strategic outlook as an aspiring great power. U.S. hegemony in its liberal and democratic forms benefits China in important ways, but through the lens of power politics it also disadvantages certain Chinese interests. Accordingly, efforts to restrain the United States characterize Beijing's latest and likely future response to globalization. In fact, mainstream Chinese strategic thinkers now believe that globalization, as manifested in transnational forces, international institutions, and a greater need for multilateralism, can be used to "democratize" the U.S. hegemonic order to minimize unilateralist power politics.

Even more broadly, China's strategic choices are increasingly designed to exploit globalization as a way of making China rich and strong and simultaneously reducing international fears of fast-growing Chinese material power. Under President Hu Jintao and Premier Wen Jiabao, the new Chinese leadership, sensitive to foreign reactions to China's growing power, has actively pursued cooperative security, win-win economic cooperation, and an increasingly multilateral approach to foreign policy in general, to an even greater extent and with greater success than their predecessors. China's new foreign policy choice highlights the potential role of globalization in transforming great-power politics from the unmitigated struggle for supremacy of earlier eras to a more cooperative form of interstate competition that increases prospects for China's peaceful rise.

The Changing Colors of Globalization

Although the term "globalization" did not enter official discourse in China until 1996, its leaders acknowledged throughout the 1990s that economic affairs were playing a growing role in post–Cold War international relations.[1] Some references to globalization appeared in academic writings in the early 1990s, but the dominant concepts in scholarly and policymaking circles were interdependence, integration, and internationalization. When globalization first entered Beijing's diplomatic lexicon, officials described it as a trend driven by advances in science and technology that were producing increased cross-national flows of capital, goods, and know-how. The emphasis on the technological drivers underlying this process conceptually restricted globalization to the economic realm in official Chinese analysis although the term was soon understood elsewhere in the world to include social, cultural, political, and security dimensions. Similarly, early attention to this emerging trend emphasized the opportunities for economic development and ignored concerns about U.S. hegemony, Westernization, national sovereignty, and other politically controversial issues.

Long before the term "globalization" became popularized worldwide in the 1990s, the benefits of China's growing participation in the world economy were undeniable. After Deng Xiaoping formally assumed power in 1978, transnational flows of capital, goods, information, and technology increased steadily throughout the 1980s, accelerating further during the 1990s as the contours of an emerging manufacturing juggernaut took shape. By the mid-1990s, economic ties to the outside world were widely seen as critical to the robust economic growth that made China the envy of industrializing countries everywhere. For example, by 1992 China stood as the world's leading recipient of foreign direct investment (FDI) among developing countries. Indeed, FDI accounted for sizable (and growing) percentages of China's domestic investment, industrial output, exports, tax revenues, and job growth before globalization became a catchphrase.

A series of events in the late 1990s tested China's initial, somewhat romantic, notions of globalization quickly and severely. The Asian financial crisis of 1997–1998 revealed the double-edged sword of globalization, that is, the challenges it presents as well as the opportunities. Although China escaped much of the turmoil, the travails of its neighbors highlighted the threats that global economic forces posed to national economic security. The crisis also reinforced suspicion that the United States and Japan seek every opportunity for strategic gain, even in ostensibly economic matters. Coupled with Washington's hard line in its ongoing negotiations over China's accession to the World Trade Organization (WTO), U.S. policy during the Asian financial crisis, namely the perceived U.S. indifference to the spreading chaos and its subsequent failure to support measures that many in East Asia sought as necessary for a quick recovery, underscored the significant economic, social, political, and even strategic risks that deeper participation in a globalizing world economy would entail for China. The economic dislocation and political upheaval in developing Thailand and Indonesia, not to mention industrialized South Korea, presented a sobering vision of the challenges to national sovereignty and well-being that can accompany greater integration into world markets.

In Beijing's view, its experience with the Asian financial crisis and the WTO revealed not only that further reform and opening would be necessary to create a modern economy capable of competing effectively in a globalizing world economy but also that severe imbalances and inequities continued to persist in the international system. Even though China's strategic position compared favorably to most developing countries, Beijing did not see itself as immune to the vagaries and injustices associated with contemporary international economic relations. Strikingly, Chinese officials publicly explained this deleterious side as the result of an improper handling (political mismanagement at the international level) of the globalization process rather than as a danger inherent in deeper and more extensive ties among national economies. Indeed, Beijing's rhetoric and behavior in the late 1990s sought to maintain a distinction between globalization (understood in terms of scientific and technological advances, the expansion of market forces, and the arrival of a new industrial revolution) and the international economic system (shorthand for Western-dominated, multilateral economic institutions and U.S. hegemony generally). Problems associated elsewhere in the world with globalization, such as widening disparities in North-South wealth, asymmetries in vulnerabilities to financial shocks between industrialized and developing countries, and unequal access to technology, were attributed to defects in the international economic system rather than to globalization per se.

By the late 1990s, even though China's official rhetoric continued to view globalization as an economic phenomenon, this belied a growing recognition in scholarly and elite discourse that globalization was also affecting great-power politics. Given the United States' advantage in technological innovation, revolution in military affairs, and cultural domination, globalization seemed to confer relative gains on the United States, enabling it to pursue its foreign policy virtually unchallenged. This belief has been reinforced by what Beijing has perceived as a series of unilateral U.S. actions threatening to Chinese interests, such as Washington's closer relationship with Taipei since the 1995–1996 Taiwan Strait crisis; the 1996–1997 strengthening of the U.S.-Japanese defense guidelines; the 1999 U.S.-led NATO intervention in Kosovo (and resulting bombing of the Chinese embassy in Belgrade); the intensification of U.S. plans for missile defense under President George W. Bush; the April 2001 EP-3 surveillance plane incident; and, most recently, the 2003 war in Iraq. The result has been a more realistic Chinese assessment of globalization's economic and security implications as well as a new recognition that globalization is not merely an economic trend but rather a process that must be actively managed politically as well.

The heightened profile of international terrorism, the spread of weapons of mass destruction, the growing problem of infectious diseases such as AIDS and the Severe Acute Respiratory Syndrome (SARS), transnational drug trafficking, and cybercrime have also influenced the evolution of China's views on globalization. Chinese officials have repeatedly acknowledged that, as security threats become increasingly globalized, the pursuit of security becomes more and more cooperative and multidimensional and, in an age of increasingly transnational threats, China's security is dependent on the security of others in unprecedented ways. Such new ideas have made "common security" and "globalized cooperation" regular features of China's foreign policy discourse in the new millennium, including then-President Jiang Zemin's analysis in 2002: "As countries increase their interdependency and common ground on security, it has become difficult for any single country to realize its security objective by itself alone. Only by strengthening international cooperation can we effectively deal with the security challenge worldwide and realize universal and sustained security."[2]

Just as globalization has prompted new thinking about security issues in China, nontraditional security threats have also significantly transformed China's understanding of globalization itself. Once restricted to economics, the discourse on globalization now extends to an expanding range of political and security matters. Such reconceptualization underscores the importance of globalization both as a real-world phenomenon and as a lens through which Beijing's grand strategy is filtered. It has facilitated China's satisfaction with, and boosted China's confidence in peaceful status mobility within, the international system.

The fact that China's support for globalization has never wavered, even in the wake of the Asian financial crisis and through a variety of subsequent foreign policy tests, reflects a strategic choice by China's leaders to deepen the country's participation in the world economy as the best means available to pursue economic modernization, cope with U.S. hegemony, and fulfill Beijing's great-power aspirations. Chinese leaders characterize globalization as an irreversible tide that no country can or should resist while emphasizing the need to manage the process proactively to maximize benefits and minimize harms. Most significantly, perhaps, Chinese policymakers and academic analysts alike have intently explored ways in which globalization can restrain U.S. power, reduce fears of a China threat, and ultimately make international relations defined more by the democratic exercise of legitimate authority and dictated less by coercive use of power.

'Democratizing' U.S. Hegemony through Multipolarization and Economic Globalization

China's official advocacy of multipolarity in world politics predated Beijing's explicit embrace of globalization by almost a decade. During much of the 1990s, political discussion treated multipolarization and globalization as two separate issues, demonstrating little concern with the implications of the combined trends for Chinese foreign policy. Having initially struggled to define the post–Cold War world, Beijing has in the new millennium propounded a new official formulation—"multipolarization and economic globalization"—that reinterprets the dual trends and their interconnectedness as the strategic context for Chinese foreign relations.[3]

Instead of predicting the imminent emergence of a dispersed power configuration, as was the case previously, China now views the trend toward multipolarization as a tortuous process of unspecified duration. Today, Chinese official media and mainstream analysts explicitly reject equating multipolarity with a hostile balancing drive against the predominant power of the United States. Notably, one Chinese scholar openly voiced his criticism of the official "multipolarity" notion for its anti-U.S. tone and implications of confrontational power politics.[4] Beginning in the second half of 2003, the government in Beijing even toned down its explicit advocacy of multipolarity, for example, preferring to pledge to promote "multilateralism" in the Sino-French Joint Statement signed in late January 2004.[5] Rhetorical deployments aside, the new interpretation of multipolarization reflects a preference for a more democratic world order that emphasizes proper management of state-to-state relations over the redistribution of power. In other words, China is less concerned with U.S. power per se and more concerned with the way that power is exercised.

As explained by the vice minister of foreign affairs, Wang Yi, the Chinese view of multipolarization differs from the traditional Western interpretation in that China seeks the "harmonious coexistence of all forces," including developing countries, rather than a confrontational great-power struggle.[6] According to this perspective, multipolarization is antithetical to the self-help, unilateralist approach to security and development associated with the traditional great-power game.

Chinese analysts and political elites clearly recognize that the United States enjoys great advantages in utilizing globalization across the military, technological, economic, political, and even cultural arenas to consolidate Washington's predominant position in the world further. These observers also recognize, however, that China's own national rejuvenation requires its active participation in such a world. The latest mainstream view recognizes that the force of interdependence and globalization is essential to convince the United States of what Joseph Nye Jr. calls "the paradox of American power," whereby U.S. power is simultaneously strengthened and restrained in the globalized world. To cope with the wide array of global challenges, cooperative and legitimate use of power is not only a virtual necessity but also strengthens the U.S. global leadership role.[7]

For example, Shen Jiru, director of strategic studies at the Institute of World Economics and Politics at the Chinese Academy of Social Sciences (CASS), argues that the United States did not retaliate against France, Germany, and Russia for their opposition to the U.S. war in Iraq because "the advance of economic globalization means that the interests of different countries are interwoven ever more closely, and this has become a powerful material force constraining U.S. hegemonism."[8] Elsewhere, Shen posits that diplomatic activism by Japan, Korea, China, Russia, and the United States on the North Korean nuclear issue is best explained by common concern over the devastating impact that a militarized conflict would have on the highly interdependent Northeast Asian regional economies.[9] Along the same lines, CASS scholar Zheng Yu argues:

[T]he rising trend of economic globalization has led to an unprecedented level of economic interdependence, thereby effectively containing the possible escalation of regional conflicts to great-power war. And it has become increasingly difficult to resort to economic coercion as a means to control the economic development of another country. As such, economic globalization has provided opportunities and favorable conditions for overall peace and development in the international community.[10]

These observations reflect the emerging Chinese interest in exploring how economic globalization can actually change the parameters of great-power politics from a traditional zero-sum game to win-win competition. "Under conditions of globalization there are no absolute winners or absolute losers," contends Luo Zhaohong, a CASS research fellow. Consequently, "the globalization age requires increased cooperation between all countries and regions, and we must apply the concept of 'both are winners' or 'all are winners' in place of the outdated 'zero-sum game' mentality."[11] Such a new concept presumably precludes Cold War–style antagonism between two great powers or two blocs. The win-win idea has been widely espoused in mainstream Chinese analyses, as it is considered a hallmark of China's new foreign strategy.

Chinese analysts and policymakers believe that economic globalization creates the open economic system necessary for China's growth. Although pressuring China to live up to international commitments, the globalized world also offers China opportunities to express its discontent, to take measures to defend its economic interests, and even to assert a leadership role in global governance, all without triggering fear that Beijing harbors revisionist intentions. China's diplomacy in the WTO provides a case in point.

Although China's leaders pursued WTO entry primarily to improve the country's own participation in the world economy, they also saw membership as a means to influence the shape of the international economic system. China's subsequent WTO participation has reiterated its new attitude toward leadership in a globalized world. In his speech at the 2001 ministerial conference in Doha, Qatar, China's trade minister, Shi Guangsheng, argued that equal attention should be paid to the "development of the world economy" and "trade and investment facilitation." In the speech, which marked the occasion of China's WTO accession, Shi referred to the "obvious defects of the existing multilateral trading system," namely its failure "to reflect the interests and demands of developing countries in a more adequate fashion."[12] In addition, in a declaration issued at the time of the Doha meeting, China insisted that the "developmental dimension" be fully incorporated into the multilateral trading system.

Similarly, at the September 2003 WTO ministerial meeting in Cancun, Mexico, Commerce Minister Lu Fuyuan assessed the positions of developed against developing countries, concluding that "their obligations are not balanced and their gains are not equal." Signaling Beijing's concern about fairness, Lu emphasized the "enormous commitment" to trade liberalization that China had made by joining the WTO. Indeed, he also noted that Beijing's accession protocol requires China to reduce trade barriers "well below the level of other developing countries."[13] By laying these rhetorical markers, Lu indicated his country's determination to prevent the Doha talks from resulting in further substantial obligations for Chinese liberalization.

Consistent with this stance, Beijing acted as a member of the Group of 22 (G-22) developing countries in Cancun to bargain collectively for a reduction in the use of agricultural subsidies by developed countries such as the United States, members of the European Union, and Japan. At first glance, Beijing's participation in the G-22 could be interpreted as evidence that China wanted to undermine the liberal international economic regime by blocking progress toward a new WTO agreement. In truth, however, China was much less strident in its criticism than were Brazil, India, and many other developing countries. Despite U.S. trade negotiators' clear disappointment that China had allied itself with the G-22 in Cancun, they praised Beijing afterward for working hard to broker a deal. Indeed, China displayed its customary pragmatism in trying to navigate the treacherous waters of agricultural policy and the so-called Singapore issues (trade facilitation, government procurement, investment rules, and competition policy). Presumably, this is why WTO Director General Supachai Panitchpakdi called on Beijing to "use its influence to be a bridge between developed and developing countries" in the wake of the collapse of the Cancun meeting.[14] This direct appeal to Chinese leaders, in which Supachai acknowledged that China is both a "developing nation" and an "emerging superpower," reflects the growing influence of Beijing in shaping the economic order from which it already benefits handsomely.

Like many developing countries, China believes that the WTO has failed to live up to the promises not only of the Doha "Development Round" launched in 2001 but also of the Uruguay Round concluded in 1994. In the latter case, developing countries were promised liberalization in agricultural and textile trade (which has been slow to materialize) in exchange for the adoption of rules advocated by developed countries on issues such as services and intellectual property rights (which have progressed further). Although there is no evidence that Beijing wishes to weaken the WTO, China does insist that any new agreement must be negotiated more inclusively and must deliver a more equitable outcome. To that end, China has recently expressed a willingness to play a more active and constructive role in reinvigorating the WTO talks that had stalled in Cancun in 2003.

By using an increasingly wide variety of economic platforms, including the WTO, the Asia-Pacific Economic Cooperation (APEC) forum, and various UN agencies, Beijing actively seeks to manage the course of globalization. Even though Beijing has attempted to assert a Chinese voice, its positions hardly constitute a confrontational, revisionist agenda vis-à-vis the existing international order. China has resisted the norms and principles of the liberal international economic system no more than most developing countries.[15]

Beijing's increased emphasis on the democratization of international relations beyond the economic arena can be seen in its promotion of the so-called new security concept. This notion was first introduced by the Chinese leadership in the context of managing relations with Russia and newly independent Central Asian states in the mid-1990s and has subsequently been applied elsewhere. This policy advocates an economic and political order in which mutual trust, benefit, equality, and cooperation characterize bilateral relations and multilateral institutions to reduce "insecurity and safeguard global strategic equilibrium and stability."[16] Also significant, and not all that surprising, the policy reflects Beijing's desire to circumvent Washington's well-established alliance networks by associating such structures with a Cold War mentality that is ill suited to an era of globalization in which security and development are positive-sum games requiring mutual cooperation, rather than the bloc politics of the past.

In this new spirit, Beijing has sought to infuse a sense of shared growth and security community into China's relations with its neighbors. The Shanghai Cooperation Organization (SCO), established in June 2001 to capitalize on earlier joint confidence-building efforts among China, Russia, Kazakhstan, Tajikistan, Kyrgyzstan, and Uzbekistan, is designed to achieve a more institutionalized form of cooperation on issues ranging from antiterrorism to trade. Chinese leaders now hail the SCO as a model of regional cooperation that enhances collective security for the participants while not threatening any outside party.

Similar motivations were behind Beijing's October 2003 signing of the Treaty of Amity and Cooperation, the nonaggression pact of the Association of Southeast Asian Nations (ASEAN). China simultaneously issued a joint declaration with ASEAN, the "Strategic Partnership for Peace and Prosperity," which included a call to establish a security dialogue between the 10 member countries of ASEAN and China. These initiatives built upon Beijing's ongoing efforts to forge a China-ASEAN free-trade agreement. China has also become an enthusiastic participant in the network of currency-swap arrangements launched by China, Japan, South Korea, and ASEAN in 2000 under the so-called Chiang Mai Initiative. Such initiatives to promote trade and monetary regionalism in East Asia reflect a comprehensive and multilateral approach to security.

Whereas interdependence served mainly as a means for advancing Chinese economic interests in the past, it now appears that China is coming to value interdependence partially for its own sake. More specifically, although China remains wary of the implications of interdependence for national autonomy, as are all nations to varying degrees, Beijing's grand strategy now shows signs of relying on formal and informal mechanisms (strengthened multilateral institutions and strong economic ties, respectively) of interdependence as a de facto strategy for restraining the United States.

For example, Beijing has deepened its involvement in the UN system in recent years, including its participation in the Security Council, where China had been extremely passive in the past. Since the 1999 NATO war in Kosovo, China has been more determined than ever to defend the relevance and authority of the UN. Elsewhere, China has actively promoted security initiatives in venues such as the ASEAN Regional Forum (ARF), in which its dialogue partners include the United States, Japan, the EU, and Russia as well as ASEAN members. At the 2003 annual ARF meeting, Beijing proposed that a security policy conference be established within ARF in which military as well as civilian personnel would participate. Only a few years earlier, because of China's victim complex originating from its century-long experience as a semicolony after the Opium War (1839–1842) and rigid notion of sovereignty, China's advocacy of such a position would have been unthinkable.

To the extent that globalization can create constraints on U.S. power—power that might otherwise be used to pursue unmitigated unilateralism—China believes it can pluralize and democratize the hegemonic order and strengthen incentives for Washington to engage Beijing rather than contain it.[17] As such, Chinese mainstream observers see globalization and multipolarization reinforcing each other to create common interests that can replace the China threat theory with the China opportunity theory. Such a world is most conducive to China's quest for economic prosperity and great-power status.

Global Threats and China's New Thinking on Security

China's concern about transnational threats such as terrorism, unregulated capital flows, weapons proliferation, epidemics, and cross-border criminal activities preceded the terrorist attacks of September 11, 2001. For example, the Asian financial crisis dramatically sensitized China to its own banking and economic vulnerabilities, given the broad similarities (such as high levels of nonperforming loans) to the conditions that contributed to weakness in neighboring countries such as Thailand, Indonesia, and South Korea. Similarly, one of the original missions of the SCO was to combat what member states call the three evil forces of terrorism, separatism, and extremism. The September 11 attacks and the SARS crisis undoubtedly raised Chinese awareness about what China's latest White Paper on National Defense specifically refers to as "diversifying and globalizing" security threats.[18]

Today, China no longer faces any imminent threat of military invasion by any foreign power. According to Chu Shulong, director of the Institute of Strategic Studies at Tsinghua University, Taiwan may be the only prominent traditional security issue currently facing China. Consequently, he argues, China should brace itself mainly against nontraditional threats that would endanger its social stability, economic vitality, and "human security."[19] Moreover, official Chinese views now also hold that effectively combating these global threats requires cooperative security rather than traditional competitive politics.

For China, no nontraditional threat hit home as abruptly as the outbreak of SARS in the first half of 2003. Originating in southern China in late 2002 (or earlier by some accounts), the epidemic quickly infected more than 8,000 people in 30-plus countries, causing nearly 800 deaths within six months. By the time the disease was finally brought under control, Beijing's initial mishandling of the crisis, as well as the SARS scourge itself, had taken a serious toll on China's economy and its international reputation. The silver lining of the tragedy, however, was the subsequent call by Chinese analysts for a comprehensive rethinking of national security with more attention to nontraditional threats to social stability and the rights and well-being of the Chinese people.[20]

When China's top leadership finally acknowledged the SARS crisis and started to mobilize the "people's war" against the epidemic in April 2003, Chinese commentators emphatically characterized SARS as a global disease posing a common threat to the international community. They even compared the outbreak to the September 11 terrorist attacks on the United States: both came from new threats facing humanity and both required joint international efforts to eradicate them.

In response, foreign leaders generally echoed Beijing's characterization of SARS as a global challenge. Whereas the foreign media were more critical of Beijing's initial cover-up, world leaders, including Bush, refrained from openly casting blame on Beijing and offered support instead for the embattled Beijing leadership, which had been newly inaugurated in March. Foreign governments and international institutions provided a financial package worth $38 million in support of Beijing's fight against SARS. This support led a prominent Chinese international relations scholar, Yan Xuetong, to declare that SARS "not only tested our country's foreign relations, but to some extent strengthened China's cooperative relationship with the international society. Moreover, SARS has provided China with experience in international cooperation and a new environment for China's further integration into the international society."[21] Of particular note, he specifically attributed the enhanced international cooperation to the nontraditional nature of the SARS threat.

The devastation of the Asian financial crisis, the fallout of the terrorist attacks, and the North Korean nuclear standoff further underscored the intertwined nature of traditional and nontraditional security threats. Chinese commentators have learned that nontraditional threats can imperil China's security environment and strike China's vital interests in social stability, national unity, and economic development. While calling for greater attention from their government to such threats, Chinese analysts also emphasize the inadequacy of an outdated, militarized, self-help approach to security. This emerging recognition among the political and intellectual elites of the need for a comprehensive, multilateralist, and cooperative model for security has resulted not only from the practical necessities in dealing with these new threats but also from China's greater interest in transforming great-power politics in ways that would improve the country's security environment.[22]

Indeed, cooperation between China and the United States on transnational threats such as terrorism and North Korean nuclear proliferation has significantly stabilized the bilateral relationship. Despite pervasive concerns about the offensive nature of Washington's hegemonic policies, the consensus within the Chinese policy community is that the global war on terrorism has defused, at least in part, U.S. strategic concerns about China becoming a peer competitor. In this way, the dark side of globalization, namely nontraditional threats, may serve to restrain U.S. power and reduce U.S. hostilities toward China. The six-party talks in Beijing on the North Korean crisis are a case in point. They have strengthened Sino-U.S. cooperation and diminished the U.S. unilateral impulse to settle the crisis through force.

Strategic Choice in a Globalized World

Despite Beijing's rhetoric bemoaning inequities in the international economic system, criticizing international military intervention, and denouncing U.S. unilateralism, Chinese foreign policy in recent years can in fact be best characterized as dynamic "system maintenance."[23] At the outset of the new millennium, China's international behavior is increasingly motivated by a desire to maintain the status quo by seeking stable relations with the United States as the world's sole current superpower and by promoting China's gradual rise in the international system.[24]

In the past decade, China has stepped up its great-power diplomacy. It has significantly improved relations with Russia, Germany, France, and the EU. As an exception, political relations with Japan have most recently stalled largely due to disputes over issues concerning Japanese wartime responsibility and a severe lack of confidence in each other's strategic intentions. President Hu Jintao's attendance of a North-South conference sponsored by the 2003 Group of Eight summit in France represented a breakthrough in China's view, which had long perceived the great-power club as Western-dominated and discriminatory. This turnabout underscores China's desire to participate in great-power forums. Individually, China has cultivated strategic partnerships with Russia, Germany, and France, not as a hostile alliance to the United States but to enhance its own international standing.

Within this broader foreign policy framework, the Chinese perception of and policy toward the United States are more nuanced and strategic than straightforward or clear-cut. Beijing prefers an enduring, robust relationship with the United States but resents the many ways in which U.S. hegemony disadvantages China's interests. To the extent that the United States remains the champion of economic liberalism, China benefits from U.S. leadership. Although Chinese elites often find U.S. hegemony objectionable, China also owes U.S. leadership for the largely tranquil and open international environment essential for its economic growth during the past three decades or so. At the regional level, Chinese officials in the past couple of years have openly accepted the U.S. role in Asia as long as that presence does not threaten China's interests.

Generally frustrated by the uncertainty and ambiguity of U.S. policy toward their government, Chinese leaders' discontent has focused specifically on what they perceive to be the United States' distrust of, and zero-sum power politics mindset toward, China. To avoid the prohibitive costs of confrontation and dispel any impressions of China's pursuit of old-style power politics, Chinese foreign policy has disavowed both all-out internal military mobilization and vigorous external military alliances. Neither China's military modernization nor its strategic partnership with Russia amounts to a classical balancing strategy. In the minds of most Chinese observers, the persistence (and even strengthening) of U.S. primacy after the end of the Cold War has rendered balancing a relatively impractical alternative.[25] Coupled with China's strategic self-restraint, the enduring power gap between China and the United States has dissuaded Beijing from trying to engage directly in peer competition with Washington.[26]

Thus, Chinese analysts have focused their attention on defining a position for their country within a global system of U.S. hegemony. It is in this context that the Chinese leadership has conceptualized the impact of globalization on China's economic agenda and security environment. By transforming the geo-economic context of interstate competition, globalization has created powerful incentives for China's participation in transnational economic structures and multilateral institutions. Pursuit of a balancing strategy, on the other hand, would require China to divert huge sums of scarce resources to a concerted arms buildup, to establish military alliances against Washington, and to withdraw from (and perhaps even actively undermine) the U.S.-led liberal international economic system—all to China's disadvantage. Such confrontational policies are likely to prove futile and self-defeating. Rather, a Chinese foreign policy that accommodates economic globalization and works toward active participation in international institutions is essential to maintaining the robust economic growth critical both to social stability and the political legitimacy of the Chinese Communist Party, let alone China's rising status and influence in international politics.

Throughout the series of foreign policy crises encountered in recent years, particularly as manifested in tensions between the United States and China, the leadership in Beijing has consistently concluded that China has no alternative but to continue and even to increase China's participation in the globalizing world economy. Nothing illustrates this commitment better than the timing and circumstances of Beijing's November 1999 agreement with Washington on China's WTO accession, when President Jiang Zemin and Prime Minister Zhu Rongji delivered politically on a deal whose terms were strenuously opposed by significant bureaucratic interests at home. Even more striking, China's top leaders had to overcome an embarrassing negotiating rebuff by the Clinton administration during Zhu's April 1999 visit to Washington as well as the bombing of China's embassy in Belgrade the following month. The latter, in particular, made it difficult domestically for Jiang and Zhu to appear as if they were making concessions to gain U.S. blessing for China's WTO membership.

In their public statements, China's leaders routinely acknowledge that globalization—economic globalization, initially, but now including its more fundamental implications—encourages broad participation in multilateral institutions both at the regional and global levels.[27] More specifically, across an increasingly wide range of trade issues, including disputes over steel tariffs, textile quotas, and antidumping duties, WTO mechanisms are proving an important means by which China can defend its interests against U.S. unilateralism. For example, China was one of the complainants who appealed to the WTO over the controversial imposition of U.S. tariffs on imported steel in March 2002. Indeed, China prepared retaliatory tariffs against U.S. imports, as allowed under WTO rules, in case the Bush administration had refused to lift the duties.

Similarly, global and regional institutions have provided a measure of support as Beijing has resisted pressure from Washington to revalue the renminbi on U.S. terms. In November 2003, for example, a majority of the International Monetary Fund's (IMF) directors found that China's currency was not substantially undervalued, noting in part the sharp decline in China's overall trade surplus.[28] This marked the third time in as many months that the Bush administration failed to secure multilateral pressure on China on this issue. In September, members of ASEAN with additional support from Australia undermined Washington's drive to have a statement issued on Beijing's currency policy at a meeting of APEC finance ministers. In October, Bush himself failed to make the U.S. case successfully at the annual APEC leaders' summit. At the October meeting, Japan went on the record in opposition to Washington's position. For their part, Chinese officials said that Beijing would consider changing its currency policy "if there was consensus in the region."[29] Any statement by the IMF or APEC would not have obliged China to take action, and Chinese officials undoubtedly expressed their willingness to consider the consensus view knowing what the outcome would be. These rejections of U.S. policy were important symbolically, however, in validating Beijing's determination to manage currency rates and undertake foreign exchange reform at its own pace.

Whereas recent emphasis has been on China's growing participation in multilateral institutions, similar arguments can be made about how informal mechanisms of interdependence, such as China's burgeoning commercial ties, have anchored its relations with other great powers. For all of China's oft-cited dependence on the United States as an export market, Washington's penchant for foreign borrowing contributes to leveling the playing field. By virtually any measure, Chinese holdings of U.S. debt, such as Treasury securities, dwarfs U.S. investment in Chinese factories. The result is a historically unusual relationship in which the rising power, developing China, provides both exports (second-leading supplier) and loans (second-leading foreign holder of government debt) to the superpower, the industrialized United States.

In this and other ways, China's economic ties with the United States are seen as weakening any impulse the United States may have to view China as a rival that needs to be contained. By many accounts, Beijing long ago adopted a conscious strategy of developing constituencies in the United States, particularly in the business community, who will support engagement policies toward China even if the noneconomic aspects of the bilateral relationship sour. Given the de facto constraints on using a balancing strategy to check the exercise of U.S. power, interdependence presents the most viable alternative currently available to China to restrain U.S. hegemony. Although deepening economic ties may produce their own tensions in the relationship, as the ongoing controversies over the proper valuation of the renminbi and the broader sources of the U.S.-Chinese trade imbalance illustrate, they still create mutual dependencies that most Chinese observers view as limiting hostilities.

Certainly, China continues to resort to power politics calculations as all states do in the still anarchic, albeit highly globalized world—for example, relying on coercive measures as an essential tool to prevent Taiwan's de jure independence—and is determined to strengthen its material power. Even in Taiwan, however, China's nicer, gentler image has made its threat of force less credible. Military confrontation over a democratic Taiwan would contradict Beijing's attempt to differentiate its own strategic choice of responsibility and peace from traditional great-power politics, characterized by the prominent role of violence and territorial conquest. In this sense, globalization and interdependence might have undercut the efficacy of China's coercive diplomacy in the short term and has no doubt drastically increased the cost of a military solution. Yet, decisionmakers in Beijing still believe that the same process has deepened cross-strait interdependence, increased international support for stability in the region, and overall held the prospect of decisively turning the tide in mainland China's favor.

Beijing still finds certain aspects of U.S. hegemony detrimental to its interests, but the bottom line is that mainstream Chinese strategic thinkers believe that attempts to change the status quo radically carry substantial risks of international instability that, particularly in terms of geo-economic fragmentation, are anathema to China's pressing developmental needs. As such, China's strategic calculus is characterized by a dynamic status quo orientation that seeks what Robert Gilpin terms "changes *in* an international system" rather than "change *of* an international system."[30] The past decade has proven China's determination to advance its interests within the globalized world.

Toward a New Great-Power Politics?

Great-power politics has traditionally been viewed in terms of an unmitigated struggle for power among nation-states. Specifically, some mainstream international relations theories attribute inevitable great-power conflict to the supreme value that states attach to superior relative power. It is from this perspective that China's economic growth and rise in power are viewed as detrimental by many observers outside China. This line of reasoning overlooks the potential role globalization can play in transforming Chinese foreign policy choice and the corresponding responses to China's rise by other great powers.

In the preceding sections, we have outlined the mainstream views among top Chinese leaders and prominent strategic researchers within leading Chinese civilian think tanks and academic institutions. To be sure, these views are contested by more traditional security thinking, particularly among military analysts.[31] Yet, the prevailing views and the strategic choices that Beijing has made in recent years raise the question of whether China has, in fact, already begun to pursue a different approach to great-power politics, one that seeks to overcome the security dilemma fueled by great-power transitions. Skillful management of the Taiwan issue in particular remains critical to entrenching such an emerging Chinese view. Assuming that is successfully navigated, such an approach emphasizes positive state-to-state relations at the expense of narrower concerns about undercutting other states in the interest of enhancing China's own relative power.

Globalization by no means negates competition, but in today's increasingly globalized world, rules and institutions may moderate competitive politics. Chinese experience with and perceptions of globalization show that globalization has facilitated its status quo orientation despite U.S. hegemony. The same process has in turn led to international responses to China's rise that are, overall, characterized by a much more constrained balance-of-power logic than was evident in traditional great-power politics. The steady rise in China's international and regional status has vindicated its cooperative diplomacy.

It is by no means certain that China will not retreat from cooperative security thinking, nor is a new great-power system solely a Chinese choice. China's strategy and the constraints imposed by both the bright and dark sides of globalization on the unilateral exercise of coercive power, however, may provide other states the kind of mutual reassurance of each other's intentions and mutually beneficial outcomes that have been largely absent in traditional great-power relations. Countries thus may increasingly engage in multifaceted, dynamic, win-win competition rather than maintain a single-minded, zero-sum power struggle. As such, beyond the changes globalization appears to be bringing to China's foreign policy in particular, mainstream Chinese global thinking suggests the possible emergence of a new kind of great-power politics where peacefully contested change may replace the worst manifestations of hostile competition.

Notes

1. The term "globalization" was introduced by then-Foreign Minister Qian Qichen during the General Debate of the United Nations General Assembly on September 25, 1996, UN document A/51/PV.8.

2. Jiang Zemin, "Together Create a New Century of Peace and Prosperity," Xinhua, April 10, 2002, in FBIS, CPP2002–0410000101. On common security, see Wu Bangguo, "Create a Hundred Years of Peace in Asia, Jointly Build Sustained Development of Asia," September 1, 2003, in FBIS, CPP2003–0901000066. On globalized cooperation, see Li Zhaoxing, speech to UN General Assembly, New York, September 24, 2003, www.un.org/webcast/ga/58/statements/chinaeng030924.htm (accessed October 9, 2003).

3. See Jiang Zemin, report to the Sixteenth Congress of the Chinese Communist Party, Beijing, November 8, 2002, in "Building a Well-off Society in an All-Out Effort, Creating a New Situation for the Cause of Chinese-Style Socialism," *Renmin Ribao* (overseas edition), November 18, 2002, pp. 1–3.

4. Ye Zicheng, "Transcend the 'Polarity' Mentality: Thoughts on China's Diplomatic Strategy," *Southern Weekend*, www.irchina.org/news/view.asp?id=297 (accessed January 20, 2004).

5. *Renmin Ribao*, (overseas edition), January 28, 2004, pp. 1, 4.

6. Wang Yi, "Safeguard Peace, Promote Development, Create a New Situation For Diplomatic Work," *Shijie Zhishi*, January 16, 2003, pp. 8–10, in FBIS, CPP2003–0204000110.

7. Joseph S. Nye Jr., *The Paradox of American Power: Why the World's Only Superpower Can't Go It Alone* (London and New York: Oxford University Press, 2002).

8. Shen Jiru, "Will the World Pattern Change?" *Renmin Ribao*, April 3, 2003, p. 13, in FBIS, CPP2003–0403000067.

9. Liao Lei, "PRC Expert Shen Jiru on Role of Economic Factors for Improving DPRK–U.S. Relations," Xinhua, August 26, 2003, in FBIS, CPP2003–0826000123.

10. Zheng Yu, "The Primary Goals of Chinese Diplomacy at the Beginning of the Century," *Huangiu Shibao*, September 5, 2003.

11. Luo Zhaohong, "Grasping Changes in the Environment from an Economic Perspective," *Xiandai Guoji Guanxi*, no. 11, November 20, 2002, in FBIS, CCP2002–1211000217, p. 2.

12. "Statement by Foreign Trade Minister Shi Guangsheng to the Fourth Ministerial Conference of the WTO Following the Adoption of the Decision on China's Accession to the WTO," November 10, 2001, http://english.mofcom.gov.cn/article/200211/20021100050101_1.xml (accessed April 4, 2004).

13. "Statement by H.E. Mr. Lu Fuyuan, Minister of Commerce," WT/MIN/(03)/ST/12, September 11, 2003, http://docsonline.wto.org/DDFDocuments/t/

WT/Min03/ST12.doc (accessed April 4, 2004) (from the Fifth Session of the Ministerial Conference, Cancun, September 10–14, 2003).

14. Rebecca Buckman, "WTO Head Asks China to Help Revive Talks," *Asian Wall Street Journal*, November 11, 2003, p. A3.

15. Margaret M. Pearson, "The Major Multilateral Economic Institutions Engage China," in *Engaging China: The Management of an Emerging Power*, eds. Alastair Iain Johnston and Robert S. Ross (London: Routledge and Kegan Paul, 1999), p. 207.

16. Jiang Zemin, "Together Create a New Century of Peace and Prosperity."

17. Wu Xinbo, "Globalization and the Restructuring of the Strategic Foundation of Sino-U.S. Relations," *Shijie Zhengzhi Yu Jingji*, September 14, 2002, pp. 55–60, in FBIS, CPP2002–1011000334.

18. China State Council, Information Office, "China's National Defense, 2002," *Renmin Ribao* (overseas edition), December 10, 2002, pp. 1–4.

19. Chu Shulong, "China's Diplomatic Strategy During the Period of Comprehensively Building a Well-Off Society," *Shijie Zhengzhi Yu Jingji*, August 2003, p. 5, www.iwep.org.cn/wep/200308/chushulong.pdf (accessed April 21, 2004).

20. See Xue Lan and Zhang Qiang, "Confronting the Crisis—SARS Predicament and the Transformation of China's Governance," *Renmin Wang*, May 19, 2003.

21. Yan Xuetong, "SARS Tests China's Foreign Relations," *Global Times*, May 23, 2003.

22. Qian Qichen, "Adjustments of the U.S. National Security Strategy and International Relations in the Early New Century," *Renmin Ribao* (domestic edition), January 19, 2004, p. 4, www.people.com.cn/GB/guoji/14549/2303998.html (accessed January 18, 2004).

23. Samuel S. Kim, "China and the United Nations," in *China Joins the World: Progress and Prospects*, eds. Elizabeth Economy and Michel Oksenberg (New York: Council on Foreign Relations, 1999), p. 46. See Alastair Iain Johnston, "Is China a Status Quo Power?" *International Security* 27, no. 4 (spring 2003): 5–56.

24. See Zhang Yunling, "How to Understand the International Environment China Faces in the Asia-Pacific Region," *Dangdai Yatai*, no. 6, June 15, 2003, pp. 3–14, in FBIS, CPP2003–0717000218, p. 3.

25. For a related discussion, see Banning Garrett, "China Faces, Debates the Contradictions of Globalization," *Asian Survey* 41, no. 3 (May–June 2001): 409–427.

26. This specific analysis on China is consistent with the general argument made in William C. Wohlforth, "The Stability of a Unipolar World," *International Security* 24, no. 1 (summer 1999): 5–41.

27. On economic affairs, one example is Jiang Zemin's speech at the Eighth APEC Informal Leadership Meeting, Brunei, November 16, 2000, www.fmprc.gov/cn/

eng/6004.html (accessed March 11, 2003). On security affairs, see Tang Jiaxuan's speech at the Ninth ASEAN Regional Forum Foreign Ministers' Meeting, Brunei, July 31, 2002, http://fmprc.gov.cn/eng/33228.html (accessed March 11, 2003). Portions of this and the following three paragraphs draw in part from Thomas G. Moore, "Chinese Foreign Policy in the Age of Globalization," in *China Rising: Power and Motivation in Chinese Foreign Policy?* eds. Yong Deng and Fei-Ling Wang (Lanham, Md.: Rowman and Littlefield, forthcoming).

28. "Risk of Divorce—Strains Grow in the U.S.-China Marriage of Convenience," *Financial Times*, November 20, 2003, p. 20.

29. "Asia Leaves U.S. to Fight Alone Over Yuan Policy," *Asian Wall Street Journal*, October 21, 2003, p. A1.

30. Robert Gilpin, *War and Change in World Politics* (Cambridge and New York: Cambridge University Press, 1981), p. 208 (emphasis in original).

31. For a representative military view, see Lt. Gen. Li Jijun, "China's National Security in the Globalization Era," *Outlook Weekly*, http://news.xinhuanet.com/2004-03/27/content_1387461.htm (accessed March 27, 2004) (reprint).

Wu Xinbo

The Promise and Limitations of a Sino-U.S. Partnership

Terrorism's emergence after September 11, 2001, as the primary threat to international security introduced a new focus to Chinese foreign policy and brought about a great opportunity for improving relations with the United States. The broadened and deepened cooperation with Washington on counterterrorism and nonproliferation raised the prospect of a Sino-U.S. partnership in a new international setting. The effects of U.S. foreign policy adjustments on U.S. relations with China, however, are mixed. Although September 11 lowered China's status on the United States' threat list, the way the Bush administration has pursued the campaign on terrorism, particularly the invasion of Iraq, has aroused strong Chinese concern about the orientation of U.S. foreign policy, thus constraining the two countries' emerging partnership.

A New Focus for Chinese Foreign Policy

Although Chinese leaders and scholars have long been aware of the rise of nontraditional security challenges, a new recognition of terrorism's capacity for destruction in the aftermath of the September 11 attacks has largely reshaped China's security concept as well as its foreign and

Wu Xinbo is a professor at the Center for American Studies, Fudan University, in Shanghai.

Copyright © 2004 by The Center for Strategic and International Studies and the Massachusetts Institute of Technology
The Washington Quarterly • 27:4 pp. 115–126.

security policies. As the Chinese Ministry of Foreign Affairs explicitly acknowledged, "the 9/11 incident underscored the imminent threat of terrorism to international peace and security."[1] New concern over the terrorist threat in the global war on terrorism in the three years since the attacks has encouraged the Chinese government to undertake a series of security and foreign policy initiatives in counterterrorism, nonproliferation, and regional security, as well as develop a greater commitment to multilateralism.

COUNTERTERRORISM

China, a nation that has faced its own terrorist threat posed by the East Turkistan terrorist forces in China's Xinjiang Province, has intensified its counterterrorism efforts in the aftermath of September 11 through a range of legal, military, and diplomatic measures.

The East Turkistan terrorist threat is the product of a movement launched by Islamic fundamentalists in the Xinjiang Uygur Autonomous Region of China in the 1980s, which seeks to found a so-called state of East Turkistan. In the 1990s, influenced by extremism, separatism, and international terrorism, part of the East Turkistan forces inside and outside China turned toward separatist and sabotage activities, with terrorist violence as their main means. According to the Chinese government, from 1990 to 2001 the East Turkistan terrorist forces were responsible for more than 200 terrorist incidents in Xinjiang, which resulted in 162 deaths and more than 440 injuries. Moreover, these forces are believed to have close connections with Al Qaeda. For example, the East Turkistan Islamic Movement (ETIM), one important group of the East Turkistan forces, is supported and directed by Osama bin Laden. Since the 1990s, bin Laden has schemed with the heads of Central and West Asian terrorist organizations many times to help the East Turkistan forces launch a holy war in Xinjiang, with the aim of establishing a theocratic Islamic state in the region.[2] Although China worked hard to cope with this terrorist threat, Beijing took a low profile on this issue before September 11, never internationally publicizing the threat or openly calling for international cooperation in fighting the East Turkistan terrorists.

The events of September 11 and the emergence of an international security environment focused on combating global terrorism has encouraged and enabled China to attract new international attention to this threat. On November 11, 2001, Chinese foreign minister Tang Jiaxuan stated in his address at the United Nations that "China also suffered from the terrorist threat. 'Eastern Turkistan' terrorist forces were trained, armed, and financially aided by international terrorist organizations. Fighting 'Eastern Turkistan' is an important dimension of the international campaign against terrorism."[3] In January 2002, China released a White Paper revealing in detail the East Turkistan organization's terrorist activities conducted in Xinjiang from 1990 to 2001.[4] Beijing's efforts to publicize East Turkistan terrorist activities in the hopes of encouraging the world to treat the organization as part of the greater international terrorist threat proved successful in the summer of 2002 when ETIM was added to the U.S. Department of State's list of terrorist organizations and the UN followed suit.

Beijing's new interest in working with international partners to meet its own terrorist threat, as well as combat global terrorism, further led China to enter into regular bilateral dialogue with other countries to promote cooperation on counterterrorism. In October 2001, China and Russia agreed to establish the Sino-Russian working group on counterterrorism. In the same month, Presidents Jiang Zemin and George W. Bush met at the Asia Pacific Economic Cooperation (APEC) summit meeting in Shanghai, where they reached an agreement to set up Sino-U.S. exchanges and to cooperate on counterterrorism. In January 2002, Beijing and New Delhi agreed to establish a bilateral working group on counterterrorism.

In addition to bilateral approaches, China turned to multilateral institutions such as the Shanghai Cooperation Organization (SCO). The organization, with China, Russia, Kazakhstan, Kyrgyzstan, Tajikistan, and Uzbekistan as its members, was founded in 2001 to fight separatism, extremism, and terrorism. In the post–September 11 era, SCO faced both challenges and opportunities. On one hand, the United States, under the flag of fighting terrorism in Central Asia, started to forge closer security ties with some SCO members and stationed troops in the region, potentially undermining the organization's cohesion and function. On the other hand, the new sense of urgency about the terrorist threat among SCO members provided an incentive to deepen the organization substantively. Beijing seized this opportunity to intensify SCO cooperation, leading to the June 2002 agreement among SCO member states to establish its regional antiterrorism institution in Bishkek, the capital of Kyrgyzstan, to enhance coordination and the exchange of intelligence in the campaign against terrorism. In the summer of 2003, China and all SCO members except Uzbekistan launched their first, joint, multilateral military exercise, rehearsing a strike on terrorist camps.

In sum, the events of September 11 heightened China's awareness of the terrorist threat. Beijing subsequently not only moved to actively seek international cooperation in meeting its own terrorist challenge, but also extended support to the global war on terrorism through bilateral and multilateral approaches.

APPROACH TO NONPROLIFERATION

The September 11 attacks coupled with subsequent international attention to the prospect that terrorists could acquire weapons of mass destruction (WMD) has also alerted China to threats posed by weapons proliferation in unprecedented ways. The terrorists' use of hijacked civilian aircraft to attack military and civilian targets in the United States has made Chinese policymakers aware that, were terrorists able to obtain them, they would indeed be likely to use nuclear, chemical, and biological weapons to wide effect. As China's Ministry of Foreign Affairs observed, "At present, proliferation of weapons of mass destruction and their delivery vehicles has posed an increasing threat to world peace and security. Putting an effective end to such a threat has become a common task for the entire international community."[5]

This escalation of the WMD threat on Beijing's foreign policy agenda has prompted the Chinese government to improve its export control practices and take a more active role in international efforts to prevent WMD proliferation. Although Beijing promised to Washington in November 2000 that it was going to publish regulations to enhance its export controls, it was slow in doing so. China's heightened concern over the spread of WMD in the post–September 11 era, however, speed up its pace. In 2002, for example, China formulated, promulgated, and enforced a series of control regulations and related lists aimed at safeguarding its sensitive materials, such as missiles, biological and chemical items and technologies, and all military products. Marking a major step forward in China's nonproliferation legislation, these new regulations and lists established detailed and stringent provisions on the scope, clearance procedure, and punishment of the export of sensitive materials and embraced the "catch-all" principle, requiring the comprehensive control of all exports that might entail proliferation risks.

Heightened concern about the spread of WMD also drove Beijing to adopt active diplomacy on the North Korean nuclear issue. Since the revelation of the North Korean nuclear program in the fall of 2002, Beijing has engaged in "its most active multilateral diplomatic efforts ever,"[6] both to avoid conflict on the Korean peninsula and to prevent the further proliferation of nuclear weapons and technology. In fact, China is more concerned about nuclear proliferation beyond Korea than it is about the prospect of a nuclear North Korea, as a nuclear North Korea is unlikely to use its weapons against China while proliferation runs the risk of weapons landing in the hands of terrorist organizations, a nightmare for every country.

REGIONAL STABILITY

The September 11 attacks highlighted the preeminence of nontraditional security threats; the transnational nature of these challenges has caused China to attach more importance to stability on its periphery. China, bordering 15 countries, has more immediate neighbors than any other country in the world. As it increasingly opens its borders for economic and people-to-people exchanges with the outside world, the state of China's neighbors' stability directly impacts its own. For instance, the disintegration of the Soviet Union led to the rise of Islamic fundamentalist influence in some of its Central Asian republics. Very quickly, these influences penetrated China's Xinjiang province, spurring the East Turkistan forces' activities in China.

To enhance stability on its periphery, Beijing used to focus on improving political ties with adjacent countries through a policy it described as *"mu lin you hao* (good neighbor and friendliness)." In recent years, however, particularly after September 11, China has paid more attention to the economic dimension of its relations with neighboring countries. Reflecting on the broad sociopolitical context of terrorism, the Chinese believe that poverty and economic inequality is the hotbed of terrorism. As former Chinese foreign minister Tang Jiaxuan commented, "The prolonged violence and impoverishment in some developing countries has made them easy prey to the manipulation of terrorists. Only when we succeed in achieving common development ... can we eradicate the root causes of terrorism."[7] The Chinese political and intellectual elite realize that, although China's economy is growing fast, most of its immediate neighbors still lag behind. Poverty in those countries may generate serious sociopolitical tensions and instability that will strain security on China's periphery, but the economic gap between a prosperous China and some of its poorer neighbors could also cause resentment against China, giving rise to tensions in their relations.

To guard against this possibility, Beijing has shown more enthusiasm for promoting economic cooperation with its neighboring countries, including the building of strong economic ties among SCO's members and the deepening of economic cooperation with states of the Association of Southeast Asian Nations. Indicative of this new focus on shared, improved economic relations, Beijing has more recently declared a policy of *"you lin, an lin, fu lin* (bringing its neighbors harmony, security, and prosperity)." It is expected that such an approach will help create a stable security environment for China and enhance its influence in regional affairs.

A Greater Commitment to Multilateralism

China's new post-9/11 awareness that terrorism in the era of globalization is transnational and requires a multilateral response has made the country a more vocal advocate of multilateralism in the last three years. Meanwhile, the U.S. penchant for unilateralism both before and since the September 11 attacks has reinforced China's commitment to multilateralism. Immediately after September 11, Beijing was very concerned that the Bush administration, which demonstrated a unilateral tendency well before the attacks, would launch a series of unilateral efforts to fight terrorism, with uncontrollable consequences for the existing international order.

From the beginning of the global response to transnational terrorism, China stressed the desirability of giving the UN the lead role in coordinating an international campaign. On October 3, 2001, in a speech to a UN session on antiterrorism, the Chinese permanent representative to the UN suggested that the UN "is an important venue for the counterterrorism cooperation among countries, and it should play a leading role in the international campaign against terrorism."[8] Although China understood and even provided support for the U.S. war in Afghanistan, the subsequent U.S. invasion of Iraq without UN authorization aggravated China's concern that the United States is determined to use military force and to abandon multilateral institutions to achieve its security goals.

Although the war in Iraq quickly drew to an end, China worries about its implications for international relations in the long run. Beijing deplored how the Iraq war and the international dispute that preceded it undermined mutual trust between countries, eroded harmony among different cultures, and detracted from the authority of an international regime of cooperation. Reflections on the Iraq war have reinforced China's commitment to multilateralism. As Chinese foreign minister Li Zhaoxing put it, "Multilateralism stands as an effective means to address the common challenges facing humankind, an important approach to solving international disputes, a strong safeguard of globalization's healthy development, and the best way to promote the democratization and legalization of international relations."[9] From China's point of view, Washington's appeal to the UN after the war to handle the Iraq issue proves that even a powerful country such as the United States cannot succeed alone, attesting to the high value of multilateralism.

The United States: Testing a New Security Concept and Practices

September 11 obviously resulted in drastic changes for the United States, both externally, including a revolutionary change in U.S. threat perceptions, the birth of the preemption doctrine, and the pursuit of freedom of action at the expense of traditional alliances, and internally, including the elevation of homeland security concerns as well as the rise of neoconservative influence. First, the September 11 attacks brought a paramount change to the United States' concept of security and national security strategy that has had profound implications for Sino-U.S. relations: the U.S. threat perception shifted from a geopolitical concern to a functional one. Prior to the attacks, the Bush administration's defense planners held that shifts in the balance of power, including the rise of major powers, and traditional major-power competition stood as the primary threat to U.S. national security. Challenges posed by a rising China particularly concerned the Pentagon, as the 2001 *Quadrennial Defense Review Report (QDR)* noted that "[m]aintaining a stable balance in Asia will be a complex task. The possibility exists that a military competitor with a formidable resource base will emerge."[10] Although the *QDR* was released in late September 2001, its draft was completed before that and thus presented the pre–September 11 security thinking in the U.S. national security establishment.

The primary perceived threat to U.S. national security then changed, as clearly conveyed in its September 2002 *National Security Strategy (NSS)* report, to "the crossroads of radicalism and technology,"[11] otherwise defined as the combination of terrorism and WMD. By fundamentally shifting the priorities on the U.S. national security agenda and U.S. threat perceptions, the September 11 terrorist attacks made terrorism a much more urgent task than balancing emerging powers. In the realm of U.S. foreign policy, China was thus transformed from a "strategic competitor" requiring imminent attention to a potential partner in the war on terrorism. As demonstrated by Bush's trips to China in October 2001 and February 2002, Washington now was interested in developing "candid, constructive, and cooperative" relations with China. Meanwhile, Beijing also saw the opportunity to improve ties with Washington and reached out to the United States by providing valuable assistance and cooperation in the war on terrorism, such as supporting all UN counterterrorism resolutions, sharing intelligence, and cracking down on the financing of terrorist activities, among others. As such, the events of September 11 transformed the mood of Sino-U.S. relations from negative to positive.

Although Beijing views the reprioritization of the U.S. security agenda as necessary and appropriate, it saw other adjustments in U.S. national security strategy, particularly the preemption doctrine, as controversial and worrisome. At a tactical level, preemption was not new in U.S. military actions, demonstrated by the U.S. invasions of Grenada and Panama. Incorporating preemption into the U.S. national security strategy, however, and using it as the basis to deal with certain types of threats, such as rogue states, caused concern in Beijing and around the world. The NSS promises that, in the pursuit of preemption, the United States "will always proceed deliberately"; pledges that it will "build better, more integrated intelligence capabilities to provide timely, accurate information on threats"; and will "coordinate closely with allies to form a common assessment of the most dangerous threats."[12] Such assurances were proven false, however, by the United States' conduct of the war in Iraq, the first application of a preemptive strike after the September 11 attacks. As it turned out, the U.S. intelligence community did not provide "accurate information" about Iraq's WMD capability or connections to Al Qaeda, nor did Washington "form a common assessment" with some of its important allies over the threats posed by Baghdad, much less seriously listen to China's opinion on the issue. While eliminating the exaggerated threat posed by Saddam Hussein, the preemptive war against Iraq derailed the counterterrorist campaign, which should focus on terrorism itself rather than the so-called axis of evil; strained transatlantic relations; and undermined U.S. credibility as a responsible power. As a group of 27 retired U.S. diplomats and military commanders complained in June 2004, "Never in the 2 1/4 centuries of our history has the United States been so isolated among nations, so broadly feared and distrusted."[13]

Beyond preemption, the Bush administration, and the Pentagon in particular, seemed to believe that the United States should seek support from, but not be constrained by, traditional allies in fighting rogue states and terrorists after September 11. Instead, the United States sought to forge a "coalition of the willing" whenever necessary to advance its objective, with the mandate determining the coalition, not vice versa. Implicit in such an approach is a quest for unlimited freedom of action. That quest and the subsequent quarrel over the war in Iraq between the United States and some of its traditional allies have been so intense that some even wonder whether they are witnessing "the beginning of the end of 'the West'—a coalition of U.S.-led, like-minded allies, bound by core shared values and strategic threats?"[14] From a Chinese perspective, this means that the United States may become less predictable and potentially more dangerous to the world.

Beyond these foreign policy changes, the fourth change to the U.S. national security strategy since September 11 is the elevation of homeland security to its core, as demonstrated by the creation of the Department of Homeland Security. From the end of World War II until September 11, 2001, U.S. strategic attention was mainly devoted to protecting its overseas interests and allies in Western Europe, the Middle East, and East Asia. Although the Soviet Union could have attacked North America during the Cold War, the U.S. capacity to retaliate deterred it. In more than half a century, amid endless conflicts and chaos around the globe, the U.S. homeland was basically safe, affording Washington the freedom of action overseas, including its involvement in Korea and Vietnam. The tragic attacks in New York and Washington, however, revealed the vulnerability of the United States in an era of globalization, particularly when the enemies are nonstate actors employing nontraditional means.

As a result of the new sense of vulnerability in homeland security, the Americans—the elite and the general public alike—have become more sensitive to perceived external threats and are more inclined to endorse the use of force to address them, even single-handedly. This explains why the U.S. invasion of Iraq, although widely and strongly opposed in the rest of the world, received a relatively high percentage of support at home. This phenomenon added to China's concern about the force-prone tendency in U.S. foreign behavior. Now with the transition of authority from

U.S. forces to the Iraqi interim government, the Chinese wonder what the United States will target next—North Korea, Iran, or even China?

In fact, the Chinese are closely watching the neoconservatives' future influence on U.S. foreign policy. Before September 11, neoconservatives saw China as the primary threat to the United States and advocated a tough China policy. The events of September 11, however, shifted their attention away from China and toward Al Qaeda and Iraq. In the post–September 11 period, although the neoconservatives have used their influence in the Bush administration, particularly in the office of Vice President Dick Cheney and in the Pentagon, to promote robust military support for Taiwan—unprecedented since normalization of Sino-U.S. ties in 1979—and limit military-to-military relations with China, they do not have much control over other dimensions of Sino-U.S. relations. If Bush is reelected in November and the neoconservatives remain influential into his second term, however, it is very likely that they will try to turn more heat on China. Yet, some U.S. watchers in China argue that there is no need to worry even if Bush is reelected because the Iraqi aftermath should have been enough to teach him to distance himself from the neoconservatives.

Overall, the Chinese have seen both opportunities and challenges from the changes that have occurred in U.S. foreign policy in the post–September 11 era. On one hand, counterterrorism's emergence as the top U.S. priority changed the context of Sino-U.S. relations and broadened the area of cooperation between China and the United States. On the other hand, the United States seems to have become more force-prone, more unilateralist, and more unpredictable. If the level of political and strategic trust between the two countries is any indication, it is fair to say that the current stability in Sino-U.S. relations is tactical, not strategic.

New Trends Shaping International Security

By successfully destroying the World Trade Center in New York City, Al Qaeda demonstrated to the world its immense capacity to inflict heavy casualities on its targets, encouraging other terrorist groups throughout the world to follow its example by building networks and launching their own attacks. The attacks highlighted two trends that had developed in the post–Cold War era. First, nontraditional security challenges such as terrorism, WMD proliferation, drug trafficking, illegal immigration, AIDS, and environmental pollution superceded traditional security threats at the forefront of national security agendas. Most countries today see nonstate actors as a greater threat to their security interests than a shift in the balance of power. The terrorist threat in particular has received unprecedented attention. Where the next major terrorist attack may occur, how to cope with terrorist threats effectively, what the root causes of terrorism are and how to address them, and how to enhance international cooperation in the campaign against terrorism have risen to the top of the international agenda. The preeminence of counterterrorism has facilitated the birth of new international regimes as well as modified the function of some existing ones. For instance, APEC—a forum created to promote trade and economic and technological cooperation as well as to liberalize investment in the Asia-Pacific region—has devoted more attention to counterterrorism.

As far as Sino-U.S. relations are concerned, the events of September 11 prompted the Bush administration to view China through a more rational lens and provided more ground for cooperation between the two countries. Even so, the United States' narrow focus on terrorism at the expense of other issues such as AIDS, poverty, and environmental degradation may strain Sino-U.S. cooperation. For China as well as for many other countries, although terrorism is a great threat to world peace and security, a more balanced agenda should be set, reflecting a wider range of concerns and serving the interests of more countries and peoples. Otherwise, cooperation on counterterrorism may not be sustainable.

Second, relations among countries are more fluid, fundamentally realigning contemporary major powers in a highly pluralistic and flexible international system of cooperation, competition, alignment, and realignment. During the Cold War, countries divided into two antagonist camps along an ideological line; today, the line of demarcation has blurred. Traditional allies may fall into serious disputes, while countries without alliance bonds can move close to each other because of common interests and similar views of the world. International relations are becoming much more dynamic.

The United States is a major source of the dynamics for change. The Bush administration's unilateralist tendency and its attitude toward traditional alliances certainly have aroused strong concern among other major powers, including China, and may disrupt the global partnership against terrorism. Many questions remain unanswered: Will the United States continue to deviate from its long-held liberal tradition in its foreign policy? Will the American people succumb to the temptation of empire in a world of only one superpower? If Senator John Kerry (D-Mass.) wins the presidential election in November 2004, will he adopt a foreign policy informed by neoliberalism and multilateralism? If Bush is reelected, will he draw lessons from his first term, distance himself from the neoconservatives and traditional nationalists, and adopt a more moderate and pragmatist foreign policy? Only three years after the September 11 attacks, it is still too early to tell which of these changes in U.S. foreign policy are permanent and which are just temporary.

Notes

1. Chinese Ministry of Foreign Affairs, *China's Foreign Affairs, 2003* (Beijing: World Affairs Press, 2003), p. 145.

2. Information Office of the State Council, "'East Turkistan' Terrorist Forces Cannot Get Away With Impunity," *Beijing Review*, January 31, 2002, pp. 14–15, 19.

3. Xinhua News Agency, November 11, 2001.

4. Information Office of the State Council, "'Eastern Turkistan' Terrorist Forces Cannot Get Away With Impunity."

5. Chinese Ministry of Foreign Affairs, *China's Foreign Affairs, 2003*, p. 141.

6. David M. Lampton and Richard Daniel Ewing, *The U.S.-China Relationship Facing International Security Crises: Three Case Studies in Post-9/11 Bilateral Relations* (Washington, D.C.: Nixon Center, 2003), p. v, http://www.nixoncenter.org/publications/monographs/US-ChinaRelations2003Intro.pdf (accessed July 12, 2004).

7. Xinhua News Agency, "PRC FM Tang Reiterates China's Stand on Counter-Terrorism," January 20, 2003.

8. *People's Daily*, October 5, 2001, p. 3.

9. Li Zhaoxing, keynote speech at the Conference of the Asia-European Foreign Ministers on Multilateralism, http://www.fmprc.gov.cn/chnwjdt/wshd/t85514. htm (accessed June 28, 2004).

10. U.S. Department of Defense, "Quadrennial Defense Review Report," September 30, 2001, p. 4, http://www.defenselink.mil/pubs/qdr2001.pdf (accessed July 12, 2004).

11. *The National Security Strategy of the United States of America*, September 2002, p. 1, http://www.whitehouse.gov/nsc/nss.pdf (accessed July 12, 2004).

12. Ibid, p. 16.

13. Peter Slevin, "Retired Envoys, Commanders Assail Bush Team," *Washington Post*, June 17, 2004, p. 22.

14. Thomas L. Friedman, "Is This the End of 'the West'?" *International Herald Tribune*, November 3, 2003, p. 6.

David Shambaugh

The New Strategic Triangle: U.S. and European Reactions to China's Rise

The transatlantic rift over the European Union's proposed lifting of its arms embargo on China is emblematic of the shifting geopolitical global order, in which the interaction of the United States, China, and the EU will be a defining feature of the international system in the years to come. These three continental powers increasingly possess the bulk of global economic and military power as well as normative and political influence. Given the combined economic, political, and strategic weight of these three principal actors on the world stage today, it behooves policymakers and analysts to pay much greater attention to the interactions of this new strategic triangle.

Along with U.S. military supremacy and unparalleled power, the EU's increasing coherence and economic weight, and the acceleration of technological and economic globalization, China's rise in world affairs is one of the four principal trends that define the new global order. In

David Shambaugh is a professor of political science and international affairs and director of the China Policy Program at the George Washington University, as well as a nonresident senior fellow in the Foreign Policy Studies Program at the Brookings Institution in Washington, D.C. He previously was on the faculty at the School of Oriental and African Studies (SOAS) of the University of London from 1988 to 1996, where he also served as editor of *The China Quarterly*. The author is grateful to John Corbett, Chas W. Freeman Jr., Bates Gill, Donald Keyser, James Moran, J. Stapleton Roy, and Michael Yahuda for their comments on earlier drafts of this article.

Copyright © 2005 by The Center for Strategic and International Studies and the Massachusetts Institute of Technology
The Washington Quarterly • 28:3 pp. 7–25.

this new order, China is becoming a more responsible player on the global stage and is involved with a growing number of issues on the international agenda, such as counterterrorism, environmental degradation and global warming, energy security, international crime, international peacekeeping and nation building, nuclear nonproliferation, public health, and the stability of the global financial system. Beijing's shift from passive nonplayer and free rider to proactive engagement in addressing these challenges reflects Chinese leaders' increasing self-confidence as well as their recognition that China's responsibilities in the global arena are growing along with their nation's rising power and influence. As China becomes more involved in the global system, the United States and Europe increasingly interact cooperatively with Beijing on these and other global governance challenges. Yet, in other areas their interests diverge.

The entanglement over the arms embargo exposes the significantly different prisms through which Europe and the United States view China's rise. To be sure, U.S. and EU approaches toward China share important commonalities that should not be minimized, but it is also essential to recognize the differences. If Europe had any significant strategic interests or military presence in East Asia, for example, or was committed to Taiwan's security, European leaders would probably be much less tempted to lift the arms embargo.

Given the deeper differences in transatlantic perspectives that the arms embargo illustrates, it is long overdue that those in the United States and Europe who work on China and Asian affairs interact considerably more with those involved in transatlantic relations. Had this interaction been occurring with any regularity in recent years, the arms embargo issue would not have surprised and shaken transatlantic ties to such a significant extent, as the U.S. government would have seen it coming and the EU would have been more sensitive to Washington's objections.

It is therefore important to probe the deeper interests and perceptions in U.S. and European approaches toward China that underlie the transatlantic tensions that have erupted over the arms embargo. Significant differences in national interests and perceptions must be clearly understood if the EU and the United States are to avoid faulty assumptions about the other's policies and priorities. Yet, these differences should not be overstated because the United States and Europe share similar views on many aspects of China's place in the international community and, on balance, those transatlantic commonalities outweigh the differences.

Transatlantic Convergences on China Policy

Although there are nuanced differences in approach, at the most basic level the United States and Europe have a shared desire to enhance China's place at the global table and to enlarge its stake in the global system. Both want China to be a status quo rather than a revisionist power and believe that enmeshing China in the widest possible range of international institutions might help ensure this outcome by socializing Beijing into international norms of behavior. Thus, the United States and the EU welcome China's growing constructive involvement in the international system. Indeed, this core premise has guided U.S. and European policies and approaches toward China since at least the 1980s.

As far back as 1968, President Richard M. Nixon argued that a China that lived in isolation from the international community was destabilizing to world affairs, and this belief was one of Nixon's expressed motivations for opening relations with China in 1972. President Jimmy Carter deeply shared this view, which guided his decision to normalize diplomatic relations between the United States and the People's Republic of China in 1979. President Ronald Reagan also came to share this perspective, and his administration did a great deal to engage Beijing bilaterally on a series of global issues and to bring China into several multilateral international institutions. President George H. W. Bush perhaps held this conviction most deeply of all recent U.S. presidents, but unfortunately the tragic events of 1989 in China prevented him from fulfilling his vision. The Clinton administration also adopted this strategy during its second term, successfully concluding negotiations for China's accession to the World Trade Organization (WTO). Even the current Bush administration, which is not known for embracing global institutions, has regularly argued that China needs to work constructively within such entities, even though in practice the administration has sought to engage China on these issues bilaterally. In some cases, such as China's quest for membership in the Missile Technology Control Regime in 2004, the Bush administration stonewalled both Beijing's application and the EU's endorsement of China's application. Yet, overall the United States has been a consistent advocate of integrating China into the international institutional order.

Europe has also long believed in the wisdom of binding China into the international institutional order, perhaps even more so than Washington. This perspective is based on several reinforcing rationales in the European worldview, which is animated by the belief that predominant powers should be counterbalanced and that a multipolar world is more stable than a hegemonic or anarchical order; that nations should adhere to international law and codified norms of behavior; that international institutions should be strengthened and empowered to achieve effective global governance; that sovereignty has its limits and, under certain conditions (such as in the EU), can be shared; and that soft power should be more influential than hard power. These core elements of Europe's *weltanschauung* all apply to the way Europeans think about China and its potential role in the international system.

Europe and the United States also share an abiding interest in the improvement of human rights in China. This shared goal has been consistent over time, even though the policy instruments and tactics used to achieve it have varied. The United States has tended toward public diplomacy, as well as the introduction of a resolution on China at the UN Human Rights Commission in Geneva. On the other hand, Europe has preferred private diplomacy and has eschewed this particular UN mechanism, although the EU has strongly encouraged China's ratification of and adherence to various UN human rights covenants.

Despite their shared humanitarian convictions, European and U.S. leaders also exhibit discernible differences in their emphasis on which human rights to promote in China. Washington has always placed a priority on the rights of political prisoners and dissidents and in recent years, particularly under President George W. Bush, on freedom of religion. Forced abortions and female infanticide have also figured prominently in Washington's condemnations of Chinese practices. Religious and cultural repression in Tibet, as well as the ideal of a free Tibet, have aroused passions in the United States and have commanded congressional attention.

Europeans seem somewhat less concerned about political dissidents and subterranean democracy activists, as well as about religious freedom. Instead, European entreaties to the Chinese government stress improving workplace safety, reducing gender discrimination, decreasing state control of the media, improving prison conditions, and eliminating the death penalty. Europe, particularly the United Kingdom, Germany, and the Netherlands and countries in Scandinavia, shares U.S. distress about Tibet, but it is part of a broader European concern about the protection of all ethnic minorities in China. Above all, Europeans have a strong desire to improve all forms of civil society in China. This approach sometimes leads to conflicts, such as those that arose over European suggestions that China permit the establishment of autonomous trade unions or over recent efforts by the Chinese government to vet and approve Chinese nongovernmental organizations (NGOs) with which the EU works. Nevertheless, on the whole, the Chinese government has been receptive to EU programs in the public sphere. Despite these differences in emphasis, human rights is an area of strong convergence for Europe and the United States, and their differing emphases should be seen as more complementary than contradictory.

The United States and Europe also stress the need to build and enforce the rule of law in China. Both believe that achieving this objective is fundamental to reaching several broader goals: respect for human rights, the smooth functioning of a market economy, predictability for international investors, rooting out corruption, and the creation of legal safeguards against an arbitrary and repressive state. Europe invests considerably more into rule of law programs in China than does the United States.[1] Only since 2003 has the U.S. Congress authorized the direct expenditure of public funds for rule of law programs in China. The U.S. government, notably the U.S. Agency for International Development, is still inhibited from undertaking many types of assistance programs in China because of congressional legislation and sanctions that have remained in place since 1989. The EU, however, as well as several individual member states, particularly Sweden and the United Kingdom, have expended significant and sustained resources for many years to establish various types of legal, judicial, and penal training programs in China and in Europe.

Transatlantic commonality also exists on the issue of China's adherence to the Nuclear Non-Proliferation Treaty (NPT), which China joined in 1992. China's past proliferation practices have long been a concern to the U.S. government, which has engaged in intensive negotiations with Beijing as well as occasionally sanctioning Chinese firms, and the EU has opened its own separate dialogue with China on nonproliferation in recent years. These joint efforts have borne fruit, as Beijing has developed its own export control regulations and has become more sensitive to the dangers of proliferation of materials associated with nuclear weapons. Beijing has also improved its controls over the proliferation of ballistic missiles and component parts.

Finally, Europe and the United States share an abiding interest in China's adherence to and full implementation of its obligations as a WTO member. Washington and Brussels worked in tandem to bring China into the WTO and now pursue parallel efforts with Beijing across a broad range of economic and financial reforms and commitments, particularly protecting intellectual property rights, liberalizing foreign financial services in China, deregulating distribution rights for retail sales of consumer goods, and curtailing Chinese nontariff barriers and dumping practices. Even though U.S. and European companies compete directly in China, at the governmental level there has been long-standing solidarity on most trade-related issues.

The EU negotiated just as hard, and in some areas even harder, than the United States in admitting China into the WTO. Since then, the EU has been a stringent enforcer of China's obligations and has been particularly tough-minded against Beijing's demands that China be granted market-economy status (MES), which would effectively eliminate antidumping tariffs. In 2004 an EU internal study concluded that China still fell far short on four of five criteria necessary to achieve MES status.[2]

Over the past year, Beijing has exerted considerable pressure on Brussels to grant MES and relax its antidumping penalties, but thus far the EU has not succumbed to this pressure. For its part, the U.S. Department of Commerce is also bringing an increasing number of antidumping cases against Chinese firms. In both cases, this trend reflects not only unfair Chinese trade practices, but also the ballooning trade deficits that the EU and United States have with China.

Transatlantic Divergences on China Policy

Although the United States and Europe agree on many important policy areas, their respective understandings of China's rise differ significantly, and consequently, many policy approaches diverge accordingly. Understanding these differences in substantive policy areas requires an appreciation of the underlying philosophical premises and prisms through which Europe and the United States analyze China and its rise.

SYSTEMIC WORLDVIEWS AND THE IMPACT OF EUROPEAN INTEGRATION

Many Europeans are disquieted by the extent and use of U.S. global power, particularly military power, and the doctrine of preemption. Most western Europeans believe that multipolarity is more conducive to global stability than unipolarity and that it can better advance Europe's own security and economic interests. This view is held most strongly in France and Germany, the Benelux countries, Scandinavia, and the Mediterranean states. Although the British government may not share this enthusiasm for multipolarity, in the wake of the war in Iraq, much of the British public is equally disquieted by U.S. unilateralism. The 10 new EU members in eastern Europe ("New Europe") tend not to support multipolarity as ardently as western European governments and publics, but even these nations firmly believe in a strong and united Europe.

As a result, with respect to the global structure of power, Europe and China find common cause in strengthening alternative poles of national power and regional organizations, such as the EU, the Association of Southeast Asian Nations (ASEAN), and the Shanghai

Cooperation Organization, and share the view that U.S. power and preeminence should be diluted and counterbalanced.[3] In addition to agreeing on the value of multipolarity, Europe and China also share similar views about multilateralism. They share the view that global institutions, particularly the United Nations, need to be strengthened, in part as a further check against a unipolar hegemon and in part because such institutions should be the central actors to address various challenges of global governance. For its part, Beijing has become more receptive to and deeply involved in global and regional institutions. The American public, on the other hand, tends to be deeply skeptical of global institutions and regimes, and the current administration has gone further than its predecessors in circumventing or undermining the authority of these entities. The United States is often scornful of the United Nations, viewing it as cumbersome and often impotent and in need of radical reform. Washington is also frequently dismissive of many regional organizations, such as the ASEAN Regional Forum, considering them hollow talk shops that have few tangible accomplishments because of their lack of enforcement mechanisms. The U.S. government tends to dismiss such institutions because they possess little, if any, hard power and legally binding responsibilities. By contrast, Europeans and Asians are much more comfortable with institutions that shape normative behavior through consensus and the exercise of soft power. This attitude may reflect their relative weaknesses in hard-power terms, but it also indicates a preference for resolving differences through consensual negotiation.

The entire European experiment of pooled sovereignty is also alien to many Americans who, despite the system of decentralized federalism on which the United States was founded, do not trust the idea of sacrificing sovereign rights to a greater pan-regional superstate. As T. R. Reid argues in his recent book, *The United States of Europe*, although many Americans may instinctively distrust the idea of European integration, it is still important that they understand its dynamics and strengths as well as the direct impact the EU has on the daily lives and economic interests of the U.S. population.[4] Jack Welch, former CEO of the General Electric Company, and many other titans of corporate America have had to learn the hard way that the EU is for real and can directly affect their businesses inside the United States.

To date, however, the powerful processes of pooled sovereignty and economic integration in Europe have not been matched by similar coherence of policy on the global stage. At present, the EU's Common Foreign and Security Policy (CFSP) remains little more than a series of declaratory ideals, but if the new European Constitution is ratified and adopted, there will be a concomitant reorganization of the European Commission and the European Council. The power and authority of the new EU minister of foreign affairs will be strengthened, and the EU will begin to act with a more coherent and authoritative voice in international diplomatic affairs.[5] U.S. pundits as politically diverse as Robert Kagan and Reid, both of whom have lived in Europe, argue that a combination of generational change in European societies, the rise of a more coherent European identity, deeply held philosophical attitudes about the use of force and interstate relations, and a stronger EU foreign policy apparatus collectively serve to exacerbate transatlantic differences.[6] Other commentators, such as British scholar Timothy Garton Ash, recognize these differences but also argue that core common values anchor U.S.-European relations and that, with renewed commitment and some policy adjustments, transatlantic relations can be reinvigorated.[7] A bevy of transatlantic think tank study groups have also debated the causes and likely consequences of U.S.-European fissures.[8] Despite the ultimate prognoses of such observers, they all agree that transatlantic differences have widened considerably since the end of the Cold War and that, if the trend is not arrested, it could undermine the bedrock of the international system. The worry is that the West is being reduced to a mere geographical designation, rather than being the powerful political actor and moral beacon the world has known since the Second World War.

UNDERSTANDING THE RISE OF CHINA

These structural and perceptual differences underlie divergences in the U.S. and EU approaches to China. The principal difference in their approaches lies in how each understands a "rising China." The public discourse in the United States concerning China invariably refers to its rise and is dominated by analysis of China's increasing hard power: the growth in Chinese military power and its effect on U.S. national security interests in East Asia, both with respect to Taiwan and more generally. This is the principal prism through which most U.S. analysts view China's rise and the main factor that animates the debate in Washington. Notwithstanding popular discontent over the loss of U.S. manufacturing jobs as a result of outsourcing to China, even China's substantial economic prowess and trade surplus with the United States take a backseat in these debates to the national security implications of China's rise.

Europe, on the other hand, considers China's rise more in terms of China's domestic transitions, that is, Europeans see China as a large developing country in the midst of multiple transitions leading it away from state socialism and toward a market economy, a more open society, and a more representative and accountable government. Unlike analysts in the United States, who focus on China's external posture, European analysts focus primarily on China's internal scene. This is a substantial difference in perspective, from which policy decisions and resources follow.

This perspective underlies the main thrust of European policies toward China: to assist China in successfully managing these internal transitions and reforms. Europe does not want China to become a failed state. The EU is more willing to accept China as it is and to assist Beijing in meeting its domestic challenges. Accordingly, European nations and the European Commission believe that they have a great deal to offer, both in advice and resources. This is the case not only because of western Europe's own long experience with social democracy and public welfare but also the ongoing eastern European states' experience as transitional economies and polities that have emerged from a similar period of state socialism. To be sure, China has not abandoned its one-party system nor is it likely to do so voluntarily, but Europeans are drawing on their own experiences with the velvet revolution and social democracy in order to contribute to the growth of civil society and the public sphere in China. They know well that these were the precursors to the democratization of Eastern Europe. Europeans are also keen to share their experiences with industrial reform, higher education, science and technology policy, media deregulation, privatization of public transport, political transparency and accountability, as well as many other areas. In brief, the EU believes it has much to offer to assist capacity building in China and is investing heavily in such programs.[9]

The strategic partnership between the EU and China, agreed to in 2003, further reflects the European view that China has already become a key player on the types of soft security issues that Europe considers significant. The EU believes that the main threats to its security are of the transnational variety: illegal immigration, international crime, contagious diseases, energy, environment, and problems related to poor governance. The EU views China as one of the major powers that will shape the outcome of these problems.

Although European and U.S. companies are locked in intense competition for market share in China, at the governmental level the difference in investment of resources is indicative of the divergent approaches to managing a rising China. The United States invests its resources primarily to monitor the growth of China's hard power and to deter potentially aggressive Chinese behavior beyond its borders, whereas the EU is investing in initiatives inside of China to increase the country's soft power and facilitate its sustainable development.

Analyzing China

Underlying the philosophical differences between the U.S. and European approaches to China is the question of how each comes to understand China. Not only does each side view China through the divergent prisms described above, but there are pedagogical differences in their respective professional China communities at the governmental and nongovernmental levels. Understanding these analytical differences as well as the varying levels of commitment of resources that Europe and the United States invest into understanding China help explain these differing approaches.

Both the U.S. government and the governments of the individual EU member states have officers in charge of China issues in their respective foreign ministries, intelligence agencies, and functional government departments. Yet, two characteristics set the United States and Europe apart: the number of such officers and their training. China specialists in the U.S. government substantially outnumber their European counterparts, and they receive a significantly greater amount of training in contemporary Chinese affairs.

At present, the Department of State has about 200 Foreign Service officers who have completed advanced Chinese language training. Many hold advanced graduate degrees in Chinese studies and will have numerous tours of duty devoted to Greater China (the mainland, Taiwan, and Hong Kong). Such "China hands" follow a long and distinguished tradition of U.S. diplomats who have served in China since the nineteenth century. The Commerce Department has a somewhat smaller (between 20 and 30) but also highly qualified cohort of China-trained Foreign Commercial Service (FCS) officers. The U.S. Departments of Energy, Education, Treasury, and others all have China desks and maintain smaller numbers of China specialists on their staffs.

In the U.S. military, the U.S. Army has a corps of about 50 China-trained foreign area officers, and the Navy and Marine Corps have started similar programs. These officers serve most of their careers doing intelligence work as military attachés in China and as staff officers advising relevant officials in the Office of the Secretary of Defense, the Joint Chiefs of Staff, or the Pacific Command in Honolulu.

The number of intelligence personnel devoted to China analysis is even greater. China has been a growth industry in the U.S. intelligence community in recent years, and the number of analysts has grown apace. Reasonable estimates are that the Central Intelligence Agency has nearly 200 analysts devoted to full-time work involving China; the Defense Intelligence Agency and the National Security Agency each has about 200; the National Geospatial Agency employs approximately 100; and the U.S. Pacific Command maintains several hundred personnel throughout the Asia-Pacific region whose full-time job is to monitor the People's Liberation Army.

These reasonable estimates provide a sense of the level of effort and resources the U.S. government devotes to tracking developments in China. Not only is the number of personnel and level of resources significant, but Chinese language capabilities and analytical training in Chinese studies is also commonplace in these communities.

Outside of government, the U.S. academic community's expertise on China is unparalleled in the world. Literally hundreds of professors specialize in contemporary China studies (post-1949), and similarly large numbers conduct research related to China's modern and premodern histories. As recently as a decade or so ago, a student wishing to study China had to attend one of about a dozen leading universities that offered programs in Chinese studies. This is no longer the case. Chinese studies programs have proliferated rapidly in state universities and private liberal arts colleges around the country in recent years. In many ways, these institutions are proving to be feeder schools, providing quality undergraduate training in Chinese studies for students who then go to the premier postgraduate programs. The vast majority of graduate students now arrive in M.A. and Ph.D. programs armed with undergraduate degrees or concentrations in Chinese studies, relative fluency in Chinese, and the experience of having lived in China for two years or more. The background and experience with which students now enter graduate school is truly impressive, and they are even better trained when they leave. Demand for Chinese studies is high and growing in universities throughout the United States, and there will be no shortfall of expertise to fill jobs in the government and private sectors in the years ahead. This is one significant way in which the United States is meeting the "China challenge."

Outside of universities, considerable expertise on China can be found in research institutes and think tanks, particularly in Washington, D.C., as well as at the Council on Foreign Relations in New York and the Seattle-based National Bureau of Asian Research. Today, virtually every leading think tank in the nation's capital has at least one China specialist on staff, and many have several. In addition to these nonprofit institutions, a number of for-profit consulting firms, frequently referred to as "Beltway bandits," such as Centra Technologies, Science Applications International Corporation (SAIC), and many others, maintain considerable research staffs of China specialists who are awarded government contracts to conduct research on China for various government agencies. Finally, a number of federally funded research and development centers, most notably the RAND Corporation and the CNA Corporation, receive substantial government grants and contracts to research China.

By contrast, in Europe one does not find anywhere near this level of institutional or financial commitment. Compared with the United States, the depth of expertise on China remains very limited. This deficiency is the result of structural and intellectual impediments.

Structurally, European universities have never done a good job of integrating area studies with the social sciences; British universities have traditionally done a better job of integrating the two. In many continental European universities, students are frequently forced to choose between the two early in their academic training. If students choose area studies, they end up learning, in the grand Sinological tradition, Chinese language, history, and culture, but little about how the contemporary Chinese system functions. If they choose one of the social sciences, they are trained in comparative systems and methods, but not necessarily in the specifics of China or its language or culture, and hence cannot use Chinese materials in their research. Today, there is a dearth of scholars in European universities who specialize in contemporary China. I am aware of only three scholars in these universities who specialize in the Chinese economy, eight who specialize in domestic Chinese politics, five who specialize in Chinese foreign policy, a handful who study contemporary Chinese society or demography, and none who specialize in Chinese military and security affairs. Chinese studies in European universities have steadily atrophied over the last two decades, and unless there is a significant EU-wide initiative to reverse the trend, European universities will continue to lag badly behind their counterparts in North America and Asia.

The situation in European think tanks is better, with some experts in these areas working in at least 10 organizations in the United Kingdom, France, Germany, and Italy and in Brussels.[10] The quality of the expertise of researchers in these institutes is quite good, but many of them suffer from the structural impediments noted above in their university training. Consequently, many do not speak Chinese or use primary Chinese sources in their research. These researchers tend to be trained in functional subjects related to China, such as security studies or economics, but not in Chinese studies per se.

To cope with the absence of expertise in China that should be coming out of European universities, European companies operating in China have opted for an arrangement that is not available to governments: they have hired significant numbers of Chinese citizens. Not only do native Chinese increasingly staff their commercial operations in China, but European corporations are also promoting many native Chinese employees into their management structures in Europe and elsewhere around the globe.

Expertise on China in government ministries across Europe is uneven. Although the British Foreign and Commonwealth Office has a long and distinguished tradition of training its career diplomats and providing them all the tools needed to understand and navigate around China, the same cannot necessarily be said about other foreign ministries in Europe. Continental European governments have a limited number of diplomats or military attachés who possess strong Chinese language skills, have earned advanced degrees in Chinese studies or have studied in Chinese universities, or have a deep grasp of the intricacies of the Chinese political scene, economy, society, or military establishment. Nor do EU member states tend to have midcareer training programs for these officers, many of whom arrive in China with little, if any, Chinese language capability or in-depth knowledge of how China works. As a result, many of these officers do rotational service in China but remain quite isolated from Chinese society and institutions while there. The European Commission does no better to train its diplomats in Chinese affairs, although the commission has some very capable and dedicated civil servants who manage EU relations with China. Europe's intelligence agencies also display the same general lack of expertise.

None of these observations is meant to imply that Europe lacks officials who are competent to manage their governments' relations with China; many handle their portfolios very capably. It is simply to note that Europe does not invest very heavily in China-specific training for their government officials, nor in university-based programs that provide the pool from which these civil servants are drawn.

An additional important feature that distinguishes European from U.S. understanding of China is the interaction between government officials and analysts and their nongovernmental counterparts. Such interaction has long been a hallmark of the U.S. system, with specialists outside of government frequently interacting with those on the inside and some serving stints in government service themselves (the revolving-door phenomenon). Over time, such synergy has substantially benefited both communities in the United States. In Europe, however, such interaction is minimal. Cooperation has improved in France and Germany in recent years, but usually only those working in government-affiliated research institutes enjoy such consulting opportunities. Sweden and Denmark offer somewhat better opportunities for interaction between university scholars and government officials. Without such interaction, a virtual firewall exists between those who make policy and those who research China. As a result, the research in Europe is very scholarly but generally lacks policy relevance. Conversely, policy toward China is developed exclusively within the governments of member states, with minimal input from nongovernmental experts. The European China Academic Network (ECAN) was created in 1996, with five years of funding from the European Commission, precisely to rectify these deficiencies, and it accomplished a great deal in its initial period of operation. ECAN's funding has not yet been renewed, however, and its future remains uncertain.

Curiously, the EU's relative lack of depth and expertise in Chinese affairs does not seem to have been a handicap for European countries as they have attempted to forge strong ties with China. Europe, both at the EU level and that of its member states, has been able to build very robust relations with China in recent years. The parameters of the Europe-China relationship have been described elsewhere.[11] They are truly impressive across the board, in trade and investment, cultural and educational exchanges, diplomatic interactions, military exchanges, and the range of programs that the EU operates in China.

Clearly, Europe's relative lack of expertise on China has not impeded this burgeoning relationship. How can this disjunction be explained? The reason is converging national interests. Europe and China share basic common interests in developing trade and investment, building exchanges at all levels of society, helping China manage its internal transitions, and promoting a multipolar and multilateral world order. Such convergences do not necessitate an enormous cadre of China experts to work in European governments or nongovernmental institutions.

Pursuit of these mutual interests are further facilitated by the lack of European strategic interests or presence of European military forces in Asia, as well as the important fact that Europe has no responsibility for the defense of Taiwan and there is not an active pro-Taiwan lobby in Europe. These differences are enormously important as Europe has the luxury to develop its relationship with China unencumbered by the strategic and security responsibilities that the United States shoulders in Asia or the domestic role that the Taiwan lobby plays in Washington. Although the United States has also built an excellent and productive relationship with China in recent years, the Taiwan issue and these strategic factors constantly lurk in the background and hang over the Sino-U.S. relationship.

Navigating the New Strategic Triangle

What should analysts think about this new strategic triangle? How is it likely to evolve, and what impact will it have on world affairs? It would be a mistake to conceive of the new strategic triangle among Beijing, Brussels, and Washington in the same way as the old one among Moscow, Washington, and Beijing during the 1970s and 1980s. The new one exhibits several key differences.

First, the respective legs of the new triangle are more fluid and less static. An action on one side of the triangle does not trigger an opposite reaction on the other sides. Nor are two nations strategically aligned against the third. Also, unlike the old strategic triangle in which China and the United States had little contact with Soviet society, the new triangle is far more interactive. Today, each economy, society, and government is interlinked in a variety of ways and is deeply interdependent with the other two. Concomitantly, this is not a zero-sum triangle of two against one; rather, it is a largely positive-sum triangle that includes some mutually shared interests among all three. The United States and Europe share a variety of common perspectives about China's integration into the international order as well as on safeguarding human rights, transitioning to a market economy, establishing the rule of law, enfranchising civil society, liberalizing the political system, making the media more independent, and protecting the environment. Europe and China have common interests in multipolarism and multilateralism, as well as commercial and cultural issues. Indeed, all three sides are in agreement on some issues, such as nuclear nonproliferation and the liberalization of global trade.

A second difference is that national security concerns do not dominate the triangle as they did during the Cold War. Although they do play a significant role in the U.S.-China relationship, especially in the context of Taiwan, the U.S.-China relationship is extraordinarily deep and operates at multiple state and substate levels, with extensive linkages between the two societies. National security is simply not a feature of the relationship between Europe and China, which is driven by commerce, an increasing cultural attraction, Europe's desire to assist China's reform programs, and a shared vision for building a more egalitarian and institutionalized international order. Thus, unlike the old strategic triangle, the new one does not hinge on the nuclear balance of terror, global competition for client states and influence, or on zero-sum assumptions about the other side's policies and behavior on the global stage.

Third, significant divergences exist along all the legs of the new strategic triangle as well. The United States and Europe have certainly had their fair share of recent disagreements about Iraq, a series of international treaties and regimes, the role of the United States in the world, and the China arms embargo. China and Europe have had a series of disputes over trade and MES classification as well as disagreements over human rights. Europe has concerns about China's proliferation practices, as well as the arms embargo. More recently, China's Europe specialists have begun to criticize the motives underlying EU programs to promote civil society in China as an ideological ruse to "Westernize and divide China" (Xi-hua, fen-Hua).[12] The United States and China have also disputed human rights, trade, and proliferation, as well as Taiwan, missile defense, and regional security in East Asia.

All these features add up to a very fluid and shifting set of relationships in which mutual positions sometimes converge and sometimes diverge. The EU and the United States sometimes side with each other, China and the EU sometimes find themselves in agreement, the United States and China sometimes work well together, and sometimes the interests and policies of all three intersect, all while each side simultaneously has disputes with the other two parties. What has not occurred, to date, is a situation where U.S. and Chinese perspectives converge against European interests.

For these and other reasons, today's strategic triangle among the United States, China, and Europe has different dynamics than the one that dominated world affairs from the Sino-U.S. opening of 1971 to the Sino-Soviet rapprochement of the late 1980s. Although tensions exist on both the U.S.-Chinese and U.S.-European axes, neither is likely to develop the competitive or adversarial character that typified relations among the powers in the Sino-Soviet-U.S. triangle. Of course, a conflict between the United States and China over Taiwan or even potentially North Korea would radically alter this prognosis. Exacerbated tensions across the Atlantic over a range of issues, such as Iraq, Iran, the UN, NATO, or trade, could also change the dynamic by increasingly pulling the United States and Europe apart.

In the near term, the EU's arms embargo on China is also potentially a very disruptive and divisive issue. When the embargo is lifted—and it is eventually likely to be lifted—no matter how much the EU's Code of Conduct and export controls over dual-use technology are strengthened, the political symbolism of lifting the embargo will not go down well in Washington and is likely to trigger substantial acrimony and punitive measures by Congress against European companies. Symbols are sometimes more important than sabers; it is difficult to imagine a worse message than the one that lifting the embargo sends to the United States at a time when China is strengthening its military capabilities and passing antisecession laws aimed at Taiwan. Lifting the embargo will also sow the seeds of substantial distrust in Washington and will have spillover effects on other aspects of transatlantic relations and cooperation.

Maintaining common diplomatic positions and managing issues such as Iran's nuclear program could become an extremely complicated task. Should European nations and companies actually begin to sell weapons and increase defense technology transfers to China, thus potentially endangering U.S. military forces and altering the security balance in East Asia, a substantial rupture in relations between Europe and the United States may occur. Such an outcome could undermine the Atlantic Alliance, which has proven to be the bedrock of the international order for the past 60 years. Therefore, getting China right between the United States and Europe is of the highest priority.

To that end, the executive branch of the U.S. government is long overdue to establish a regular dialogue about China with Europe, a dialogue the EU has suggested in the wake of the arms embargo imbroglio. Congress also needs to increase its understanding of EU-China relations. To its credit, the U.S.-China Economic and Security Review Commission, a congressionally mandated body set up in 1999 to monitor China, traveled to Belgium and the Czech Republic in late 2004 to hear testimony of European officials and experts and to learn more about relations between Europe and China.[13] But efforts cannot stop there. In Europe, officials and analysts need not only to develop a much better grasp of U.S. national security interests in East Asia and the complexities of Sino-U.S. relations, but also to deepen their own understanding of contemporary China. Such increased transatlantic consultation and interaction on China is intrinsically important for both sides to learn from each other and will also decrease China's propensity to play the United States and Europe off against each other.

Most fundamentally, all three sides of the new strategic triangle are in agreement on the most important and overarching issue: to manage China's integration into the established global system smoothly and peacefully. Historically, rising powers, including Europe and the United States, have often catastrophically disrupted the global order, and it is incumbent on all three to ensure that history does not repeat itself. This effort will require all three to keep their eye on this macro issue, while not getting bogged down in minor disputes. It will also require intensified dialogue not only along all three individual legs of the triangle, but among all three together. An annual or semiannual triangular summit of the heads of state of China, the EU, and the United States would be a very useful mechanism, while functional working groups drawn from all three governments could regularly meet to coordinate common approaches to global challenges. If these three leading global powers could find their way to such positive dialogue, policy coordination, and tangible cooperation, the world would be much more stable. The new strategic triangle should be thought of as a positive-sum instrument for effective global governance.

Notes

1. See "EU-China Legal and Judicial Co-operation Programme - Introduction," http://www.legaljudicial.org:9280/euc/contents/en/programme_overview/Folder.2004-04-03.7022221162/Document.2004-04-03.7039919760.

2. European Commission officials conversations with author, Brussels, July 2004.

3. See Information Office of the State Council, *China's EU Policy Paper* (October 2003), http://www.english.peopledaily.com.cn/200310/13/print20031013_125906.html (accessed October 24, 2003).

4. T. R. Reid, *The United States of Europe: The New Superpower and the End of American Supremacy* (New York: Penguin Press, 2004).

5. "EU Foreign Policy Under the European Constitutional Treaty," *EU Focus*, Washington, D.C, March 2005, p. 6.

6. Reid, *United States of Europe*. See Robert Kagan, *Of Paradise and Power: America and Europe in the New World Order* (New York: Knopf, 2003).

7. Timothy Garton Ash, *Free World: America, Europe, and the Surprising Future of the West* (New York: Random House, 2004).

8. See, for example, Giuliano Amato et al., "Test of Will, Tests of Efficacy," *Initiative for a Renewed Transatlantic Partnership* (Washington, D.C.: Center for Strategic and International Studies, 2005); *Renewing the Atlantic Partnership* (New York: Council on Foreign Relations, 2004), http://www.cfr.org/pdf/Europe_TF.pdf.

9. See "Commission Policy Paper for Transmission to the Council and the European Parliament: A Maturing Partnership—Shared Interests and Challenges in EU-China Relations," COM(2003) 533 fin., October 9, 2003, http://europa.eu.int/comm/external_relations/china/com_03_533/com_533_en.pdf; "Joint

Statement of the Seventh EU-China Summit," December 8, 2004, http://europa.eu.int/comm/external_relations/china/summit_1204/conclusions.pdf. The EU's "capacity building" initiatives are also well chronicled in *EU-China News*, a monthly publication of the Delegation of the European Union to China, available at http://www.delchn.cec.eu.int.

10. The International Institute of Strategic Studies in London; the Stiftung Wissenschaft ünd Politik (SWP) (German Institute of International and Security Affairs); Deutschen Gesellschaft für Auswärtige Politik (DGAP) (Research Institute of the German Council for Foreign Affairs) in Berlin; the Institute für Asienkunde (Institute for Asian Studies) in Hamburg; the Akademie für Politische Bildung (Political Academy) in Tutzing, outside of Munich; the Centre Asie of the Institut Francais Relations Internationales (IFRI) (Asia Center at IFRI), Institut de Relations Internationales et Stratégiques (Institute of International Relations & Strategic Studies), and Center d'Etudes des Relations Internationales (CERI) (Center for Studies of International Relations) in Paris; the Aspen Institute Italia in Rome; the European Institute of Asian Studies; and the European Policy Center in Brussels.

11. For a survey, see David Shambaugh, "China and Europe: The Emerging Axis," *Current History* (September 2004): 243–248. See also "The EU's Relations With China – Overview," http://europa.eu.int/comm/external_relations/china/intro/index.htm (series of European Commission policy documents related to China published since 1995).

12. See Huo Zhengde, "On the China-EU Strategic Relationship," *International Studies*, no. 2 (March 2005): 13.

13. See U.S.-China Economic and Security Review Commission, *Symposia on Transatlantic Perspectives on Economic and Security Relations With China* (Washington, D.C.: U.S. Government Printing Office, 2004).

Part III:
Resurgent Russia

Zbigniew Brzezinski

Putin's Choice

Dressed all in black, including a black turtleneck sweater—a color scheme once favored by Benito Mussolini—the former KGB lieutenant colonel and now president, Vladimir Putin, addressed thousands of enthusiastic young supporters filling a Moscow sport stadium on November 21, 2007. His message was a xenophobic warning against national disloyalty on the part of Russian democratic nongovernmental organizations subsidized from outside. "Unfortunately, there are still those people in our country who act like jackals at foreign embassies ... who count on the support of foreign friends and foreign governments but not on the support of their own people," Putin bellowed to the accompaniment of Soviet-era patriotic songs blaring from the stadium's loudspeakers as the crowd waved national banners.

A few days later, the same Putin made a seeming bow to Russia's constitutional legitimacy by reaffirming that he would yield the presidency as scheduled on the expiration of his second term in March 2008. That action, however, was accompanied by the anointment of his handpicked successor, Dmitry Medvedev, a long-standing bureaucratic subordinate and business associate. Within a day, the designated next president indicated his hope that Putin would agree to serve as the state's next prime minister. Given Russia's political power realities, the electoral process

Zbigniew Brzezinski is a CSIS counselor and trustee and cochairs the CSIS Advisory Board. He would like to thank Brett Edkins for his editing and research assistance.

The Washington Quarterly • 31:2 pp. 95–116.

was thereby turned into a farce, and the authority of Putin's successor was effectively emaciated. As one leading Russian commentator said, "Putin is not an outgoing president; he is simply changing his status. He was the country's 'national manager,' and after March he will become its national leader."[1] In fascist Italy, the nominal head of state was the king, but real power rested in the hands of the "national leader," Il Duce.

How will history judge the legacy of the man once proclaimed by a U.S. president to be his soul mate and feted by a British queen at a ceremonial dinner at Buckingham Palace, for whom a French president wanted to turn a NATO members–only meeting into a celebratory birthday party (without consulting the meeting's Latvian hosts), who was able to buy the commercial collaboration of a former German chancellor, and before whom a former Italian prime minister practically genuflected? The adulation of the Western press boosted Putin's meteoric emergence as a global celebrity to a degree unprecedented for any Russian leader in history, exceeding even the favors once bestowed on Tsar Alexander I by adoring ladies in the salons of London, Paris, and Vienna in the wake of Napoleon's defeat.

Part of the answer to that question rests in the negative long-term effects that Putin's decisions, despite their apparent short-term success, are likely to have on the Russian political system, economy, and geopolitical prospects. Part of the answer also requires comparing more closely the realities now emerging in Russia as a consequence of the policies pursued by Putin as president with what might have been the alternative fruits of his presidency, given the complex realities prevailing in Russia at the beginning of 2000 when Putin was similarly handpicked for the presidency by his ailing predecessor's worried entourage. The resulting contrast between what is emerging and what might have been can then provide the basis for a more informed historical appraisal.

Putin's Motivations

First, it is appropriate to speculate briefly on the few clues available regarding the inner motivations of a man who in the course of eight years admittedly succeeded in stabilizing the Russian economy and in restoring Russia's national pride, largely by politically exploiting the financial windfall of the international demand for Russian energy resources. Putin earned widespread domestic support for ending the social chaos unleashed by the collapse of the Soviet Union and by the subsequent pell-mell privatization of the state-owned economy, which in the process scandalously enriched the more enterprising Russian "privatizers" as well as some of their Western "consultants."

Many Russians have been mesmerized, as have foreign visitors and eager would-be foreign investors, by the new glitter of Moscow and the restored glamour of St. Petersburg. Russia's revived self-pride is understandable, given the widespread sense of humiliation after the sudden fall of the Soviet Union and the disconcerting identification of the Yeltsin years with anarchy and rapacious capitalism. Many Russians derive personal satisfaction from Putin's global grandstanding, and they are impressed by the Kremlin's return to the ceremonial pomposity of the days of the great tsars. Thanks to television, Russians are now periodically guests at the Kremlin as trumpets blare and theatrically costumed guards grandly swing open enormous gates of a gilded hall in which the elite of Russia stands bowing on the sides of a long red carpet while Putin strides in with the cultivated gait of an athlete.

It is evident that the restoration of Russia's power and prestige were paramount in Putin's mind from the start. Yet, that still does not reveal how that power and prestige were to be defined, what basic beliefs motivated his quest, what values in Putin's mind Russia should represent, and what attitude it should entertain regarding its own recent past. Putin himself has never spoken explicitly regarding his motivations. Thus, only a few sparse and sporadic clues, in addition to weighing the tangible consequences of his policies, can serve as the basis for some speculative judgments regarding his driving personal impulses.

Perhaps the most telling was Putin's public comment in 2005 in his annual address to the Russian federal assembly. Without much elaboration, he declared almost as a self-evident truth that the breakup of the Soviet Union was "the greatest geopolitical catastrophe of the twentieth century." Not a casual statement, the assertion sharply demarcated him from his two immediate predecessors, each of whom had hailed the peaceful dismantling of the Soviet empire as a victory for the Russian people on their way to democracy. Even though in the course of a single century, his nation had experienced two extraordinarily bloody and devastating world wars as well as the ravages of Communist terror and the gulag, Putin revealed his preoccupation with restoring Moscow's status as a global power.

The remarkable assertion also suggests there may have been more substance to what initially appeared merely to have been a jocular gesture, namely Putin's strange salute to his former KGB superiors at the annual observance in December 2000 of Chekist's Day in honor of the Soviet security apparatus known as the Cheka, NKVD, or KGB. Although appearing at its notorious Lyublyanka headquarters as Russia's president, Putin behaved as if still a functionary, saluting his former commanders and mysteriously reporting: "Instruction Number One for obtaining full power fulfilled." Might this have been an oblique reference to a goal that perhaps some young and highly motivated KGB functionaries, Putin among them, displaced and outraged by the whimpering collapse of Soviet power, had set for themselves?

In the waning days of the Soviet Union, the KGB was the privileged elite, the ablest and most ambitious that the Soviet system could produce. As president, Putin surrounded himself in the Kremlin with graduates of that particular organization, the so-called *siloviki*. One can surmise that resentment over the Soviet Union's collapse was especially intense among those who had not yet reached the apex of the prevailing system but already had had a foretaste of its benefits. The desire to reverse the consequences of that collapse and to restore the intoxicating sense of power was probably more widespread within this cluster than anywhere else in former Soviet officialdom.

Putin's own view of Josef Stalin's crimes has never been expressed fully nor with any feeling. His occasional condemnations of Stalinism have been perfunctory, and his honoring of Stalin's victims has been minimal. In one of his rare interviews addressing his family background, he expressed special affection for his grandfather, notwithstanding the fact— it sounded somewhat as if because of the fact—that he had served in

Vladimir Lenin's and then in Stalin's personal security entourage. For any German leader, anything even remotely similar regarding a relative devotedly loyal to Adolf Hitler would be viewed internationally as intolerable. Putin's public celebration in honor of the founder of the Soviet secret police, his official opposition to Ukraine's decision to label as genocide the mass starvation induced by Stalin's collectivization, and his resentment of Baltic and Polish commemorations of Soviet mass killings point to a very selective view of the Soviet past.

In addition, the special venom with which Putin tackled the Chechen challenge immediately after assuming high office, including his vulgar public reference to where the Chechen resisters should die, conveys the impression of a leader who from the start set for himself the goal not just of ending the post-Soviet crisis but of restoring the intimidating might of the Soviet era.[2] Putin categorically rebuffed several attempts by more moderate Chechens and some foreign intermediaries to find a compromise formula for a peaceful accommodation based on enhanced autonomy. In any case, the unremitting years-long warfare to repress the Chechens, which killed probably more than 100,000 Chechens, had two immediate but significant systemic consequences. It reconsolidated and rehabilitated the weakened and demoralized Soviet security apparatus, creating a power base for the political domination in the Kremlin of the siloviki, and it channeled Russian nationalism toward undemocratic xenophobia.

By 2004, Putin's two immediate predecessors, Boris Yeltsin and Mikhail Gorbachev, had both spoken up against the pernicious political effects of the unremitting warfare against the Chechens. Yeltsin put it with his characteristic bluntness: "[T]he suppression of liberties and the rolling back of democratic rights is, among other things, a victory for the terrorists."[3] Gorbachev went even farther in urging a political process: "So it is again necessary to enter into negotiations with moderate militants, and to separate them from the irreconcilable extremists." Putin was unmoved.

A further clue emerges from Putin's evident personal animus toward the one Russian oligarch who had the temerity to claim that the lines separating the political and the financial sectors of post-Soviet Russia should not again be blurred. Whatever may have been Mikhail Khodorkovsky's transgressions during the "survival of the richest" privatization of the Yeltsin era, by the turn of the century Khodorkovsky and his oil company Yukos had come to stand for an economic system that would more closely resemble a Western free market. At the same time, the oligarch's increasingly active role within Russia and outside as well on behalf of privately sponsored, pro-democracy activism implied a concept of political pluralism alien to Putin's more traditional notion of a restored Russia.

Khodorkovsky was arrested on October 25, 2003, and sentenced to nine years in prison on May 31, 2005. His arrest, prosecution, and prolonged imprisonment had, rather like the anti-Chechen campaign, far-reaching systemic consequences. It wedded political power with financial wealth, setting Russia on the way to state capitalism. The other oligarchs, intimidated like the *boyars* before them, bowed to power but were then allowed to share their wealth with power. Oligarchic sycophancy became the norm.

Putin himself has been reported in Russian sources as having become extraordinarily and thus suspiciously wealthy. During the early Yeltsin era, Putin was a deputy to the mayor of St. Petersburg, Anatoly Sobchak, widely rumored to have been quite corrupt. Some rumors resurfaced during Putin's second presidential term linking Putin to alleged deals involving Finland. In November 2007, Anders Aslund, a senior fellow at the Peterson Institute for International Economics, recapitulated specific allegations from Russian and German sources regarding Putin's private wealth and calculated that it totaled no less than $41 billion. Much of the foregoing was said to consist of shares in state-controlled energy enterprises, including 37 percent of Surgutneftegaz shares and 4.5 percent of Gazprom.[4]

How to protect that wealth once out of power might well have been one of the principal reasons for Putin's eventual reluctance to yield political power. The siloviki also became rich, following the model of state owners in Nigeria or Saudi Arabia, with some of their wealth stashed abroad. The corrupting conflation of political power and personal wealth in contemporary Russia makes the "yellow curtains" that disguised privilege during the days of Soviet communism into a trifling indiscretion.

Medvedev, the long-term head of Putin's presidential administration while also serving as the chairman of the board of Gazprom and now heir apparent, personalizes that nexus.

The pervasive corruption among power-wielders is likely to have an additional, unintended consequence. In the long run, as in other energy-rich countries that have generated a similar tendency, elite corruption, including massive deployment of personal wealth abroad, can become a rallying cry for public resentment, especially once the wells turn dry. In the short run, such corruption makes the corrupters instinctively self-defensive, hence Putin's opportunistic inclination to rely on nationalist xenophobia to mobilize public support for those in power and to divert public attention from power-based privilege.

The picture that emerges is not that of a doctrinaire political fanatic, seeking to revive either Stalinism or the Soviet Union. Putin comes across as a ruthless KGB product who is a disciplined and determined nationalist seeking to restore Russia's power and as an opportunistic beneficiary of Russia's unexpected financial bonanza, not above quietly enjoying and secretly husbanding the material benefits of that political power. His Soviet upbringing makes him fear democracy while his Soviet pride makes him reluctant to condemn Stalinism as a crime. To Putin and his siloviki, a truly democratic system would threaten their power and their wealth. The combination of nationalist pride and material self-interest thus dictate a state that, although neither embracing Stalinist totalitarianism nor reviving Soviet collectivism, rejects political pluralism and a genuinely free-market mechanism. The state and the economy are conflated in theory and practice.

Rather reminiscent of fascism's flamboyant style but ideologically barren content is the fact that Putin's rhetorical contributions do not reflect any comprehensive view of what the Russian state, economy, and society ought to become. Nationalist exultation of the past and vague talk of a "sovereign democracy" do not provide much guidance for Russia's future. Putin tends to focus more on the short term and is noteworthy for his emphasis on pride, power, global status, and economic progress, but does not draw on any larger doctrinal design. Strengthening the state and maximizing its wealth while demonizing its domestic or foreign enemies tend to be his dominant motifs. As a political symbol, whether in posters or television appearances, he personalizes the triumph of will.

In any case, his effective control over the state's political power and its financial assets as well as a disoriented public have made it possible for Putin to make decisions that cumulatively are pushing Russia in three basic directions: politically toward an increasingly repressive state authoritarianism, economically in favor of centralized corporate statism, and internationally toward a more explicitly revisionist posture. Each reflects not only Putin's personal predispositions but also the shared interests of his like-minded top elite. Yet, each also contains longer-range dangers for Russia's future. A critical appraisal of Putin's ongoing record therefore requires asking whether there were any practical longer-term alternatives to the choices he has been making for Russia.

The State: Repressive Authoritarianism Instead of Progressive Institutionalization of an Increasingly Democratic Constitutional State

Russia admittedly was in socioeconomic disorder when Putin assumed power. Contrary to the claims of Putin's apologists, the end of that socioeconomic disorder was not attained specifically or even cumulatively because of the ruthless crushing of the Chechens; Khodorkovsky's show trial and the expropriation of his assets; the progressive subordination of television and radio to political control; the step-by-step reimposition of highly centralized political control over Russia's socioeconomically diverse regions; the manipulation of the electoral process; the growing interference by the state with the functioning of nongovernmental democratic organizations on the grounds that they threaten Russia's independence; the creation of state-sponsored political parties with privileged access to the mass media; the reliance on police measures to limit the activities of opposition parties; the officially sponsored highly nationalistic youth movement Nashi dedicated to Putin himself; or the deliberate propagation by state-controlled media of xenophobic themes to promote "national unity." All of the above culminated in the unabashed manipulation of the constitution, which on its adoption had been celebrated as confirming Russia's enduring entry into the democratic community of nations.

Russia's political atmosphere has been further poisoned by the mysterious killings of independent journalists; Putin's apparent indifference to the assassination of the leading critic of his Chechnya policy, Anna Politkovskaya; and the publicly announced grant of authority to the FSB to conduct lethal operations abroad, not long thereafter followed by the shocking killing in London of a troublesome defector from the FSB, Alexander Litvinenko. The method chosen to kill Litvinenko suggests a deliberate effort to mask the origins of the killing while inflicting the maximum amount of suffering on the victim as an object lesson to any disaffected would-be political defector from the FSB. The fact that the principal suspect in the killing as identified by the British was subsequently elected to the Duma testifies to the degree to which Russia's political values have undergone a significant transformation over the last eight years.

Although they have received more media attention, the murders of Politkovskaya and Litvinenko are far from isolated incidents, as table 1 demonstrates. In the majority of these cases, the victim had an inconvenient political profile and the perpetrators were not arrested, reinforcing the suspicion that the killings were political in motivation and undertaken under the state's protective umbrella.

If the desire to make an example of the Chechens and then of Khodorkovsky played a catalytic role in Putin's early decisions, personal as well as collective elite insecurity seems to have been instrumental in unleashing the intensifying assault on the remnants of the constitutional legacy of the Yeltsin years. It was precipitated by the democratic elections conducted in two nearby former Soviet republics. The triumphs of the Revolution of the Roses in Georgia in late 2003 and of the Orange Revolution in Ukraine in late 2004 generated reactions in the Kremlin that were nothing short of panic. The outcomes were fiercely denounced as U.S.-engineered upheavals and as a foretaste of similar, foreign-inspired designs on Russia's sovereign democracy.

The public and officially inspired campaign against foreign subversion soon acquired a domestic focus. Its result was the overt and increasingly

Table I. Politically Significant Killings

On July 27, 2006, prior to Anna Politkovskaya's murder, Reporters Without Borders claimed that "[a] t least 13 journalists have been killed in [Russia] because of their work since 2000 and none of these cases has been solved by the authorities." According to the nonprofit Committee to Protect Journalists, 14 journalists have been killed in Russia since 2000 in retaliation for their journalism. None of the murders have been solved, and 13 bear marks of contract hits.

JOURNALISTS			
Name	Position	Date Killed	Method
Eduard Markevich	newspaper editor	September 18, 2001	shot
Natalya Skryl	journalist	March 8, 2002	beaten
Valery Ivanov	*Tolyatinskoye Oborzreniye* newspaper editor, independent television station director	April 29, 2002	shot
Yuri Shchekochikhin	reporter, politician	July 3, 2003	thallium poisoning
Alexei Sidorov	Valery Ivanov's successor	October 9, 2003	stabbed
Paul Klebnikov	editor of *Forbes* Russian edition	July 6, 2004	shot
Yevgeny Gerasimenko	newspaper correspondent	July 26, 2006	tortured and suffocated
Anna Politkovskaya	journalist	October 7, 2006	shot
BUSINESSMEN			
Name	Position	Date Killed	Method
Sergei Panamarev	chairman, Akademkhimbank	June 29, 2000	
Oleg Belonenko	chief executive, Uralmash	July 11, 2000	shot
Pavel Shcherbakov	chairman, Alfavit financial group	June 3, 2002	
Igor Klimov	acting general director, defense contractor Almaz-Antei	June 6, 2003	shot

Global Powers in the 21st Century: Strategies and Relations

Sergei Shchitko	commercial director, RATEP defense plant	June 7, 2003	shot
Aleksandr Slesarev	former owner of two Russian banks	October 16, 2005	shot
Andrei Kozlov	first deputy chairman, Central Bank of the Russian Federation	September 14, 2006	shot
Enver Ziganshin	chief engineer, Rusia Petroleum	September 30, 2006	shot
Anatoly Voronin	head of property management department, ITAR-TASS news agency	October 15, 2006	stabbed
Zelimkhan Magomedov	director, National Oil Institute Fund	November 14, 2006	shot
Alexander Samoylenko	general director of operations, Itera	December 4, 2006	

POLITICIANS

Name	Position	Date Killed	Method
Valentin Tsvetkov	governor, Magadan Oblast	October 18, 2002	shot
Sergei Yushenkov	liberal member of the Duma	April 17, 2003	shot
Valery Maryasov	deputy mayor, Novosibirsk	March 2, 2004	shot
Aleksandr Semyonov	city council member, Irbit	October 15, 2006	shot
Dmitry Fotyanov	mayoral candidate, Dalnegorsk	October 19, 2006	shot

POLITICAL OPPONENTS ABROAD

Name	Position	Date Killed	Method
Zelimkhan Yandarbiyev	writer, acting president of Chechen Republic of Ichkeria	February 13, 2004	assassination bomb
Alexander Litvinenko	former security agent	November 23, 2006	polonium poisoning

arbitrary political manipulation of Russia's political processes, culminating in the elections to the Duma in late 2007 that were not much more than a state-controlled public plebiscite. The ultimate irony was that, at the time, Putin could have in all probability prevailed even in a truly contested electoral process.

Some make the case that the suspension and then reversal of democratic development in Russia was necessary to end the country's economic and social malaise. It has also been argued that the 70-year-long demoralizing Soviet experience left behind a political culture uncongenial to democracy. Yet, these arguments ignore the striking fact that Ukraine next door, a country long linked with and culturally close to Russia that shared the same Soviet experience and suffered from a similar free fall after the Soviet Union's collapse, managed to overcome its internal difficulties without a turn toward a nationalistic dictatorship. Ukraine has held several presidential elections in which the outcome was not predetermined prior to the actual vote, and it has managed to preserve a functioning parliamentary system and a free mass media. Its political culture is now more European than is Russia's, and Ukraine itself is now closer to Europe than is Russia. Neither was the case two decades ago.

It is important to note, however, that the cumulative result of Putin's retreat from democracy is the emergence of a political system that neither imitates the former Soviet Union, nor Nazi Germany, nor contemporary China. It is certainly not a totalitarian system, such as that of Stalin or Hitler. It has neither a gulag nor a genocidal aspiration, nor is it asserting pervasive social control or engaging in mass terror. Unlike totalitarianism, Russia's current repressive authoritarianism still leaves some room for individual dissent and private free speech and even more for private nonpolitical life. Politically significant in the longer run is that travel abroad remains relatively open, especially for those who can afford it. Unlike China's transformation, Russia's social change is also not guided by any programmatic design.

Ultimately, the political strength of Putin's authoritarian political system is derivative of and dependent on the country's sudden but potentially transient wealth. That wealth yields passive popular consent and more focused positive support for Putin himself. Yet, the system's dependence on capital inflows derived from the extraction and export of natural resources is also its fundamental weakness. The resulting and increasingly visible concentration of wealth at the top is corrosive and eventually demoralizing. As long as enough of it is shared to ensure a wider sense of social progress, it defers social restlessness. Eventually, however, individual, local, and regional resentments are likely to accumulate, creating a fertile soil for social unrest on the part of a public no longer hermetically sealed off from the world. Russia's public, unlike that in Saudi Arabia or Nigeria, increasingly identifies itself socio-culturally with the lifestyle of the West, and that over time may contribute to a more critically assertive political consciousness.

In any case, Putin has arrested and then reversed Russia's political evolution toward a genuine constitutional democracy. March 2008 could have been a watershed in Russia's history. Russia's democratic evolution under Yeltsin was erratic, often contradictory and at times conflicting. Nonetheless, Russia was freer 10 years ago than it is today. It was not yet an institutionalized liberal democracy, but it was moving, even if occasionally stumbling, in that direction. In such a Russia, Putin could still have dominated the political scene, benefiting from Russia's improving financial circumstances, while consolidating the beginnings of democracy in the realms of civil rights, freedom of expression, and civility in political conduct. His KGB background, his Soviet big-power hubris, and ultimately the insecurity of his wealth pushed him in another direction to Russia's historical detriment.

In brief, Putin's eight years were a regression toward capricious and repressive politics, but they could have been at least a modest progression toward a constitutional system of rule. The turn toward political authoritarianism in Russia was a choice, not a necessity.

The Economy: Centralized Corporate Statism Instead of an Increasingly Transparent and Law-Based Mixed Economy

To strengthen the state, rather than to promote social initiative to renew Russian society, was the ultimate purpose of the economic system shaped by Putin. When serving as deputy mayor of St. Petersburg under the freewheeling Sobchak, Putin had his first direct exposure to the attractions of money and to the benefits of hidden wealth. That had to be a new and heady experience for the formerly modestly salaried KGB officer. It doubtfully made him nostalgic for the mediocre lifestyle of the Soviet era. It also must have made him conscious that the combination of political power and private wealth was a potent formula.

Once in charge of post-Soviet Russia, Putin's practical application of that insight was reinforced by the imperatives of Russia's disrupted, derailed, and disoriented economic life. The country's gross national product (GNP) had fallen precipitously, to a degree ominously reminiscent of the U.S. Great Depression. The modestly living and bureaucratized Soviet middle class was hit especially hard. Suddenly, areas governed by Moscow for centuries were now independent states, insisting on respect for their boundaries and for their national assets. Typical was the fate of the once-huge Aeroflot: the newly independent states inherited portions of its air fleet, depending on where Aeroflot planes were parked on the day the Soviet Union was dissolved. The "grab as grab can" privatization of the previously state-owned and "planned" industrial assets resulted in the legally dubious but enormous enrichment of the very few. Meanwhile, state-managed retail trade simply collapsed, to be replaced initially by pitiful private and often street-based merchandising.

In these circumstances, the reassertion of political control over the country's economic life was a tempting short-term option. The enforced symbiosis between Putin's siloviki and the new oligarchs was almost literally oiled by the felicitously increasing inflow of liquidity and foreign investment, largely thanks to growing European demand for Russian energy exports. As a result, Russia's overall trade balance at the end of 2007 was a hefty $128 billion, and its international reserves equaled $466 billion.[5] As the recovery of the country's GNP accelerated, reaching by 2005 its pre-crisis 1990 levels and growing at about 6 percent annually, the benefits of the cohabitation in the Kremlin between public power and private wealth became more widespread but also more unevenly distributed.

The most visible effects of the recovery are strikingly evident in Moscow and St. Petersburg, in part because of political decisions to emphasize high-visibility, prestige-enhancing projects testifying to Russia's restored international standing, in part because the two cities have traditionally been the centers of Russia's political and social elites. Although the rest of the country changed less, and the countryside practically not at all, the recovery has also had a wider social effect. It stimulated the beginnings of an increasingly self-employed or at least non–state-employed middle class whose more privileged lifestyle aspirations became shaped increasingly by the globalized standards of urban consumption. For the emerging new middle class, not to mention the powerful new really rich, the lifestyle of the Soviet era became the unmourned past.

The picture is more mixed when the focus moves from the shorter term, primarily involving the desperately needed economic recovery, to the longer term, involving Russia's future social well-being and international economic competitiveness. In the latter case, two defining characteristics of Russia's economy under Putin are likely to have a negative impact on Russia's prospects. The first is the concentration of national economic decisions in the hands of a narrow circle of politically powerful and often personally wealthy officials. The second involves the emergence in the national economy of a cluster of murkily owned corporations (key energy companies, industrial enterprises, and banks, for example) that cumulatively dominate the day-to-day economic life of the country. The number of those owning small private businesses has remained static over the last few years, while large corporations have grown dramatically. The result is a system of corporative statism in which power holders act as if they were the owners without legally being so, while the often-hidden legal owners share the benefits with political power-holders while partaking with them in decisionmaking.

The case for the proposition that, under Putin, Russia "has become a corporate state" has been made most eloquently by Putin's erstwhile economic adviser turned severe critic, Andrei Illarionov. He has been scathing in his analysis of the implications of this development for Russia's future: "[T]oday, at the start of the twenty-first century, choosing this model is nothing other than a conscious choice in favor of a Third World social model," which he identified with Iran, Saudi Arabia, and Venezuela. He also explicitly noted some significant similarities with

"Mussolini's corporate state."[6] Such a system has a natural bias in favor of the politically opportune and toward financially rewarding the short term to the detriment of the longer-range national interest and social well-being.

Moreover, the political concentration of nationwide economic and financial decisionmaking, simultaneously combined with the symbiotic wedding of political power and economic wealth, has generated a parasitic ruling class while stifling competitive innovation. For that ruling class driven by self-interest, strengthening the state was an obvious choice. Initially, the term "federation" in Russia's self-definition as a state after the economy-owning Soviet Union's fall was to have substantive meaning, especially in regard to self-government and hence to regional financial management. Constitutional recognition of the economic diversity of the territorially vast Russia was meant to enhance grassroots democracy while stimulating local enterprise and initiative.

Alas, before long, all this was undone by Putin's very deliberate and arbitrary decision to eviscerate the federation. Local governors were no longer to be locally elected, but appointed by the president. Budgetary allocations were again to be the exclusive prerogative of the center, with national development again subject to a top-down bureaucratic process of decisionmaking. The centuries-long tsarist and then Soviet tradition of central monopoly of power and money in the hands of the socially parasitic and economically stifling, Moscow-based ruling bureaucracy was thus reasserted. The average income of Russia's richest 10 percent in early 2005 was 14.8 times higher than the income of the poorest 10 percent, while in Moscow the richest 10 percent made 51 times what the poorest 10 percent earned.[7]

That moneyed ruling class has not been above deploying billions of its dubiously acquired wealth abroad, both legally and by money laundering. Even though Putin has publicly complained, "We are seeing the laundering of billions of rubles every month within the country. We are seeing the movement of enormous financial resources abroad," official complicity has to be assumed, at least initially.[8] Although precise amounts are difficult to determine, the cumulative scale of open and disguised capital outflows from Russia have been considerably larger than Moscow's budgetary allocations for the development of long-neglected regions of Russia. Russia's wealthy siloviki and oligarchs, their nationalism notwithstanding, have preferred to invest in real estate on the Riviera and in London or simply deploy their cash to Cyprus or the Cayman Islands.

Russia's Far East, including the Vladivostok region and Kamchatka as well as the northern stretches of Siberia, have long been seeking major allocations for infrastructural modernization, housing development, and general upgrading. Disbursements, however, have dramatically lagged behind stipulated investments. Neglect by the center and limited local means have resulted in the outflow of local inhabitants to the more favored west-central parts of Russia, thereby geopolitically compounding the nation's grave ongoing demographic crisis while reducing the likelihood that greater regional autonomy could foster economically advantageous cooperation with proximate and more advanced foreign neighbors, such as China, Japan, South Korea, and the nations of Scandinavia.

Also symptomatic of the indifference by the center to Russia's outer regions is the antiquated and underdeveloped character of Russia's transportation. The country has only one transcontinental railroad and no modern transcontinental highway. In fact, it still has no equivalent to the U.S. interstate highway system constructed decades ago or the European autobahns initiated in the late 1930s. Even worse, China in the last decade has constructed a network of more than 30,000 miles of modern, multilane highways, while Russia is only now building its very first, at last upgrading the two-lane paved road between Moscow and St. Petersburg on the tract built centuries ago by Peter the Great.

Informed Russian observers are also increasingly concerned that Russia's reliance on capital inflows in return for Russia's oil and gas is breeding a decline in the country's capacity to sustain technological innovation and industrial dynamism in the global competition for economic preeminence. The renewal of Russia's industrial infrastructure, which in the Soviet times was being replaced at an annual rate of 8 percent, has declined to 1–2 percent, in contrast to the 12 percent of the developed world.[9] No wonder that the World Bank reported in 2005 that fuels, mining products, and agriculture accounted for 74 percent of Russia's total exports, while manufactures accounted for 80 percent of Russia's total imports.[10]

Not only is Russia said to be about 20 years behind the developed countries in industrial technology, but it also develops 20 times fewer innovative technologies than does China and devotes considerably less money to research and development than its rapidly transforming eastern geopolitical rival does.[11] Prime Minister Wen Jiabao of China, when visiting Russia in 2007, noted with satisfaction that Chinese-Russian trade in machinery products reached an annual level of $6.33 billion. Out of politeness, however, he refrained from adding that $6.1 billion of that sum involved Chinese machinery exports to Russia, leaving only $230 million of Russian machinery exports to China. Making matters worse, projections by the Organization for Economic Cooperation and Development for the year 2020 envisage not only China's gross domestic product as approximately four times larger than Russia's, but with India ahead of Russia as well.[12]

The absence of an ambitiously grand program to shape a truly advanced Russian society that exploits the opportunity provided by the significant price increase of Russia's rapidly expanded energy exports is the most glaring deficiency of the Putin years. That comprehensive vision has been lacking, and nationalist boasting about Russia's status as a world energy power cannot provide a productive substitute. Such a program would have to be more than a set of targets. It would have to be imbued with relevant notions of what it takes to generate a dynamically modern, socially prosperous, technologically innovative, creatively competitive, and legally transparent system capable of engaging in sustained competition on the global arena with the technologically innovative leading powers. Such a programmatic vision would have to focus on the need to remedy the painfully revealing shortcomings of Russia's competitive standing in the world, as table 2 indicates.

Putin's management of Russia's national economy was clearly a short-term success of recovery, stabilization, and growth, but it also represents a missed longer-range opportunity to set Russia firmly on a course toward becoming a truly advanced society with a productive mixed economy. Putin failed to make that choice.

Table 2. Russia's Mixed Standing in the Global Hierarchy

Category	Russian Ranking/Standing	U.S. Ranking
Land Mass	1st, followed by Canada	3rd
Population	8th, preceded by Bangladesh, followed by Nigeria	3rd
Gross Domestic Product (GDP)	11th, preceded by Brazil, followed by India	1st
GDP per capita	79th, preceded by Botswana, followed by Lebanon	10th
GDP, Purchasing Power Parity	10th, preceded by Brazil, followed by Spain	1st
Exports	12th, preceded by Hong Kong, followed by Singapore	2nd
Imports	18th, preceded by India, followed by Switzerland	1st
Foreign Direct Investment, inflows	13th, preceded by Australia, followed by Brazil	1st
Global Competitiveness	58th, preceded by Croatia, followed by Panama	1st
Business Competitiveness	71st, preceded by Egypt, followed by Kazakhstan	1st
Perceived Corruption, ranked from least to most corrupt	143rd, preceded by Syria and Pakistan, followed by Angola and Nigeria	20th
Human Development Index, based on living standards, health, and education	67th, preceded by Bosnia and Herzegovina, followed by Albania	12th
Enrollment in Tertiary Education	12th, preceded by Lithuania, followed by Slovenia	
Life Expectancy	119th, preceded by Guyana, followed by Sao Tome and Principe	29th
Political and Civil Freedoms	Labeled "not free" by Freedom House, with 44 other nations. There are 58 "partly free" nations and 90 "free" nations.	"free"

Sources: CIA World Factbook; World Bank, World Development Indicators database; *Economist*; International Monetary Fund, World Economic Outlook Database; UN Development Program, "Human Development Report 2007/2008"; Freedom House, "Freedom in the World 2007"; World Economic Forum, "Global Competitiveness Report 2007–2008"; Transparency International, "Corruption Perceptions Index 2007."

The World: Nostalgic Preoccupation with Superpower Status Instead of Aiming to Become an Influential Partner of the Advanced Democratic World

The world was startled in February 2007 when, at the Wehrkunde international conference on global security, Putin suddenly unleashed a sharp attack on U.S. foreign policy, accusing it of "plunging the world into an abyss of conflicts" because of its reliance on "an almost uncontained hyper use of force." Although Putin's stand capitalized on the widespread international sentiment that U.S. policy since 2003 had become imperialist in its reliance on force, not credible in its presidential pronouncements, and illegitimate in many of its practices, the shock effect of his salvo, followed shortly by a series of other abrasive attacks on U.S. policies, was gratifying domestically. It signaled to many Russians that their leader was no longer the protégé of the U.S. president but his global challenger and that the end of Russian subservience to the United States marked Russia's return to the days of global preeminence.

In the eyes of many members of the Russian elite, that preeminence is grounded in three decisive realities: Russia's relative coequality with the United States in nuclear weaponry, its newly claimed and frequently cited status as "an energy superstate," and deeply rooted national pride regarding Russia's huge territorial size not even closely matched by any other state. Cumulatively, these considerations make many Russians, especially in the political elite, embrace the argument that, in spite of its recent travails, Russia as a leading world power is entitled to its own exclusive sphere of influence.

Fewer Russians, however, are aware that Russia's nuclear capabilities are reduced in their political significance by its weakness in the versatile nonstrategic dimensions of military power, leaving Russia with the capacity only to engage in mutual self-destruction with the United States but with limited means for the politically effective projection of military power. The importance of the energy claim is reduced by the fact that it breeds a parasitic politico-economic elite indifferent to the need for long-range comprehensive economic development while, as Dmitri Trenin, a leading Russian foreign policy analyst, observed, the claim of being an "energy superpower is a myth, and a dangerous one."[13] Territorial intoxication overlooks the basic fact that almost one-half of Russia's landmass is located in frigid permafrost zones that actually handicap national economic prospects.[14] Last but not least, unlike the defunct Soviet Union, contemporary Russia no longer exercises any worldwide ideological appeal. To some extent, Moscow can now compensate for that deficiency by simply buying influence in key foreign capitals, be it Washington or Berlin; but money can only purchase opportunistic service, not fervent commitment.[15]

In that context, the pursuit of a foreign policy strongly motivated by resentment of the U.S. superpower status, while seeking to limit the access of the European Union and China to the energy resources of the non-Russian portions of the former Soviet Union, tends to isolate Moscow. Russia's fear of China's long-term potential makes for a Sino-Russian relationship that is tactically cooperative but strategically mutually suspicious. Russian resentment that it no longer dominates central Europe complicates its relationship not only with the EU but with the United States as well.

Of particular concern to Russia's longer-term geopolitical prospects should be the fact that politically and economically vital areas to its west and to its east are organizing themselves in a fashion that is likely to reduce Russia's influence further. In the West, the EU is steadily consolidating its economic integration, sporadically developing a political identity, and still expanding. Heavy-handed efforts to monopolize the EU's downstream and upstream dependence on Russia's energy exports are also stimulating a more deliberate effort by the EU to develop alternative energy sources and a supranational energy policy. The presence in the EU of states with vivid memories of Russian domination has also worked to Russia's detriment.

In the fast growing far eastern and southeastern Asian mainland, not only is China rising as a technologically advanced power, but Beijing is making steady headway in promoting China-led regional cooperation. China's constructive role in the six-party talks on North Korea's nuclear program has also reinforced the subtle U.S. tendency to quietly forge a

U.S.-Chinese-Japanese strategic accommodation designed to enhance stability and security in the Far East. The combination of China's industrial might and enormous human capital is bound to cast an ominous shadow over the empty and underdeveloped eastern regions of Russia.

Iran, to the south of Russia, although unstable and volatile, will almost certainly be oriented toward the EU and China. At the same time, its history predisposes Iran toward anti-Russian hostility. Moreover, Iran shares with Turkey an interest in opening up formerly Soviet-controlled Central Asia to international economic access, which collides with Moscow's evident interest in monopoly control over the flow of Central Asian energy to global markets. It is unlikely that Moscow can for long prevent the EU (with U.S. support), China, India, Iran, and Turkey from enlarging their direct access to the newly independent Central Asian states, which also quietly desire to be accessible. The Shanghai Cooperation Organization (SCO), which Putin sponsored in the hope of consolidating Russia's preeminent position in Central Asia, has already backfired, as it legitimated China's increasing interest in the former Soviet backyard. The recent presence in joint SCO maneuvers of Chinese troops in Kazakhstan for the first time since the Mongol Empire testified to China's enhanced role in the region but hardly to Russia's.[16]

Given the potentially threatening geopolitical isolation of Russia, future Russian leaders will have to face the fact that Putin's foreign policy is self-defeating. Some Russians already perceive that danger.[17] An attempt to create an exclusive but depopulated Russian sphere of influence between the West and the East in the area of the former Soviet Union, including in it a reluctant Georgia and Ukraine, is a prescription for a national disaster. Nostalgia for the imperial past is not only incompatible with modern-day realities, it is counterproductive.

A case in point is the belligerence of Russia toward Georgia because of the strategically important role that the Baku-Ceyhan pipeline plays in providing access for the EU to the Caspian Sea and Central Asian regions. The dynamics of globalization work against efforts to seal off Central Asia. Moreover, if pressed hard, Georgia and Ukraine can count on external support. Also, neither the EU nor NATO will pull back from central Europe in order to accommodate Russia. The expansion of the EU and NATO has made Europe more secure. Failure to expand would have reawakened Moscow's ambitions regarding the Baltic states and Poland, and in any case, it cannot be undone.

In that setting, Russia's only constructive choice is to assert its European cultural heritage by becoming an increasingly democratic constitutional state based on a legally transparent mixed economy, with expanding links to the EU. Paradoxically, Ukraine's gravitation toward the West, which the current rulers in the Kremlin so resent, is likely both to pave the road westward for Russia while foreclosing Moscow's imperial temptations. A Ukraine solidly in Europe is in fact the precondition for an eventually European Russia. The consequent emergence of trans-Eurasian cooperation from Lisbon to Vladivostok would enhance Russia's security while advancing its social modernization. It would also make it easier for Russia and the United States to collaborate more closely in reducing the size of their nuclear arsenals and in more effectively forestalling nuclear weapons proliferation.

To conclude, nationalist authoritarianism and corporate statism with touches of outdated imperial nostalgia freeze Russia's historical evolution for the time being. Yet, there have been some encouraging signs that more enlightened tendencies have occasionally percolated even within Putin's own regime. At the widely attended St. Petersburg Economic Forum in June 2007, the recently dismissed minister for economic development and trade, German Gref, contested the views of First Deputy Prime Minister Sergey Ivanov, at the time a presumed successor to Putin, who stressed that Russia's economic innovation should be promoted predominantly by state-controlled industries. Gref's own scenario for Russia's future, contained in his ministry's draft, "Concept of Russia's Long-Term Social and Economic Development Through 2020," argued the importance of constitutional rights, initiative, and legally protected economic freedoms as the turnkey to Russia's competitive prospects.[18]

Moreover, even though disfranchised, open opposition to Putin's political and economic decisions continues to exist. There are now politicians in Russia who dare to denounce the basic choices that the currently popular national leader has espoused. They are denied access to the mass media, but their very existence testifies not only to their courage but also to the potential for political renewal once current policies begin to lose their appeal and corruption gives rise to more widespread social resentments.

Most importantly, the younger Russian generation, which in the course of the next decade will replace the KGB remnants of the Soviet era, is well educated and has been exposed virtually or directly to the West. It is significantly more democratic in its outlook than the older generation. According to the Gallup Organization's Russian affiliate, 71 percent of Russians under the age of 30 believe that democracy is the best political system, whereas only 50 percent of those over the age of 50 believe this.[19] Whatever its current political views, before too long such exposure is bound to have a political effect, gradually redefining the outlook of Russia's elite. Such a redefinition is essential to Russia's future. Indicative of their good common sense, 80 percent of Russians doubt that their country is currently governed by the will of its people.[20] In the words of Russian political scientist Lilia Shevtsova, "Russia's basic problem does not lie in the citizenry, it lies in Russia's ruling class. And here we run up against the peculiarity of Russia's development: the ruling class in this country is far less progressive than the people.... The people have never been offered a convincing liberal democratic alternative."[21] Indeed, not offering one was both Putin's choice and his grave failing.

A basic lesson thus stands out from the West's disappointing experience with Putin: competitive courtship of the Kremlin leader's ego is not as productive as coordinated shaping of a compelling geopolitical context for Russia. Personal enticements can be easily pocketed as privileged entitlements, with Putin's membership in the Group of Eight failing miserably to convert him into a devoted democrat. External conditions need to be deliberately shaped so that future Kremlin leaders conclude that democracy and becoming part of the West are in Russia's interest as well as their own. Fortunately, because the Russian people can no longer be isolated, the chances are growing that they may reach this conclusion ahead of the Kremlin.

Notes

1. Yekaterina Vlasova, "What Will Happen After the Elections?" *Rossiyskaya gazeta*, December 4, 2007 (in Russian).

2. Michael Wines, "In Moscow, a Whiff of Terror From Afar," *New York Times*, September 26, 1999, http://query.nytimes.com/gst/fullpage.html?res=9E0CE3 DC103FF935A1575AC0A96F958260.

3. *Moskovskiye Novosti*, September 14, 2004.

4. Anders Aslund, "Unmasking President Putin's Grandiose Myth," *Moscow Times*, November 28, 2007, p. 9; Manfred Quiring, "Man sollte die active rolle Putins nicht überschätzen," *Die Welt*, November 12, 2007; Maksim Kvasha, "For Us, the Party Is Represented by the Power Bloc Headed by Ignor Ivanovich Sechin," *Kommersant*, November 30, 2007 (in Russian) (interview with a Russian investment banker); Jonas Bernstein, "Finansgroup: How Russia's *Siloviki* Do Business," *Eurasia Daily Monitor*, November 30, 2007.

5. *Economist*, January 19, 2008, pp. 109–110.

6. Andrei Illarionov, "A Different Country," *Kommersant*, January 23, 2006 (in Russian); Boris Nemtsov, "The Chekists Have Become Oligarchs," *Novaya gazeta*, February 9, 2006 (in Russian). For a comprehensive and truly incisive overall critique, see Celeste Wallander, "Russia: The Domestic Sources of a Less-than-Grand Strategy," in *Strategic Asia 2007–08: Political Change and Grand Strategy*, ed. Ashley J. Tellis and Michael Wills (Washington, D.C.: National Bureau for Asian Research, 2007).

7. Natalia Biyanova, "Increasing Income Differentiation Could Lead to a Social Explosion," *Gazeta*, February 8, 2005 (in Russian).

8. Anna Smolchenko and Oksana Yablokova, "Putin Calls for a Banking Cleanup," *Moscow Times*, September 18, 2006.

9. Mikhail Vorobiev, "Restaurants, Taxis, Girls; Grigori Yavlinsky Diagnoses the Russian Political-Economic System," *Vremya novosti*, June 7, 2006 (in Russian).

10. Economic Management and Policy Unit, World Bank Russian Country Office, "Russian Economic Report," no. 15 (November 2007), http://siteresources. worldbank.org/INTRUSSIANFEDERATION/Resources/RER15_Eng.pdf.

11. Viktoria Zavyalova, "Russia in Need of Foreign Technology," *Kommersant*, April 19, 2006 (in Russian).

12. Organization for Economic Cooperation and Development, *OECD Economic Outlook*, no. 82 (December 2007).

13. Dmitri Trenin, "Russia's Strategic Choices," *Carnegie Policy Brief*, no. 70 (June 2007), http://www.carnegieendowment.org/files/pb50_trenin_final.pdf.

14. See Fiona Hill and Clifford Gaddy, *Siberian Curse: How Communist Planners Left Russia Out in the Cold* (Washington, D.C.: Brookings Institution Press, 2003).

15. Glenn R. Simpson and Mary Jacoby, "How Lobbyists Help Ex-Soviets Woo Washington," *Wall Street Journal*, April 17, 2007, p. A1.

16. See Alexei Matveyev, "Beijing Moves Into Central Asia," *Voenno-promyshlennyi kurier*, December 6, 2007 (in Russian).

17. See Andrei Ryabov, "Loneliness in the Midst of Democracy," *Novaia gazeta*, June 8, 2007 (in Russian).

18. Mikhail Vorobiev, "Half and Half With Gref," *Vremya novosti*, July 26, 2007 (in Russian).

19. Jonas Bernstein, "Almost Two-Thirds of Russians Believe Democracy Is the Best Political System," *Eurasia Daily Monitor*, January 16, 2008, http://jamestown. org/edm/article.php?article_id=2372720.

20. Ibid.

21. Lilia Shevtsova, "Russia in 2005: The Logic of Rollback," *Nezavisimaya gazeta*, January 31, 2005 (in Russian); Lilia Shevtsova, *Russia: Lost in Transition* (Washington, D.C.: Carnegie Endowment for International Peace, 2007). See Michael McFaul and Kathryn Stoner-Weiss, "The Myth of the Authoritarian Model," *Foreign Affairs* 87, no. 1 (January/February 2008): 68–84. McFaul and Stoner-Weiss's article, which coincided with the completion of this article, is somewhat less optimistic about Russia's longer-range evolution than my own assessment.

Clifford G. Gaddy and Andrew C. Kuchins

Putin's Plan

Some of the uncertainty surrounding Russia's political future has passed. The December 2007 parliamentary elections are history, the presidential succession seems clear, and the range of options for Vladimir Putin's future role has been considerably narrowed. Yet, at each turn, other uncertainties remain and new ones arise.

In the eyes of most of the outside world, at least those of Europe and the United States, the Russian electoral process so far has failed to measure up to benchmarks of democracy and free choice of policies and personalities. Rather, this process has been about legitimizing the notion of entrusting the country's future to something called "Putin's Plan," thus ensuring *preyemstvennost' politiki* (continuity of policy) beyond the scheduled end of Putin's term of office in May 2008.

What exactly is Putin's Plan, and from where does it come? What are its goals? What are its implications for Russia's domestic and international relations?

Clifford G. Gaddy is a senior fellow at the Brookings Institution. He may be reached at cgaddy@brookings.edu. Andrew C. Kuchins is a senior fellow with and director of the CSIS Russia and Eurasia Program. He may be reached at akuchins@csis.org. The authors thank Amy Beavin, Anna Bryndza, and Igor Danchenko for their excellent research assistance.

© 2008 by The Center for Strategic and International Studies and the Massachusetts Institute of Technology
The Washington Quarterly • 31:2 pp. 117–129.

Putin's Political Course: A Different Kind of Plan

The phrase "Putin's Plan" was introduced into political vocabulary by the chairman of the United Russia party, Boris Gryzlov, in a speech in May 2007.[1] Although the term was new, Gryzlov emphasized that the concept was not. It had been "in effect since 2000," he said. Yet, when pressed more recently to specify what it is, Gryzlov admits that it does not exist as a defined statement. "Putin's Plan is simply the political course of the current president.... Putin is the leader in charge of national strategy and this is why we have dubbed his ideas 'Putin's Plan.'"[2]

Putin's Plan, in other words, is whatever Putin thinks and wants, and the Russian public seems to know this. In October 2007, a poll reported that the overwhelming majority of Russians could not describe Putin's Plan or had even heard of it. Yet, an equally large majority was nevertheless confident that Putin had one.[3] Furthermore, as the results of the December parliamentary elections showed, Russians want the country to be guided by that strategy, whatever it is.

Putin's chosen successor in the office of president, Dmitry Medvedev, clearly recognizes the inseparability of Putin's Plan from the person of Putin himself. After accepting the endorsement of the United Russia party and repeatedly thereafter, Medvedev assured Russians that he would faithfully continue Putin's strategic course and that he would need to do that in close cooperation with the "author of that strategy."[4]

The cloudiness of Gryzlov's and Medvedev's references to Putin's Plan should make it clear that although talk of the Plan with a capital P might evoke memories of Russia's Soviet history, Putin's Plan is different. In the Soviet Union, the famous five-year plans became the foremost symbol and feature of society as a whole. Those plans were highly precise and comprehensive. The Soviet Union was, after all, a centrally planned economy, and the plans did very much control everything. They included targets for the inputs and outputs of virtually every major item produced and consumed in the country.

Putin's concept of planning is nothing like that, and it has very different roots. Its roots lie not in Marxism-Leninism but in Western business theory via a book with which he most likely became acquainted during his KGB career. The KGB in which Putin trained and served, Yuri Andropov's KGB, was at the forefront of the search for an answer to the Soviet economic dilemma in the post-Stalin era, namely how to achieve increased efficiency without losing control. Part of that effort involved canvassing Western literature on theories of planning as applied to large corporations and other organizations. In the late 1970s and early 1980s, a handful of the most relevant foreign texts were translated into Russian in limited editions. One of those works, *Strategic Planning and Policy* by William R. King and David I. Cleland of the University of Pittsburgh,[5] turned out to be the one later used extensively by Putin several years after he had left the KGB in a dissertation he presented for his postgraduate economics degree.

Putin's dissertation, entitled "Strategic Planning of the Reproduction of the Mineral Resource Base of a Region,"[6] later received attention because of the prescience Putin displayed in choosing the topic of natural resources and their role in Russia's economy at a time before he was even considered for a post at the national government level. Equally important was that he had based his work on the specific notion of strategic planning defined by King and Cleland, namely planning for an unpredictable, changing environment.

In retrospect, the particular appeal of the King and Cleland text to an enlightened segment of the Soviet elite is clear. In the early 1980s, the Soviet Union had been shocked by an unexpected collapse of world oil prices. The resulting changes in the world economy wrought havoc on the USSR and its ability to sustain its empire, in large part simply because the country's leadership had failed to be flexible enough in its plans. This book spoke exactly to that point: true strategic planning has to take into account unforeseen changes. Even the best detailed plans are useless if the assumptions on which they are based, explicitly or implicitly, are rendered false by circumstances outside one's own control. What was needed was an approach that could accommodate such changes.

The intellectual origins of his notion of management shed light on Putin's future leadership style:

If the organization is to be effective in the long run ... organizational changes must be *contrived responses to anticipated future environments* rather than conditioned responses to the past and current environmental situations. However, since the future environments on which the plans are based are necessarily uncertain ... the plans should be *adaptable* to the evolving circumstances. Viewed in this way, plans are not irrevocable guides from which deviation is sinful; rather, they are adaptive mechanisms that should permit the organization to confidently face an uncertain environment.[7]

Putin's appreciation for planning under conditions of uncertainty undoubtedly grew after the collapse of the Soviet Union, not least as a result of his own experience in helping to manage the economy of the city of St. Petersburg in the tumultuous and unpredictable years from 1991 to 1997, when it seemed nothing could be taken for granted and any one of a number of sudden and unexpected changes could bring catastrophe.

Change versus Stability

There is, however, a dilemma inherent in this kind of planning under uncertainty. To be most easily understood and capable of smooth implementation, a plan has to be detailed, clear, and precise. Yet, the more precise the plan is, the more it reflects a "single image of the future," the more vulnerable it is to unexpected changes in the external circumstances.[8]

The answer, wrote King and Cleland (and after them, Putin), is that true strategic planning should not aim at producing a single, simple plan but rather establish a hierarchical system of interrelated subplans that address different dimensions of the problems being faced. The system starts from the very top by defining the most enduring objectives and moves downward to more and more detailed, time-specific tasks. Planning proceeds through a series of phases. It begins by defining the organization's mission (in a "challenging, even shocking" statement that "tells what it is, why it exists, and the unique contribution it can make") and then sets objectives ("broad and timeless statements" of destinations to be achieved), goals ("specific, time-based points of measurement" that are to be stated "as specifically and as quantitatively as possible"), and, finally, investment programs and projects ("identifiable activities pursuing specific goals with identifiable resources").[9]

Responsibility for managing the various levels of plans falls to different levels of the organizational hierarchy. The most important division in this respect is between the very highest level, that of strategic planner, and the so-called operational managers. The strategic planner defines the mission of the organization and formulates its objectives. He ensures that the objectives, goals, programs, and projects are consistent with the overall mission and serve to fulfill it. There is only one strategic planner; in the corporation, it is the CEO.

Fundamentally, the division between the strategic planner and the operational managers also has to do with uncertainty. Programs and projects—day-to-day tasks—should be free of uncertainty. People should be able to focus on a task and ignore the possibility that the environment can radically change. That can only work if, at the higher level, the strategic planner (the CEO) assumes full responsibility for making the adjustments needed when they are needed. In other words, the task of coping with uncertainty is concentrated at the top. The strategic planner defines a course that appears stable and predictable to those below, while actually leaving room for adjustment, even radical shifts, if needed.

As president of Russia, Putin has not only assumed the role of strategic planner, but he has also followed this logical order of planning remarkably closely. On the eve of his assumption of office as acting president on January 1, 2000, he issued his mission statement: "Russia on the Threshold of the Millennium," a visionary document produced with the assistance of his newly established Center for Strategic Reform.[10] The Center for Strategic Reform was initially headed by the future minister of economic development and trade, German Gref.[11] In this so-called Millennium Statement, Putin pledged first to give Russians what they long for most of all: "stability, certainty, and the possibility of planning for the future—their own and that of their children—not one month at a time, but for years and decades."[12] He identified the long-term objective of restoring Russia's status as a great power and the well-being of its people and also for the first time set up a time-specific goal of bringing Russia's per capita gross domestic product (GDP) to the level of Portugal by the year 2015. (In his 2003 address to the Federal Assembly, Putin would revise that goal to be a doubling of the GDP by 2010.) Programs and projects have followed in abundance, most notably the four so-called national projects (in agriculture, housing, education, and health care) articulated by Putin in 2004 and subsequently placed under Medvedev's leadership.

Politics in Service of the Plan

One of the major themes of Putin's Millennium Statement was the need for unity and cohesion in Russian society if the nation's destiny was to be fulfilled and the objectives met. In Putin's scheme, parties and electoral politics play a specific role in this regard. Political parties must serve the objective of unity and stability, something they cannot do if they primarily present competing policies and platforms. Rather, the purpose of political parties becomes to mold a diverse electorate into a unified body of support for his policy.

This suggests one reason why three other parties in addition to United Russia were allowed to make it into the Duma. The Kremlin's democracy managers pragmatically understand that one party cannot appeal to all segments of the Russian electorate. Vladimir Zhirinovsky's Liberal Democratic Party, which won 8.1 percent of the vote in the December 2007 parliamentary election, helps address the most xenophobic and nationalist constituencies while the Communists and Just Russia, which received 11.6 percent and 7.7 percent of the vote, respectively, appeal to poorer and older voters.

At the staged event at which four party leaders announced their support for Medvedev's candidacy and "urged" Putin to do the same, Putin identified a similar role for the approved "opposition" parties in the presidential election: "The fact that this proposal comes from representatives of four parties [that] unquestionably are based on the most different strata of Russian society and represent the interests of various groups of the population of Russia—all that tells us that we together have a chance to form a stable regime [*vlast'*] in the Russian Federation after the March 2008 elections."[13]

Nonetheless, the most reliable guarantee of unity is the thoroughly dominant role of a single party, the aptly named United Russia, which received 64.2 percent of the vote in the December 2007 election. Because the plan changes, it is essential to have a vehicle to educate and mobilize. United Russia's role, therefore, is to publicize the appropriate level of the plan and mobilize support for it, that is, to give it legitimacy. It will do it either directly with its own substantial membership or by recommending policies to be seconded by the other parties.

Some around Putin believe United Russia must play this role for decades at least, giving it a status similar to that of the Liberal Democratic Party in Japan or the Institutional Revolutionary Party in Mexico. This vision accords with that espoused by the Kremlin's chief political strategist, Vladislav Surkov, deputy chief of staff of the presidential administration, when in February 2006 he admonished members that their goal was not simply to prevail in the upcoming parliamentary elections, but to serve as Russia's ruling party for the next generation or so.[14]

This vision of United Russia ruling for several decades in order to oversee the nation's revival reflects the mentality of today's ruling elite. Most of them were born in the 1950s and 1960s, so it is natural for them to view their leadership taking Russia to 2020–2030. In their view, the task of maintaining continuity of policy and, specifically, of the individuals who are responsible for shaping that policy is not something that can be left to democratic politics. True to the roots of his notion of strategic planning, Putin is orchestrating the election of someone to succeed him as strategic planner, the CEO of Russia Incorporated. In fact, in a statement concerning the parliamentary elections that was remarkable in its frankness, Central Election Commission Chairman Vladimir Churov said as much when he told NTV on August 31, 2007, that Russia has formed "a corporate state": "We have a state corporation and we are electing the top management of our state corporation."[15]

The crux of Russia's domestic political dilemma now is that, according to the statutes of Russia Inc.—the country's December 1993 constitution—the current CEO, Putin, must step down after eight years. As of now, it appears that Putin is attempting to resolve this dilemma by entrusting the office of president to his longtime protégé Medvedev, while he himself assumes the post of prime minister. A recent public opinion poll suggests Russian society is prepared to accept Medvedev as chief executive and prefers stability over the risk of reconfiguring the Russian political system.[16] Perhaps most significantly, 80 percent of those polled expect Medvedev to continue to implement Putin's Plan. Whether or not Putin intends to relinquish his real role to Medvedev remains uncertain. For now, Putin is keeping all options open, likely waiting to see how circumstances play out and perhaps to judge whether Medvedev is capable not merely of implementing Putin's Plan but of independently adapting it to changing circumstances, the quality that distinguishes the true strategic planner.

Searching for External Stability

Stability inside Russian society has been Putin's first priority. Yet, as demonstrated in the Soviet Union in the 1980s and Russia in the 1990s, the source of greatest uncertainty lies in the external environment. From the 1997 Asian financial crisis that catalyzed Russia's default a year later to the support of international terrorist networks for the opposition in the Chechen war to the perception of the West's role in promoting "Color revolutions" in the former Soviet Union, Putin could confirm that Russia is dangerously vulnerable to "uncontrollable environmental forces in the outside environment."[17]

Putin's conviction that a nation can make meaningful plans for the future only to the extent that it has control over its own fate bears on his repeated references to and particular definition of the notion of sovereignty. For him and most of the Russian elites, sovereignty means being able to shape one's own destiny independently. It is often defined in negative terms: let no one else determine Russia's fate. Putin and his colleagues believe that Russia essentially lost its sovereignty in the late 1980s and 1990s under Mikhail Gorbachev and Boris Yeltsin.

Russia's greatest weakness was its financial state, and its removal was a precondition for dealing with other weaknesses. When Putin assumed the post of prime minister in August 1999, Russia was bankrupt and effectively in receivership. The nation owed $16.6 billion to the International Monetary Fund (IMF) alone, while its foreign currency reserves were under $8 billion and shrinking. Prospects for easily turning the situation around seemed dim.

What would eventually change the situation was the boom in world oil prices. Putin had initially benefited from a rebound in oil prices as he became prime minister in August 1999. The $20 per barrel price of Urals oil at that time was twice what it had been barely a year before, and the upward trend continued. By September 2000, it was up to more than $35 a barrel. Then it turned downward again, dipping under $17 a barrel by June 2002, before booming again in mid-2004.

Such uncertainty over Russia's oil wealth dictated a very conservative policy of financial management. A stabilization fund was established in January 2004 to absorb the extra profits of the oil companies and redirect them to paying off the country's foreign debt. The subsequent surge in oil prices then greatly accelerated Russia's capacity to restore financial sovereignty. On January 31, 2005, Russia paid off the entire balance of Russia's debt to the IMF three and a half years ahead of schedule. In the summer of 2006, it paid off the remaining $23 billion of debt owed to the Paris Club creditors.

Restoring financial sovereignty went hand in hand with Russia's perception of restoring its international political sovereignty. It is not a coincidence that the controversial term "sovereign democracy" entered the Russian political lexicon in 2005–2006, at the same time its financial dependence on the West was removed. The Kremlin's newfound sovereignty was boosted by the downturn in the momentum of regional Color revolutions beginning in the second half of 2006.[18] The Kremlin viewed Western-supported nongovernmental organizations in Georgia, Ukraine, and Russia itself as threats to regional stability and thus to the very sovereignty of the Russian Federation.

Having regained financial independence, Russia now faces the question of how to deal with the changes that took place in its environment during its period of financial weakness that began in the late 1980s. Today's Russia regards many elements of the international system that evolved during that period of weakness as illegitimate. This is most evident on a range of security issues including Kosovo, the role of NATO, missile defense, the Conventional Armed Forces in Europe Treaty, and others where the United States (in particular with the usual accusation of unilateralism) and the West are viewed as having taken undue advantage of Russia. With every action that Russia takes to defy the existing order, there are stronger calls from Western countries to exclude Russia further from the international system. In return, Russian rhetoric has heated up.

Putin alarmed many in the West with his sharp criticism of U.S. foreign policy in his February 2007 speech at the Munich Conference on Security Policy. At the core of Putin's frustration and anger is his view of the United States dangerously intervening into the sovereign affairs of others: "[T]he United States has overstepped its national borders in every way. This is visible in the economic, political, cultural and educational policies it imposes on other nations."[19] This speech and subsequent remarks by Putin and other Kremlin leaders later in 2007 sparked a furor in Western policy circles and endless commentary about an alleged "new Cold War." Russia and the West seem to be at an impasse.

A Stake in the International Economic System

A possible first step to break through this impasse is to acknowledge Russia's quest for stability and to recognize that its core concern is the risks to stability represented by the interdependent global economy. The growing mismatch between economic power and the architecture of international economic relations has become a popular theme for Putin. In that same Munich speech, Putin noted:

> The combined GDP measured in purchasing power parity [PPP] of countries such as India and China is already greater than that of the United States. And a similar calculation with the GDP of the BRIC countries—

Brazil, Russia, India and China—surpasses the cumulative GDP of the [European Union]. And according to experts this gap will only increase in the future…. There is no reason to doubt that the economic potential of the new centres of global economic growth will inevitably be converted into political influence and will strengthen multipolarity.[20]

Russia today finds itself regaining economic strength faster than anyone inside or outside of the Kremlin expected. In less than 10 years, Russia has emerged from bankruptcy to being one of the largest financiers of the U.S. current account deficit. Now the ninth-largest economy in the world according to PPP GDP estimates, Russia has set itself the goal of advancing to fifth place by 2020. By that time, Moscow projects itself to be one of the world's top five financial centers.[21] To many skeptics in the Washington policy community, this sounds like a fairy tale. Yet, much of the Russian and international investment banking community and large multinational companies take these projections quite seriously.[22]

It is in this context of rapid recovery and perception of the lack of a voice in reforming the international order for the last 20 years that the campaign message taken from a United Russia 2007 campaign brochure entitled "Putin's Plan: Victory of Russia" can be interpreted: "[This means] victory in the competitive battle of leading world powers. The result of this victory will be a dignified place for Russia in the international division of labor and distribution of assets…. The victory of Russia is a new architecture of the world in which our country can influence global politics for the benefit of security and the well-being of its citizens."[23]

In Putin's view, it is not just Russia's reversal of fortune that calls for a new architecture. Russia's resurgence is just a piece, albeit a significant one, of a changing global economic balance of power or, to put it in economic terms, a massive wealth transfer. So far, the principal beneficiaries have been the major oil exporters and large emerging market economies. Russia fits prominently into both categories.

In his speech at the St. Petersburg World Economic Forum in June 2007, Putin elaborated on the nature of change he envisioned:

> The new architecture of economic relations implies a principally new approach to the work of international organizations. It has become increasingly apparent of late that the existing organizations are not always up to

the measure in regulating global international relations and the global market. Organizations originally designed with only a small number of active players in mind sometimes look archaic, undemocratic, and unwieldy in today's conditions. They are far from taking into consideration the balance of force [sic] that has emerged in the world today.[24]

Putin's words were put into practice a few weeks later when Russia surprisingly nominated former governor of the Czech National Bank Jozef Tosovsky as an alternative candidate to the EU-supported Frenchman Dominique Strauss-Kahn for managing director of the IMF. The Russians wanted to make the point that the selection process was unfair, but they also believed that Tosovsky was a more qualified candidate given his performance over Czech finances during the challenging transitional period of the 1990s. Much of the initial response by the press and pundits either dismissed this act as just more Russian meddling and blustering or as an effort to woo the Czech government away from deploying a U.S. theater missile defense radar. A *Financial Times* editorial, however, got it right:

> It is depressing when the Russian executive director speaks more sense about the future of the International Monetary Fund than does the [EU]. Yet Alexei Mozhin did so when he criticized the EU's decision to foist ... Strauss-Kahn ... on the IMF. Only those who want the Fund to be irrelevant can applaud the decision. This is the wrong candidate, chosen in the wrong way. Mr. Mozhin was right when he said "the IMF is facing a severe crisis of legitimacy." He was correct to insist that "we must select the best candidate" if the institution is to remain relevant for developing countries.[25]

The "crisis of legitimacy" is especially acute at the IMF in large part because its voting power quotas are so convoluted and archaic. China's voting share of 3.7 percent is less than that of France or the United Kingdom, with 4.9 percent each, and India's 1.9 percent is less than Belgium's 2.1 percent. Global wealth is moving east and south, whereas the IMF distribution of voting power reflects the latter days of the colonial era. This deficit of legitimacy spills over to the World Bank, with the cozy 60-year-old agreement that an American heads the World Bank and a western European leads the IMF.

Russia's proposal was defeated in the end, thanks to the unbalanced voting system that gives the EU and the United States more than 49 percent of the vote. Yet, many developing and emerging market countries, including China and India, followed Russia's lead in support of the Tosovsky nomination. As a result of this episode, it is more likely today that the multitude of structural challenges the IMF faces to maintain legitimacy and budgetary financing will be addressed sooner rather than later. In the opinion of Prime Minister Jean-Claude Juncker of Luxembourg, the Strauss-Kahn appointment would likely be the last time the head of the IMF was selected according to the existing rules and conventions.[26]

The Tosovsky case demonstrates an instance of the Russian government taking a genuinely constructive initiative on an issue of global significance. Russia is integrated into the world economy today more deeply than ever. It recognizes the importance of financial stability and the need to reform global institutions, not only to reflect a changing economic order but also because new tools are required to address new challenges. To their credit, today's Russian leaders have learned much from the mistakes that their Soviet predecessors made during the Cold War. One such mistake was Moscow's decision not to take part in the establishment of the Bretton Woods system in 1944. There is increasing recognition around the world that the Bretton Woods institutions for global economic management require a major overhaul, and the United States should welcome the fact that Russia is emerging on the scene as a constructive player in this endeavor.

Minimizing Future Risks

Russians have learned that the vagaries of the modern global economy can pose as great a threat to a nation's existence as do military threats. The Soviet Union survived World War II, but it could not survive a collapse of world oil prices. During Putin's tenure, therefore, the Russians have acted to insulate themselves better, making the economy and society as robust as possible to external shocks.

Increasingly, however, Russia has come to realize that a purely defensive and inward-oriented approach is not enough. Russia is increasingly linked to the international economy, and if growth is to continue, that trend cannot be reversed. Indeed, it is accelerating as Russian companies and capital seek trade and investment opportunities abroad. Consequently, Russia will have to play an active role in promoting global stability. This realization fuels many of Putin's critical comments about the U.S. role in world affairs. Putin believes that the United States is simply not capable of keeping the global system stable. Moreover, if a crisis does happen, the current unipolar system will inevitably result in an attempt by the dominant nation to secure its own interests first, even at the expense of others.

Putin's Plan, as such, may or may not endure, as it is dependent on the future political role of Putin himself. Whatever Russian politician assumes the role of strategic planner, however, the goals of long-term stability and predictability will endure because the Russian people want their children to live better and their country to endure as a strong power. External events combined with governmental incompetence conspired to thwart this goal twice in the twentieth century, nearly 100 years ago with World War I and a little more than 20 years ago with the collapse of oil prices. Putin and his colleagues will continue to seek to minimize the risk of major internal and external shocks disrupting Russia's stable growth path.

Notes

1. "Boris Gryzlov: Plan Putina my obyazany realizovat' v polnom ob"eme" [We are obliged to realize Putin's plan in its entirety], United Russia, May 22, 2007, http://www.edinros.ru/news.html?id=120703 (in Russian).

2. Anna Zakatnova, "Putin's Plan," *Russia Beyond the Headlines*, December 13, 2007, http://www.rbth.rg.ru/articles/putin_plan.html.

3. "Plan Putina: Otsenki Rossiyan" [Putin's plan: Russians' evaluation], VTSIOM Press Release no. 794, October 18, 2007, http://wciom.ru/arkhiv/tematicheskii-arkhiv/item/single/8992.html (in Russian).

4. "Dmitriy Medvedev: Vmestye my dob'yemsya mirovogo liderstva rossii" [Dmitry Medvedev: Together we will achieve the global leadership of Russia], United

Russia, December 17, 2007, http://www.edinros.ru/news.html?id=126322 (in Russian).

5. William King and David Cleland, *Strategic Planning and Policy* (New York: Nostrand Reinhold, 1978).

6. Vladimir Putin, "Strategicheskoye planirovaniye vosproizvodstva mineral'no-syr'evoy bazy regiona v usloviyakh formirovaniya rynochnykh otnosheniy: Sankt-Peterburg i Leningradskaya oblast'" [Strategic planning of the reproduction of the mineral resource base of a region under conditions of the formation of market relations: The case of St. Petersburg and Leningrad region], (dissertation, St. Petersburg State Mining Institute, St. Petersburg, 1997).

7. King and Cleland, *Strategic Planning and Policy*, pp. 46–47 (emphasis in original).

8. Ibid., p. 55.

9. Ibid., pp. 28, 47, 50, 51, 53.

10. Vladimir Putin, "Rossiya na rubezhe tysyacheletii" [Russia on the Threshold of the Millennium], *Nezavisimaya gazeta*, December 30, 1999, http://www.ng.ru/politics/1999-12-30/4_millenium.html (in Russian) (hereinafter Putin, "Russia on the Threshold of the Millennium").

11. See Richard Sakwa, *Putin: Russia's Choice* (London: Routledge, 2003), pp. 52, 56.

12. Putin, "Russia on the Threshold of the Millennium."

13. "Beginning of Meeting With Political Parties United Russia, A Just Russia, Citizens' Strength, and the Agrarian Party," December 10, 2007, http://www.kremlin.ru/eng/text/speeches/2007/12/10/1804_type82912type84779_153811.shtml.

14. Vladislav Surkov, "Suverenitet—Eto politicheskiy sinonim konkurentosposobnosti" [Sovereignty is a political synonym of competitive ability], (speech, Center of Party Studies and Personnel Qualification of the United Russia Party, February 7, 2006), http://www.edinros.ru/news.html?id=111148 (in Russian).

15. Victor Yasmann, "From Silovik Power to a Corporate State," *Radio Free Europe/Radio Liberty*, September 25, 2007, http://www.rferl.org/featuresarticle/2007/09/72d3efd3-7c5c-4cec-af91-9a609ff08218.html.

16. Aleksei Levinson, "Nashe 'my': Preyemnika prinyali" [Our 'we': They have accepted the successor], *Vedomosti*, January 15, 2008.

17. King and Cleland, *Strategic Planning and Policy*, p. 15.

18. Andrew C. Kuchins, "Look Who's Back," *Wall Street Journal Europe*, May 9, 2006, http://online.wsj.com/article/SB114712273454746989.html.

19. "Speech and the Following Discussion at the Munich Conference on Security Policy," February 10, 2007, http://www.kremlin.ru/eng/speeches/2007/02/10/0138_type82912type82914type82917type84779_118123.shtml (Putin speech).

20. Ibid.

21. Sergei Ivanov, "Russia—Scenarios 2020" (speech, St. Petersburg, June 9, 2007).

22. Investment bankers, interviews with author, Moscow, May, September, and October 2007.

23. United Russia, "Putin's Plan: Victory of Russia" (2007) (campaign brochure).

24. "Speech at the XI St. Petersburg International Economic Forum," June 10, 2007, http://www.president.kremlin.ru/eng/speeches/2007/06/10/1823_type84779_133777.shtml (Putin speech).

25. "Not Strauss-Kahn," *Financial Times*, August 28, 2007, http://search.ft.com/ftArticle?queryText=not+strauss+kahn&aje=true&id=070828000677&ct=0&nclick_check=1.

26. Christopher Swann, "Strauss-Kahn to Inherit IMF Job With Reduced 'Clout' (Update 3)," Bloomberg, August 31, 2007, http://www.bloomberg.com/apps/news?pid=20670001&refer=&sid=az7CI_oU9vvM.

Celeste A. Wallander

Russian Transimperialism and Its Implications

There is a new reality on the global scene: a Russian foreign policy that is proactive and strategic. In Central Asia, the Shanghai Cooperation Organization (SCO) is an increasingly effective instrument of Russian-Chinese security and economic cooperation, one that includes Iran as an observer and not the United States. Russian energy negotiations with Kazakhstan, Turkmenistan, Ukraine, and China have yielded exclusive contracts for Russian energy exports at higher prices, agreements for Russian control over strategic pipelines, and even joint investment arrangements for Russian companies abroad.

After a decade of inaction on separatist conflicts in Georgia and Moldova, Russia has developed a new policy stance leveraged on international norms for self-determination and the potential precedent of an independent Kosovo that may result in outright Russian control of those regions. In the past two years, Moscow has opposed Western democratization policies in post-Soviet countries such as Belarus and Uzbekistan by forging partnerships with like-minded nondemocratic leaderships in strategically important neighboring countries. Although the outcome of

Celeste A. Wallander is a visiting associate professor in the School of Foreign Service at Georgetown University in Washington, D.C., and a member of the Editorial Board of *The Washington Quarterly*. A French version of this article is available in *Politique étrangère* 72, no. 1, as "La Russie face à la mondialisation: la voie du transimpérialisme."

Copyright © 2007 by The Center for Strategic and International Studies and the Massachusetts Institute of Technology
The Washington Quarterly • 30:2 pp. 107–122.

international bargaining on Iran's nuclear programs is far from certain, Moscow is poised to advance an emerging strategic partnership with the Middle East's most important regional power.

In Europe, President Vladimir Putin's Russia has had breathtaking success in effecting a bilateralization of Russia's relations with key countries, primarily Germany and France, undermining the European Union as a unified force and eliminating any advantage European countries might have had in insisting on a multilateral approach in their strategic, political, and economic relations with Russia. Toward the United States, it is fair to say that Washington now needs Moscow on vital U.S. priorities such as North Korea, Iran, Eurasian security, and energy more than Moscow believes it needs Washington.

To some extent, Moscow's newly effective strategic foreign policy is a matter of luck brought about by high energy prices, the United States' ongoing nightmare in Iraq, the backlash against democratization and liberalization in Eurasia, and the autonomous forces behind the rise of the twenty-first century's likely global powers in Asia. Nevertheless, Russia must have had a strategy poised to take advantage of this favorable environment.

What is behind this new strategic reality? Is it a postimperial Russia that pursues its national interests through global cooperation and healthy economic competition while respecting the sovereignty, independence, and legitimate national interests even of its weak neighbors? Is it a neoimperial one that defines Russian security in terms of establishing control over the foreign and domestic policies of weaker powers, as the Russian empire did for centuries and as the Soviet Union did in modern form in the last century?

A postimperial Russia can be an integrated member of the international community and a worthy partner among the emerging ranks of postmodern great powers. Such a Russia could help to develop effective responses to the range of emerging twenty-first-century security threats, including substate actors, transnational networks, and traditional nation-states. It could be an effective partner in the ongoing and long-term challenge of Eurasian security, including the region's potential for weapons proliferation. Moreover, a postimperial Russia, with its hydrocarbon energy wealth, nuclear energy technology, and advanced capacities in science and engineering, could be a major player in addressing the global energy transformation challenge in the coming decades.

A neoimperial Russia, however, would be of little help in solving these challenges, and it could create important challenges and problems itself that might drain Western resources and divert a strategic focus from global problems. A neoimperial Russia would reverse the opening of Eurasia to global and transatlantic security, political, and economic integration. It would be a force against liberalization and democratization in Eurasia, objectives of U.S. and European foreign policy on both principled and pragmatic grounds. This Russia would be more likely to define its national interests in zero-sum terms vis-à-vis other regional or global powers, including the United States and Europe. Further, a neoimperial Russia would be very unlikely to be a successfully integrated and dynamic economy because power and state control, instead of markets and growth, would play a dominant role in its commercial relations.

Not surprisingly, debate about Russia's motivations and strategy has been quietly occupying analysts and policymakers in Western capitals. That quiet debate has begun to take public form in disagreements. These quarrels have included, for example, whether it is reasonable for the Russian state to exclude foreign investors in the energy sector, to insist on bilateral negotiations on energy prices, or to restrict foreign-funded nongovernmental organizations (NGOs). For the United States and Europe to develop effective strategies to cope with whatever kind of Russia there may be and to avoid more of the ineffective tactical policy adjustments that have preoccupied the West in dealing with Russia of late, they will need to better understand what is motivating Russian foreign and security strategies, what that implies for the next decade, and what kinds of Western strategies will best secure transatlantic interests.

Analysts and policymakers are engaged in a fruitless debate over postimperialism versus neoimperialism.[1] Neither adequately explains the range of Russian policy and behavior, and both are partially correct. Instead, both the twenty-first century's globalized strategic context and the nature of the authoritarian political-economic system that has been consolidated within Russia during the Putin years are the keys to explaining Russian foreign and security policy. These causal roots have shaped a Russian strategy that is modern and transnational as well as imperialist—in other words, transimperialist.

The Contradictions of Putin's Russia

Russian foreign policy has dual and mutually reinforcing objectives: increase economic growth and global power. Economic growth, at least six percent annually since 1999, provides the state with resources and leverage in its diplomatic relations. During the 1990s, high inflation and severe economic dislocation made President Boris Yeltsin dependent on International Monetary Fund credits and Western goodwill in negotiations on debt payments and trade concessions.

Putin's Russia, on the other hand, can pay its bills, has a booming economy, and has among the world's largest aggregate carbon-based energy reserves, counting oil and natural gas. Strong demand for Russian energy, defense goods, and industrial products such as steel does not merely contribute to economic growth but also affords Russia diplomatic stature in forums such as the Group of Eight. Foreign investor interest in Russia's still largely underserved domestic consumer economy draws global businesses in the consumer sectors with major investors such as Procter and Gamble, Coca-Cola, and Daimler-Chrysler. The prospect of further growth drives interest in Russia's stock market and financial services companies.

Thus, it is not surprising that Putin cites strengthening the Russian state, growing the economy while paying foreign debt, and restoring Russia's international status as his three main achievements.[2] They are the pillars of Russia's successful foreign policies in recent years. Yet, although Russia's great-power stature and influence are built on its participation in the international economy, Putin's foreign policy is not one of integration or liberalization. In Russia's international economic strategy, the state plays a central role in managing the domestic economy and society as well as in interacting with the outside world.

Russia is engaged with the international economy, but on terms antithetical to economic liberalism. Transactions, negotiations, and relationships are channeled primarily through the state; and the state controls major sectors of the Russian economy, particularly in sectors deemed strategic, including energy, metals, and defense. The trend toward privatization, particularly in important sectors such as energy, defense, high technology, and natural resources, has been reversed. Foreign direct investment outside of the consumer goods sector and agriculture is increasingly unwelcome. Foreign investment in strategic sectors must be limited to less than 50 percent and perhaps as little as 30 percent of a firm's value, with close state oversight of foreign investors and their proposed purchases requiring state approval.[3]

Energy, of course, has become the single most important issue in Russian foreign policy, occupying the place of importance and emphasis that military relations used to have in Soviet foreign policy and creating speculation about Russia as an energy superpower, Putin's recent denials notwithstanding.[4] Energy dominates Russia's relations with almost every important country or region, namely its post-Soviet neighbors, Europe, China, and Iran. It is less dominant in relations with the United States, reflecting a larger diplomatic agenda that includes counterterrorism and the nonproliferation of weapons of mass destruction. Furthermore, the United States is not directly dependent on Russian energy exports. Because the vast majority of Russian natural gas must be exported directly to customers through pipelines and cannot be shipped by tankers across oceans as oil is, the United States has little to gain directly in the energy sphere from warm relations with Russia. Yet, U.S. preoccupation with the problem of energy supply and prices keeps the issue on its main Russia agenda as well.

Moscow has used its importance in global energy markets to fracture the EU's common trade policies; to limit its neighbors' willingness to pursue political and security relations that Russia opposes (influencing Ukraine's new reticence on NATO membership, for example); to lay the groundwork for multifaceted cooperation with a rising China; and to create leverage for Russia's entry into the global economy as an investor and owner. Sometimes this has been quite obvious. In November 2006,

Belarus and Russia faced off in a confrontation over the state-owned gas company Gazprom's demand that it be allowed to buy 50 percent of Beltransgas or it would triple or even quadruple the price Belarus pays for Russian natural gas.

In other cases, it has been subtler. Gazprom is joint owner with a company called Centragas Holding (the ownership of which remains a mystery) of RosUkrEnergo, a Swiss-registered company that serves as an intermediary for selling Russian and Central Asian gas to Europe. Instead of buying natural gas directly from Gazprom, Ukraine's state energy company Naftogaz buys it at a negotiated price from RosUkrEnergo, leading corruption experts to believe that the company's sole purpose is to generate and siphon rents in interstate energy deals.

The subtlety increases the further one gets from Russia's post-Soviet borders. In western Europe, Gazprom created a subsidiary company with minority German ownership chaired by former German chancellor Gerhard Schroeder, conveniently not long after Schroeder as chancellor had approved the agreement to build the new Northern European Gas Pipeline. Gazprom is seeking to build a new pipeline to Germany that bypasses transit countries such as Ukraine and Belarus, an objective that many in Europe viewed with concern insofar as it would increase European dependence on Russian energy exports. By creating a subsidiary in which German political and business interests have a direct stake, Gazprom succeeded in persuading key players to go ahead with the deal.

The spectacle of Western companies such as Hydro, Statoil, Chevron, ConocoPhillips, and Total vying to become the chosen foreign investor in the Shtokman natural gas project is yet another example of Russia's ability to leverage its potential energy exports to facilitate close international ties. That competition, however, ended with the Kremlin's decision in October 2006 to retain control by excluding foreign ownership.[5]

Russia's interest in entangling foreign investors has extended to industrial and defense sectors as well. The state-owned Vneshtorgbank bought five percent of the European defense giant EADS in 2006, with Russian sources calling for a 25 percent controlling stake and Putin raising the idea of a Russian seat on the board. Russian steel giant Severstal sought unsuccessfully to acquire European steel firm Arcelor. Russian steel and iron ore firms have large investments in Ukraine's steel sector and related industrial sectors.

Investment and internationalization are, in principle, positive aspects of a modernizing Russia. The key question is whether the investment conforms to global standards for transparency as well as commercial interests and is consistent with competition, profit, and growth. Russian investments driven by private firms in a competitive and transparent economy would have implications for Russia's foreign policy, but they would not be of major concern. Investments managed or even owned by the Russian state, however, are a different matter.

Recent patterns suggest that Russian international investment is not consistent with liberal integration. Moscow uses political relations for economic benefit and economic leverage for political benefit and increasingly resists transparency and international oversight in its domestic and international commercial relations. Furthermore, this new element in Russia's international economic presence comes at the same time that the Putin leadership has taken a very strong interest in the internal domestic political-economic orders of its post-Soviet neighbors.

Namely, Moscow exhibits a strong dislike and even fear of the recent Color Revolutions in Georgia, Ukraine, and Kyrgyzstan. In addition to assisting the Kuchma regime in conducting fraudulent elections in the fall of 2004 to ensure the victory of Viktor Yanukovych in Ukraine—a successful effort that was nonetheless overturned by the Orange Revolution—the Russian leadership has sought to strengthen relations with other authoritarian regimes, most notably in Uzbekistan, with the explicit objective of helping them to fend off democratization. With Georgia appearing to move forward on its transatlantic course with a NATO Intensified Dialogue on its membership aspirations and reforms, Georgian-Russian relations have escalated to confrontation in the aftermath of Georgia's arrest of alleged Russian spies and Russia's virtual blockade of the country.

Neoimperialism or Postimperialism?

Given these trends, the question is unavoidable: Is Russia going through understandable bumpy patches in a transition to postimperialism, or is it constructing a form of neoimperialism? A postimperialist Russia would explain recent policies as those of a normal middle-power seeking security and prosperity. In this view, Russia is undergoing an economic and political transformation that is gradually creating a political and economic system with elements of political freedom and economic competition. With involvement in the international economy, Russia will come to have a stake in the global economic system and will begin to play by the rules. As the stakes for Russia rise in foreign investment and trade, the cost-benefit ratio of hegemonic or imperialistic strategies in the definition of Russian national interests and the developments of its foreign and security policies will change in favor of liberalization.

A neoimperial Russia, on the other hand, would explain Russian policies as the establishment of an informal empire as a vehicle for Russia's emergence as a quasi-modern great power. It points to the importance of a geopolitical definition of Russian national interests heavily influenced by Eurasianist thought and Russian nationalism. This neoimperial Russia would seek wealth, power, and security through a position of strength vis-à-vis the West, as well as other powers, such as Iran and China, by exercising power over dependent neocolonies, primarily the former Soviet states. This Russia would be primarily focused on zero-sum competition with the United States, but also potentially with regional competitors.

Both explanations have elements of truth and fit with aspects of Russian policy and behavior. Neither, however, can account for the range and variety of Russian policies and behaviors. Postimperialism cannot explain Russia's obstructionist stance on frozen conflicts in Moldova and Georgia, blatant use of energy as a tool of power in its foreign policy, or interests in special commercial deals with Iran and Venezuela. It is entirely contradicted by Russia's reliance on authoritarian regimes in Belarus, Uzbekistan, and Kazakhstan.

Most importantly, postimperialism cannot explain Russia's refusal to accept international rules of the game as defined by the liberal international economic order, including contracts and private investment in the energy sector. For example, by threatening massive fines and investigations based on accusations of environmental damage in the international joint venture Sakhalin-2 to develop natural gas exports in the

Far East, accusations to be viewed with considerable skepticism given the Russian government's poor track record on environmentally sound policies and practices, the Russian government has forced Mitsubishi, Mitsui, and Royal Dutch/Shell to sell enough of their majority stake in the venture to cede majority ownership to Gazprom. The Russian government has also refused to ratify the European Energy Charter, which it signed in 1994, because implementation of the charter would require transparency and competition in Russia's pipeline systems, currently monopolized by the state companies Gazprom and Transneft.

Neoimperialism as an explanation for Russian foreign and security policy is flawed as well. If the Russian leadership is bent on reestablishing an informal Russian/Soviet empire, why does the Kremlin continue on the path of the malign neglect and failure to reform the Russian military? In contrast to the expectations of a neoimperial model, Russia has been very restrained in the use of force toward its post-Soviet neighbors. Russia played a constructive role in resolving the crisis over Ajaria in 2004 and has been withdrawing military forces from Georgia. Although Russia did endorse fraudulent elections in Ukraine, it also accepted the results of the Orange Revolution and the free and fair elections that ultimately made Viktor Yushchenko president. Russia is now poised to join the World Trade Organization (WTO) and its leadership remains active in pursuit of that goal, having compromised a great deal and made substantial progress in its negotiations with the United States. The disputes that delayed its WTO accession agreement were not those of an empire and are all too familiar in the normal trade realm of the international economic system.

Perhaps the most important anomaly both for neoimperialism and postimperialism as explanations for Russian foreign policy is the deep complicity of leaderships abroad in Russia's new activism in international politics and economics. Russia's favorable gas deal with Ukraine in January 2006, which keeps Ukraine largely vulnerable and dependent on Russian energy and goodwill, was not imposed on an unwilling Ukrainian leadership. The winning government of the Orange Revolution agreed to it, and the deal profits not only Gazprom but also the Ukrainian joint owners of RosUkrEnergo.

Gazprom may be pressuring Belarusian president Aleksandr Lukashenka for partial ownership and thus control of gas pipelines, but without the billions of dollars in implicit and explicit subsidies received over the past years, Lukashenka would face domestic discontent and potentially more effective opposition. Georgia is vulnerable to a Russian blockade precisely because so many illicit economic and commercial relations with Russia sustain the Georgian economy. Uzbek president Islam Karimov did not expel the U.S. military presence in 2005 because of Russian neoimperialist pressure. Rather, he saw a common interest in joining with Russia to resist the perceived threat of a Color Revolution that would shake his authoritarian rule.

Both models ignore an essential dynamic of Russia's foreign policy: how the Russian leadership pursues power and wealth. At the level of the international system, this means globalization. At the level of Russia's emergent domestic political-economic system, the key factor is patrimonial authoritarianism.

Globalization Shapes Russia's Choices

Globalization is created by networks of interdependence on a global scale. Although it has taken place in previous historical periods, its current scale, speed, and multiplicity are unique, and it is the defining feature of the contemporary global system.[6] One of globalization's attractions is that it can increase trade, spur innovation, and create efficiencies. It leads to economic growth and development and affects the power and wealth of nations. Yet, globalization creates challenges as well as opportunities. It brings information, ideas, resources, wealth, disease, and external threats. Increased interaction can challenge existing social and political institutions, especially their ability to regulate and control the lives and behaviors of citizens. As a result of globalization, states must often cope with shifting configurations of power and interest within their own societies.

Leaders can respond by adapting well to the new challenges, developing capacities for dealing with new areas of economic policy, and cooperating with other governments to create international institutions to manage transnational global challenges. States can also erect barriers to globalization's networks of interdependence, however, insulating the country. In doing so, the state may forgo the opportunities of globalization. Barriers to trade maximize control and minimize foreign influence over the state and its society but limit the growth effects of free trade that competitive and integrated economies enjoy. In the modern world, no country can aspire to prosperity or greatness by isolating itself from globalization, especially if, like Russia, its economic base requires exports. If Russia wishes to be a wealthy great power, it is going to have to participate in the globalized international system.

Therein lies the dilemma. In order to participate successfully in the globalized economy and to benefit from it, Russia would have to open its economy, following liberal practices such as transparency, rule of law, and the sanctity of contracts. To compete and innovate, it would have to allow its citizens access to information, ideas, the global media, and ultimately the right to hold the government accountable for its policies. A globalized Russia would in fact be a postimperial Russia. This would be consistent with Russia's national interests and its stated objectives for prosperity and security. It is not consistent with Russia's internal political-economic system, however, and thus not consistent with the interests of the current Putin regime.[7]

Moscow's Patrimonial Authoritarianism

Russia is neither the Soviet Union nor a partial democracy. The Russian political system is not totalitarian; the state does not control every aspect of life or aspire to do so. Neither is it a democracy. The conditions for democracy, including competitive political parties, independent media, free and fair elections, and government accountability to a constitution, are not only lacking but have been systematically dismantled.

Russia is an authoritarian system based on centralization, control, and rule by an elite that is not accountable to its society. It is a special variant, which I term "patrimonial." "Patrimonial" means that the primary relationship in the system is that between patron and client.[8] Patron-client relationships are dependent on control and distribution of "rents," wealth created not by productive economic activity but by the political manipulation of economic exchange.

Patrimonial authoritarianism is a political system based on holding power in order to create, access, and distribute rents. It is well known that Russia is deeply corrupt,[9] but corruption in the Russian system of patrimonial authoritarianism is not merely a feature of the system; it is essential to the very functioning of political power. The political system is based on the political control of economic resources in order to enrich those within patron-client clans.[10] The patron remains in power by rewarding clients, and the clients are rewarded by supporting their patron. The patron requires support from his clients, and he must access and distribute rents for that support. Without the creation and control of rents, political power disappears. At the top of the political system, Putin manages relations among competing patron-client clans headed by top government and business figures, such as Development and Trade Minister German Gref, Deputy Prime Minister and Gazprom chairman Dmitry Medvedev, Gazprom president Alexei Miller, and Igor Sechin, deputy head of the presidential administration and chairman of Rosneft. Each of these individuals in turn has his own set of clients, who are in turn patrons of their own clans, and so on, creating a complex web of relationships that sustain political power and distribute patronage rents.

Obviously, patrimonial authoritarianism is wholly inconsistent with transparency, rule of law, and political competition. The true purpose of the political system is not to mediate among citizens, businesses, or interest groups but to manage and control them so that they do not impinge on the ability of the patron-client clans to use their political power to generate, access, and distribute rents. Patrimonial authoritarianism requires a nontransparent, nonaccountable, nonpermeable, vertical, and centralized political system.

It also requires a central role for the state in the economy. For the political system to work, the state must control at least the most important economic assets of the country, and it must do so in a nontransparent way. Patrimonial authoritarianism is thus incompatible with liberal capitalism, which requires contracts, commercial accountability, and ownership rights. All these would interfere with the ability to generate, access, and distribute rents. They would bring independent sources of power, with interests and competition outside the patron-client system.

This partially explains why the Kremlin was and remains so threatened by the Color Revolutions in post-Soviet countries, why it seeks to control NGOs and their foreign funding, and why it has turned against foreign investors. The Russian political system of patrimonial authoritarianism and the personal interests of its elite in rents need self-isolation to prevent the loss of control, to resist transparency, and to prevent any kind of competition.

There are two problems for the Russian elite. First, this domestic political system is fundamentally inconsistent with globalization, in which a great deal of economic growth, wealth, and thus potential rent is to be found. Second, as the state increases its control of the Russian economy, the economy is beginning to falter. In the energy sector, the very linchpin of the Kremlin's power and wealth, growth has been slowed as the sector comes under state control. Growth in oil production is leveling off, and Gazprom's failure to increase its natural gas production means that the only way it can fulfill its international contracts is by buying cheap natural gas in Central Asia and reselling it abroad. Russia faces electricity shortages in the coming year and may have to import electricity from neighbors such as Ukraine.

There are still resources and rents within Russia, but because state control is depressing economic growth, the big money lies in participation in the globalized international economy. Because of the effects of state control, elites must seek out rents abroad. Because the political system at home depends on rents to sustain the patron-client relationships, the internal political system will need access to international trade and investment. Russia needs to export to the West, China, India, and nearby neighbors, all of whom are to some extent participating in the globalized system.

Transimperialism

The dilemma for the Kremlin is that the logic of its domestic politicaleconomic system requires isolation, but sustaining power requires the wealth generated by participation in globalization, which would undermine that very system. So, how can Moscow deal with the international context of globalization and yet sustain patrimonial authoritarianism at home? The answer is transimperialism. Transimperialism is the extension of Russian patrimonial authoritarianism into a globalized world. Russia can trade and invest without being open and permeable by selectively integrating transnational elite networks in the globalized international economic system and replicating the patron-client relations of power, dependency, and rent seeking and distribution at the transnational level.

Russian foreign policy is increasingly focused on creating transnational elite networks for access to rent-creating opportunities in the globalized international economy. Moscow functions as the arbiter and control point for Russia's interaction with the outside economy to ensure that Russia is not exposed to the liberalizing effects of marketization, competition, and diversification of interests and social power. If that were to happen, the political system that keeps the present leadership in power would be at risk of failing. In this sense, globalization is a threat not to Russian national interests but to the interests of Russia's political leadership.

In the transimperialist framework, it is not surprising that Russia is withdrawing military forces from the Caucasus while extending Russian ownership of gas pipelines through joint projects with its post-Soviet neighbors. Military power is not key to sustaining the patrimonial networks at home and abroad. Instead, nontransparent transnational companies and state-to-state negotiations beyond the scope of normal commercial relations create the rents and mechanism for accessing and distributing them. Russia can live with the Yushchenko government, for example, as long as Ukraine's internal political economy is sufficiently patrimonial and corrupt to prevent transatlantic standards of transparency and rule of law in its commercial dealings with Russia.

In Central Asia, Russian state control of Gazprom and pipelines creates the mechanism for nontransparent agreements between Russia and Turkmenistan for the purchase of Turkmen gas at below-market rates and for Russian sales of that gas through RosUkrEnergo to Ukraine.

Rent-seeking opportunities are thus facilitated through global energy networks kept under Russian state control and impervious to Western scrutiny.

Transparency is more of an obstacle for Russia in energy deals with Europe, but the same mechanism of relying on transnational patron-client relations and the control of commercial ventures for generating and distributing wealth is apparent. Witness the commercial transnational manifestation of the Putin-Schroeder relationship in the latter's chairmanship of the company extended from Gazprom to manage a northern European gas pipeline. We should expect to see more Russian efforts to create special transnational commercial relationships with friendly Western leaders.

Western companies tend to expect Western standard business practices in their investments globally, and such practices would threaten Russian patrimonial authoritarianism at home. The Russian government has responded by passing legislation requiring majority Russian ownership and thus control of oversight and composition of management in increasing sectors of the economy, particularly growth areas such as energy, metals, and heavy industry. Royal Dutch/Shell is now a minority owner in the Sakhalin-2 natural gas project and will have no veto over how the project is managed. BP-TNK is under constant pressure regarding its energy investments in Russia, and industry experts expect that Gazprom will make a move to buy out TNK, gaining a controlling stake in the transnational company.

Such privately owned, joint transnational ventures, along with the now effectively defunct, nonstate oil company Yukos, seemed in the early years of the Putin era to herald Russia's global commercial integration and thus its transition to postimperialism. Yukos was broken apart through state claims for enormous back taxes and the consequent sale of its most valuable component, Yuganskneftegaz, to Rosneft, which is chaired by Putin associate Sechin. Mikhail Khodorkovsky, Yukos's chief executive officer, was sentenced to nine years in prison. The elimination of such competition and establishment of new joint ventures have become the leading examples of Russia's transimperial modus operandi to access global networks, wealth, and rents. The common elements are

Russian state control, mutual gain for elites in nontransparent commercial deals in global markets, and Russia's growing leverage as a result of such dealings with the United States and Europe.

Transimperialism is not consistent with integration. It includes involvement in the international economy, but only insofar as it can be managed from Moscow in cooperation with corrupt elites in partner countries. It is based on a form of political-economic management highly dependent on personal relationships. This would have been difficult to achieve on an international scale in the past, but in a globalized world, such transnational networks are easy to build and are even the norm. Nontransparent commercial and political relationships are essential, allowing rents to be acquired and distributed. Political and commercial openness and oversight would drive the system to competition and accountability. Those attributes would allow for profits but not rents. Profits would accrue to the productive, the innovative, and accountable business and political leaders rather than to the current Russian leadership.

Transimperialism is a form of geopolitics through commercial relationships and transnational patron-client relationships. The interests at stake are not national security interests arising from geopolitics or national wealth. Searching for meaning in the foreign relations of Russia with its neighbors in such concepts leads nowhere. The interests at stake are those of the Russian elite and the transnationalized elites in the former Soviet republics, China, India, Iran, and even the West who profit from Russia's interest in the rent-seeking opportunities of a globalized system. The hope that Russia's genuine need for investment, expertise, and technology would liberalize the Russian economy has proven to be a false one. The price would be to undermine the Russian political-economic system of patrimonial authoritarianism, and that price is too high for the Kremlin to pay.

How the West Should Respond

Were the West to face a neoimperial Russia, the policy prescription would be neocontainment. A neoimperial Russia would be a threat to the sovereignty and security of countries in Europe and Eurasia. Were the West to face a postimperial Russia, the policy prescription would be integration. If Russia were postimperial, it would be ready to play by the rules of the game of the globalized economy. It would benefit from investment and healthy competition in markets and politics. Russian partners would represent the wide array of Russian societal interests, and the Russian political system would become accountable and responsive to citizen demands, as political systems in the West ultimately are.

If neither is the case, however, neither policy is the right one. Integration of an illiberal, patrimonial, authoritarian Russia would give the Kremlin the resources of globalization without the rules, constraints, and competition-inducing aspects of political and economic liberalization. It would feed Moscow's power and leverage. Neocontainment of an illiberal Russia would be a flawed policy as well. It would reinforce the ability of the Kremlin to isolate and control its commercial and business interests, society, media, and potential political challengers. Because the transnational relations among Russian and post-Soviet leaderships are welcomed by many of the latter that profit very well from them, neocontainment might limit the range of Russia's access to international rents, but it would not eliminate them. Furthermore, neocontainment would feed the image of the outside world as a threat to Russia, helping to justify isolation and patrimonial authoritarianism.

Instead, transimperialism requires a policy of liberal engagement. Liberal engagement involves Russia, but not exclusively through the Kremlin and not on the Kremlin's terms. It refuses to accept nontransparency in global commercial relations and engages Russian society, including the broadest array of business interests, as widely and deeply as possible. Russia should become a member of the WTO as long as it plays by the rules. Foreign investors should go to Russia but invest only when their standards for rule of law and good corporate governance are met. The transatlantic community should pursue every opportunity to negotiate with the Kremlin, but never to agree to commercial initiatives that require nontransparency or lowered standards. The West should welcome Russian investment, but on the most stringent Western rules and to the standards required of Western companies.[11]

Transimperialism is not sustainable if liberal economic and political conditions for Russian participation in the globalized international system are upheld. Over the next decade or so, Moscow will not be able to sustain state control over increasing sections of the Russian economy unless it can participate in globalized economic networks without adhering to the system's rules. The Russian system cannot generate sufficient rents without international participation, but it cannot both participate internationally and sustain patrimonial authoritarianism at home.

Such a policy can only be effectively sustained transatlantically, with cooperation between an effective EU and a strategic United States. The Russian leadership's recent successes in bilateralizing its relations with Europe is evidence of how important a common approach is in sustaining the rules and effectiveness of the international system built over the past 60 years. For a secure and prosperous Russia, an objective in the interests of the transatlantic community, the West must be idealistic in its hope for an integrated modern Russia and realistic that such a Russia will not emerge from the Kremlin's transimperialism.

Notes

1. For contrasting arguments, see Jackson Diehl, "Russia's Unchecked Ambitions," *Washington Post*, December 6, 2004, p. A21; Eugene B. Rumer, "Why Contain Russia?" *Washington Post*, December 17, 2004, p. A33.

2. "Full Text: Vladimir Putin Interview," September 9, 2006, http://en.valday2006.rian.ru/materials/20060910/52329444.html (hereinafter Putin interview).

3. Organization for Economic Co-operation and Development (OECD), *Investment Policy Review of Russia 2006: Enhancing Policy Transparency* (Paris: OECD, 2006), ch. 4.

4. Putin interview.

5. Agata Loskot-Strachota, *Russian Gas for Europe* (Warsaw: Centre for Eastern Studies, 2006).

6. Thomas L. Friedman, *The Lexus and the Olive Tree* (New York: Random House, 1999), ch. 1.

7. See Celeste A. Wallander, "Global Challenges and Russian Foreign Policy," *Twenty-First Century Russian Foreign Policy and the Shadow of the Past*, ed. Robert Legvold (New York: Columbia University Press, 2007).

8. On patrimonialism, see Georgi Derluguian, "The Coming Revolutions in the North Caucasus," *PONARS Policy Memo*, no. 378 (2005).

9. See Transparency International, "Corruption Perceptions Index 2006," http://www.infoplease.com/ipa/A0781359.html; Tom Parfitt, "Corrupt Bureaucrats Cost Russia £125bn a Year, Prosecutor Says," *Guardian*, November 8, 2006, http://www.guardian.co.uk/russia/article/0,,1941743,00.html.

10. See Thomas Graham, "The New Russian Regime," *Nezavisimaya gazeta*, November 23, 1995, http://www.prospect-magazine.co.uk/article_details.php?id=4909.

11. For a similar conclusion, see Roderic Lyne, Strobe Talbott, and Koji Watanabe, *Engaging With Russia: The Next Phase* (Washington, D.C.: Trilateral Commission, 2006), ch. 9.

Dmitri Trenin

Russia Redefines Itself and Its Relations with the West

Russian foreign policy's modern-day motives are completely dissimilar to those of the recent Soviet and the more distant czarist past. Whereas the empire was predominantly about Eurasian geopolitics and the Soviet Union promoted a global ideological as well as political project backed up by military power, Russia's business is Russia itself. Seen from a different angle, Russia's business is business. In stark contrast to its Soviet past, postimperial Russia stands among the least ideological countries around the world. Ideas hardly matter, whereas interests reign supreme. It is not surprising then that the worldview of Russian elites is focused on financial interests. Their practical deeds in fact declare "In capital we trust." Values are secondary or tertiary issues, and even traditional military power is hardly appealing. Fluctuating energy prices, not nuclear warheads, are what really matter to Moscow.

Geopolitics is important primarily as it affects economic interests, but not as a guiding theory. Private and corporate interests are behind most of Moscow's major policy decisions, as Russia is ruled by people who largely own it. Although the unofficial slogan says "What is good for Gazprom is good for Russia," in reality "Russia" stands for a rather

Dmitri Trenin is a senior associate at the Carnegie Endowment for International Peace and director of studies at the Carnegie Moscow Center. A French version of this article is available in *Politique étrangère* 72, no. 1, as "Le Business russe entre l'Europe et l'Amérique."

Copyright © 2007 by The Center for Strategic and International Studies and the Massachusetts Institute of Technology
The Washington Quarterly • 30:2 pp. 95–105.

small group of people. These people have not inherited their power and property but fought hard to get where they are today. Not a single one among them is a public politician; practically everyone is a bureaucratic capitalist. Under President Vladimir Putin's watch, the Russian state has turned into something like Russia Inc., with top Kremlin staffers and senior ministers sitting on the boards of various state-owned corporations and taking an active interest in their progress and profits. In a major conflict of interest, for example, between terminating gas subsidies to former Soviet republics and keeping them in Moscow's political orbit, material interest wins. Russian leaders want to be and be seen as powerful and wealthy individually, but also as a group, which helps to achieve their individual goals.

Having survived in a ruthless domestic business and political environment, Russian leaders are well adjusted to rough competition and will take that mindset to the world stage. From their perspective, everyone can be a partner, from U.S. president George W. Bush to Hamas leader Khaled Meshal and from the Council of Europe's rapporteur on Chechnya, Lord Frank Judd, to Iranian president Mahmoud Ahmadinejad. Equally, anyone can become an adversary, even Belarusian president Alexander Lukashenko. It's nothing personal, it's business.

This does not mean, however, that Russian leaders do not know the difference between the diverse parties with which they are dealing. Russian tycoons thrive primarily on the business they conduct with Europe and the United States, and they desire fast, personal integration with the West. Although some would take risky shortcuts to riches through China, Iran, or Venezuela, most probably keep their principal assets in the West instead of Asia or Russia. If things went sour at home, they would probably leave Moscow for London or Zurich, not Shanghai or Mumbai.

From Moscow's perspective, Russian-Western relations are competitive but not antagonistic. Russia does not crave world domination, and its leaders do not dream of restoring the Soviet Union. They plan to rebuild Russia as a great power with a global reach, organized as a supercorporation. They are convinced that the only way to succeed is to get their way, and they are prepared to be ruthless. Virtually for the first time, Russia is turning into a *homo economicus*, and it is emerging as a major player in the highly sensitive field of energy. This naturally disturbs many Europeans and Americans.

This disturbance extends to political and strategic areas. Although Westerners usually reject moral equality between their countries and Russia, namely the "values gap," Russians no longer recognize U.S. or European moral authority. Moscow is prepared to deal with its Western partners on the basis of interests or agree to disagree and compete where necessary. The principal underlying issue between Russia and the West at the start of the twenty-first century is the terms of engagement.

The View from Moscow

Ironically, at the beginning of the twentieth century the Soviets were fiercely ideological, and the West was essentially practical and pragmatic. Now, the Russians have transformed themselves into raw-and-ready capitalists, and the West is lecturing them on values. From the Russian perspective, there is no absolute freedom anywhere in the world, no perfect democracy, and no government that does not lie to its people. In essence, all are equal by virtue of sharing the same imperfections. Some are more powerful than others, however, and that is what really counts.

Buoyed by high oil prices, Russian leaders are standing tall for the first time in almost two decades. Their level of self-confidence can only be compared to the early 1970s, when the Soviet Union achieved strategic nuclear parity with the United States and the United States suffered defeat in Vietnam. Once begging for loans, Russia has now paid off its debts. Russia is sovereign at last and fiercely independent, no longer a poor ward of the West, and on the way to becoming a power on par with others. For each concession the Russians are now asked to make, they will quote a price.

Power and property are inextricably linked in Russia itself, and Russian leaders, though primarily business oriented, are not oblivious to the political influence that comes with ownership or market dominance. They reason that economic dependencies lead to political dependencies, which result in privileges. The oil and gas business, they believe, is essentially political. For decades, Western oil companies were major political players in the Third World countries in which they operated. Since the 1973 oil boycott, decisions by the Organization of the Petroleum Exporting Countries have been essentially political. The Baku-Tbilisi-Ceyhan pipeline was a U.S.-driven political project, with the aim of bypassing Russia. Transit countries, such as Ukraine and Belarus, have used their critical geopolitics to win concessions from their Russian suppliers. The Russians thus make no apologies for being the principal purveyor of oil and gas to the Western markets. They see it as a strength that stands out among so many Russian weaknesses. They enjoy being an energy power.

Ironically, despite the geographical distance, Russia is in some ways more similar to the United States in its outlook and key characteristics than it is to the European Union. The United States is a nation-state, and postimperial Russia is on the way to becoming one. The role of religion is more prominent than it is in most EU states, although, needless to say, very different than it is in the United States. Russia shares a predilection and propensity toward using force in international disputes and certainly has a residual superpower mentality, now manifested in energy power. The role of money is preeminent, and social democracy is not a major force. Russia is becoming markedly individualistic, although in a very crude fashion. Given all of these characteristics, Russia will modernize and will become more Western, but it will not necessarily become European.

This means that Russia's future foreign policy is likely to be global, assertive, and driven by the national interest as defined by the country's elite. It will be couched in the universalist language of international law and moral values. It will not be tied to the United States or the EU. The idea will be to develop what many Russians believe is their nation's unique capacity to understand different cultures and, if need be, mediate between them. Russia will seek to strengthen its relations with the leading countries of Asia as well as Latin America and continue to be at peace with the Muslim world.

Russia and Europe: Seeking Equality and Reciprocity

Russia's long daydream about uniting with Europe is history. Soviet leader Mikhail Gorbachev's idea of a "common European home" and other

Russians' more recent concept of a greater Europe are now regarded as conceptual flights of fancy. Old thinking about integration, which even included EU membership in some cases, has been shelved. The new talk is centered on sovereignty, with the United States as the role model and China as an object of admiration and envy. Present-day Russia wants a Europe without dividing lines: a pragmatic business proposition that assumes the essential equality of two partners.

Russia does not seek to dominate Europe, but it will exploit the EU's various vulnerabilities at a tactical level. To capitalize on the EU's internal divisions, Moscow prefers to deal with the EU's members separately, rather than as a group. It will take advantage of its links to Germany, France, and other important countries such as Italy, Spain, Greece, and Portugal. Based primarily on strong business interests, these relationships are relatively stable, being subject to periodic corrections, such as the recent post-Schroeder "readjustment" of German-Russian relations, but are not in any real danger of sharp reversals. Relying on these productive ties, the Kremlin will work to offset the influence of the recent group of EU entrants, which includes some traditional Russia skeptics such as Poland and the Baltic states.

Having consigned central Europe, including the Balkans, to the EU sphere politically, Russia seeks to acquire assets there and in the Baltic states. Rather than a nostalgic move, this is a pragmatic decision to exploit opportunities where competition is still relatively light. At the same time, the Russians want to keep the post-Soviet neighborhood largely to themselves. From their perspective, NATO and EU enlargement should stop at the Commonwealth of Independent States' doorstep. Gazprom's sharp increase in gas prices in late 2005, leading to the cessation of supplies to Ukraine on New Year's Day in 2006, was the ultimate coup de grace for the former Soviet Union. A similar move led to cutting off Belarus one year later. Moscow sent the message to its neighbors that there would be no special relations or subsidies anymore, even for political loyalists such as Armenia or Belarus. This is as much about geoeconomics as it is about geopolitics. Although the former Soviet states are now considered abroad, Russia still sees these neighbors as economic spaces in which it continues to enjoy some comparative advantages over third-party competitors.

Pipelines are essential to Russia's policy of economic expansion. As Putin mentioned at a meeting with EU leaders in Lahti in October 2006, Europe relies on Russia for 44 percent of the natural gas it consumes, and 67 percent of Russia's natural gas sales are to Europe. The EU will seek to lower its dependence on Russian gas, but pipeline projects that bypass Russia promise bitter rivalry. The underlying cause of the Kremlin's ongoing spat with Georgia is Tbilisi's Westward political orientation, which among other things would allow Western companies to build a pipeline to pump Caspian gas to Europe, bypassing Russia. In Turkmenistan, Russia and the West are already struggling over Turkmenistan's vast natural-gas inheritance.

This energy interdependence will keep the EU-Russian relationship relatively stable in the medium to long term. In 2010 the North European gas pipeline, traveling under the Baltic Sea, will further link Russia and Germany. The development of the giant Shtokman gas field in the Arctic Sea will require cooperation on an even larger scale, due to the massive requirements of expertise and advanced technology, and much of the gas from that project will be shipped to Europe. Russian leaders want to deepen this relationship through asset swaps. In return for allowing Europeans to acquire some of Russia's upstream assets, Russians want a piece of the downstream distribution business in the EU. They see this as a fair trade and are prepared to bargain hard.

Russian companies will continue to seek lucrative assets in other industries as well, proceeding with initial public offerings in Europe, opening Russian businesses to Western buyers. In some sectors, such as the aircraft industry, Russian producers may enter into cooperative arrangements with European companies to acquire lucrative industrial assets. In particular, they have been eyeing the French-German aerospace company EADS, with which there has been some industrial cooperation since 2004. In 2006 a Russian state-owned bank bought five percent of EADS's shares. Russian defense minister Sergei Ivanov, who as vice premier also oversees the defense and technology industries, subsequently singled out EADS as a possible future strategic partner in civilian aircraft production. Russians are angered but not deterred by the stiff competition they meet and will keep trying despite occasional setbacks, such as the recent failed bid by Severstal to merge with European steel manufacturer Arcelor.

Outside of government and business relations, European-Russian personal contacts will gradually increase to include ever more diverse interests of societal groups and individuals. Visa-free travel to the EU for ordinary Russians may be decades away, but Russian diplomatic passport holders, that is, the Russian elite, already have that access. Europe's general attractiveness to Russians and its geographic proximity will lead to a gradual social rapprochement between the EU and Russia.

This process will hardly be smooth or easy. In the short term, the European media and publics will become even warier of Russia. The transfer of power in the Kremlin in the spring of 2008 or, as the case may be, the extension of Putin's mandate is likely to be accompanied by events that will drive Russia's image still further into the ground. Political assassinations, large-scale ethnic violence, and terrorist attacks would serve as a pretext for anyone trying to exploit isolation from the West and stir up turmoil at home to create an emergency situation in Russia that would freeze the existing power and property balance.

New members of the EU, particularly Poland and the Baltic states, will negatively affect the EU's attitudes toward Russia. The recent signals from the deepening and widening of the EU are not particularly encouraging. In a dispute over its meat exports to Russia, Poland has succeeded in delaying the start of an EU-Russia negotiation, due in 2006, on a new overarching document to replace the Partnership and Cooperation Agreement. Along with the Baltic states, Poland is wary of the North European gas pipeline and is calling for an EU-wide energy security policy to oppose Russia's domination. The current acrimony of Russian-Georgian relations and the uncertainties regarding Ukraine's foreign policy orientation will also complicate the picture. True statesmanship on each side will be required to keep the relationship from hitting the rocks.

Russia and the United States: Damage Control

U.S.-Russian relations do not benefit from the same economic interconnectedness. With their interactions therefore based mostly on geopolitics, the United States and Russia are in unstable territory. The Kremlin has basically written off Washington as a partner in useful diplomatic business for the foreseeable future. Russian decisionmakers see the United States, with its Iraq turmoil, as distracted and disinterested. To the extent that they must deal with the United States, they view it mostly as a problem. The U.S. opinion on Russia is to an extent a mirror image. Most of the meager news about Russia in the United States is negative as well.

The U.S. and Russian foreign policy agendas are very different. Washington's agenda is currently dominated by Iraq, Islam, terrorism, and the proliferation of weapons of mass destruction. Russia puts the post-Soviet neighborhood front and center. In principle, these plans could complement each other and lead to a measure of productive interaction, but the ideological bent of the Bush administration on democracy promotion and the Kremlin's domestic heavy-handedness and suspicion about democracy promotion prevent any chance of serious, long-term engagement.

The only positive goal the Russian government is currently pursuing with the United States is accession to the World Trade Organization (WTO), likely to be completed in 2007. Moscow recognizes that keeping the issue unresolved indefinitely would mean more problems later. Now that Georgia has recalled its signature from its bilateral WTO protocol with Russia to protest Moscow's economic sanctions, Russian wants to avoid Ukraine acceding first and using its membership as a bargaining chip during gas talks. Yet, reaching agreement with the United States has turned out to be exceedingly difficult. Even signing the bilateral protocol in November 2006 is only a prologue to dealing with the Jackson-Vanik Amendment. This piece of U.S. legislation, passed in 1974, originally conditioned normal trading relations with the Soviet Union on Moscow permitting its Jewish citizens to emigrate. Although the original purpose of the amendment is no longer relevant, the legislation continues to block Russia from acquiring normal trading status in the United States.

Washington and Moscow conflict more directly on the issue of U.S. influence in the post-Soviet area. Russia is adamantly opposed to NATO membership for Ukraine, Georgia, and Azerbaijan. Capitalizing on Uzbekistan's decision to remove the U.S. military presence there, Russia is trying to ease U.S. forces out of Central Asia altogether. Moscow has been somewhat relieved by the August 2006 election of Russia-friendly Ukrainian premier Viktor Yanukovych, who will counterbalance the pro-Western, liberal president Viktor Yushchenko. Obviously, the Russians would like to see President Mikhail Saakashvili's government in Georgia replaced by some who would take Russian interests more seriously. Saakashvili, to many Russian leaders, is what Venezuelan president Hugo Chavez is to the United States. There is little, however, that the Kremlin can do about the Georgian president.

As a permanent member of the UN Security Council, Russia is an important factor in several areas of major significance to the United States. Moscow's cooperation is a necessary part of any solution to the Iranian nuclear issue that is negotiated in the UN context. It is similarly vital to the North Korean problem, even though China is playing a leading role there. A common position of the five countries negotiating with Pyongyang, including Russia, is a sine qua non for North Korea taking the six-party talks seriously. Across the greater Middle East, with U.S. policies in Iraq, Afghanistan, and Lebanon and toward the Israeli-Palestinian dispute in crisis, Russia could be a useful partner. It keeps a presence in Central Asia and maintains contacts with the elements of the former Northern Alliance in Afghanistan, which opposed the Taliban for years and joined with the United States to end the Taliban's rule in 2001. It has a long-standing relationship with Syria, having supplied arms to Damascus for two generations. It has useful contacts among the Palestinians and the Lebanese factions and a very vibrant relationship with Israel, approximately one-fifth of whose population is Russian-speaking. Despite the very different lenses through which the White House and the Kremlin view the war on terrorism, the core interests of each call for collaboration against Islamist extremists.

Russia could move somewhat on these top U.S. priorities, but it will not budge without a serious quid pro quo. Essentially, the Kremlin wants the United States to stop being a spoiler in the Russian neighborhood. Yet, even if the United States was willing to make certain concessions, Russian flexibility has its limits. Russian leaders will not subscribe to anything at the UN Security Council that would sanction the use of force against Iran. From the Russian perspective, a preventive war over Iran is worse than a nuclear Iran. They believe that a war would only delay Iran's nuclear program, but at the price of a major regional crisis, political radicalization, and Muslim-Western confrontation. Looking at Iraq and Afghanistan, Russians are skeptical about U.S. staying power and its effectiveness. They suspect that the United States might try to disarm Iran, fail, and have to withdraw, leaving others in the neighborhood, including Russia, to inherit the mess. As Russian foreign minister Sergei Lavrov put it, Russia will not make the mistake it made in 1914 when it became involved in other peoples' war (World War I) and lost everything.

With the U.S.-Russian economic anchor being essentially absent, political relations can and probably will become substantially worse. A crisis could arise over some provocation or miscalculation in Georgia or Ukraine, should the main Ukrainian factions resume their bitter internecine fight. A resumption of hostilities in Abkhazia or South Ossetia would draw Russia in, resulting in a Russian-Georgian military confrontation, with Tbilisi appealing to the United States and Europe for protection and support. A major political split within Ukraine could also put the territorial unity of the country in question, encouraging Russian irredentists to propose holding a referendum in overwhelmingly Russian-speaking Crimea. Russia is turning nationalist, with clear anti-U.S. overtones, while the U.S. public sees Russia in an increasingly negative light. The rhetoric of both countries' 2008 presidential elections is likely to strain relations even further. During the U.S. campaign, Russia's membership in the Group of Eight may become an issue; and in Russia, the United States can be cast as the one country that seeks to prevent the recovery and rise of Russia. If the legitimacy of the new Russian president is questioned, the damage could be truly severe.

Russian business, of course, is intensely interested in gaining access to the U.S. market and acquiring little bits of the United States. Future energy deals, including nuclear energy, and other business agreements could give the U.S.-Russian relationship context and stability. Gazprom, Rosatom, Russian Aluminium, Lukoil, and Rosneft all want to enter or to expand their U.S. presence, but the going is difficult. The Russians are impatient and often lack specific knowledge about the workings of the U.S. business and political environments, so they make mistakes and suffer setbacks. Gazprom's 2006 decision to use Shtokman to supply piped gas to Europe rather than liquid natural gas to North America is in part a result of Russia's disappointment over the desired acquisition of gas networks along the U.S. East Coast.

Russia's Future with the West

Russian-Western relations are likely to be rocky for the foreseeable future, as they are separated by a value gap over several decades. Russia is very old Europe. It could be reminiscent of Germany in the 1920s, with its vibrancy and intense feeling of unfair treatment by others; France in the 1940s, when it was trying to heal its traumas; or Italy in the 1960s, as far as the nexus of power, money, and crime is concerned. Russia is not a democracy—not even a failed one—but it is a rough, capitalist reality powered by private interest, which sometimes poses as the state interest.

The future of Russia itself is key to any discussion of its future foreign relations. Will it actually be able to modernize, or will it fail again, collapsing once and for all? Will property and globalization, the two forces unleashed in the 20 years since the start of perestroika, be enough to put Russia on track? Will Russia succeed in using two decades of stability to build capitalism? The last time it tried, the Bolshevik Revolution cut the effort short in 1917, before even the first decade was out. It may or may not become a democracy, but this outcome will not be known until the mid–twenty-first century.

To the extent that Russian capitalism embraces the rule of law, constitutionalism, and eventually some form of democracy built on civic responsibility, this gap with the West will likely narrow, but the process will be very slow. Aside from a general preference for economic expansion over integration, Moscow is pursuing few long-term strategies. Tactics prevail, medium-term thinking is just emerging, and no national interest worth the name has surfaced. In Russia's contemporary bureaucratic capitalism, the state itself has been informally but effectively privatized and will take some time to coalesce.

Despite its transitional character, Russia is too important to be ignored, neglected, or stereotyped. The West will not only miss opportunities but may run real risks if it misjudges Russia's movements, overreacting or reacting inappropriately to them as a result. Russia could be a party to a future U.S.-initiated exercise in global governance, or it could become isolationist and anti-American. The West would do best by dealing with Russia on Russia's own terms, reaching for an acceptable balance of reciprocity, and not on the basis of normative principles such as democratic reform. Ideology is not a good guide in a valueless yet vibrant Russian environment. Public preaching only shows the powerlessness of EU and U.S. politicians to change realities within Russia and allows Russian officials to portray these protests, even meaningful ones, as meant for Western political consumption.

New realities and evolving interests may make Russia correct its trajectory in the long term. If some future Russian leadership were to decide in favor of economic and political integration with a body that is larger than Russia, it would have only one candidate: the EU. The EU must therefore consider its relations with Russia from a long-term perspective. For the EU, Russia is the immediate neighborhood and the ultimate frontier. In principle, Russia alone, not Africa or the Middle East, could give Europe strategic depth. Culturally, geographically, and historically European, Russia would project the EU all the way to the Pacific, strengthen the Europeans' global outlook, and provide the EU with a range of resources and materially add to its power. This would enhance Europe's overall competitiveness vis-à-vis other major players. Eventually, a pan-European energy system could emerge, or Russian companies could join the EU's aerospace consortium as a substantial minority shareholder. Russians could even visit Paris and Berlin without visas. The resultant whole would be larger than the sum of its parts. This vision, however, has a caveat. A poor and failing Russia would never be a suitable party for the EU, but a rich and successful one would not find joining the EU particularly attractive.

The potential of U.S.-Russian relations can be realized if and when the United States makes a strategic decision to prioritize world leadership and integration, reaching out to the major players, including Russia, in an effort to consolidate the system over which it presides. By that time, the present Russian foreign policy philosophy would probably have had to change, toward more community-conscious behavior. This is not impossible, if the analogy with rough robber barons turning, usually in the next generation, into socially responsible capitalists holds true for nation-states. For those with a long view, a positive partnership is possible, even if difficult to see for quite some time.

Of course, Western countries should diversify their energy supplies, but they must be realistic about the extent to which this is possible. Turning energy into an area of power relations, such as by adding an energy dimension to NATO, is not a well-considered proposition. Outside of the energy sector, building defenses against the invasion of Russian capital is bad business and bad politics. Russia will not take over the EU or the United States, of course, but it could eventually become a responsible shareholder in the system, allowing Westerners to own pieces of Russia in an inevitable quid pro quo.

The main hope for both sets of relationships is more business ties. Essentially, this would mean more of the United States and Europe in Russia and more of Russia in the EU and the United States. This would create a more solid foundation for political relations, especially between the United States and Russia, a far better understanding of each party's goals, and a convergence of interests. As capitalism in Russia continues to evolve and as the country, on the threshold of WTO membership, integrates further into the global web of economic, political, and social relationships, Russian standards can be expected to grow more modern and closer to the sets of values now espoused by Americans and western Europeans.

Sarah E. Mendelson and Theodore P. Gerber

Us and Them: Anti-American Views of the Putin Generation

For months, pundits from San Francisco to Vladivostok have energetically debated whether Vladimir Putin will retain power in Russia and under what rubric: president, prime minister, national leader, or something else. Although obviously critical to Russia's future, this narrow focus on one man overlooks an important political and social development inside Russia. As the eminent Soviet-era dissident Sergei Kovalev has observed, "'Putin' now stands for an entire set of policies" and a "web of political concepts generated in the bowels of the KGB."[1] Our recent nationally representative surveys in Russia indicate that Russians ages 16 to 29 gravitate enthusiastically to this ideological platform that Putin has built.

These young people, born between 1976 and 1991, are aptly labeled "the Putin generation." Instead of the Helsinki generation or the fall-of-the-Berlin-Wall generation bound together by an embrace of international human rights norms and democracy as core values, young Russians now tend to reflect and support the values and aspirations expressed by Putin. They favor the restoration of a hypersovereign Russia that

Sarah E. Mendelson is director of the Human Rights and Security Initiative at CSIS. She may be reached at smendelson@csis.org. Theodore P. Gerber is a professor of sociology at the University of Wisconsin-Madison. He has served as a consultant for CSIS. The survey discussed in this article was supported by grants from the Ford Foundation and the Charles Stewart Mott Foundation and was written in collaboration with the Russian information agency MEMO.RU.

Copyright © 2008 by The Center for Strategic and International Studies and the Massachusetts Institute of Technology
The Washington Quarterly • 31:2 pp. 131–150.

remains outside the Euro-Atlantic community and resists or rejects international legal norms. Were Putin himself to leave the national stage any time soon, his views would likely live on in the Putin generation for years to come.

The first building block in Putin's national concept is Soviet nostalgia, an effort to restore a sense of pride in the putative accomplishments of the Soviet Union and to harness this pride to the current Russian state. One manifestation is the theme that "the collapse of the Soviet Union [was] the greatest geopolitical catastrophe of the twentieth century."[2] First pronounced during Putin's State of the Union address in April 2005, this sentiment has become so familiar and widely accepted that young Russians discuss why they agree with it even in casual conversation with Western reporters.[3] Another aspect of Soviet nostalgia is ambivalence toward Joseph Stalin. A survey we conducted in 2005 showed that four in five young Russians agreed with Putin's assessment of the Soviet collapse, and a majority failed the "Stalin test," agreeing, for example, that Stalin did "more good than bad."[4] Our 2007 survey data confirmed these findings, providing additional evidence that these Putin themes resonate deeply with young Russians. The rewriting of Soviet history in a positive light effaces historical memory and facilitates Russia's development as an authoritarian state.

The second building block, the focus of this article, involves the manufacturing of enemies within and outside Russia. Kremlin authorities and Putin himself repeatedly stir up anxiety among the population concerning dangerous foreign influences, suggesting that enemies encircle Russia and claiming that the foreign governments that help finance Russian nongovernmental organizations are meddling in Russia's internal affairs.[5] Recently, official rhetoric has turned explicitly anti-American. Putin has accused the United States of seeking to impose its ideas and interests on the rest of world, going so far as to liken recent U.S. policies to those of the Third Reich. "One state and, of course, first and foremost the United States, has overstepped its national borders in every way. This is visible in the economic, political, cultural and educational policies it imposes on other nations," he told a stunned audience in Munich in February 2007.[6]

At home, the Kremlin-supported youth group Nashi (Russian for "Ours") actively promotes the belief that foreign enemies pose a threat to Russia.[7] Although young Russians have been generally apathetic and apolitical, our 2007 survey shows a surprising jump in awareness of Nashi and growing desire to join its ranks. We illustrate these definitive sentiments of the Putin generation using data from our surveys, particularly the 2007 study, which contains a number of questions concerning views of the United States. First, we explore how extensively young Russians support the Putin path. Then we examine how young Russians ages 16 to 29 view the United States based on a series of indicators from our survey. Next, we analyze social, demographic, and subjective factors that correlate with views toward the United States among young Russians. To conclude, we assess the challenges that Russia's current political situation presents to U.S. and European policymakers.

Why Youth Views Matter for U.S.-Russian Relations

Understanding young Russians' attitudes about the United States is important for multiple reasons. First, Putin's anti-American turn seems to be motivated at least in part by domestic political considerations. The creation of foreign "enemies" is a classic tactic used by political leaders, including, to be sure, Soviet leaders, to distract their populations from the shortcomings of their own government and rally support behind authoritarian measures. The Russian government is beset by widespread corruption, incompetence, and failure at many levels. Despite resource-driven economic growth, many government institutions—the police, the military, federal bureaucracies, local inspectors, and schools—are deeply dysfunctional.

As the economic situation continues to improve, young Russians may start to demand that the government commit resources to reforming the many public institutions that make their lives more difficult and dangerous instead of easier and safer. To date, rather than confront the problems posed by Russia's public institutions and undertake difficult reforms, Putin has instead chosen to eliminate dissent and raise the specter of enemies, both internal (immigrants) and external. These so-called enemies help his circle maintain power by implying that any dissent advances the agenda of Russia's external foes and thus jeopardizes Russia's sovereignty. Putin appears to have chosen the United States in particular as the new incarnation of the foreign threat, one that should scare Russian citizens away from critical thought or action directed against his administration. In the face of a supposed foreign threat, any challenge to the regime can easily be portrayed as treasonous.

An empirical assessment of how young Russians view the United States can demonstrate whether or not this strategy has been effective. If so, it bodes poorly for U.S.-Russian relations in the near term. The U.S. government and the next administration in particular will have to contend with the diplomatic challenges posed by the belligerent tone and confrontational actions of Russian government officials. Moreover, leaving aside the immediate issue of how the United States can effectively counter Putin's newly aggressive stance, if young Russians have turned decidedly against U.S. policies or people, U.S. officials will need to develop longer-term strategies to restore a more positive image within the current generation of young Russians. Young adults are an especially key population in Russian politics because they will obviously be around for years to come.

Not long ago, many policymakers and analysts assumed or expected that young Russians would overwhelmingly demand democracy in Russia. This assumption seemed reasonable given that many students in the Soviet period were the "chief milieu for underground or semi-underground circles."[8] In fact, the only known protest against Stalin came from a small student group.[9] Today, although young Russians have embraced lattes, iPods, and other consumer goods enjoyed by youth in Western countries, their political views tend to be neither pro-Western nor pro-democracy.

Young Russians are not, however, monolithic. Although majorities largely embrace Putin's anti-American message, we do find that substantial numbers are pro-American or at least neutral. The next logical question to ask is which social, demographic, and subjective variables are related to views toward the United States. Moreover, our data permit us to assess, albeit in a preliminary manner, the claims raised by some critics of U.S. counterterrorism polices that these very policies have eroded U.S. soft power. Additionally, the conventional wisdom holds that individuals who believe that the United States practices or facilitates human rights abuses such as torture and the indefinite detention of terrorist suspects are more likely to hold anti-American views.

Although our data cannot be used to assess causal relationships among these views, they do permit us to see whether perceptions of human rights violations associated with U.S. policies correlate with negative views of the United States. Such a correlation is not sufficient to establish a causal link, but it is consistent with the argument that U.S. policies have helped contribute to the erosion of the U.S. reputation. This information, along with additional survey data, will be helpful in the campaign to restore U.S. soft power. Finally, we investigate whether anti-American views are related to support for the pro-Kremlin group Nashi, for the Moscow-based human rights organization Memorial, and for Putin's assertion that the collapse of the Soviet Union is the greatest geopolitical catastrophe of the twentieth century.

Youth Support for the Putin Path

The most direct evidence as to what young Russians think about Putin's policies and ideas is how they feel about Russia's current path and about Putin himself. By both counts, our surveys show very strong support for the Putin path. Although Western observers have grown increasingly worried about Russia's trajectory, especially since 2005, when Russia paid off all of its foreign debt and Putin's antidemocratic tendencies became more evident, young Russians have become increasingly likely to agree that Russia is on the "right path." In 2005, 45 percent thought that Russia was on the right path, while 44 percent disagreed. By 2007, there is distinct growth in support for the current policies. In the most recent survey, a solid majority (56 percent) of respondents concurred, while fewer than three in 10 disagreed.[10]

This widespread perception that Russia is on track is rooted in support for Putin himself, not in a positive assessment of the performance of other Russian institutions. We asked respondents to indicate how much they trust specific institutions, including the president (fig. 1). Confidence in the president is substantially higher than trust for any other institution, and it is growing: 82 percent trusted the president in 2007, whereas 78 percent did in 2005. Young Russians are substantially less likely to express trust in other government institutions, such as the police and the army, and trust in them is on the decline. Trust in the media also seems unusually high given extensive government control, suggesting that young Russians buy into Putin's project of asserting state control over information.[11]

Clearly, young Russians support Putin and tend to have an optimistic outlook on their country's trajectory despite the growing encroachment of the government on civil society, the loss of civic freedoms, and the poor performance of other institutions. Dysfunctional public institutions in Russia include the military, the police, and other security organs; federal, regional, and local governments; inspectorates and license administrators; and educational institutions, especially universities.

Figure I. How Much Do Russians Trust...

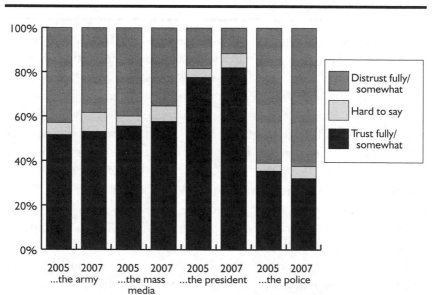

Note: All changes from 2005 to 2007 are statistically significant.

For example, violent hazing and economic exploitation of soldiers are endemic and persistent problems, as evidenced by the brutal beating in early 2006 by senior officers of one young man that cost him his legs and his genitals. Rather than take responsibility for such crimes and the overall lack of reform in the army, government officials then blamed society for the abuse.[12] Police corruption and arbitrary violence against citizens are so widespread that Russia conforms to a model of "predatory policing" in which the police do more to harm than to protect public well-being.[13] Although *Time* proclaimed Putin "Man of the Year" in 2007 for the "stability" that he has brought to Russia, nearly every day someone in the North Caucasus disappears or is assassinated from bomb explosions. Literally hundreds of such incidents have occurred during Putin's second term, including the Beslan school siege.[14]

Despite evidence of institutional dysfunction, the Putin message appeals to the current generation of young Russians, perhaps fulfilling a psychological need to believe in a strong Russia. Members of this cohort were very young when the Soviet Union collapsed, the last of the travel bans were lifted, and shortages of material goods ended. Most probably cannot recall a Russia without foreign imports. They came of age during the 1990s, a time of rampant political chaos and economic crisis, including crippling inflation. The failure of Russian leaders during that period to construct and promote an alternative, positive concept of the Russian state likely contributed to the current appeal of the Putin path, filling an ideological vacuum. Its themes of past glory and achievement, blaming Russia's troubles on external and internal enemies, and promise of economic growth and political order seem to satisfy a visceral yearning for a radiant future in response to an unstable and troubled present. Increasing revenues from oil and natural gas undoubtedly help as well.

Anti-American Sentiment

Given the apparent appeal of the Putin path, we should perhaps not be surprised to find considerable antipathy toward the United States.

Putin's rhetoric has been especially harsh concerning those who accept funding from foreign sources, calling them "jackals" and warning foreigners against "sticking their snotty nose[s] into our affair[s]."[15] The 2007 survey contains a variety of questions measuring how fully young Russians share these views. We asked respondents whether they agree or disagree with three statements about the United States. The first is a standard assertion of Russian officials and news media: "The United States tries to impose its norms and way of life on the rest of the world." Nearly 80 percent of respondents agreed with this statement.

We reversed the polarity of the responses for the next statement, to make sure that the first set of responses does not merely indicate that respondents are likely to agree with the questioner. In this instance, only 20 percent agreed that "the United States does more good than bad in the world." Finally, about three-quarters agreed that "the United States provides aid to other countries only in order to influence their internal affairs." These three questions clearly indicate that a large majority of young Russians, 70 to 80 percent, hold anti-American views. Apparently, Putin's anti-American rhetoric has resonated with a large portion of Russia's youth.

More evidence that young Russians have embraced Putin's depiction of the United States comes from the responses to a question regarding how best to describe the relationship between the United States and Russia (fig. 2). Sixty-four percent of the respondents viewed the United States as either an "enemy" or a "rival." This overwhelming tendency to see the United States as a threat stands out in comparison to views on other countries. We asked the same question about six other countries. The only one that comes close to the United States, in terms of the percentage of respondents who viewed it either as an enemy or a rival, is another target of Putin's bellicose rhetoric: Georgia, at a distant 44 percent. The remaining countries are even less likely to be viewed in such negative terms, even though some of them (Iran and China) arguably pose a greater or equal threat: Belarus (12 percent), Germany (13 percent), Iran (21 percent), Ukraine (21 percent), and China (27 percent). Young Russians are three times more likely to see the United States as a threat than to see Iran as such. Correspondingly, young Russians are

Figure 2. What Is the Relationship of [country] to Russia?

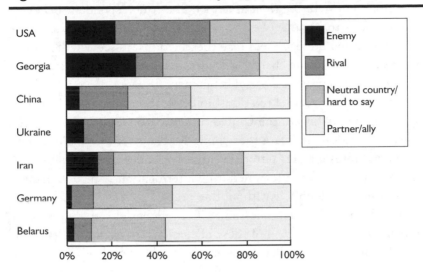

more likely to see Belarus, China, Germany, and Ukraine either as partners or allies than they are to see the United States or Georgia as such.

Views of U.S. Counterterrorism Policies

Although we believe that Putin's rhetoric is the main factor shaping the Putin generation's perceptions of the United States and foreign influence, their views of the Bush administration's counterterrorism policies may also encourage anti-American sentiment. In light of the argument that these policies have contributed to the loss of U.S. soft power, it is worth considering the possibility that young Russians who perceive the United States as violating human rights are also more likely to adhere to the broad anti-American message that Putin has been promoting.

In order to test at the individual level whether perceptions of human rights violations in U.S. counterterrorism policies are associated with more critical views of the United States, we included three questions measuring whether respondents believe the United States engages in such practices. We explained to each respondent that there are reports that the United States has taken certain actions but that these reports have been contested. We then asked whether the respondent believed the allegations to be true. We also asked whether the respondent believed the United States should take these actions, to see whether some Russians might advocate "harsh" measures against suspected terrorists.

These data can provide a useful benchmark for more rigorous analyses in the future of any causal relationship between U.S. counterterrorism policies and views toward the United States, particularly if the policies change. The results indicate that young Russians tend to believe that the United States tortures terrorism suspects, renders them from justice to countries that practice torture during interrogations, and detains terrorism suspects indefinitely without due process or legal representation (fig. 3). Although for each question, a fair number of respondents had "no opinion" as to the truth of these allegations, in every case roughly one-half stated that the allegations are definitely or probably true. Very few, 9 to 13 percent, believed these allegations to be false.

We also assessed whether young Russians support these policies. In fact, majorities opposed rendition from justice and indefinite detention; fewer than 20 percent supported either. Perhaps surprisingly, views

Figure 3. Do You Agree or Disagree With the Following Statements?

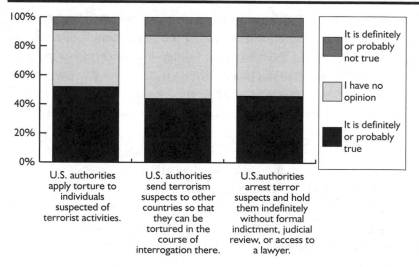

on torture were somewhat more balanced, with 30 percent saying the United States probably or definitely should torture terrorism suspects. Nonetheless, here too there was more disapproval than approval, with 42 percent opposed. Thus, despite some ambivalence with respect to torture, the broad finding is that young Russians oppose policies, such as rendition and indefinite detention, that have resulted in violations of human rights and that the Bush administration has sought to justify as part of the "war on terror."

Who Is Anti-American and Why?

One criticism raised against the Bush administration's counterterrorism policies focuses on the practical global cost of human rights violations, which are alleged to tarnish the United States' traditional image as a protector of individual rights and freedoms. In short, counterterrorism policies that violate human rights foster anti-American sentiment throughout the world. Although this argument seems logical and plausible, we have not seen it tested empirically.

If U.S. human rights violations undermine America's image abroad, we should expect to find that those young Russians who believe that the United States engages in such violations have more negative opinions of the United States than those who do not believe such allegations. That is not to say that a correlation of this nature proves that the Bush administration policies promote anti-American views, because the causal arrow could point in the opposite direction; that is, those who are more anti-American at the outset could be more likely to give credence to the allegations of U.S. human rights violations. The absence of such a correlation, however, would effectively disprove the argument, so if we find it in our data, we can at least conclude that the argument is plausible and merits further study. Thus, we bring empirical evidence, albeit preliminary, to bear in the larger debate over the consequences of these policies for U.S. soft power. Moreover, this issue is practical as well as theoretical. Although U.S. policymakers cannot control the Kremlin's rhetoric, they can reverse policies that undermine the international image of the United States as a guarantor of human rights norms and as an alternative to authoritarian regimes around the world.

More broadly, our data provide an opportunity to discern what factors are related to the intensity of anti-American sentiment among young Russians. Are some demographic groups more inclined toward criticism of the United States than others? Perhaps, for example, better-educated, more urbanized young Russians take a more favorable view. Do supporters of Nashi differ in any meaningful way from others in their views of America? The Kremlin has poured money into Nashi in an effort to create an institution that fosters nationalistic and pro-Putin sentiments among young Russians. Our data suggest that awareness of this group is growing. Thirty-three percent of the respondents to the 2007 survey said that they had heard of Nashi, up from 20 percent in the 2005 survey.

If the organization is serving its designed purpose, we would expect to find that those who support it, by which we mean the 9 percent of our sample who either are current members or say they would like to join, are more likely to embrace the Putin administration's anti-American message. On the other end of the political spectrum, the 3 percent of our respondents who support Memorial may also have distinctive views toward the United States. Although we would generally expect supporters of human rights to hold the United States in high esteem, recent U.S. policies may have undermined that positive image. Finally, if the two building blocks of Putin's platform create a coherent ideology, we would expect that those who see the Soviet collapse as a catastrophe also to hold more negative views toward the United States.

To examine how, if at all, these factors are related to anti-American sentiment, we first created a single scale measuring anti-American views based on the answers to the four questions regarding the United States discussed above, as well as a fifth question asking whether respondents like or dislike the U.S. president.[16] The resulting "anti-Americanism" scale runs from 1 to 5, with higher values denoting stronger anti-American views. The sample mean on the scale is 3.72.[17]

Next, a multiple regression analysis obtained precise measures of how the variables of interest relate to anti-Americanism when the other variables are held constant. The results are presented in figure 4.[18] The

Figure 4. Factors Associated with More Anti-American Views

Note: Bars represent estimated increase in the anti-American scale associated with the corresponding category, holding constant the other variables. All results are statistically significant except for "rural resident."

length of each bar in the figure represents the factor's average effect on anti-Americanism on the 5-point scale, all else being equal. For example, the first bar indicates that young Russian men have, on average, a 0.19 higher value on the anti-Americanism scale than do young Russian women who are otherwise identical in terms of the variables measured—education, age, place of residence, etc.

The regression results reveal that highly educated males living in Moscow are actually the most anti-American within Russia's youth. Their average values on the anti-Americanism scale are 0.49 higher than females without college education who do not live in Moscow but are otherwise the same with respect to the other variables in the figure. Given that the standard deviation of the scale is 0.76, this represents a substantial effect. This finding is cause for particular concern. The most educated young Russians, who, given their gender and residence in the country's power center, are likely to figure prominently in the next generation of elites, are the most anti-American.

Two other demographic effects also merit commentary. First, ethnic Russians are somewhat more anti-American than non-ethnic Russians, which may point to greater Russian nationalism as one source of anti-American views. Second, young Muslim Russians hold the United States in substantially higher esteem (0.29 on the scale) than non-Muslims. Although this finding is not too surprising considering the potential tensions between Russia's Muslim population and the Putin administration, it is nonetheless quite striking. Where else in the world, apart from perhaps Albania and Kosovo, might we find that the Muslim population is more pro-American than other religious or ethnic groups?[19]

Young Russians who believe the United States tortures or indefinitely and unlawfully detains terrorism suspects have considerably more negative views of the U.S. government than do those who place little or no credence in the allegations. Those who have no opinion as to the validity of either allegation fall in between those who believe and those who do not. Our regression model provides clear, direct evidence supporting the hypothesized link between beliefs about U.S. human rights violations and the declining image of the United States among foreign publics.

Statistical analysis of our cross-sectional data cannot demonstrate that the linkage between perceptions of U.S. abuses and anti-American sentiment is causal. Yet, our analysis demonstrates that, at the individual level, the perception of U.S. human rights abuses and anti-American sentiment are strongly correlated, even when other variables are controlled statistically. Our findings are thus consistent with the argument that the Bush administration's counterterrorism policies have damaged the reputation of the United States among young Russians. It is plausible that Russians who are inclined to dislike the United States in the first place may be more likely to believe reports of U.S. human rights abuses than are Russians who are positively inclined toward the United States. Yet, even under this scenario, reports of abuses at Abu Ghraib and Guantanamo clearly reinforce anti-American inclinations.

Supporters of Nashi are also significantly, although only slightly, more anti-American than young people who do not support Nashi, and supporters of Memorial are less anti-American than nonsupporters. Nashi has yet to attract the attention and interest of a majority of young people. Only one-third of our sample has even heard of the organization, and only 9 percent are members or want to join. This 9 percent, however, is more anti-American than other young people (again, controlling for the other variables in the model), suggesting that as this constituency grows, so too might support for anti-American sentiment. The fact that we see growth in support for Nashi from less than 3 percent in 2005 is also noteworthy. U.S. policymakers should therefore closely monitor the trajectory of this youth organization and any of its successors.

At the other end of the spectrum, Memorial had less recognition and support in 2007 than Nashi and slightly less support than it did in 2005. Only 17 percent said that they had even heard of Memorial, one of the oldest indigenous human rights organizations in Russia with branches in most regions of the country. The mission of Memorial is to document political crimes committed during the Soviet period against citizens and to monitor current human rights abuses in Chechnya and elsewhere in Russia. Memorial is often a partner and a source of information for the work of Human Rights Watch. Strikingly, only 3 percent of the respondents are members or would like to join. Yet, despite the recent U.S. record regarding human rights, the Memorial constituency remains more pro-American, after controlling for the other variables. Anything the United States can do to encourage the expansion of that constituency could reap longer-term benefits in terms of swaying Russian public opinion toward more favorable views of America.

Supporting this particular organization is challenging in the current political climate; overt funding of Memorial by U.S. government entities could well make the organization a target of the Russian government. Moreover, as an organization, it faces its own demographic crisis, as the majority of its active members are senior citizens, who themselves were repressed by Stalin or who lost relatives in the gulag, the Soviet system of forced labor camps. Nonetheless, U.S. policymakers and other donors should explore creative ways of supporting the organization and helping expand its appeal to young Russians.

We find clear evidence that those who agree that the Soviet collapse was the greatest catastrophe of the twentieth century are more anti-American than otherwise similar young Russians who do not agree with that statement. This association between nostalgia for the Soviet period and anti-American views suggests that the two pillars of Putin's platform combine into a unified political ideology.

Policymakers should also be aware that anti-American sentiment seems to be driven by responses to U.S. government policies as opposed to prejudices about the U.S. population. In the survey, we asked, "How do you feel about Americans?" meaning the American people. This question was part of a series of similarly worded questions regarding feelings about 12 different national, ethnic, religious, or political groups. Although more respondents expressed negative views (19 percent) toward Americans than expressed positive views (14 percent), the most common response was neutrality (64 percent), and the level of anti-Americanism by this measure is considerably lower than the level of hostility toward the U.S. government's policies. This suggests that, although the Putin generation holds largely negative views toward the U.S. government, this sentiment has not translated into widespread animosity toward the American people.

Finally, although hostility to the United States in particular has been especially salient in Putin's rhetoric and in the views of young Russians, we also have evidence of broader fears of foreign influence and motives, which Putin has fanned. Seventy-eight percent of respondents agree that "Russia would be better off if foreigners stopped imposing their ideas on us," and 65 percent agree that "foreigners who assist Russian organizations financially are trying to meddle in our affairs." One-third even agree with the view that "foreigners introduced AIDS in Russia in order to weaken it." Fewer (only 30 percent) agree that "Russia should strive to become a European country rather than pursue its own path."

The Need for a New U.S. Policy on Russia

Policymakers in the United States need to calibrate their approach to Russia based on where Russia is today politically, rather than where they wanted Russia to be when the Soviet Union collapsed. The dream of a democratic Russia embedded in the Euro-Atlantic community is, for the time being, over.[20] This reality raises several delicate and interconnected policy dilemmas that the West and particularly the next U.S. president will confront in its relations with Russia: What should a new policy toward Russia emphasize? How can we avoid a new Cold War? How should the United States engage Russia on issues related to human rights and democracy? How stable and durable is the current Russian political situation?

Putin's Russia is not the Soviet Union. Yet, the ambiguous nature of this relationship, in which Russia is not exactly friend yet not exactly foe, is difficult to navigate politically. On one hand, Russia does not currently pose an existential threat to the United States, despite its nuclear arsenal. There is no inherent reason why a return to the Cold War is necessary or likely, notwithstanding potential fault lines, such as differing approaches to Iran's nuclear program or Kosovo's quest for independence.[21] Policymakers in the United States and in Europe should continue to engage Russia, as they did during the Soviet period, on common interests and, where possible, in joint projects, such as health promotion campaigns.[22] Policymakers need to carefully monitor Russia's relations with states that are hostile to U.S. and European interests, such as Belarus, Iran, and Venezuela.

Through some of its actions, the Russian government has attempted to take advantage of declining U.S. influence and challenge the current international order, advancing a hypersovereign model to replace one that emerged from the Helsinki accords of 1976. Of late, Russia has had much greater impact on the international human rights and democracy machinery than vice versa.[23] Russian authorities have successfully used divide-and-conquer strategies inside international organizations, blocking the condemnation of gross human rights violations that occur inside states and challenging the practice of international election-monitoring. In the UN Security Council, for example, they joined China to prevent, weaken, and ultimately delay international responses in Darfur and Burma.[24] At least one human rights organization claims the Russian and Chinese governments have supplied Sudan with arms or dual-use technologies that were diverted to Darfur despite the arms embargo in place since 2005.[25] These and other actions suggest an urgent need to generate recommendations and political will to repair the weakened international human rights machinery, including within the United Nations, the Council of Europe, and the European Union.

When Russia demands special rules for itself or departs from accepted norms, such as rejecting international election observation by the Organization for Security and Cooperation in Europe as it did in December 2007 before its parliamentary elections, international organizations and member states should respond. The United States should coordinate strategy with European states. The use of administrative means to pressure voters and the brazenness and impunity with which the Putin administration orchestrated the events leading up to the election marked a new, negative stage in Russia's post-Soviet trajectory. Yet, Putin received calls of congratulations from President Nicholas Sarkozy of France and former prime minister Tony Blair of the United Kingdom.[26] These actions suggest that European policymakers are oblivious or indifferent to the threats that human rights defenders and journalists experience in Russia today. Coordinated transatlantic responses are more likely to deter repressions against these targets, while the recent mixed messages only enable the authoritarian drift.

European policymakers are not the only ones enabling Russia's departure from international norms and laws. Although not intuitively connected to a new Russia policy, reestablishing the United States as a generator of human rights norms will have important repercussions for engaging Russia and other authoritarian and semiauthoritarian regimes. These are more than just fuzzy, feel-good recommendations. Our data suggest that U.S. counterterrorism policies have a corrosive effect, possibly stimulating negative views among young Russians. Part of the repair work, therefore, requires new U.S. policies on a range of issues and should be driven by a desire to opt back into the international legal framework that generations of Americans helped create. This shift toward international legal frameworks will require a dramatic departure from current U.S. policies on counterterrorism, including adopting new detention and interrogation policies for alleged terrorist suspects.

The repair work will also require a radical shift in how the United States approaches the thorny issue of foreign assistance, particularly democracy promotion. The Russian government is rich, with plans for not one but two stabilization funds worth hundreds of billions of dollars.[27] Yet, assistance should not end for important groups such as Memorial and other human rights organizations that will surely see none of the emergent oil wealth. Instead, assistance requires radical restructuring. The top-down approach of the Bush administration's "F" process offers exactly the wrong model.[28] Instead of listening and responding to local needs, existing approaches are likely to benefit Washington insiders.

In contrast, new approaches must be geared to Russian needs and designed to encourage Russian civil society to engage local populations. What forms of engagement do Russians want? Are they hostile to all forms of assistance? By responding to their needs rather than our own, assistance can dramatically leverage its impact as well as inoculate donors and activists against accusations that the assistance constitutes foreign interference. Young Russians are generally neutral or positive about Russian organizations that accept foreign financial contributions for work on health issues such as HIV prevention or human rights issues that matter to them, such as police abuse. They feel negative about support for political organizations, such as those that protest against the government. U.S. policymakers will need to find a way to respect the wishes of Russians while not enabling the hypersovereign tendencies that reject international norms and laws. Again, the need for the United States to repair the damage done in the human rights sphere will be critical to any possible future engagement with Russia, as well as other authoritarian states, on these issues. Equally important, solid opinion data on what Russians support in terms of foreign engagement can bring to life a policy that is based on listening and responding.

Contacts between the United States and Russia need to be multiplied and diversified, rather than relying mainly on high-level meetings, as the Bush administration has done with the encouragement of the Kremlin. The overpersonalization of presidential politics that marked both the Clinton and Bush administrations has not helped U.S.-Russian relations. The new approach should, if the Russian government is willing, support concrete cooperation between different parts of societies (mayors, legislators, university presidents) on a range of issues of common concern, such as public health, counterterrorism, youth alienation, or even urban decay, where stakeholders may share best practices. Youth exchange programs might be highlighted to reverse the trend revealed in the current generation of 16- to 29-year-old Russians. Additionally, one could imagine a sister-school program bringing children in the United States and Russia into direct contact over the Internet.

Congressional contacts with the Russian Duma and Federation Council have dropped off in recent years and need to be restored, not because these are important centers of power in Russia, but because there is widespread misperception among Duma deputies of the U.S. Congress's relationship with the executive branch. This lack of understanding of how politics works in the United States is another ingredient feeding Russian misperceptions. Is this situation something that the Kremlin seeks to perpetuate, or will there be willingness to challenge misperceptions? Will the Kremlin allow, support, or be neutral about diversifying or multiplying contacts? The answers to these questions will offer a useful metric to gauge the Russian government's desire for hostile or neutral relations with the United States.

We may well be in for a decade of Putin or Putin-like policies, with Russia slipping farther from the Euro-Atlantic community and creating its own set of allies and networks while shutting down voices of opposition internally. Burdened by dissent, corruption, and poorly functioning public institutions, the future could be less bright than the current oil-flush economy suggests. A day may come, if not next year or the year after, then perhaps within a decade or two, when either a middle-aged Putin generation tires of the manufactured Soviet nostalgia or the children of the Putin generation, having grown up with more knowledge of the world outside of Russia, demand political structures that are more consistent with the dreams many had for Russia when the Soviet Union collapsed. Perhaps the post-Putin generation will eventually view Russia as not so distinct from Europe. It may be that the most we can hope for is that young Russians might share the nuanced vision of the United States expressed by Andrei Sakharov: "[W]e don't idealize America and see a lot that is bad or foolish in it, but America is a vital force, a positive factor in our chaotic world."[29] From where we stand today, that would be progress.

Notes

1. Sergei Kovalev, "Why Putin Wins," *New York Review of Books*, November 22, 2007, http://www.nybooks.com/articles/20836.

2. Vladimir Putin, "Annual Address to the Federal Assembly of the Russian Federation," April 25, 2005, http://www.kremlin.ru/eng/speeches/2005/04/25/2031_type70029type82912_87086.shtml.

3. See "Viewpoint: Pro-Putin Cheerleader," *BBC News*, November 26, 2007, http://news.bbc.co.uk/2/hi/europe/7113253.stm.

4. Sarah E. Mendelson and Theodore P. Gerber, "Soviet Nostalgia: An Impediment to Russian Democratization," *The Washington Quarterly* 29, no. 1 (Winter 2005–06): 83–96; Sarah E. Mendelson and Theodore P. Gerber, "Failing the Stalin Test: Russians and Their Dictator," *Foreign Affairs* 85, no. 1 (January/February 2006): 2–8.

5. Sophia Kishkovsky, "Outside Political Aid Forbidden, Putin Says; Kremlin Fears Meddling of Westerners," *International Herald Tribune*, July 22, 2005, http://www.iht.com/articles/2005/07/21/news/russia.php; Vladimir Putin, "An-

nual Address to the Federal Assembly," April 26, 2007, http://www.kremlin.ru/eng/speeches/2007/04/26/1209_type70029type82912_125670.shtml.

6. "Speech and the Following Discussion at the Munich Conference on Security Policy," February 10, 2007, http://www.kremlin.ru/eng/speeches/2007/02/10/0138_type82912type82914type82917type84779_118123.shtml; Vladimir Putin, "Speech at the Military Parade Celebrating the 62nd Anniversary of Victory in the Great Patriotic War," May 9, 2007, http://www.kremlin.ru/eng/speeches/2007/05/09/1432_type82912type127286_127675.shtml (Putin speech).

7. See Nickolai Butkevich, "Pro-Kremlin Youth Group's Brochure Exposes Rabidly Paranoid Worldview," Coalition Against Hate, May 16, 2007, http://www.coalitionagainsthate.org/2007/05/16/pro-kremlin-youth-groups-brochure-exposes-rabidly-paranoid-worldview.

8. Ludmila Alexeeva, *Soviet Dissent* (Middletown, Conn.: Wesleyan University, 1985), p. 395.

9. Adam Hoschschild, *The Unquiet Ghost: Russians Remember Stalin* (Boston: Houghton Mifflin, 2003), pp. 28–40.

10. Throughout this article, we aggregate categories such as "fully agree" and "agree somewhat" in order to simplify our presentation of the results. Disaggregating the categories adds some nuances but does not affect any of our arguments or conclusions.

11. We also asked about trust in political parties and the courts. Trust in political parties is even lower than trust in the police, while trust in the courts is about equivalent to trust in the mass media.

12. Steve Gutterman, "Russian Army Abuse Blamed on Society," Associated Press, February 15, 2006.

13. See Theodore P. Gerber and Sarah E. Mendelson, "Public Experiences of Police Violence and Corruption in Contemporary Russia: A Case of Predatory Policing?" *Law and Society Review* 42, no. 1 (2008): 1–43.

14. Detailed charts available on request from Mendelson.

15. Clifford Levy, "Putin Accuses U.S. of Trying to Discredit Russian Vote," *New York Times*, November 27, 2007, http://www.nytimes.com/2007/11/27/world/europe/27russia.html.

16. Fifty-two percent disliked "the American president," 27 percent liked the president, and 21 percent found it difficult to say. We created the scale by recoding all variables to run from 1 to 5, with higher values denoting greater animosity for the United States. We used factor analysis and reliability analysis to verify that these variables should all be combined into a single scale.

17. The standard deviation is 0.76.

18. All the coefficients differ statistically from zero (that is, they are "statistically significant"), except for that contrasting rural residence to residence in "other

urban" areas. Overall, the independent variables we identified as possibly relating to anti-Americanism account for 15.4 percent of the variance in the scale, which is relatively high for a social science analysis.

19. See Maxim Artemiev, "Pervasive Anti-Americanism," *Vedomosti*, July 31, 2007, http://www.vedomosti.ru/newspaper/article.shtml?2007/07/31/130154.

20. Sarah E. Mendelson, "Dreaming of a Democratic Russia," *American Scholar* 77, no. 1 (Winter 2008): 35–43.

21. Mark MacKinnon, *The New Cold War: Revolutions, Rigged Elections, and Pipeline Politics in the Former Soviet Union* (New York: Carroll & Graf Publishers, 2007); Edward Lucas, *The New Cold War: How the Kremlin Menaces Both Russia and the West* (Bloomsbury and Palgrave, forthcoming).

22. Ted Gerber and Sarah Mendelson, "A Survey of Russian Doctors on HIV/AIDS," CSIS, January 2006, http://www.csis.org/media/csis/pubs/060707_ruseura_mendelsondocrepjan06.pdf; William H. Frist, "Improving Russian-U.S. Collaboration on Health," *The Washington Quarterly* 30, no. 4 (Autumn 2007): 7–19.

23. See Sarah E. Mendelson, "Anatomy of Ambivalence: The International Community and Human Rights Abuse in the North Caucasus," *Problems of Post-Communism* 53, no. 6 (November/December 2006): 3–15; Mark Leonard and Nicu Popescu, "A Power Audit of EU-Russia Relations," European Council on Foreign Relations, November 2, 2007, http://ecfr.3cdn.net/456050fa3e8ce1034 1_9zm6i2293.pdf.

24. Colum Lynch, "Russia, China Veto Resolution on Burma; Security Council Action Blocks U.S. Human Rights Effort," *Washington Post*, January 13, 2007, http://www.washingtonpost.com/wp-dyn/content/article/2007/01/12/AR2007011201115.html; Edith M. Lederer, "U.S. Push for Sanctions Opposed," *Washington Post*, April 18, 2007, http://www.washingtonpost.com/wp-dyn/content/article/2007/04/18/AR2007041800368.html; Richard Waddington, "China, Russia Seek to Block UN Report on Darfur," Reuters, March 16, 2007, http://www.reuters.com/article/worldNews/idUSL1682479200703167pageNumber=1.

25. "Sudan, Arms Continuing to Fuel Serious Human Rights Violations in Darfur," Amnesty International, May 2007, http://www.amnesty.org/en/alfresco_asset/8bfe199c-a2b8-11dc-8d74-6f45f39984e5/afr540192007en.pdf.

26. "Vladimir Putin Had a Telephone Conversation With Tony Blair, the Special Representative of the Middle Eastern Quartet," December 3, 2007, http://president.kremlin.ru/eng/sdocs/news.shtml?month=12&day=03&year=2007; "Sarkozy's Congratulatory Call to Putin Irks EU Members," *Deutsche Welle*, December 4, 2007, http://www.dw-world.de/dw/article/0,1433,2987505,00.html.

27. "Stabilization Fund to Be Converted Into National Prosperity," Kommersant.com, August 2, 2007, http://www.kommersant.com/p791856/r_500/new_fund_to_specialize_on_portfolio_investment.

28. See Randall Tobias, "Foreign Assistance: A Strategic New Direction" (speech, CSIS Statesmen's Forum, Washington, D.C., February 5, 2007), http://www.csis.org/component/option,com_csis_events/task,view/id,1191/.

29. Andrei Sakharov, *Memoirs* (New York: Alfred A. Knopf, 1990), p. 563.

Part IV:
Europe's Power and
Its Natural Limits

Robert E. Hunter

Europe's Leverage

The destinies of the United States and Europe are now intertwined in such critical ways as to be inseparable. Policies, programs, and practices of states on each side of the Atlantic must be measured against this reality. Some Europeans believe that Europe, Russia, and China can create a bloc to balance U.S. power, and some Americans believe the United States can divide European states from one another or simply ignore them. These attitudes and actions, however, are and will continue to be based more on fantasy than analysis or understanding. The United States in particular, with all of its power and potential, ambitions and aspirations, must grasp this notion and act according to its logic.

Nothing has happened to lessen the importance of the continent of Europe as the most important landmass—economically and politically—to be kept free of a hegemonic power at odds with U.S. interests, values, and objectives (the stuff of three world wars in the twentieth century). Europe still depends on U.S. power, influence, engagement, and leadership to be fully assured of its own independence, security, long-term prosperity, and in some places even domestic tranquility. Meanwhile, the U.S. and European economies, especially those of the European Union, are now so intermingled that both sides would suffer grievous

Robert E. Hunter is a senior fellow at the RAND Corporation in Washington, D.C. During 1993–1998, he was U.S. ambassador to NATO.

Copyright © 2003 by The Center for Strategic and International Studies and the Massachusetts Institute of Technology
The Washington Quarterly • 27:1 pp. 91–110.

injury if either tried to lessen their level of entanglement with one an-other significantly. The panoply of economic interaction between the United States and the EU, including trade in goods and services, invest-ment, cross-ownership, travel, and finance, must now be valued in the trillions of dollars, with the power to control and influence rarely having a clear locus on one side of the Atlantic or the other; certainly neither side is able to claim decisive predominance. Indeed, transatlantic eco-nomic interdependence is now so much a fact of life that the concept is no longer even questioned. At the same time, a broad array of relatively common values and institutions of incalculable worth bind the United States and Europe together, creating an interpenetration of influence unrivaled among any other set of major powers. Much of what the Unit-ed States seeks to do elsewhere in the world will depend on its ability to gain the support and active engagement of European power—and Euro-pean powers—politically, economically, and militarily.

The Five Transformations

Radical changes have taken place in the nature of global politics, mili-tary strength and effectiveness, economics, society, and even culture—in a phrase, in the nature of power and influence in today's world. Taken together, these changes have made Europe a new repository of capacity to act in the world and thus have given new significance to the relationship between Europe and the United States. In recent years, five significant changes have redefined the position and role of Europe in the world.

END OF THE COLD WAR

With the collapse of the Soviet Union's internal as well as external em-pires and of communism's order and appeal in Europe, the European continent suddenly ceased to be the cockpit, the primary locus, of com-petition for global power and the place on which U.S. attention abroad had to be riveted. Europe's political and strategic independence is still critical to the United States, and if this wheel squeaked, it would be first in U.S. priorities for oiling. Yet, it is not now squeaking, and the United

States has had the luxury, if not the compulsion, for the foreseeable future to look elsewhere in pursuit of many of its most important strategic requirements. No, Europe has not become a backwater, but no longer is it the central focus of global politics—at least as defined by the most important power in the international system—as arguably it had been previously without serious interruption since the inception of that concept a few hundred years ago.

CONSOLIDATION OF THE EUROPEAN UNION

Although Europe's significance as a geostrategic entity at the top of the list of regions that must be actively kept free of anti-Western hegemonic or ideological dominance has radically declined, its internal development has preserved its inherent importance on the world stage. With some limited exceptions, notably the United Kingdom, European military power has decreased apace with the retreat of the continental threat; but Europe's economic and political power have increased, in part because the EU has bounded forward on a number of fronts. Vigorous debates of a decade ago about whether the European Community should emphasize widening (admitting more members) or deepening (advancing economic and political integration among existing members) have been decisively answered with "Both." Although tension between the two projects continues, especially as the EU tries to admit 10 new countries while writing a constitution that can ideally chart a single course for all EU member states and the union as a whole, the overall success of the European experiment continues driving forward, despite its recurring fits and starts.

THE RISE OF GLOBALIZATION

The end of the Cold War and of the threats it posed to the security of virtually all Western states, and even to the prospects for the survival of humankind, altered the reality and widespread perceptions of the efficacy of traditional forms of state power in international relations. To be sure, central European countries recently freed from Soviet and Communist dominance still placed security, including military guarantees and membership in NATO, well ahead of domestic prosperity and links to the EU; and residual concern remained about the reemergence of a challenge from post-Soviet Russia. The economically and politically dominant western part of the continent, however, judged military power to be of diminishing importance, EU economic and political integration to be of rapidly rising importance, the role of international institutions to be of increasing benefit, and nonstate interactions with other parts of the world to be of steadily growing significance.

Meanwhile, from the mid–twentieth century onward, historical barriers among nations and people were increasingly surmounted by technology, leading to the rise of globalization, defined here in shorthand as "those developments that are increasing the pace and extent of interaction among nations, societies, and peoples and of the speed with which information can be transmitted and processed"[1] plus its myriad effects on individual societies. Clearly, Europe has become as globalized as any other part of the world, with a profound impact on European perceptions of international society; instruments of power and influence; and relationships among governments, international institutions, and the nongovernmental and private sectors. In brief, in contrast to the Cold War era, the immediate territory of Europe as well as that of nearby regions has become more important to virtually all Europeans, with nonmilitary instruments increasingly the coin of the realm.

EMERGENCE OF THE SOLE SUPERPOWER

By the 1990s, the United States' 75-year vocation of eliminating European-based threats to U.S. security in the form of German and then Soviet efforts to dominate the continent had come to an unexpected and thoroughly successful end. With the sudden recognition that Soviet power and purpose had for some years been hollowing out from within, the United States found itself to be the world's sole superpower. Indeed, for years it had been steadily amassing, relatively and absolutely, more incipient military, economic, political, and even cultural power than any other country in centuries—some historians have argued since the Roman Empire. At the same time, the United States discovered that, at least geostrategically though not in terms of the rise of globalization, it had largely regained the sanctity of its two broad oceans with the end of the Cold War as the nuclear balance of terror with the Soviet Union disintegrated. For the first time since the bombing of Pearl Harbor, serious, direct threats to the U.S. homeland appeared to have receded into the realms of either strategic theory or the distant future.

For post–Cold War relations across the Atlantic, the United States could have emerged as an unmatchable strategic competitor for Europe, had either side had any interest in such a competition; it is striking that neither did, reflecting nearly a century of shared strategic perspective and an even longer history of shared values. Even in economic relations, where the demands of the Cold War had required that the United States and the European Community essentially bury their differences, no radical change occurred when the apparatus of confrontation with communism and Soviet power collapsed: both sides of the Atlantic discovered that they were destined to sail together in the same economic boat.

At the same time, the emergence of the United States as sole superpower also seemed to mean that European states and institutions no longer had to provide the military and economic sinews of power in pursuit of common security interests on the continent. Soon, however, this generalization was confounded as allies on both sides of the Atlantic realized that their strategic partnership was still useful and indeed necessary to secure the future of the continent. These reasons included preservation and reform of the NATO alliance and its historically unique, integrated command structure; the continued embedding of a now unified Germany into NATO and the EU; grounding central Europe firmly and fully in the West, not least to end its tragic history as *casus belli* and battleground of great wars; drawing the Russian Federation into the Western system of security, politics, and economics; stopping all conflict on the continent; and, to all these ends, keeping the United States engaged as a European power.[2] Nevertheless, the degree of European engagement in these efforts, certainly in terms of providing classic tools of power, was concomitantly reduced from Cold War requirements.

Yet, the United States' role of sole superpower also meant that it could no longer require other countries, including its long-term strategic partner Europe, to respond to its definition of challenge, as had been patent during the Cold War. In this sense, superpowers come in pairs: without the Soviet Union or a strategic replacement for it, it hardly seemed possible that developments anywhere in the world could escalate to conflict necessarily embroiling Europeans and Europe. For Europe and generally for the United States as well, ending the Arab-Israeli conflict was desirable but not strategically necessary; the Indo-Pakistani conflict could erupt again into violence but was far away and largely out of sight; proliferation of nuclear weapons and of other weapons of mass destruction (WMD) was believed to be a relatively managed, secondary matter; international terrorism attracted so little attention on either side of the Atlantic that it merited a scant four words in the 1999 NATO Strategic Concept[3]; and China's potential emergence as a rival to overall Western power and position was only a distant prospect.

Thus, throughout the 1990s and into the new century, it was difficult for the United States to enlist support from European allies to develop and modernize relevant instruments of power, especially military power, for potential use elsewhere and certainly not to apply it toward any of the situations noted above. At NATO, after all, the term "outside of area" in the mid-1990s meant Bosnia and Kosovo, even though both were demonstrably within Europe. Further, although some European states did engage in peacekeeping and nation building, virtually all could safely cede responsibility to the United States to manage most problems external to Europe that might, unmanaged, at some point seriously affect European interests. These included, after the 1991 Persian Gulf War, developments in the greater Middle East of unimpeachable interest to Europe, indeed, arguably of even greater interest to Europe than to the United States. Sole superpower thus tended to be a lonely position.

EUROPE AS AN INTERNATIONAL SYSTEM

Looking backward, Americans may be tempted to characterize Europe's post–Cold War behavior as free riding. In fact, some Americans made such arguments throughout the 1990s and continue to do so, especially in light of major reductions in military spending; little European progress in developing particular military capabilities—so-called interoperability—that would permit allied militaries to fight together in an information-dense environment; and, in this U.S. view, Europe's commensurate failure to share the burdens—seemingly even in prosecuting the 1999 air war over Kosovo, despite the fact that this conflict was occurring in Europe and thus was in Europe's interest.

Judging the EU so negatively obscures some additional factors. Certainly, in terms of responsibility for the functioning of the global economy, key European states and the EU were then and are now playing substantial and effective roles more or less commensurate with their economic weight in the world. Europe was similarly coming to terms with what were then almost exclusively nonmilitary challenges of the emerging phenomenon of globalization, such as environmental damage, the movement of crime across borders, disruption of societies, the spread of disease such as HIV/AIDS, and waves of immigration.[4] Viewed objectively, the European role in responding to the challenges of globalization was also helping to shape the future battlefield, so to speak, in the sense that it helped directly and indirectly reduce the long-term likelihood of conflict in many parts of the world. Thus, European states have consistently outpaced the United States in foreign aid as a percentage of gross domestic product; and European governments, private industry, and nongovernmental organizations have done more than their fair share in trying to deal with the congeries of economic, political, social, and human factors that, left unaddressed, can contribute to conflict and to support for terrorism. These efforts show a capacity and the political will to act on behalf of interests that are also shared by the United States and others.

In judging Europe's contributions to overall Western security and its ability and willingness to employ power to that end, many outside observers also tend to overlook Europe's own system of international politics: sufficiently large, complex, modern, interconnected, productive, and sophisticated in all dimensions that its effective functioning is itself of vital importance in global politics, security, and economics, including of course for the United States. Indeed, the question of whether Europe is prepared to project power abroad, which has been a major U.S. objective for several years, must not obscure the necessity, first, for Europe to project power within Europe itself. Among top U.S. strategic interests is that Europe not be dominated by a potentially hostile, hegemonic power. A corollary is that Europe be able to organize and conduct itself successfully, within itself, in part to ensure that the United States will not have to intervene once again, perhaps militarily, in pursuit of its own strategic interests. The United States championed European economic and political integration as well as military defense from the late 1940s onward largely because of this same rationale. That mission, now turned essentially to the east of the existing EU, is still critical to U.S. interests.

The European system, therefore, includes the major projection of power within Europe itself in direct support of U.S. interests. NATO's redefined purpose within Europe in the 1990s to fulfill the remaining items on the twentieth-century transatlantic security agenda was conducted in parallel with EU actions geared toward complementary ends. Yet, although the United States played the leading role in NATO's transformation and has contributed significantly to Europe's future—all the while standing ready to be the guarantor of last resort of Russia's behavior—the Europeans have successfully undertaken most of the effort. This is especially true financially and economically, where Europe took on the lion's share of burdens, including the deepening and widening of the EU; West Germany's massive subventions to former East Germany; sovereign investment in central Europe, the Baltics, the Balkans, and even the Russian Federation; and the integration of these societies into the West.

Furthermore, European militaries, with limited exceptions, have in truth not kept pace with qualitative and high-technology developments in the U.S. military, but the vast proportion of Western military personnel in the Balkans are European, not American, and they would have borne most of the brunt of ground combat in Kosovo had it been necessary. Europeans share the military burden with the United States in postwar Afghanistan as well.

European Military Power: America Finds It Wanting

For the past several years, most aspects of European power projection capabilities and political will relevant to the interests and concerns of the United

States have generally been found wanting in prevailing U.S. analysis. This reference is to Europe's projection of military power beyond Europe, which has been the principal criterion for U.S. judgment of European power and Europe's willingness to use it. Some U.S. criticism has been based on the unspoken assumption that, as during the Cold War, the existence of the Atlantic Alliance implies that European interests elsewhere in the world, including interests in projecting power, should be similar to those of the United States. Indeed, in many cases, U.S. success in dealing with regional challenges and conflict also benefits Europeans, even as far afield as the South Asian subcontinent and Northeast Asia. Perhaps, also, the 50-year existence of the Atlantic Alliance, coupled with the fact, almost unique in history, that it was not dismantled when its principal purpose was achieved, has led to a natural if unwarranted assumption that one set of common interests necessarily carries over to a second.

This notion holds that modern-day allies, unlike traditional, independent sovereign states acting entirely according to their individual interests, instead form a community of interests that can reliably produce new common analysis and new common action. That result would certainly be unprecedented; indeed, a major part of NATO's reform during the 1990s was directed toward defying the classic history of alliances that had outlived their initial purposes. The United States led in nurturing the proposition that the Atlantic Alliance had an integrity and purpose that did not depend entirely on the Cold War from which it was born. Allies fearing that the United States would reduce or end its military engagement in Europe particularly supported this sentiment. This effort included preserving NATO for its own sake (16 countries jointly defending themselves rather than renationalizing military affairs); emphasizing the completion of the security work of the twentieth century that was listed above; nation building and fostering values as shared strategic interests as well as worthwhile in their own right; retaining an unprecedented and unsurpassed integrated military command structure (Allied Command Europe); and the slow recognition that some interests and challenges exist beyond Europe that could affect everyone sooner or later. The last-named notion was not a ringing endorsement for preserving an alliance, but it was better than nothing.

The United States, meanwhile, pressed its European allies to maintain defense spending at the highest possible level and to develop capabilities that would promote interoperability and power projection. Thus, the United States accepted, in principle and to a great degree in practice, the EU's development of a European Security and Defense Policy (ESDP) in part because that could provide incentives for European states to take defense seriously for the cause of European integration, even if they would not do so for the cause of NATO's continued effectiveness. At the same time, the United States, supported by some key allies, also argued forcefully for NATO's continued primacy. As part of this understanding, the NATO allies agreed that the EU's so-called Headline Goal Task Force (the Rapid Reaction Force) could have direct NATO support to give it any real chance of being militarily effective.[5] Even so, few expected that European capabilities for power projection outside of the NATO framework would amount to much beyond some limited cases such as interventions in Africa, search-and-rescue operations, or extracting civilians from conflicts. In fact, within ESDP, the EU took on military responsibility in the Congo in 2003 and has promoted security in Macedonia; in 2004, it may do the same in Bosnia, where NATO now has lead responsibility.

ESDP is also allied to another important, long-term EU development, the Common Foreign and Security Policy (CFSP). Both are designed, progressively, to give the EU competence in foreign policy and security matters, among the last of the areas of sovereignty that any state is willing to see reduced. Along with ESDP, CFSP has a virtue that is unmatched by NATO because the EU institutions can act seamlessly on a crisis from its inception at the political level through the employment of military force, whereas NATO can only act when requested to do so by member states or the United Nations, often after a crisis has passed the point of nonmilitary resolution.

In a low-key way, the United States also chivvied its European allies to look beyond the continent to regions in which the United States was beginning to see emerging problems. Even so, the general interpretation of Senator Richard Lugar's (R-Ind.) famous 1990s slogan for NATO—"Out of area or out of business"—was of NATO's admitting new members rather than of its militarily engaging beyond Europe. Emblematic of this view, NATO's Partnership for Peace (PFP), whose membership came to include every constituent element of the former Soviet Union, was essentially a U.S. show in terms of resources committed and day-to-day involvement of U.S. personnel in PFP countries. Washington did not make a particular point of asking allies to play similar roles.

Not surprisingly, therefore, in the relative absence of major challenges either to U.S. or to European interests from beyond Europe, much of the intra-alliance debate on issues of European military capabilities and political will to use those capabilities had something of an academic quality. The Europeans made commitments and pledges to increase their defense capabilities, including two rounds of a NATO Defense Capabilities Initiative at the 1999 Washington summit and the 2002 Prague summit, but rarely redeemed these promises[6]; and the WMD issue was placed under the mandate of three separate NATO committees as early as 1994 but largely languished.[7] In effect, the United States and Europe may have valued the continuation of transatlantic military cooperation, the preservation of Allied Command Europe, and the development of contingent capabilities, but hiding behind the intra-allied debate was a lack of clarity about where such capabilities might actually need to be used. Thus, in response to U.S. requests for increased military capacities, the European answer in large part was rhetorically sound but reticent in practice, related less to analysis of what the future could hold than to the felt European need to influence the United States and retain U.S. engagement on the continent. Concomitantly, the Europeans' lagging effort toward creating military capabilities for the future was not a critical matter for the United States. Although the United States continued to press its allies, with the exception of the potential use of allied airpower in Kosovo—within Europe—no particularly compelling case existed where the United States wanted the Europeans to project military power and the Europeans were unable to respond.

The Impact of 9/11

From September 11, 2001, onward, different perspectives between the United States and most of its European allies regarding instruments of power and power projection beyond Europe gained a more tangible quality. The United States knew and the Europeans understood that the tragic attacks demanded a military response and that the United States alone had to define precisely where and what that would mean as well as take full command of operations. Purely on European and Canadian initiative, without being asked to do so by Washington, the alliance took the unprecedented step of invoking Article 5 of the 1949 North Atlantic Treaty.[8] Although many Europeans later expressed regret that the United States preferred to conduct military operations in Afghanistan through a U.S.-led coalition of the willing and able, rather than through the NATO military command, they understood what the United States had to do. Indeed, much of the later regret was based on the European concern that a U.S. vision of Europe's military backwardness would negatively impact Europe's influence in Washington and future U.S willingness to take NATO seriously.

Most importantly, so far in the U.S. global war on terrorism, no fundamental fault lines have developed between the two sides of the Atlantic in terms of the use of power and other instruments for combating terrorism in its immediate expression (distinct, for example, from debates about what constitutes international terrorism or about the relative emphasis that should be placed on different elements of counterterrorism activity, such as trying to prevent terrorism's development and emergence as opposed to targeting its practitioners and supporters). Europe has fully supported the U.S. use of military power, particularly but not exclusively in Afghanistan where in fact NATO formally assumed command of the International Security Assistance Force in August 2003.[9] Individual allies, the EU, and other institutions have contributed greatly to countering international terrorism in a wide range of areas, including intelligence, police work, border control, financial assets blocking, and a host of other activities that can be at least as important as direct military action and on which the success of military action depends.[10] Some allies have also provided fighting forces, notably special forces of the United Kingdom, France, Denmark, Germany, and Turkey in Afghanistan.[11]

Thus, allies do not diverge from the United States on the application of these elements of power, and the Europeans have capabilities—plus the locus of a number of counterterrorism efforts on European soil—of great and immediate benefit to the United States. The United States has appropriately acknowledged that contribution. Therefore, in helping to meet the most important current threat to U.S. security, the European allies have the capacity to be of direct value, they have been willing to use those capacities, and the United States depends in significant part on European actions. Of course, this is not just European willingness to support U.S. needs—putting power and influence at U.S. disposal. Although some assessments of the nature and extent of the challenge from international terrorism differ between most European countries and the United States—and every European state believes that major progress in settling the Israeli-Palestinian conflict is crucial in limiting terrorists' appeal in the Arab and Islamic worlds—few in Europe can rule out their own vulnerability or the need to take at least prophylactic steps to counter terrorism.

On to Iraq

Despite a significant degree of transatlantic understanding on practical and short- to medium-term steps to counter international terrorism, especially that emanating from the Europe-proximate Middle East, the same cannot be said to exist regarding the U.S. view of Iraq during the past two years; the arguments for the war in Iraq and the conduct of the postwar period; and overall issues related to WMD. Differences of view do not necessarily pit the United States on the one hand versus all European allies on the other; a variety of assessments and viewpoints can be found within countries on both sides of the Atlantic. Much has been written about these differences and need not be rehearsed here. For purposes of this discussion, important questions can be limited to a focus on instruments of and attitudes toward power and influence in terms of (1) what Europe can and will do; (2) how that response relates to U.S. expectations, thus either influencing or failing to influence U.S. views of the place, power, role, and potential of European countries and Europe as a whole; (3) how the United States should judge the future European role in terms of these criteria; and (4) how the United States should view the future in general in terms of instruments, processes, countries, and institutions needed to secure its national interests.

Unlike the conflict in Afghanistan, as part of the war on terrorism, most European allies were not able, much less willing, to contribute to the anti-Saddam military effort as defined by the United States. With some notable exceptions, most prominently the United Kingdom,[12] a number of leading European countries and much of public opinion diverged from the United States in terms of what should be done, why it should be done, when it should be done, and who could as well as would take part under U.S. leadership and command. This divergence deeply affected U.S. views of European power and influence in terms of subjective assessments and objective capacities, regardless of whether European countries would employ those capacities. Further, this disagreement created a two-part problem, both parts of which are important but the nonmilitary one more so than the military because, at least in combat, the United States has less need for allies than it has in either pre-combat diplomacy or providing security and other forms of support after combat is over.

This last point is of particular concern in regard to the European role within NATO and the projection of military power to places such as the greater Middle East. Experience in Afghanistan and Iraq argues against trying to get European states to spend more money on defense for its own sake and, except for a few more advanced militaries, against emphasizing high-technology weapons capabilities (advanced tactical aircraft, precision-guided munitions), and in favor of convincing allies to create other military capacities that are also important to common action and potentially a useful supplement to U.S. action outside the framework of the alliance. These capacities must focus not only on integration of forces across the battlefield (emphasizing C^4ISR, or command, control, communications, computers, intelligence, surveillance, and reconnaissance) but also on special forces, peacekeeping units, strategic and tactical airlift and sealift, other steps needed to increase force deployability, and the full range of paramilitary activities that have proved so important in every venture from Bosnia through Iraq—activities at which several European countries excel.

These possibilities have played a major role in NATO's formation of a new NATO Response Force (NRF). It is the complement to the EU's rapid reaction force and is designed "to be a robust, high readiness, fully trained and certified force that is prepared to tackle the full spectrum of missions, including force."[13] Among other things, it can be a vehicle for European allies to provide what capabilities they can to joint military operations relevant to twenty-first-century challenges and deployable beyond Europe. The NRF can be the nucleus of increased European defense efforts, a renewed military partnership with the United States, and perhaps even the core of NATO's capabilities in the future.[14] Of key significance are the NRF's practical rather than theoretical approach to European military contributions to the alliance, the maintenance of integrated military efforts by a number of allies, and the creation of a force that can actually act militarily in useful and effective ways, however limited, at least at first. Although unlikely to blunt U.S. criticism of European defense efforts at least in its early days, the NRF is a start;[15] it is also a start on Europeans regaining some limited influence over the U.S. approach to the use of force.

Seeking a Role for European Power and Ceding Some Influence

At least in theory, the United States could provide all of these military capabilities on its own, developing and deploying those it currently lacks, without recourse to allies. Of course, the United States would be considerably constrained if particular European allies actively opposed a U.S. military action that required transiting Europe to get there (i.e., almost anywhere in the greater Middle East). That did not happen during the Iraq war.[16] Whatever any European state might have felt about that war, once it began, none could wish the United States to fail, just as none can wish the United States to fail in Iraq in the conflict's aftermath. All Europeans still depend on U.S. effectiveness, leadership, and commitment to Europe, which could be eroded if there were active efforts to impede the U.S. pursuit of its critical interests. Moreover, in regard to the greater Middle East, there is a common understanding that all Western states are in the same boat together in the end. It is in part for this reason that the

European Council has begun debate on a set of far-reaching concepts, dubbed the "Solana Report" for its author, CFSP High Representative Javier Solana, that goes a fair distance in meeting U.S. concerns regarding European attitudes about threats and responses to them.[17]

The United States could also foot the bill for the conflict and aftermath by itself, without serious impact on the management of the U.S. economy or even the alternative potential uses of moneys spent on Iraq. Such a U.S. go-it-alone approach could thus depreciate the importance of any European role in securing U.S. national interests. Nevertheless, four primary reasons exist for the United States to reject this reasoning, instead looking to allies to deploy niche capabilities in Afghanistan and Iraq; to provide military, paramilitary, and police forces for peacekeeping duties; to help provide logistical support for others' military efforts; and to engage directly and financially in nation building.

The first reason is instrumental: a division of labor can save the United States resources, so long as confidence is high that so-called niche capabilities provided by allies are either not critical to the United States or will be provided in any likely scenario. Furthermore, in some circumstances, as in postwar Iraq, both the United States and the United Kingdom (the latter as a former colonial nation) would benefit from decreasing their profiles and increasing the visible presence of personnel from other nations, both European and—especially—the non-Western and Islamic.[18]

The second reason is alliance-political: to do what is possible to keep differing transatlantic perspectives of what is important in terms of national and alliance-wide security from further diverging. In this regard, preparing for joint military action can sometimes be as important as actually fighting together. That was certainly true in the conflict-free Cold War in Europe, and it is far from clear how many more wars, if any, like that in Iraq in 2003 there will be to fight in the foreseeable future, even in the U.S. estimation.

The third reason for the United States not to go it alone where it can gain the support of allies is that the greater the cooperation, the greater the chances of minimizing other problems across the Atlantic. This is about preserving the Atlantic Alliance not just for its own sake but also for the sake of continuing to promote a broader community of interests and values, not least in economic and other nonmilitary areas. This view also has strong resonance in Europe; thus, Poland assumed command of the Multinational Division Central South in Iraq in September 2003, and NATO actively supported it,[19] while some allied forces, notably French, continue to serve with U.S. fighting units in Afghanistan.

The fourth and most important reason is domestic-political within the United States. Although most Americans continue to be willing to pay a significant price to secure national interests and values in wartime, public and congressional opinion are reluctant to pay heavy costs, in either U.S. blood or treasure, following the end of formal hostilities. They certainly are not comfortable with the impression that the United States is bearing burdens without the support of the European allies. Naturally, therefore, following an initial period of trying largely to go it alone, the United States has begun turning to allies and others for postwar support in Iraq. Also naturally, several allies and other states have conditioned that support on U.S. willingness to share perspectives and decisions, as well as costs and responsibilities, concerning what happens in Iraq as well as, for some European allies, concerning what the United States might do elsewhere, especially in the Middle East, for example, regarding Iran and the Israeli-Palestinian conflict.

In short, allies are prepared to trade needed support for influence or, put differently, to trade something that the United States needs, even if largely for domestic political reasons, for U.S. recognition and appreciation of European power to shape events and to help decide how and where this is done. That is clearly in the common interest.

Beyond Military Power

Events surrounding the war on terrorism, the defeat of Iraq, efforts to stop the spread of WMD, and the congeries of new U.S. responsibilities for rebuilding a system of security, economics, and politics in the greater Middle East—responsibilities perhaps to be shared with other states—should be leading to a reassessment of the critical elements in the realm of power: what is it that the United States and, in this case, its European allies need to be able to do to influence events in the Middle East and elsewhere to their liking, especially in a rapidly globalizing world? What do they need in order to shape the future, rather than just respond to it?[20]

Further, what forms of European power are relevant within this context, for European ends and as judged important by the United States in the pursuit of its own national objectives? Discussed above have been the roles of European economic power and influence, European actions to stabilize and transform emerging democracies in the former Warsaw Pact, European active engagement in the war on terrorism, European military efforts in the Balkans and as far afield as postwar Afghanistan, and European niche and other military capabilities and willingness to deploy them, including the dispatch of the Polish multinational division in Iraq.

Yet, European countries and the EU can and will act in other ways that can significantly shape events and in some cases reduce the likelihood of conflict or other threats to Western security interests. Terminology used in discussion and debate of these matters, such as "hard" versus "soft" power, is often fuzzy and imprecise, especially as between diplomacy and force and as between military and nonmilitary instruments. Analysts and commentators often rate military force as most significant, without reference to what outcome is desired, simply because it is widely believed to be most clearly decisive. Yet, shaping the future and building security can depend as much on what is done effectively in advance of situations emerging that could then require more robust capabilities and intense action, especially the use of military force. Of course, this proposition is nothing new, nor is the aphorism that recourse to war in the absence of outright aggression by one or another party usually reflects failure to use nonmilitary instruments and methods effectively beforehand.

At the same time, to borrow a term in vogue in strategic analysis—the notion that certain military capabilities can become "force multipliers"—European nonmilitary, crisis-shaping capacities and the willingness to use them can become "influence multipliers" in relations with the United States.

Whether timely U.S. and European joint efforts can forestall the emergence of key challenges to Western security interests, including international terrorism and the spread of WMD, is of course now being deeply debated. Debates about preventing terrorism, for example, turn on complex questions, such as whether changing conditions in societies that produce terrorists or at least the political and personal support for terrorism, can help to dry up the sea within which the terrorist fish swim.[21] For his part, U.S. president George W. Bush has said, "We fight against poverty because hope is an answer to terror."[22]

More generally, Western security, as broadly understood, faces a wide range of actual and potential challenges where nonmilitary instruments are important. Preventing communicable diseases from coming to a nation's shores, especially in a world of easy and frequent travel, is one such case; less well understood is the value of promoting health in countries where its absence can help produce conflict, support for terrorism, and social and economic breakdown—potential security as well as humanitarian concerns that can operate beyond the borders of the immediately affected country or region. Health is not alone; the full range of issues that cluster under the rubrics of development and environment, broadly understood, are part of this canon.

Strategic Partnership to Shape the Future

These points may seem far afield from the original discussion of what power and influence Europe can wield, how Europe relates to the United States, and how seriously the United States should take Europe, but they are not. Indeed, the greatest potential for agreement and reinforcement of action in the transatlantic world falls in the area of advance effort, of trying to prevent the emergence of threats in common to the United States and Europe. The United States and the European states should be looking for means to augment traditional political-military security cooperation, that is, the mutual harnessing and rationalizing to common ends of the military power on the two sides of the Atlantic, primarily through NATO. Even though that cooperation continues to be important to both sides, they should also be looking for ways to build on the obvious and ineluctable intertwining of their respective economies, shared leadership of the global economy, and interests and capabilities in a wide range of third areas, especially health, education, development, promotion of human rights, democracy, and the rule of law as well as other aspects of society, nation, and institution building.

One such means should be the creation of a strategic partnership between the United States and the EU, in league with the NATO alliance partnership, reflecting a wide range of shared goals, similar threats and challenges, and complementary means to meet them. This U.S.-EU strategic partnership would not primarily be about military relations, left largely to NATO, but rather about marshalling the economic strength, talents, leadership, and commitments that are common to all these nations, to a greater degree than any other set of nations, for purposes of working together on critical elements of a twenty-first-century agenda, as introduced above, that must be pursued even to deal with more exigent matters such as the threat of terrorism.

Such a scenario for U.S.-European engagement would harness each side's capabilities to produce effects that neither can produce alone, even to promote its own national security. It also looks very much like the pattern of U.S.-European relations during the past half century, which included a heavy reliance on working with others, forging and fostering international institutions, and promoting the rule of law—old lessons being learned all over again, not out of textbooks but from hard, practical experience. Given that events have once again demonstrated that neither the United States nor the European states can achieve their national goals alone—or at least that each will better be able to do so in cooperation with, rather than opposition to or abstention from, the other—and given the wide range of areas in which the two sides are ineluctably interdependent, moving in a cooperative direction is the course of wisdom for the twenty-first century, just as it was in the latter half of the twentieth century.

Turning U.S. Incipient Power into Lasting Influence

As argued above, the United States emerged from the Cold War with more incipient power than any other nation or empire since the collapse of the Roman Empire. Yet, even a decade ago it was also clear to many observers—and it becomes ever more clear with each passing month—

that the emphasis has to be on the word incipient and that the core task for the United States in the years ahead is to turn this incipient power into lasting influence. The method for doing so was evident from 1945 until the end of the Cold War and it is becoming clear again: the United States can only make this critical transition of power to influence by once again building institutions, attitudes, policies, and practices that can fulfill U.S. interests precisely because they also meet the interests of other countries and peoples. This insight, which should in fact be self-evident, is only now beginning to be relearned, and it must still be fully adapted to the post–September 11, post-Iraq era. It very much validates the proposition that Europe—its people, power, influence, and institutions—matters decisively not just to the prosecution of European interests and values but also to those of the United States and of other peoples and societies across the inevitably globalizing world.

Notes

1. Robert E. Hunter, "Global Economics and Unsteady Regional Geopolitics," in Richard L. Kugler and Ellen L. Frost (eds.), *The Global Century: Globalization and National Security* (Washington, D.C.: National Defense University, 2001), www.ndu.edu/inss/books/books%20-%202001/Global%20Century%20-%20June%202001/JDSChap4Hunter(ri)FinalCr.htm (accessed October 29, 2003).

2. See Robert E. Hunter, "Maximizing NATO: A Relevant Alliance Knows How to Reach," *Foreign Affairs* 78, no. 3 (May/June 1999), www.foreignaffairs.org/19990501faessay1037/robert-e-hunter/nato-at-fifty-maximizing-nato-a-relevant-alliance-knows-how-to-reach.html (accessed October 10, 2003).

3. "Alliance security must also take account of the global context. Alliance security interests can be affected by other risks of a wider nature, including acts of terrorism, sabotage and organised crime, and by the disruption of the flow of vital resources." "The Alliance's Strategic Concept," NATO Press Release NAC-S(99)65, April 24, 1999, www.nato.int/docu/pr/1999/p99-065e.htm (accessed October 10, 2003).

4. For further information on the significant migration of Muslims into Europe, see Shireen T. Hunter, ed., *Islam: Europe's Second Religion* (New York: Praeger, 2002).

5. See Robert E. Hunter, *European Security and Defense Policy: NATO's Companion—or Competitor?* (Washington, D.C.: RAND, 2002), www.rand.org/publications/MR/MR1463/ (accessed October 6, 2003).

6. "Defence Capabilities Initiative," NATO Press Release NAC-S(99)69, April 25, 1999, www.nato.int/docu/pr/1999/p99s069e.htm (accessed October 12, 2003); "Prague Capabilities Commitment—individual Allies have made firm and specific political commitments to improve their capabilities in areas key to modern military operations, such as strategic air and sea lift and air-to-ground surveillance." "NATO Transformed: New Members, Capabilities, and Partnerships," *NATO Update*, November 21, 2002, www.nato.int/docu/update/2002/11-november/e1121e.htm (accessed October 12, 2003).

7. The Senior Politico-Military Group on Proliferation (SGP) and the NATO Senior Defence Group on Proliferation (DGP), under the authority of the Joint Committee on Proliferation (CJP). See Crispin Hain-Cole, "The Summit Initiative on Weapons of Mass Destruction: Rationale and Aims," *NATO Review* 47, no. 2 (summer 1999): 33–34, www.nato.int/docu/review/1999/9902-08.htm (accessed October 10, 2003).

8. "The Parties agree that an armed attack against one or more of them in Europe or North America shall be considered an attack against them all and ... will assist the Party or Parties so attacked by taking forthwith ... such action as it deems necessary, including the use of armed force." "North Atlantic Treaty," April 4, 1949, www.nato.int/docu/basictxt/treaty.htm (accessed October 12, 2003). Note that this act is still discretionary, thus emphasizing the political significance of invoking this provision.

9. Although little noted, before NATO assumed command of the International Security Assistance Force (ISAF), the United Kingdom and Turkey, as well as Germany and the Netherlands in joint cooperation, had in turn exercised command of ISAF.

10. "European Union Steps Up Fight Against Terrorism," European Union News Releases No. 67/01, September 20, 2001, www.eurunion.org/news/press/2001/2001067.htm (accessed October 10, 2003).

11. "Operation Enduring Freedom—Order of Battle," www.globalsecurity.org/military/ops/enduring-freedom_orbat-01.htm (accessed October 10, 2003).

12. Other NATO countries formally supporting U.S. policy on the war in Iraq were Spain, Portugal, Italy, Hungary, Poland, Denmark, and the Czech Republic. Also, the so-called Vilnius 10 group of central European states agreed to a common declaration of support for U.S. policy. See "Eight European Leaders Support Disarming of Iraq," January 30, 2003, www.useu.be/Categories/GlobalAffairs/Iraq/Jan3003EuropeLetterIraq.html (accessed October 10, 2003). See also Quentin Peel et al., "The Plot That Split Old and New Europe," *Financial Times*, May 27, 2003, www.globalpolicy.org/security/issues/iraq/attack/2003/0527plot.htm (accessed October 10, 2003).

13. "NATO Response Force—NRF," www.nato.int/shape/issues/shape_nrf/nrf_intro.htm (accessed October 10, 2003).

14. The NRF was formally "stood up"—became active—on October 15, 2003. It

could be the vehicle for any alliance-agreed, NATO-wide engagement in Iraq peacekeeping. It could also serve as the framework for a NATO peace-enabling force in support of an Israeli-Palestinian peace agreement. In time, an augmented NRF could become the key institution for organizing and projecting NATO military power, perhaps becoming the dominant element of the integrated military command structure. See Robert E. Hunter, "The Perfect Army for Iraq: NATO," *New York Times*, September 13, 2003.

15. Notably, French forces are playing a leading role in the NRF.

16. Only Turkey and Austria, for different reasons, refused the use of their air space to coalition overflights.

17. See "Draft European Security Strategy Presented by the EU High Representative for the Common Foreign and Security Policy, Javier Solana, to the European Council, 20 June 2003 in Thessaloniki, Greece," *Internationale Politik* 4, no. 3 (autumn 2003), www.dgap.org/english/tip/tip0303/solana200603.htm (accessed October 10, 2003).

18. This was a principal strategy of U.S. president George H. W. Bush during Operation Desert Storm in 1991.

19. On June 2, the North Atlantic Council agreed to a request from the Polish [r]epresentative to support Poland in the context of its leadership of a sector in Iraq. That NATO support has consisted of providing intelligence, logistics expertise, movement coordination, force generation, and secure communications support. … Several NATO and [p]artner countries are among the nations contributing to the Polish-led multinational division. Spain provides a substantial presence and the [d]eputy [c]ommander, while Ukraine is the second[-]largest force contributor. Other [a]llied and [p]artner contributors include Bulgaria, Denmark, Hungary, Latvia, Lithuania, Kazakhstan, [t]he Netherlands, Norway, Romania, Slovakia and the United States.

"Poland Assumes Command of Multinational Division in Iraq With NATO Support," NATO Press Release (2003)93, September 3, 2003, www.nato.int/docu/pr/2003/p03-093e.htm (accessed October 12, 2003).

20. This concept was a central component of U.S. military strategy from 1995 until 2002: "Shape, prepare, respond." Jim Garamone, "Capabilities, Strategy Must Converge to Face New Threats," American Forces Information Service, June 22, 2001, www.defenselink.mil/news/Jun2001/n06222001_200106221.html (accessed October 10, 2003).

21. "The people may be likened to water, and guerrillas to the fish that swim in it." Mao Tse-Tung, *On Guerrilla Warfare* (1937), www.bellum.nu/wp/mtt/mttogw.html (accessed October 10, 2003).

22. Office of the Press Secretary, The White House, "President Outlines U.S. Plan to Help World's Poor," March 22, 2002, www.whitehouse.gov/news/releases/2002/03/20020322-1.html (accessed October 6, 2003).

Timothy M. Savage

Europe and Islam: Crescent Waxing, Cultures Clashing

As it has historically, the world of Islam may do more to define and shape Europe in the twenty-first century than the United States, Russia, or even the European Union.[1] The Islamic challenge that Europe faces today is twofold. Internally, Europe must integrate a ghettoized but rapidly growing Muslim minority that many Europeans view as encroaching upon the collective identity and public values of European society. Externally, Europe needs to devise a viable approach to the primarily Muslim-populated volatile states, stretching from Casablanca to the Caucasus, that are a central focus of the EU's recently adopted security strategy "A Secure Europe in a Better World"[2] and its nascent "Wider Europe— New Neighborhood" initiative. Recognizing that "the Union's capacity to provide security, stability, and sustainable development to its citizens will no longer be distinguishable from its interest in close cooperation with the neighbors," the New Neighborhood initiative seeks to define a new framework for relations with 14 states or entities—Algeria, Egypt, Israel, Jordan, Lebanon, Libya, Morocco, the Palestinian Authority, Syria, Tunisia, Ukraine, Moldova, Belarus, and Russia—and their 385 million

---

Timothy M. Savage is a career U.S. foreign service officer, currently serving as a division chief in the Office of European Analysis at the Department of State in Washington, D.C. He recently served as U.S. consul general in Leipzig, Germany. The views and opinions in this article are those of the author alone and do not necessarily represent those of the State Department.

Copyright © 2004 by The Center for Strategic and International Studies and the Massachusetts Institute of Technology
The Washington Quarterly • 27:3 pp. 25–50.

inhabitants now along the EU's eastern and southern borders following its May 1 enlargement.[3] The Muslim factor is adding contours to Europe's domestic and foreign policy landscape in more than just demographic and geographical terms. The European-Islamic nexus is spinning off a variety of new phenomena, including the rise of terrorism; the emergence of a new anti-Semitism; the shift of established European political parties to the right; the recalibration of European national political calculations; additional complications for achieving an ever closer EU; and a refocusing, if not a reformulation, of European foreign policy.

Novel and dynamic but still inchoate, Europe's reencounter with Islam in both its domestic and foreign dimensions offers a range of opportunities for positive change in the world. Yet, Europe's track record of engagement with Islam over the last 1,350 years is not encouraging. Although exploring some new initiatives, Europeans today seem inclined to pursue a status quo approach at home and abroad, preferring caution, predictability, control, and established structures over the boldness, adaptability, engagement, and redefined relationships that the new situation requires. A similar mind-set is evident among Europe's Muslim population.

If accommodation is not reached, current dynamics will likely yield a Europe that not only faces increased social strife, national retrenchment, and even civil conflict domestically but also could well succumb to a "Fortress Europe" posture and decline on the international stage. The situation has not deteriorated to this point yet, but the tipping point[4] may be closer than is generally realized.

Demographic Dynamics

Few European states have gathered comprehensive data on the number and nature of the Muslim presence within their national borders. A number of states in Europe, notably Belgium, Denmark, France, Greece, Hungary, Italy, Luxembourg, and Spain, actually bar questions on religion in censuses and other official questionnaires, as does the United States. Thirteen countries still do not recognize Islam as a religion, even though it is at least the second-largest religion in 16 of 37 European countries (including the Baltic states but not including the other former Soviet republics or Turkey). In many countries, Muslims are an unrecognized minority, excluded from most minority rights safeguards and protection against discrimination because they do not fit national definitions of minorities that are based primarily on ethnic and racial criteria.

More than 23 million Muslims reside in Europe, comprising nearly 5 percent of the population, according to data compiled in the U.S. Department of State's *Annual Report on International Religious Freedom 2003* (see table 1). This number is significantly larger than the estimated 13–18 million typically cited by the media or in academic studies, which are based on dated and often incomplete information. When Turkey is included, the figures balloon to 90 million and 15 percent, respectively. More important than the current numbers, however, is the trend that is emerging. The Muslim population more than doubled in the last three decades, and the rate of growth is accelerating.

Most European countries closed their doors to labor immigration in the 1970s, following the first Arab oil embargo and the subsequent economic downturn, yet some 500,000 immigrants—primarily family reunification cases—and 400,000 asylum seekers arrive in western Europe

Table I: Muslims in Europe

Country Grouping	Number of Muslims[1]		Percent of Total Population[1]	
	1982	2003	1982	2003
EU-15	6.8 mil.	15.2 mil.	1.9	4.0
New EU Members	208,000	290,000	0.4	0.4
EU-15 plus New EU Members	7.0 mil.	15.5 mil.	1.6	3.4
Other European States (incl. Turkey)	56.0 mil.	74.8 mil.	50.0	56.0
Other European States (not Turkey)	8.8 mil.	7.7 mil.	14.0	10.0
All European States (incl. Turkey)	62.9 mil.	90.3 mil.	11.6	15.0
All European States (not incl. Turkey)	15.6 mil.	23.2 mil.	3.2	4.5

Note:

1. Current numbers from U.S. Department of State, *Annual Report on International Religious Freedom 2003*; 1982 estimates in brackets for comparison, from M. Ali Kettani, *Muslim Minorities in the World Today* (London: Mansell Publishing Ltd., 1986).

each year. According to the International Organization for Migration, Muslims make up a large and increasing proportion of both groups, coming primarily from Algeria, Morocco, Turkey, and the former Yugoslavia.[5] Muslims probably also make up a significant proportion of western Europe's illegal immigrants (between 120,000 and 500,000 enter the EU annually).[6] Indeed, in a number of European countries, the words "Muslim" and "immigrant" are virtually synonymous.

Currently, the waves of immigrants and asylum seekers from the Middle East and North Africa (MENA)—the region with the world's second-highest fertility rate—have had more to do with the worsening conditions in the MENA countries than with labor shortages in Europe, the region with the world's lowest fertility rate. As the MENA population doubles in the next three decades and Europe's shrinks, increased migratory flows from south to north appear unavoidable—a trend augmented by Europe's graying population, as opposed to the youthful MENA average. In 2000 the UN projected that, to counterbalance their increasingly graying populations, EU states annually would need 949,000 migrants to maintain their 1995 populations; 1,588,000 migrants to maintain their 1995 working-age populations; or 13,480,000 migrants to maintain their population support ratios (the ratio of people aged 15–64 to those aged 65 and older).[7] Furthermore, rather than help alleviate the problem, the demographics of the 10 new EU member states increase these gaps. Whichever goal is pursued, most of these individuals will be Muslims.

Today, approximately 50 percent of Muslims in western Europe were born there.[8] More importantly, the Muslim birth rate in Europe is currently more than three times that of non-Muslims, contributing to the burgeoning numbers of Muslims in Europe.[9] As a result, Muslim communities in Europe are significantly younger than the non-Muslim population, and Europe's "Generation X" and "Millennium Generation" include considerably more Muslims than does the continent's population as a whole.[10] One-third of France's five million Muslims are under the age of 20 (compared to 21 percent of the French population as a whole); one-third of Germany's four million Muslims are under 18 (compared to 18 percent of the German population as a whole); one-third of the United Kingdom's 1.6 million Muslims are under 15 (compared to 20 percent of the British population as a whole); and one-third of Belgium's 364,000 Muslims are under 15 (compared to 18 percent of the country's population as a whole).[11]

To date, conversion to Islam has been a minor factor in the increased Muslim presence in Europe, making up less than 1 percent of all Muslims in Europe. From this low base, however, conversions could develop as a new and potentially significant source not only of the growth of the Muslim presence in Europe but also of its voice and visibility, particularly if Islam gains official recognition, becomes more established and institutionalized in Europe, and enters a proselytizing phase.

By 2015, Europe's Muslim population is expected to double, whereas Europe's non-Muslim population is projected to fall by at least 3.5 percent.[12] Looking further ahead, conservative projections estimate that, compared to today's 5 percent, Muslims will comprise at least 20 percent of Europe's population by 2050. Some even predict that one-fourth of France's population could be Muslim by 2025 and that, if trends continue, Muslims could outnumber non-Muslims in France and perhaps in all of western Europe by mid-century.[13] Although these projections seem incredible at first glance, they may not be far off the mark. At present, more than 15 percent of the 16–25-year-old cohort in France is Muslim; in Brussels, 25 percent of the population under the age of 25 is Muslim. A factor in this equation that is as important as the dramatic increase in the Muslim population is the dramatic decline of the general European population, which, according to UN projections, will drop by more than 100 million from 728 million in 2000 to approximately 600 million, and possibly as low as 565 million, by 2050.[14]

GHETTOIZATION

The growing Muslim presence in Europe has tended to cluster geographically within individual states, particularly in industrialized, urban areas within clearly defined, if not self-encapsulated, poorer neighborhoods such as Berlin's Kreuzberg district, London's Tower Hamlets, and the *banlieues* (suburbs) of major French cities, further augmenting its visibility and impact yet circumscribing day-to-day contact with the general population. Two-fifths of Muslims in the United Kingdom reside in the greater London area; one-third of Muslims in France live in or around Paris; and one-third of Muslims in Germany are concentrated in the Ruhr industrial area.[15] Muslims now constitute more than 25 percent of the population of Marseille; 20 percent of Malmo, Sweden; 15 percent of Brussels and Birmingham, as well as Paris; and 10 percent or more of London, Amsterdam, Rotterdam, The Hague, Oslo, and Copenhagen.[16]

The recent increase in Europe's Muslim population has occurred primarily in western Europe. In the decade following the fall of the Berlin Wall, the western European Muslim presence grew at a pace nearly six times faster than that in North America. Austria, Denmark, the Netherlands, Norway, and Sweden were among the states with the most dramatic immigration and asylum-driven Muslim growth in Europe in the 1990s. In the rest of this decade, Spain, Italy, and perhaps Greece—west European states with the lowest fertility rates, the oldest populations, the most porous borders, the closest proximity to countries of migration, and the highest number of illegal residents—appear destined to experience comparable increases in their Muslim populations.

The indigenous Muslim populations in southeastern Europe, by contrast, have declined by some 15 percent during the last 20 years as a result of, among other things, Turkish emigration from Bulgaria, Albanian immigration to Italy and Greece, and emigration and deaths caused by the Balkan wars. In central and eastern Europe, Muslim populations remain virtually nonexistent.

IDENTITY

The nature of the Muslim presence in Europe is also changing. No longer "temporary guest workers," Muslims are now a permanent part of western European national landscapes, as they have been for centuries in southeastern Europe. The institutionalization of Islam in Europe has begun, as has a "re-Islamization" of Muslims in Europe.

To talk of a single Muslim community in Europe, however, is misleading. Even within individual countries, ethnic diversity, sectarian differences, cleavages within communities arising from sociopolitical and generational splits, and the nonhierarchical nature of Islam itself mean that Europe's Muslims will be more divided than united for decades to come. Like European Christians and Jews, European Muslims are not a monolithic group. Nonetheless, Muslims increasingly identify first with Islam rather than with either their family's country of origin or the European country in which they now reside.[17] Moreover, this phenomenon is significantly more pronounced among younger Muslims.

Some ethnic barriers between Muslims are beginning to lose their significance, again especially among the young, in part also because of an emerging cohort of religious leaders who are not financed or sponsored by individual Muslim states, who use the vernacular, and who address the concerns of young European Muslims. The current generation is also modernizing and acculturating to aspects of contemporary European society at a faster rate than the first waves of Muslim immigrants did. Younger Muslims are adopting attributes of the European societies in which they were born and raised, such as language; socialization through schooling; and, in many cases, some of the secular perspectives of the country in which they reside. Yet, generally they do not feel part of the larger society nor that they have a stake in it. Conversely, even though they may be third-generation citizens, they often are not viewed as fellow citizens by the general public but are still identified as foreigners and immigrants instead.

Nevertheless, the proportion of Muslims holding European citizenship is increasing. With more Muslims being born in western Europe and with recently eased naturalization procedures in many countries, particularly in Germany, this trend will accelerate. More than three-fifths of Muslims in France and the United Kingdom are already citizens of those countries. In Germany, the proportion is only 15–20 percent; of the remainder, 11 percent have applied for citizenship and a further 48 percent plan to do so, according to a survey conducted by the Konrad Adenauer Foundation in 2001.[18] These figures indicate that Germany could soon have up to 2.4 million new citizens and, significantly, potential voters. A similar surge can be expected at some point from the approximately one million Muslims currently living in Italy, where less than 10 percent have Italian citizenship. The same is true for Spain and its estimated one million Muslims. In Scandinavia, where naturalization is generally obtainable after five years of residency, the percentage of Muslims who have citizenship can be expected to increase significantly in the near future from the current 15–30 percent levels (see table 2).

Table 2: Muslims in the EU-I5

Islam		Total No. of Muslims[2] [1982 est.]	% of Population[2] [1982 est.]	Muslim Citizenship		Muslims' Ethnicity/ Country of Origin
Recognized?	Rank[1]			%	No.	(% of Muslims[3])
Austria Yes (1979)	3rd	338,988 [80,000]	4.2 [1.1]	28	96,052	Turkey (50) Bosnia (25) Kosovo (10)
Belgium Yes (1974)	2nd	364,000 [350,000]	3.5 [3.6]	NK[4]	NK	Morocco (55) Turkey (33)
Denmark No	2nd	162,000 [35,000]	3.0 [0.7]	11	18,000	Turkey (27) Yugoslav (22) Lebanon (11) Pakistan (10)
Finland Yes (1980s)	4th	20,000	0.4	NK	NK	Somalia (23) Yugoslav (20) Iraq (17) Iran (11)
France Yes (2002)	2nd	5 mil. [2.5 mil.]	8.3 [4.6]	60	3 mil.	Algeria (30) Morocco (20) Turkey (10)
Germany No	4 mil. 3rd	4.9 [1.8 mil.]	15 [2.9]		500,000	Turkey (68) Yugoslav
Greece Yes (1923)	2nd	450,000 [160,000]	4.1 [1.6]	22	100,000	Turkish (50) Pomak (25) Romani (15)
Ireland No	3rd	19,147	0.5	NK	NK	
Italy No	2nd	1 mil. [120,000]	1.8 [0.2]	7	70,000	Morocco (34) Albania (27) Tunisia (10)
Luxembourg No	3rd	6,000	1.4	NK	NK	Montenegro (25)
Netherlands Yes (1988)	3rd	886,000 [400,000]	5.5 [2.8]	50	450,000	Turkey (40) Morocco (34)
Portugal Yes (1976)	2nd	35,000	0.4	NK	NK	Mozambique Guinea
Spain Yes (1992)	2nd	1 mil. [120,000]	2.4 [0.3]	NK	NK	Morocco
Sweden Yes (1979)	2nd	350,000 [30,000]	3.9 [0.3]	15– 30	50,000– 100,000	Yugoslav (25) Iran (14) Iraq (14) Turkey (13) Bosnia (13)
UK No	3rd	1.6 mil. [1.25 mil.]	2.7 [2.2]	60	1 mil.	Pakistan (45) India (19) Bangladesh (13–16)
Total		15.2 mil. [6.8 mil.]	4.0 [1.9]			

Notes: (1) Rank among the five major religions: Catholic, Islamic, Jewish, Orthodox, and Protestant. (2) Current numbers from U.S. Department of State, *Annual Report on International Religious Freedom 2003*; 1982 estimates in brackets for comparison, from M. Ali Kettani, *Muslim Minorities in the World Today* (London: Mansell Publishing Ltd., 1986). (3) Data provided for groups greater than 10 percent; percentages provided where known. (4) NK = not known.

Despite these trends in citizenship, younger Muslims are resisting assimilation into secular European societies even more steadfastly than the older generation did. Europe's Muslims, including the younger generation, are willing to integrate and respect national norms and institutions as long as they can, at the same time, maintain their distinct Islamic identity and practices. They fear that assimilation, that is, total immersion into European society, will strip them of this identity. Yet, this is the price many Muslims increasingly see European governments and publics demanding: to have Europe become a melting pot without accommodation by or modifications of the existing culture. Studies in France and Germany find that second- and particularly third-generation Muslims are less integrated into European societies than their parents or grandparents were.[19] The recent headscarf affairs in France and Germany underscore and further exacerbate this basic clash.

Perceived discrimination in European societies affecting employment, education, housing, and religious practices is compelling many second- and third-generation Muslims to embrace Islam as their badge of identity. Indeed, the unemployment rate among Muslims is generally double that of non-Muslims, and it is worse than that of non-Muslim immigrants. Educational achievement and skill levels are relatively low, participation by Muslim women in the workforce is minimal, opportunities for advancement are limited, and biases against Muslims are strong. Such factors contribute to the isolation—and self-encapsulation—of Muslim communities in Europe. Thus, it is not surprising that a survey conducted in France, for example, revealed that Muslim identification with Islam was stronger in 2001 than it was in 1994 or 1989, with the number of those declaring themselves "believing and practicing" Muslims increasing by 25 percent between 1994 and 2001.[20]

Strategic Implications

Europe's reencounter with Islam is spinning off a range of developments with far-reaching implications.

INCUBATOR FOR TERRORIST RECRUITMENT?

Europe's counterterrorism officials estimate that 1–2 percent of the continent's Muslims—between 250,000 and 500,000 individuals—are involved in some type of extremist activity. How many of these Muslims would actually support terrorism or commit terrorist acts is unclear. The key point is not that Europe's legal environment and location offer a convenient platform from which terrorists can operate, but that the chemistry resulting from Muslims' encounter with Europe seems to make certain individuals more susceptible to recruitment into terrorist networks.

The September 11 hijackers were not simply based in Europe; they were Arabs whose outlook had been radically transformed by their experiences in Europe. Of the approximately 660 original detainees from 42 countries held by the United States in Guantanamo, more than 20 were citizens of at least six different western European states, and perhaps a similar number were permanent residents. (By comparison, two were U.S. citizens.) The total number of Guantanamo detainees from Europe is significantly greater, statistically, than one would expect, suggesting that there may be something about the European environment that contributes to certain Muslims embracing terrorism. In this regard, Michael Radu of the Foreign Policy Research Institute has reportedly noted that, since September 11, 2001, European countries have arrested 20 times more terrorism suspects than the United States.[21]

According to German and French experts, only a minority of European Islamist terrorists had been passionate fanatics in their Muslim home countries prior to coming to Europe.[22] A larger group of terrorists by far is recruited from the masses of young men, many of them middle-class, who experience a sort of culture shock in Europe and become radicalized, "born-again" Islamists. Not accepted as an integral part of European society and at the same time repulsed by its secularism and materialism, a few individuals with a Muslim background, especially when confronted by a significant personal crisis, apparently find solidarity, meaning, and direction in radical Islamist groups that are actively looking for such recruits.

Few radicalized Muslims in Europe return to their families' homelands to take up the fight. Rather, these young men embark on a jihad in places such as Afghanistan, Bosnia, or Chechnya; some do so in the West. As the French expert Olivier Roy has observed, the sociological background of western Europe's violent Islamic militants fits a pattern common to most of the western European radical leftists of the 1970s and 1980s (e.g., Germany's Rote Armee Faktion, Italy's Brigatta Rosso, and France's Action Directe).[23] The cells tend to be amalgams of disaffected, European-educated, single males (often with university-level technical or scientific training) and working-class dropouts (including jailhouse converts) who share a common, marginal culture. Their backgrounds have nothing to do with Islamist struggles against specific Middle Eastern governments or, except for the Saudis and the Yemenis, traditional religious education. Nor are these militants or the cells to which they belong linked to any Middle Eastern state intelligence services or radical movements. Rather, the recruits seem to be simple foot soldiers controlled and directed by Islamist groups, pursuing their own global agenda.

A NEW TYPE OF ANTI-SEMITISM

In France, which has Europe's largest Jewish and Muslim populations, there is concern about the sixfold increase in acts of violence against Jewish property and persons in 2002 as compared with 2001.[24] According to a recent statement by Israeli minister Natan Sharansky, the number of anti-Semitic incidents in France rose from 77 in 2002 to 141 in 2003, accounting for 47 percent of all anti-Semitic attacks in western Europe.[25] Accompanying this violence, emigration by French Jews to Israel doubled between 2001 and 2002—to the largest number since 1972.[26] According to figures released by the Israeli government in late January 2004, 2,380 French Jews emigrated to Israel in 2003, and 2,556 emigrated in 2002, as compared to the 1990s, when approximately 800 French Jews emigrated to Israel each year. Also significant, the majority of emigrants are reportedly between the age of 16 and 25.[27]

Many of the more frequent anti-Semitic incidents in France and elsewhere in Europe are linked mostly to Arab Muslims who are channeling growing frustration over their own and fellow Muslims' social and economic disenfranchisement at Israel's handling of the Palestinian Intifada, as well as to a few young Muslims who are displacing this anger onto another immigrant minority group whose own place in European society has been frequently questioned.[28] This is a development that France's minister of education, Luc Ferry, has called "a real danger—all the greater because today's anti-Semitism is of a new type, coming from parts of society that are more 'acceptable' than the extreme right: from Arabs and Muslims."[29]

In January 2003, the German government banned the radical Islamist organization Hizb ut-Tahrir (HuT) for propagating anti-Semitism in Germany and urging violence against German Jews. HuT maintained at least some ties with the neo-Nazi National Party of Germany, which participated in an anti-U.S./anti-Israeli HuT demonstration in Berlin in October 2002. Recent developments in Belgium, Denmark, Italy, and the United Kingdom have also made European governments sensitive to this new source and type of anti-Semitism, including its possible exploitation by extremist organizations of the Left as well as the Right.

POLITICAL SHIFT TO THE RIGHT

In the last decade, the growth and visibility of Europe's Muslim population have also given new life to radical right-wing parties, which have played on xenophobia and popular fears of Islam. Just as important, advances by parties of the far Right (e.g., Belgium's Flemish Bloc, the British National Party, Denmark's People's Party, Jean-Marie Le Pen's French National Front, Italy's Northern League, and Switzerland's People's Party) have led to right-leaning adjustments in the political priorities of mainstream parties. In a number of cases (Austria, Denmark, Italy, Norway, and Switzerland, as well as the previous government of the Netherlands), European coalition or minority governments depend on the support of right-wing parties with pronounced anti-Muslim views to remain in office. This rightward shift has been most evident in actions to restrict immigration and an increased emphasis on national interests in EU policy debates, but it is also reflected in recent moves such as those in France and Germany to ban the wearing of the Muslim headscarf in public schools and by the Netherlands to expel up to 26,000 asylum seekers.

The kind of impact that a fast-growing Muslim citizenry will have on national politics in European states remains to be seen. To date, Europe's Muslims have not engaged broadly in European party politics, although a few political steps have been taken, such as mobilization during the September 2003 by-elections to defeat British Labour Party members of Parliament who backed the war in Iraq.[30]

In general, however, political activism among Muslims to date has been rather limited. In France, where 92 percent of adult citizens have registered to vote, the corresponding figure among Muslim citizens is only 37 percent.[31] In a March 2004 poll, nearly half of surveyed Muslims in the

Table 3: Muslims in New EU Member States

Islam		Total No. of Muslims[2] [1982 est.]	% of Population[2] [1982 est.]	Muslim Citizenship		Muslims' Ethnicity/ Country of Origin (% of Muslims[3])
Recognized?	Rank[1]			%	No.	
Cyprus		200,000	26.0	100	200,000	Turkish Cypriot/
Yes	2nd	[155,000]	[24.4]			Turkey
Czech Rep.		20,000–	0.2–	NK[4]	NK	
No	4th	30,000	0.3			
Estonia		<6,000	0.4	NK	NK	Tatar
Yes	5th					
Hungary		NK	<0.1	NK	NK	
No	5th					
Latvia		300	<0.1	NK	NK	Tatar
Yes	5th					
Lithuania		2,700	0.1	NK	NK	Tatar
Yes	5th					
Malta		3,000	0.8	25	750	
No	3rd					
Poland		5,123	<0.1	NK	NK	Tatar
No	4th	[22,000]	[<0.1]			
Slovakia		<5,000	<0.1	NK	NK	
No	5th					
Slovenia		47,488	2.4	NK	NK	Bosnian
Yes	4th	[20,000]	[1.1]			
Total		290,000 [208,000]	0.4 [0.4]			

Notes: (1) Rank among the five major religions: Catholic, Islamic, Jewish, Orthodox, and Protestant; (2) Current numbers from U.S. Department of State, *Annual Report on International Religious Freedom 2003*; 1982 estimates in brackets for comparison, from M. Ali Kettani, *Muslim Minorities in the World Today* (London: Mansell Publishing Ltd., 1986); (3) Data provided for groups greater than 10 percent; (4) NK = not known.

United Kingdom claimed that, in the next general election, they would not vote.[32] Although Muslims in the United Kingdom and elsewhere in Europe generally express a basic degree of confidence in national institutions (e.g., judiciary, legislature, political parties, armed forces), they seem inclined to remain disconnected politically, giving priority to apolitical concerns (e.g., family, faith, and honor) over engagement with larger, organized structures. With the exceptions of Belgium and the Netherlands, Muslims are greatly underrepresented, and in many cases unrepresented, in European national parliaments and governments, as they are in the United States.

As mainly first- and second-generation immigrants, Muslims who do vote have tended to lean strongly toward the social welfare and assistance programs of left-of-center parties; for example, 85 percent of the Muslim vote in the United Kingdom went to the Labour Party in the 1997 elections. A few European political analysts, however, recently have detected a possible shift in some Muslim quarters toward center and right-of-center parties, with some Muslims apparently beginning to identify more with conservative values on family, social, and moral issues, as well as entrepreneurship.[33]

For the immediate future, there is likely to be an inclination by right-of-center parties to play the "Muslim card" in certain contexts, particularly as an aging and dwindling European population worries about the influx of foreigners, a strained welfare system, and constant reminders of the threats of terrorism. Some observers have suggested that the European Right should actively pursue the Muslim vote, just as Republicans are now courting the Hispanic vote in the United States.[34] The existence of far-right parties in Europe, however, probably precludes such a strategy, for far-right parties offer an alternative home for that portion of the center-right's base that would oppose Muslim incorporation.

For their part, Muslim voters in the future will probably play a greater, albeit localized political role. Attempts at forming Islamic parties in Europe have failed. Over the long term, it is likely that the Muslim voter, similar to individual Christian and Jewish voters in Europe today, will choose his or her party affiliation on the basis of personal interests and status, not religious identification. Still, where specific political issues touch on deeply felt religious briefs and practices, the Muslim citizen, as his or her Christian and Jewish counterpart, may become a swing voter. Engagement in the political process offers a path for Muslims to achieve the goal of integrating into European society, while maintaining their distinct Islamic identity.

NATIONAL POLITICAL CALCULATIONS

European politicians are beginning routinely to interject calculations of the "Muslim factor"—the impact of Europe's growing Muslim population at the ballot box as well as on the Muslim street—into their decisionmaking processes. This consideration played a significant role in President Jacques Chirac's stance on Iraq and probably also factored into Chancellor Gerhard Schröder's calculus. Although peaceful protest as well as violence (including terrorism) are the immediate concerns, European politicians are also sensitive to the geographical clustering of actual and potential Muslim voters, specifically their significant presence in blue-collar, traditionally left-of-center districts.

Politicians must also be aware of the potentially far-reaching consequences should Muslims start to vote in larger numbers and shift to voting for center and right-of-center parties. This consideration does not apply solely to France and Germany. In the United Kingdom, the Labour Party's margin of victory for seven seats in the House of Commons in the 2002 elections was less than the Muslim population in those districts.[35] This, for example, may have played a role in British support of Pakistan's draft UN Security Council resolution on protecting cultural monuments during the 2003 war in Iraq, particularly given Foreign Secretary Jack Straw's Blackburn constituency, which has the third-largest proportion of Muslims in the United Kingdom (nearly 20 percent).

COMPLICATING ATTEMPTS TO FORM A CLOSER EU

As the EU seeks to move forward on its agenda of broadening and deepening Europe, the world of Islam poses complications on various fronts. The ongoing debate on whether to mention Christianity in the EU's

Table 4: Muslims in Other European States (Non-EU)

Islam		Total No. of Muslims[2]	% of Population[2]	Muslim Citizenship		Muslims' Ethnicity/ Country of Origin
Recognized?	Rank[1]	[1982 est.]	[1982 est.]	%	No.	(% of Muslims[3])
Albania		2.15 mil.	70.0	100	2.15 mil.	Albanian
Yes	1st	[2.11 mil.]	[75.0]			
Bosnia		1.52 mil.	40.0	100	1.52 mil.	Bosnian
No	1st	[2.13 mil.]	[51.6]			
Bulgaria		963,800	12.2	100	963,800	Turkish (75)
Yes	2nd	[1.7 mil.]	[19.3]			Pomak (20) Tatar
Croatia		44,370	1.0	100	44,370	Bosnian
Yes	3rd	[150,000]	[3.3]			
Iceland		229	<0.1	NK[5]	NK	
Yes	3rd					
Liechtenstein		1347	4.0	NK	NK	
Yes	3rd					
Macedonia		600,000	30.0	100	600,000	Albanian
Yes	2nd	[600,000]	[31.4]			
Norway		68,899	1.5	15–	10,000–	Pakistan (31)
Yes	2nd	[12,000]	[0.4]	30	20,000	Bosnia (17) Turkey (13) Iraq (11) Iran (11) Somalia (11)
Romania		67,257	0.3	100	67,257	Turkish
Yes	4th	[65,000]	[0.3]			Tatar
Serb-Mont.		2.02 mil.[4]	19.0	100	2.02 mil.	Albanian
Yes	2nd	[1.93 mil.]	[19.7]			Bosnian
Switzerland		310,807	4.3	10	36,481	Turkey (43)
No	3rd	[70,000]	[1.1]			Yugoslav (36)
Turkey		67.1 mil.	99.0	100	67.1 mil.	Turkish/
Yes	1st	[46.9 mil.]	[99.0]			Kurdish
Total		74.8 mil.	56.0			
		[56.0 mil.]	[50.0]			
without Turkey		7.7 mil.	10.0			
		[8.8 mil.]	[14.0]			

Notes: (1) Rank among the five major religions: Catholic, Islamic, Jewish, Orthodox, and Protestant; (2) Current numbers from U.S. Department of State, *Annual Report on International Religious Freedom 2003*; 1982 estimates in brackets for comparison, from M. Ali Kettani, *Muslim Minorities in the World Today* (London: Mansell Publishing Ltd., 1986); (3) Data provided for groups greater than 10 percent; percentages provided where known; (4) Total for Serbia-Montenegro includes Kosovo; (5) NK = not known.

draft constitution is one example, as is the perennial issue of Turkey's membership. The increasing Muslim presence in Europe has reopened debates on several issues: the place of religion in public life, social tolerance in Europe, secularism as the only path to modernity, and Europe's very identity. The Muslim factor has also highlighted a potential contradiction in the nature of the union itself, namely that the EU is still primarily a common market with arguably a social as well as a democracy deficit.[36] Finally, former EU official Fraser Cameron has noted that, thus far, Muslims in Europe have not tried to affect EU foreign policy but this "could change in the future."[37]

The dynamics unleashed by the process of European integration coupled with the forces of globalization, Europe's demographic decline, and its economic doldrums are generating wrenching identity-related tensions for many Europeans. The impact of the burgeoning Muslim presence on individual European societies as well as their collective identity is further exacerbating European anxiety by adding nationalist—albeit muted—and xenophobic overtones to the discourse. Some Scandinavian analysts have attributed the negative Danish votes in 1992 and 2000 and the near-negative votes in 1993 on referenda on the Maastricht Treaty and EU monetary union partly to this climate, which has fostered a degree of renationalization in European politics.[38] EU integration and Muslim integration, though vastly different issues (at least on the surface), seem to strike a common, sensitive nerve among many Europeans, reflecting growing concerns with such core issues as control and identity.

REFOCUSING FOREIGN POLICY

Over time, the political salience of the Muslim factor in Europe will be most evident in the domestic realm. In large measure, the influence of Muslims on European societies will be a function of whether and when Muslims get involved in the electoral process on a significant scale, how political parties will include Muslims in day-to-day political life, what economic role they will play, and what degree of social mobility they will achieve. In the near term, however, the impact of the Muslim factor may be most visible on the foreign policy stage for at least three reasons.

First, as a group, Europe's Muslims are energized more quickly and forcefully by developments in the international arena, notably those in which the *umma* (universal Muslim community) is viewed as endangered and the *dar al-Islam* (abode of peace, or Islamic territory) is involved, such as the Israeli-Palestinian conflict and the crises in Iraq and Bosnia, than by domestic issues, such as employment and education. For example, the Muslim Association of Britain and the Stop the War Coalition jointly sponsored the mid-February 2003 demonstration in London involving an estimated one million persons—the largest protest in British history—under the dual banners "Don't Attack Iraq" and "Freedom for Palestine."

Second, for governments and politicians, in cost-benefit terms it is generally easier to respond to Muslims' concerns about foreign policy than to those about domestic matters, given both the generally limited political and financial resources required and the views of their non-Muslim constituencies. Those constituencies may ignore or sympathize with international causes but view specific, domestic benefits for Muslims as coming at their expense.

Third, Europe has many Muslim neighbors, and its foreign and national security policies are necessarily defined in good measure by its Islamic "near abroad," as the EU's New Neighborhood initiative explicitly acknowledges. Growing unrest in the adjacent Islamic world, which also resonates among Europe's own Muslim minorities; concerns about unwanted immigrants, Islamic fundamentalist terrorism, and weapons of mass destruction emanating from the region; as well as energy dependence all make stability in the "crescent of crisis" a priority for Europeans.[39]

Europe's Risky Stability Strategy

European states have a widespread aversion to supporting change that has uncertain and potentially destabilizing consequences in Europe's immediate neighborhood in North Africa, the Middle East, and the Caucasus, even when the governments involved are recognized as corrupt and oppressive. As part of its strategy for dealing with this situation, European governments have sought to cultivate ties with existing regimes, at times propping them up at great cost to seek their assistance to staunch the unregulated flow of immigrants into Europe and to quarantine the Islamic fundamentalist contagion.

The EU, along with non-EU European states, would prefer to see stronger economies operating with greater transparency and under better governance along Europe's periphery. Yet, in contrast to its readiness to use the prospect of EU membership to foster economic, democratic, and human rights change in central and eastern Europe, Brussels has to date been unwilling to exercise the leverage afforded by its Euro-Mediterranean partnership to encourage reform along Europe's Muslim edge. The partnership is a potentially potent tool, with an annual budget from its inception in 1995 through 2006 of nearly one billion euros plus nearly three times that amount available via loans from the European Investment Bank. This is more than half of the funds earmarked for the 10 new central and eastern European members of the EU during the same period. The Euro-Med program, however, does not demand fulfillment of political and human rights requirements by its Mediterranean partners, such as those spelled out in the Copenhagen Criteria for new EU members, in exchange for this financial, trade, and developmental assistance.

In May 2003, British foreign secretary Straw acknowledged this shortcoming, stating that "there is a pressing need to develop a stronger relationship with the Muslim world. I hope Europe will refocus its programmes, including Euro-Med, to work in partnership with North Africa on issues that really matter: good governance, the rule of law, and transfer of expertise."[40] It remains to be seen whether the EU's nascent New Neighborhood initiative will move decisively in this direction and become the platform for a common, inclusive approach with the United States toward the greater Middle East.[41]

In domestic policy, Europe's quest for stability is manifest in European governments' attempts during the last decade to manage their Muslim populations by effectively nationalizing, if not secularizing, Islam. These governments are trying to foster nationally oriented Islams subordinate to the state as well as to established European norms stretching back to the Treaty of Westphalia, the Enlightenment, and Napoleonic rule that were developed in different times, for different religions, in very different environments. By nationalizing Islam and putting it squarely within existing structures in the tradition of state churches, governments are seeking to contain a sensitive issue on familiar ground, maintaining the leverage established structures afford.

These efforts favor certain Muslim groups over others; seek to educate imams locally, require them to speak the vernacular, and understand the local culture; facilitate construction of mosques and religious instruction in the hopes of reducing Arab state financing and influence; restrict wearing the *hijab* (Islamic head scarf); and virtually shoehorn Muslim organizations into structures that correspond to national criteria and objectives, such as Belgium's Central Body for the Islamic Religion, Germany's Central Council of Muslims, and the French Council of the Muslim Religion. In all too many cases, state-established Muslim councils have failed the tests of fair and equal treatment and are not truly representative. States have excluded certain Muslim groups, predetermined and/or selected-out individual representatives, and taken a "one size fits all" approach that fails to take into account the diversity and variety of the Muslim communities in most European states, including their sectarian differences, the inherently nonhierarchical nature of Islam, and other functional and structural differences from Christian religions.

The problem with this approach is that, although it ostensibly puts Islam on the same plane as traditional European religions, it fails to integrate Muslims into European society. This outcome is not all that surprising, given that the governmental goals are primarily control and regulation, not outreach and accommodation. To date, not a single national Islamic council created by a European state has become an effective interlocutor with the government, facilitating a fruitful two-way dialogue. Most have foundered. The attempt to promote a nationally oriented Islam artificially, however, may accentuate the trend toward Muslim alienation, prompting further movement toward communalism. By promoting the establishment of private Islamic schools or by deliberately excluding or failing to foster structures that permit the full range of Muslim sectarian groups to have a voice in the dialogue and by prompting a search for channels and associations outside of the state's purview or direction, devoid of attachments to Europe, European governments further segregate Muslim communities, limiting the possibilities for engagement with the broader society.

For their part, Europe's Muslims have a tendency to move in a similar direction, reinforced by the statist approach of trying to nationalize Islam, in Europe or elsewhere. Roy has described this path as "recommunalization along supranational lines, which is defined in essence by European Muslims' identification with a universal umma, or community of the faithful. ... It is with this ... phenomenon that radicalism and violence become potentially serious issues."[42]

Attempts to nationalize and secularize Islam, moreover, hinder the development of a modern Euro-Islamic identity that amalgamates Western culture with Islamic orthopraxy, parallel to the distinct Arab Islamic, South Asian–Islamic, and East Asian–Islamic cultures and identities that have emerged elsewhere in the world. The Arab Islamic culture has most profoundly shaped the practices of Muslims in continental Europe, but much of this influence derives from Arab customs and traditions, not Islamic orthopraxy. Although not surprising given the origins of most of Europe's Muslims, this development in a sense represents a form of reverse Arab colonialism in Europe. The development of a parallel Euro-Islamic model[43] could provide a framework for Muslims to make the adjustments necessary to integrate into European society while maintaining their Islamic identity and for European societies to make appropriate accommodations and adaptations to encompass a growing segment of Europe's citizenry.

Islamophobia and Europhobia

Ironically, 1989 saw the acceleration of European integration, with the fall of the Berlin Wall, and rising tensions with the Muslim world, over the Salman Rushdie affair in the United Kingdom and the initial hijab controversy in France. Since that time, a series of events have polarized popular attitudes toward Europe's Muslim communities and galvanized Islamic identity within them. Europe's Muslim population is now more than merely an immigration issue. Increasingly, the Muslim presence in Europe has become a challenge to domestic social unity; *The Economist* has warned that this "could be a huge long-term threat to Europe."[44]

As they publicly advocate integration, many Europeans and Muslims in Europe remain convinced that their respective values are not only incompatible with each other but also that the other's values directly challenge their own identity. These perceptions thus perpetuate each group's separate existence within Europe. Although many European Muslims are open to a milder form of integration, overwhelming majorities of Muslims in France, the United Kingdom, and Germany resist assimilation, preferring to be a part of Europe while maintaining their own Islamic identity. If anything, the trend toward Muslim differentiation and alienation appears to be growing stronger, with the younger generation in the vanguard. In a 2003 Ipsos poll, for example, three-fourths of French Muslim respondents considered the values of Islam to be compatible with those of the French Republic, but only one-fourth of those under 25 shared that view.[45] Conversely, an Ipsos poll conducted around the same time indicated that 62 percent of the general French population believed that the values of Islam were not compatible with those of the French Republic.[46]

In a 2002 survey conducted in Germany, 19 percent of respondents said that Muslims should not be allowed to practice their religion in Germany, 43 percent voiced doubts about Islam's capacity to be tolerant, and 67 percent said that, when practicing their religion, Muslims should be more respectful of the views of the German public.[47] According to the 2000 European Values Survey, in comparison with people of a different race, immigrants, and Jews, Muslims are the societal group that Europeans least want as a neighbor and, in some cases, by significant margins.

The rapidly growing Muslim populations seem to be overwhelming the ability of European governments to draw the lines of tolerance rationally, consistently, and convincingly. Europeans see Muslims as a direct challenge to the collective identity, traditional values, and public policies of their societies, as demonstrated by the heated controversies over the hijab, Muslim food (*halal*), the construction of mosques, the teaching of Islam in schools, and Muslim burial rites. This attitude is also reflected in intense debates over women's rights, church-state relations, and Islam's compatibility with democracy. Politicians, pundits, and ordinary citizens are all seized with the "Islamic challenge."

The fact that European governments and publics tend to view and respond to all Muslims as an undifferentiated whole further reinforces the tendency among Europeans to see the Muslim presence not as a potential boon but as a real threat, which, in some respects, becomes a self-fulfilling prophecy. The threat is framed in terms of security (terrorism) and economics (jobs); yet, the core issue is identity and the perceived cultural threat Islam poses to the European way of life. Europeans have even coined a name for it: Islamophobia. Conversely, this tendency to see Muslims as a monolith has its reverse image in Muslim allegiance to the umma, which transcends other loyalties; tends to reinforce the "we/them" perspective; and is part of the reason why Muslims resist assimilation—the total loss of identity-related indicators of existing differences from European societies—and insist on integration—a reconstituted identity that stresses remaining differences—or, in some cases, recommunalization—a physical presence in Europe but no accommodation with European society. In other words, Muslims tend to seek a physical presence in Europe but no accommodation with European society.[48]

Although Europeans, Muslim and non-Muslim alike, are divided on how to handle this new Islamic challenge, the dynamics of the situation argue that both Muslim and non-Muslim Europeans will need to undergo, individually and jointly, a wrenching, far-reaching, and probably prolonged adjustment in mind-set to avoid a spiral of future clashes. Whether Europe will be transformed and strengthened or torn apart is still an open question. In many ways, the process of integration in Europe ahead is akin to what a generation of Americans, black and white, experienced during the civil rights movement in the United States 50 years ago, following the Supreme Court's 1954 *Brown v. Board of Education* decision. Yet in other ways, the challenge for Europe seems more daunting because it involves not only integration and tolerance but also redefining both parties' identities. Each side will have to change and move toward the other. Europe's Muslims will need to accept the norms, customs, and cultures of the states in which they live and reject efforts to establish a parallel society, while the general European population will need to broaden its horizons to embrace and accommodate diversity, accepting integration and not just complete assimilation as a valid relationship to society.

The centuries-old question of whether Europe and Islam can coexist will have to be confronted. In the estimates of some, Europe is entering a period of demographic,[49] economic,[50] psychological, and political decline, which will make it all the more difficult to address the additional challenges of integration, tolerance, and identity posed by Europe's Muslim population.

For their part, Muslims in Europe, who must confront poverty, bigotry, de facto segregation, and limited social mobility, are likely to find it difficult to embrace Europe's liberal democratic views on gender equality; sexual liberalization; and the principles of compromise, egalitarianism, and identification with the state. These are all issues that challenge the traditional views not only of Muslims but also of individuals with an Arab, Turkish, or South Asian heritage, as the vast majority of Europe's Muslims are. These cultural backgrounds have not included the Enlightenment as a central pillar, and the idea of a secular society is for the most part alien. Moreover, as Mustafa Malik notes, in these societies, "[R]esistance to liberalism was heightened by hatred for European colonialists, who represented liberal values."[51] Lack of organization and political standing, diversity of views and interests, economic weakness, and the absence of clear leadership pose major complicating hurdles, all of which Europe's Muslims will need to address if they are to contribute their part to Europe's transformation.

Approaching a Tipping Point?

Changing minds on questions of identity is no small task. Yet, the alternative—entrenchment of such conflicting perspectives—sets a clear course for conflict. If Europe and its Muslim communities fail to reach an accommodation, increased social strife, national retrenchment, and potentially significant civil conflict are likely to overwhelm the vision of a continent that is whole, free, and united.

Although the situation in Europe is not quite there, the tipping point may be closer than is generally realized. As intolerance toward Muslim communities grows in Europe, European Muslims are growing more self-confident but also more dissatisfied, particularly as Europe's economy continues to sputter. The percentage of Muslims in France is rapidly approaching that of African-Americans in the United States in 1950 (10 percent), and the percentage of Muslims in Europe as a whole will pass that benchmark within the next decade. Muslim and non-Muslim moderates participating in the Euro-Islamic dialogue are being squeezed and marginalized, with core issues and representative standpoints being distorted. Alarm bells are being set off in various quarters, highlighting and reinforcing the extremes on both sides.

Increasingly, public attention is focusing on polarizing statements such as the finding of the French commission, which recommended that the Islamic head scarf be banned in public primary and secondary schools and declared that the secular state was under "guerrilla assault" by Muslims. Commission Chairman Bernard Stasi even warned that "forces in France ... are trying to destabilize the republic, and it's time for the republic to react."[52] Meanwhile, the Middle East editor of the influential German nationwide daily *Frankfurter Allgemeine Zeitung* depicts the situation as "frightening," questions the prospects of integrating Germany's growing Muslim population into society, and maintains that at least 10 percent of Germany's Muslim population—400,000 individuals—are followers and supporters of radical Islam, whose aim is the establishment of an Islamic state.[53]

Such views are not isolated. They reflect many Europeans' tacit and widespread fear of the inevitability of social conflict stemming from the burgeoning Muslim population; the Muslims' demands for more control, greater entitlements, and preservation of their Islamic identity; and Europe's ongoing struggle with a multicultural identity that most members of the middle and upper classes resent. These fears are not new but rather deeply ingrained and growing.

Following the fall of the Berlin Wall, an older, revived version of the Muslim threat at home and abroad seems to have replaced the Communist threat in Europe. Indeed, during his brief tenure as NATO secretary general in the mid-1990s, Belgian Willy Claes claimed that the new threat to the alliance was Islam.[54] Thus, it is not surprising that Samuel P. Huntington's *The Clash of Civilizations and the Remaking of the World Order* had and continues to have far greater resonance in Europe than it does in the United States.

Whether owing to a self-fulfilling prophecy, the transcendence of contemporary dynamics over political acumen and resources, or truly intractable differences between Europe and Islam, many inside and outside Europe will consider the failure to address and avert the looming crisis arising from the clash of cultures within European borders as confirmation of Huntington's thesis. These same observers will view this outcome as one that sets the stage for the larger, predicted twenty-first-century clash of civilizations along the frontiers where the West and Islam meet.[55]

Conversely, however, a success in dealing with the building clash of cultures and identities, which results in a shift of both Muslim and non-Muslim European mind-sets, and crafts a societal framework that encourages integration and respects individual as well as national identities would negate Huntington's thesis of the inevitable incompatibility of Islam and the West. It would require change in European society, to be sure. As with all change, there would be winners and losers. Yet, success holds out the hope of reinvigorating and redefining Europe, proffering a possible corrective to its projected political, economic, and demographic decline as well as moving European integration to a new level and giving it new meaning.

As Mark Twain reportedly remarked, history does not repeat itself, but it sometimes rhymes. It would indeed be ironic if Islam provided the impetus for redefining Europe, as it did more than a millennium ago, and the basis for a new, second European renaissance, as it did for the first. Although that may be expecting too much, success in addressing this clash of cultures, at a minimum, would open the door to a range of opportunities for positive change in Europe and perhaps beyond.

Notes

1. See Timothy Garton Ash, "The Price of Parsley," *Guardian*, July 25, 2002; Norman Davies, *Europe: A History* (Oxford University Press, 1996), pp. 7–16, 251–258.

2. Adopted on December 12, 2003.

3. See European Commission, Communication from the Commission, "Wider Europe–Neighborhood: A New Framework for Relations With Our Eastern and Southern Neighbors," Brussels, March 11, 2003, p. 3 (hereinafter Wider Europe communication).

4. See Malcolm Gladwell, *The Tipping Point: How Little Things Can Make a Big Difference* (New York: Little, Brown & Co., 2000).

5. International Organization for Migration (IOM), *World Migration Report 2000* (IOM: Geneva, 2000), p. 195.

6. IOM, "Facts and Figures on International Migration," *Migration Policy Issues* no. 2

(March 2003): 2, www.iom.int/DOCUMENTS/PUBLICATION/EN/MPI_series_No_2_eng.PDF (accessed March 21, 2004).

7. Population Division, Department of Economic and Social Affairs, United Nations Secretariat, "Replacement Migration: Is It a Solution to Declining and Aging Populations?" ESA/P/WP.160, March 21, 2000," www.un.org/esa/population/publications/migration/migration.htm (accessed March 27, 2004).

8. Mustafa Malik, "Islam in Europe: Quest for a Paradigm," *Middle East Policy* 8, no. 2 (June 2001): 100; "How Restive Are Europe's Muslims?" *Economist*, October 18, 2001, www.economist.com/world/europe/displayStory.cfm?Story_ID=824394 (accessed March 27, 2004).

9. Christopher Caldwell, "The Cresent and the Tricolor," *Atlantic Monthly*, November 2000, p. 22.

10. See Peter Mandaville, "Muslim Youth in Europe," in *Islam, Europe's Second Religion*, ed. Shireen T. Hunter (Westport, Conn.: Praeger, 2002), pp. 219–230.

11. Olivier Roy, "EuroIslam: The Jihad Within?" *National Interest* (spring 2003): 65, fn. 2; "Germany," *Muslim Voices in the European Union*, vol. 5, Phase One Report, p. 33; "Census 2001—Ethnicity and Region in England and Wales," www.statistics. gov.uk/census2001/profiles/commentaries/ethnicity.asp (accessed March 27, 2004); Fabienne Brion and Ural Manao, "Belgian Country Report," *Muslim Voices in the European Union*, vol. 2, p. 31.

12. Omer Taspinar, "Europe's Muslim Street," *Foreign Policy*, March–April 2003, p. 77.

13. See Michel Gurkinkiel, "Islam in France: Is the French Way of Life in Danger?" *Middle East Quarterly* 4, no. 1 (March 1997): 19, fn. 2, and 21; John L. Allen Jr., "Europe's Muslims Worry Bishops," *National Catholic Reporter*, October 22, 1999, p. 3; Roy, "EuroIslam," p. 65; John Esposito, "Introduction: Modernizing Islam and Re-Islamization in Global Perspective," in *Modernizing Islam: Religion in the Public Sphere in the Middle East and Europe*, eds. John L. Esposito and Francois Burgat (New Brunswick, N.J.: Rutgers University Press, 2003), p. 11; Oussama Cherribi, "The Growing Islamization of Europe," in *Modernizing Islam: Religion in the Public Sphere in the Middle East and Europe*, eds. John L. Esposito and Francois Burgat (New Brunswick, N.J.: Rutgers University Press, 2003), p. 195.

14. See Population Division, Department of Economic and Social Affairs, United Nations Secretariat, "World Population Prospects: The 2002 Revision—Highlights," ESA/P/WP.180, February 26, 2003, p. 1, www.un.org/esa/population/publications/wpp2002/WPP2002-HIGHLIGHTSrev1.PDF (accessed March 28, 2004) (Table 1. Estimated and Projected Population of the World, Major Development Groups and Major Areas, 1950, 2003, 2003 and 2050 According to Fertility Variant).

15. M. Ali Kettani, *Muslim Minorities in the World Today* (New York: Mansell Publishing Limited, 1986), p. 41; Remy Leveau and Shireen T. Hunter, "Islam in France," in *Islam, Europe's Second Religion*, ed. Shireen T. Hunter (Westport, Conn.: Praeger,

2002), p. 8; Jorgen S. Nielson, *Muslims in Western Europe*, 2d ed. (Edinburgh: Edinburgh University Press, 1995), p. 26.

16. Leveau and Hunter, "Islam in France," p. 8; Anne Sofie Roald, "From 'People's Home' to 'Multiculturalism': Muslims in Sweden," in *Muslims in the West: From Sojourners to Citizens*, ed. Yvonne Yazbeek Haddad (New York: Oxford University Press, 2002), p. 110; Brion and Manao, "Belgian Country Report," p. 44; Open Society Institute 2002, "The Situation of Muslims in the UK," *Monitoring the EU Accession Process: Minority Protection*, pp. 368, 447, www.eumpa.org/reports/2002/content/09/250/2002_m_uk.pdf (accessed March 24, 2004); Eltje Buur, Anne Havelarr, and Paul Abell, "The Netherlands," *Muslim Voices in the European Union*, vol. 2, Phase One Report, p. 20; Kari Vogt, "Integration through Islam? Muslims in Norway," in *Muslims in the West: From Sojourners to Citizens*, ed. Yvonne Yazbeek Haddad (New York: Oxford University Press, 2002), p. 88.

17. "How Restive Are Europe's Muslims?"

18. Ulrich von Wilamowitz-Moellendorff, *Türken in Deutschland* (Sankt Augustin, Germany: Konrad Adenauer Foundation, 2001), pp. 1–2, www.kas.de/db_files/dokumente/arbeitspapiere/7_dokument_dok_pdf_12_1.pdf (accessed March 21, 2004).

19. Jim House, "Muslim Communities in France," in *Muslim Communities in the New Europe*, eds. Gerd Nonneman, Tim Niblock, and Bogdan Szajkowski (Reading, UK: Garnet Publishing, 1996), p. 222, fn. 14; Zachory Shore, "Uncommon Threats: Germany's Muslims, Transatlantic Relations, and the War on Terror," *AICGS Policy Report* #5 (2003), www.aicgs.org/publications/pubonline_ar-pr.shtml (accessed March 21, 2004).

20. Open Society Institute 2002, *EU Accession Monitoring Program*, p. 76.

21. Frederick S. Kempe, "Europe's Middle East Side Story," *Wall Street Journal*, July 29, 2003.

22. Olivier Roy, "European Muslims Try to Find a Balance Between European Culture and Values and Islam," National Public Radio's *All Things Considered*, February 28, 2003.

23. This paragraph draws heavily on the insights found in Roy, "EuroIslam," pp. 63–73.

24. Elaine Sciolino, "French Rallies Against War Shift Focus to Israel," *New York Times*, March 30, 2003.

25. Philip Delves Broughton, "French Anti-Semitism Drives More Jews to Settle in Israel," *Telegraph*, January 29, 2004, www.telegraph.co.uk/news/main.jhtml?xml=/news/2004/01/29/wsemit29.xml (accessed February 20, 2004).

26. Craig S. Smith, "French Jews Tell of a New and Threatening Wave of Anti-Semitism," *New York Times*, March 22, 2003.

27. Broughton, "French Anti-Semitism Drives More Jews to Settle in Israel."

28. See Jean-Marc Dreyfus and Jonathan Laurence, "Anti-Semitism in France," May 14, 2002, www.brookings.edu/fp/cusf/analysis/dreyfus.pdf (accessed March 28, 2004).

29. Luc Ferry, radio interview, February 27, 2003.

30. See Severin Carrell, "Labour Faces 'Muslim Backlash,'" *Independent*, September 21, 2003.

31. Thierry Portes and Cecilia Gabizon, "Sondage: pour les valeurs de la Republique, mais contre la victoire des Etats-Unis," *Le Figaro*, April 5, 2003, www.lefigaro.fr/cgi/perm/archives/find?url=http://newportal.cedromsni.com/httpref/intro.asp&user=lefigaro&part_ID=lefigaro (accessed April 14, 2004) (hereinafter *Le Figaro* survey).

32. Poll of 500 Muslims over 18 years of age taken March3–11, 2004, by ICM polls, 10 percent were undecided, and 7 percent said they were ineligible to vote, www.icmresearch.co.uk/reviews/2004/guardian-muslims-march-2004.htm (accessed April 14, 2004).

33. See Anne Sofie Roald, "Muslims in Sweden," in *Muslims in the West: From Sojourners to Citizens*, ed. Yvonne Yazbeck Haddad (New York: Oxford University Press, 2002), pp. 116–117; Andrew Rawnsley, "A Catastrophic Success for the Tories," *Observer*, May 4, 2003.

34. Cem Ozdemir, "Europe's Awkward Embrace," *Foreign Policy*, January/February 2004, pp. 68–69.

35. Kevin Maguire, "Wake-up Call for Party That Took Votes for Granted," *Guardian*, June 18, 2002.

36. See Jan Hjarno, "Muslims in Denmark," in *Muslim Communities in the New Europe*, eds. Gerd Nonneman, Tim Niblock, and Bogdan Szajkowski (Berkshire, UK: Garnet Publishing, 1996), pp. 297–298.

37. Fraser Cameron, "The Islamic Factor in the European Union's Foreign Policy," in *Islam, Europe's Second Religion*, ed. Shireen T. Hunter (Westport, Conn.: Praeger, 2002), p. 269.

38. See Hjarno, "Muslims in Denmark," p. 297; Lief Stenberg, "Islam in Scandinavia," in *Islam, Europe's Second Religion*, ed. Shireen T. Hunter (Westport, Conn.: Praeger, 2002), p. 137.

39. See Geoffrey Kemp, "Europe's Middle East Challenges," *The Washington Quarterly* 27, no. 1 (winter 2003–04): 163–177.

40. Jack Straw, "Europe in the World," address at the Center for European Reform, Brussels, May 19, 2003.

41. See Wider Europe communication; European Commission, Communication from the Commission, "Paving the Way for a New Neighbourhood Instrument," no. 393 (final), Brussels, July 1, 2003.

42. Roy, "EuroIslam," p. 63.

43. See Tariq Ramadan, *Western Muslims and the Future of Islam* (London and New York: Oxford University Press, 2004).

44. "Forget Asylum-Seekers: It's the People Inside Who Count," *Economist*, May 8, 2003.

45. *Le Figaro* survey.

46. Jerome Cordelier, "IPSOS-LCI-Le Point Poll: Islam Is a Worry for the French," *Le Point*, May 16, 2003.

47. Ulrich von Wilamowitz-Moellendorff, "Was Halten die Deutschen von Islam?" Konrad Adenauer Foundation working paper, May 2003.

48. Roy, "EuroIslam," pp. 64–65.

49. In addition to previously cited UN studies, see Wolfgang Lutz, Brian C. O'Neill, and Sergei Scherbov, "Europe's Population at a Turning Point," *Science*, March 28, 2003, pp. 1991–1992 (noting that, "[a]round the year 2000, the population [of Europe] began to generate 'negative momentum'").

50. See Kieran McMorrow and Werner Roger, "Economic and Financial Market Consequences of Aging Populations," *European Commission Economic Paper* no. 182, Brussels, April 2003; John Vinocur, "A Doomsday Scenario for Europe's Economy," *International Herald Tribune*, May 13, 2003 (summarizing a report by the Institute Français de Relations Internationales entitled *World Trade in the 21st Century*).

51. Mustafa Malik, "Islam's Missing Link to the West," *Middle East Policy* 10, no. 1 (spring 2003): 126.

52. Ken Dilanian, "France Struggles to Integrate Its Muslim Minority," *Philadelphia Inquirer*, January 5, 2004.

53. Udo Ulfkottte, "Network of Radical Islamic Organizations in Germany," speech to German-Atlantic Society, Bonn, February 5, 2004. See Udo Ulfkotte, *Der Krieg in Unseren Städten: Wie Radikale Islamisten Deutschland Unterwandern* (Frankfurt am Main: Eichborn Verlag, 2003).

54. Sami Zemni and Christopher Parker, "Islam, the European Union, and the Challenge of Multiculturalism," in *Islam, Europe's Second Religion*, ed. Shireen T. Hunter (Westport, Conn.: Praeger, 2002), p. 233.

55. Milton Viorst, "The Muslims of France," *Foreign Affairs* (September/October 1996): 96.

Gideon Rachman

The Death of Enlargement

For many years, European politicians could broadly be divided into two camps: deepeners and wideners. The deepeners, such as former head of the European Commission Jacques Delors and current Belgian prime minister Guy Verhofstadt, believed above all in pursuing the political integration of the European Union. Their aim was, as Verhofstadt writes frankly in the title of a recent book, to create a "United States of Europe."[1] The wideners, epitomized by former British prime minister Margaret Thatcher (Delors's arch enemy), were keen to expand the membership of the EU to include all the post-Communist countries of eastern and central Europe. They wanted to spread the political and economic benefits of EU membership as broadly as possible, but they were also often attracted to EU enlargement for other, more self-serving reasons. They believed that the larger the EU was, the more diverse it would become, and the more difficult it would be to achieve the deepeners' goal of a united Europe.

Not surprisingly, wideners and deepeners were often highly suspicious of each other. Each side suspected, often correctly, that the other was intent on sabotaging their pet project. Yet, each side missed an essential point: for at least 20 years, the widening and deepening of the EU

Gideon Rachman is business editor of the *Economist* and was its Brussels bureau chief from 2001 to 2005.

Copyright © 2006 by The Center for Strategic and International Studies and the Massachusetts Institute of Technology
The Washington Quarterly • 29:3 pp. 51–56.

have not been opposing and hostile projects. On the contrary, they have proceeded in tandem. The EU kept expanding, but the process of "ever closer union," laid out in the Treaty of Rome in 1957, also kept rolling forward. Spain, Greece, and Portugal were admitted to the European club in the 1980s after undergoing democratic revolutions. In the Maastricht Treaty of 1992, the EU committed to creating a single currency, the euro, and a common foreign policy. In 2004, 10 central European countries were finally formally admitted to the EU as full members, alongside Cyprus and Malta, expanding EU membership to 25 countries. That same year, EU leaders agreed on the union's first written constitution, a move intended to push it toward a new and deeper level of political integration.

There was a certain logic to the fact that widening and deepening were proceeding alongside each other. The EU works by compromise and trade-off; a concession to the wideners was often matched by a concession to the deepeners. Each position in the EU's widening versus deepening debate can be identified with particular national positions. The British were always wideners, viscerally opposed to all moves toward political union. The French were always deepeners, wary of the impact of enlargement on France's traditional preeminence within the EU. The Germans, however, have traditionally supported both positions. Because it would create new markets for German industry and stabilize Germany's borders, they could see a strong national interest in expanding the EU eastward. Yet, the German establishment was also still profoundly attached to the idea of a united Europe that could aspire to an assertive international role still unthinkable for modern Germany.

Some politicians, leading German ones such as former chancellor Helmut Kohl and former foreign minister Joschka Fischer in particular, therefore managed to be enthusiastic wideners and deepeners at the same time. They argued that enlarging the EU and pushing for a political union, far from being mutually antagonistic policies, only made sense if pursued simultaneously. According to this argument, it was precisely because enlargement would make the EU more diverse that a closer political union was increasingly necessary. Without moves toward political union, the EU would become ungovernable.

The Germans' characteristically dialectical position, that two apparently opposing policies could be united to create a new synthesis that would advance the European project as a whole, seemed for many years to be more prescient and generous spirited than the more fearful and competitive British and French positions. It helped that the German position was also shared by the Brussels establishment, above all by the permanent, powerful civil service of the European Commission, both for practical and ideological reasons. The commission supported enlargement partly because it was a project that it managed and partly because its successful completion could only add to the EU's as well as its own size and grandeur. For similar reasons, the commission was also traditionally the most federalist, i.e., pro–political union, institution within the EU. The commission, after all, tends to attract employees who believe in "Europe." And more power for Europe tends also to mean more power for the commission.

The French and Dutch Referenda

The Germans and the commission were correct to believe that enlargement and the promotion of political union could go hand in hand. Yet, it is now becoming clear that the reverse is also true. If the process of political union is blocked, then enlargement could be stopped in its tracks.

This new logic has become apparent in the wake of the French referendum on the EU constitution in May 2005. France rejected the constitution by 54 percent to 46 percent. A few days later, Dutch voters rejected the constitution by an even greater margin. The French vote in particular was widely interpreted as a vote against the EU enlargement that had taken place a year earlier as much as against the constitutional text that that had been placed before French voters. The iconic figure during the campaign was the "Polish plumber" who was apparently poised to move to France, driving down wages and social standards through his willingness to work for low wages and in inhumane conditions. The services directive, a draft European law that made it easier for Polish plumbers and other service providers to work across the EU, became a subject of fierce debate in the French campaign, even though it did not feature in the constitutional text.

The fact that the French vote appeared to be driven by issues that were not strictly germane to the constitutional text has confirmed the worst fears of many political analysts about direct democracy and referenda. The problem is that, as the late French president François Mitterand is reputed to have remarked, the voters never answer the question you ask them. Yet, in fact, it was not entirely irrational for French voters to link their fear of enlargement with their dislike of the constitution. The constitutional treaty consolidated all previous European treaties and laws into a single text. Exasperated pro-Europeans pointed out that many of the items to which French rejectionists objected, such as free movement of people between all EU countries, had been part of European law for many years. That was true, but in a post-enlargement environment it was also arguably beside the point. Agreeing to a single market between countries with broadly similar income levels and similar cultures is one thing. Given that some of the new EU member states had wage levels that were just 20 percent of those in France, however, it is not entirely surprising that French voters were slightly alarmed by the prospect of head-to-head competition with Polish plumbers and Slovak auto workers.

The question of culture also loomed large in the French and Dutch referendum campaigns. Caucasian Polish Catholics were not regarded as particularly threatening, but voters were acutely aware that the largest country sitting in the EU's waiting room is Turkey, a Muslim nation on Europe's periphery with alarming neighbors such as Iraq. Whenever French and Dutch politicians protested that the prospect of Turkish membership was still a very long way off, the "no" campaigns could point out that the Turks were present at the constitutional convention that drew up the treaty and that the Turkish prime minister was among the European leaders who signed the document at a formal ceremony in Rome. The idea of untrammelled immigration from Turkey was always likely to be highly controversial in two countries where Muslim immigration has helped created political upheaval in recent years, leading to the rise of an entirely new political movement in the Netherlands, the List Pim Fortuyn, and contributing to the embarrassing appearance of a far-right candidate, Jean-Marie Le Pen, in the final runoff for the French presidency in 2002.

In an effort to win their referendum and head off a revolt based on fear of enlargement in general and Turkey in particular, the French government made a fateful promise. After the admission of Romania, Bulgaria, and Croatia to the EU, all future enlargements would be subjected to a referendum. This is not an entirely new departure. The French had a referendum on British membership in the 1970s. (Amazingly enough, given the history of mutual antagonism between the two countries, they voted in favor.) In general, however, successive EU enlargements have been passed in parliaments without direct consultation with the people.

Because all member states have to ratify any enlargement, parliamentary ratification may be the only practical route to pursue in a 25-member EU. By abandoning this tradition and writing the promise to have a referendum on future enlargements into the French constitution, France has thrown grave doubt on the future of EU enlargement. It is not alone. Austria, where skepticism about eventual Turkish membership is also rampant, has also promised its people that they will get to vote on Turkish membership. Because referendum promises tend to snowball, it is likely that many EU countries will eventually feel compelled to vote on future enlargements.

Tough Choices Ahead: Turkey, the Balkans, and Ukraine

Because Europe's most difficult cases now beckon, this anxiety is all the more acute. There is little doubt that the current political climate within the EU is unfavorable to Turkey, which excites western European fears of Muslim immigration and competition from low-wage labor. Because many EU laws are passed by majority vote and a country's voting power is based on its population, the fact that Turkey might be the largest single nation within the EU by 2030 based on current population trends also counts against it.

It is less than a decade since Europeans and Americans had to intervene militarily in the Balkans. The area is now at peace but clearly remains unstable, with final state boundaries still to be settled and old enmities lurking just beneath the surface. Almost all foreign observers closely involved with the region are convinced that the prospect of eventual EU membership is indispensable to driving further political reform and cementing democracy. The fear is that if the prospect of EU membership disappears off the political agenda, the Balkans may slip back into instability. Olli Rehn, the EU's enlargement commissioner, warned bluntly on March 15, 2006, that "[i]f we were to go wobbly about the western Balkans' European perspective, our beneficial influence would be severely eroded, just when the region enters a difficult period for talks on Kosovo's status."[2] Signs of just such a wobble became apparent at an EU summit in Salzburg that same month, when EU leaders for the first time qualified their commitment to enlargement with a reference to the EU's "absorption capacity."[3]

The countries of the western Balkans have at least been explicitly offered the prospect of eventual EU membership. No such promise has been made to Ukraine, however, and the political consequences of that lack of generosity may now be emerging. After Ukraine's Orange Revolution, newly elected president Victor Yushchenko made the drive for eventual EU membership a central part of his political strategy. Yet, he was undermined by his failure to receive almost any encouragement from Brussels, which also may well have contributed to his defeat in parliamentary elections in March 2006. The setback for Yushchenko and the rebound in the fortunes of the pro-Russian Viktor Yanukovych threaten to undermine all efforts to bring Ukraine into a stable, democratic, and prosperous European community and to pull the country away from Russia's orbit. If Ukraine, with its size and strategic significance, is rebuffed, other smaller countries such as Belarus, which is still under authoritarian rule, and newly democratic Georgia are likely to be similarly discouraged.

The threat that the EU enlargement process may now die a lingering and public death is potentially a huge blow to the EU and its goal of spreading prosperity and democracy into its wider neighborhood. The EU's aspirations to have a powerful, common foreign policy have generally not met with much success in the wider world, but in its "near abroad," the EU has had one extremely powerful foreign policy tool: the promise of eventual membership, with all the benefits in terms of security, prosperity, and personal opportunity for prospective new members it implies. A senior EU official joked that, "[o]nce a country applies to join the European Union, they become our slaves."[4] That is not quite the case, but it is certainly true that proud countries such as Poland have proved willing to rewrite their domestic law from top to bottom to qualify for EU membership. EU diplomats have proudly compared their ability to spread democracy and the rule of law through peaceful persuasion with the more muscular approach that the United States has favored in Iraq. Yet, the awful prospect is now dawning that the EU, if it were to discard enlargement, would be throwing away its only effective foreign policy tool.

Although eventual EU membership for the countries of the Balkans and Turkey is now clearly in doubt, this does not mean that the prospect of EU membership has completely lost its potency as a spur to reform in those countries. Fortunately, it is not in the interests of either the Brussels authorities or the applicant countries to acknowledge just how much trouble the enlargement process is in. The Turkish government, for example, has placed so much emphasis on its drive for EU membership that to accept that the prospect of membership is actually receding would involve a serious and destabilizing loss of face. The government of Turkish prime minister Recip Tayyip Erdogan may also find the demands made by Brussels a useful spur to domestic reforms that it wants to make anyway, regardless of whether negotiations eventually lead to membership.

For their part, the European authorities in Brussels do not want to admit the difficulties the enlargement process is now facing because to do so would involve acknowledging the deep troubles faced by the EU as an institution as well as jettisoning a powerful tool for influencing the behavior of the EU's neighbors. For the moment, therefore, the enlargement dance can continue, but when the music stops and the lights go up, all parties involved risk suffering a bitter disillusionment.

Notes

1. Guy Verhofstadt, *The United States of Europe* (London: Federal Trust for Education and Research, 2006).
2. "Rehn and MEPs Warn Against 'Wobbly' Messages to Balkans," *EU Observer*, March 16, 2006.
3. Ibid.
4. EU official, conversation with author, Brussels, January 2003.

Robin Niblett

Europe Inside Out

Six months after the French and Dutch rejections of the European Union's constitutional treaty, Europe is still in shock. Member states remain in a self-mandated period of reflection in the hope that they can reach a new consensus on how to achieve their "ever-closer union."[1] Yet, the more time that passes, the more it becomes apparent that the basic foundations on which the process of European integration has been built over the past 50 years are now under assault. The EU's expansion from 15 to 25 members in May 2004 created new fissures that cannot be smoothed over with the sorts of trade-offs arranged in the past by its original West European member states, led by France and Germany. Is this then just the most recent in a series of temporary crises that have punctuated the EU's history and have generally served, in the end, to provide a new impetus for the process of integration, or should a gradual loosening of the EU or even a collapse of its key institutions be expected?

Rather than presaging the unraveling of the EU, the current crisis appears to announce a recalibration of the emphasis that EU governments have placed on each of the three pillars of integration established by the Maastricht Treaty of 1991, which launched a new phase of European integration after German unification and the end of the Cold War. The

Robin Niblett is director of the Europe Program and executive vice president at CSIS.

Copyright © 2005 by The Center for Strategic and International Studies and the Massachusetts Institute of Technology
The Washington Quarterly • 29:1 pp. 41–59.

first pillar encompasses primarily the EU's program of economic integration, including the single market and single currency. The second involves the development and implementation of common foreign and security policies among the EU member states. The third pillar refers to the nascent efforts by EU governments to coordinate their policies in the field of justice and home affairs. Although economic integration has led the European unification process since its inception, it is less likely to serve as the engine of European integration in the near future. As the focus on economic reform becomes firmly a national preoccupation, with the EU playing a facilitating rather than a driving role, the search for common foreign policies and closer cooperation on issues of domestic security will become the primary, if still gradual, drivers of European integration. This recalibration is necessary and one from which the EU could emerge stronger in the decade ahead.

The Aftershocks of May 2005

From its inception, the EU has offered a formal framework within which France and Germany turned their backs on the competition for relative power that had bedeviled their relations and Europe as a whole during the nineteenth and twentieth centuries. The two countries and an expanding group of their West European neighbors chose instead to pool their sovereignty, offering a model of cooperative governance whose fruits—peace and economic prosperity—served both as a standard and a beacon for the rest of Europe. After the Cold War, the EU took on a second vocation, becoming the agent for continental European unification, at first through trade and cooperation agreements between the EU and its East European neighbors and then, after the fall of the Berlin Wall, through a road map to membership for all European nations that met the so-called Copenhagen criteria of democratic governance and market openness established in 1993.

By the spring of 2005, both of these goals had for the most part been met. In the west, the fear of Franco-German conflict has ended. In the east, the EU has begun to overcome Europe's division, drawing most of the members of the former Communist Eastern Bloc into the EU's institutions and offering a path to membership for those that remain on the threshold. The failure to ratify the constitutional treaty thus exposed a new and growing challenge: the yawning divide between member states' governmental ambitions for the EU and popular frustrations with its performance, especially the disconnection between what governments promised through Europe and what Europe could deliver. The depth of this divide was apparent in the decisive majorities that rejected the treaty in the relatively pro-Atlanticist, free-market Netherlands and the traditionally pro-Europe, statist France. Opposition to the treaty also united many of those on the left and right of the political spectrums in each country.[2]

At the heart of these twin rejections lay at least four driving forces, each of which transcended the treaty's actual content and is relevant to Europe's future direction. First, opposition to the treaty reflected a deep and pervasive frustration with the lackluster economic growth and persistently high levels of unemployment that have blighted much of continental Europe for the past two years. In this context, it was difficult to believe politicians' claims that "more Europe" could be the solution to economic malaise. A poll conducted in France in June 2005 revealed that 31 percent of voters believed that the constitution would have a negative impact on French employment rates.[3]

Second, many of those who voted against the constitutional treaty did so to voice their opposition to the EU's May 2004 enlargement, which they perceived as undercutting western Europe's economic competitiveness and driving down their standards of living. For this cadre of voters, the constitutional treaty also offered the opportunity to register a preemptive vote against further EU enlargement, both to the east and, most of all, toward Turkey.

Third, efforts by the constitution's drafters to develop new decision-making procedures for a 25-member Europe merely reminded French and Dutch voters of their relative loss of influence in an enlarged EU. France saw its voting parity with Germany broken for the first time. Smaller states such as the Netherlands saw their relative weight diluted under the proposed double-majority voting system, which swung the pendulum of power further toward the more populous states while weakening the role of the European Commission as the guarantor of a Community-wide perspective. These changes in the relative weight of the member states were all the more significant as the treaty appeared to be ceding even more national power over important social decisions to the EU and its centralized institutions.

Finally, the referenda on the constitutional treaty gave voters the chance to rebel against the high-handedness with which European governments and officials have managed the process of European integration. Monetary union, enlargement to the east, and the adoption of the Maastricht criteria of fiscal discipline had all entailed significant concessions of national sovereignty to Brussels but with little improvement in people's daily lives to show for it. Voters now had the chance to say "no" to their governments' next big European idea and demand instead that they stop pedaling forward on the integrationist bicycle.

All in all, by the summer of 2005 it was clear that the process of European integration had been shorn from its post–World War II and Cold War roots. What does "an ever-closer union" mean when it encompasses at least 25 disparate states in the twenty-first century? The idea that governments could simply return to business as usual in their European conclaves is simply not credible. How then is change likely to manifest itself within the EU over the coming years? The first and most noticeable change will occur in the economic realm.

The Changing Drivers of Economic Integration

The creation of the European Coal and Steel Community in 1952 and the establishment of the European Economic Community in 1957 initiated nearly 50 years of steadily increasing economic integration among an expanding number of EU member states. The milestones in this process are remarkable: the elimination of all tariffs to trade, the creation of a customs union, and the dismantling of most nontariff barriers to trade and investment within the union; free capital movement; border-free travel for visitors and workers across much of the EU; the creation of a single currency; and the establishment of a European Central Bank that has taken over monetary policy for 12 of the EU's member states. These steps both drove and were enabled by the continued development of EU political institutions, including the introduction of qualified majority voting on an ever-expanding range of microeconomic and social questions as well as by strengthening the role of the European Parliament alongside the European Council and the European Commission. From 1965 to 1995, European economies grew to become among the world's most prosperous and among the most generous in terms of social welfare.

STUCK IN A RUT

Today, however, there exists a profound sense that the process of European economic integration is failing to help EU member states cope with their most pressing challenge: remaining competitive under the pressures of economic globalization. This is not simply a case of EU economic growth continuing to lag behind U.S. and global progress. During the last decade, significant structural European economic weaknesses have been allowed to deteriorate further. Most significant among these is the lack of preparedness of the majority of national European retirement and health care systems for the impending demographic time bomb that will hit them within the first quarter of this century. In Germany, for example, it is estimated that in 2025 there will be 14 percent fewer Germans of working age than there are today, and that figure is projected to more than double to 32 percent by 2050.[4] In the nearer term, the ability of European governments to prepare for this demographic crisis is constrained by the fiscal costs of paying for continental Europe's persistently high levels of unemployment, which in turn are entrenched largely by restrictive labor policies in countries such as Spain, Germany, and France that protect existing workers at the expense of generating new positions for the unemployed. The EU faces other structural challenges to its competitiveness in the global economy, such as underdeveloped capital markets and insufficient investment in information and communications technologies to drive growth in Europe's economic productivity.[5]

In 2000, EU leaders launched the Lisbon Agenda to make the European economy "the most competitive and dynamic knowledge-driven economy by 2010."[6] The agenda contained a series of detailed proposals, including opening EU markets to financial services and energy, as well as other business-friendly measures. Yet, as noted in the recent report by Wim Kok, the former Dutch prime minister, the Lisbon Agenda relied heavily on national governments to undertake structural reforms in areas that lay outside EU competence.[7] In the lead-up to the constitutional treaty, EU member states' governments evaded the tough choices necessary to keep the agenda on track, discrediting the idea of using the EU as a vehicle for promoting national structural economic reforms.

A LACK OF CONSENSUS

What effect then is the failure to ratify the constitutional treaty likely to have on the EU's future ability to serve as a catalyst for driving European economic growth forward? Leaders of Europe's three largest economies have each pointed to the failure as a clarion call for a dramatic change in the EU's economic focus, but each government proposes a different approach based on its domestic politics and national preferences. British prime minister Tony Blair points to his country's experience over the last eight years and challenges the idea that EU governments need to choose between social justice and market efficiency, although unions admittedly are weak in the United Kingdom today and do not offer much opposition. Blair has argued for "a modern social policy, not regulation and job protection that may save some jobs for a time at the expense of many jobs in the future."[8] French prime minister Dominique de Villepin points to widespread demands in Europe for "more protection" and "greater job security," and he argues that Europe "cannot be constructed through market forces alone,"[9] least of all in France, where unions still hold a great deal of sway and the public sector, be it civil servants or state-owned enterprises, account for a substantial portion of the workforce. The candidates for the chancellorship in the recent German elections disagreed over how much reform is really needed to save the best aspects of the German model, but neither they nor the electorate want to jettison its main features.

The rest of the EU is equally divided on issues of economic reform. On the question of opening up the EU market to the provision of services, which make up 60 percent of the EU economy but are still largely exempt from the rules of the Single Market program, countries such as the Netherlands, Poland, and Slovakia joined the United Kingdom in supporting this proposal. Others, such as Spain, joined France and Germany in the opposite camp. Nor is it the case that all EU member countries can be neatly classified as either pro– or anti–market liberalization. The previous Polish government, for example, supported opening the market for services but was opposed to passing a more liberal EU takeover directive and efforts to scale back spending on the Common Agricultural Policy.

New German chancellor Angela Merkel's inability to secure majority supprt for her reform agenda has thrown into doubt the scenario whereby Germany would join the United Kingdom and others, possibly including a post-Chirac France after the 2007 election, to help overcome these national divergences and play a leadership role in promoting structural economic change across the EU. When combined with anxieties over the economic implications of the EU's eastern enlargement, it now seems unlikely that these three EU countries can come together to build a common agenda for economic reform, as they did in 1985 when they were instrumental in launching the Single Market program. As a result, it is also unlikely that bold economic initiatives at the EU level will be forthcoming over the next few years. A telling indicator is that the European Commission, which is typically the motor of European economic liberalization, has decided instead not only to scale back its regulatory agenda but also to conduct a "bonfire of inanities" by abolishing some 60 impending pieces of EU regulation.[10]

BACK TO THE CAPITALS

Nevertheless, the current stalemate on economic integration at the EU level need not mean that economic reform will be stalled in Europe. Instead, member states' governments are likely to look less to cooperative solutions and rely instead on promoting reforms at the national level.

Most EU policymakers today, even those in France and Germany, realize that the Franco-German socioeconomic model of the last four decades, which emphasized high levels of worker protection as well as social welfare provision, cannot serve as a successful model either for their own countries or for other European governments. At the same time, there is a growing realization that the harsher Anglo-Saxon model, with its less generous levels of welfare provison and preference for unregulated labor markets, need not be the only viable alternative. Countries such as Denmark, Finland, the Netherlands, and Sweden have been relatively successful economically in recent years by blending high public spending on education, social protection, and welfare provision with relatively unregulated labor markets. This approach could encourage other European governments to pursue national-level experiments designed to achieve the right mix of social protection and market incentives to suit their domestic political economies and social aspirations.[11] As Merkel noted before the German elections, "[P]olarisation does not help us anymore in Europe. Within the tradition of each country—and we have the tradition of the social market economy in Germany—we should try to learn from the successes of others. There is no single continental social model. There are only strengths and weaknesses."[12]

A shift toward the national level for answers to Europe's economic inertia does not necessarily foretell a corresponding unraveling of EU roles or competencies. Instead, the EU and its institutions are likely to play more of a supporting role rather than a leading one in Europe's economic development over the coming years. This outcome is hardly surprising. With the EU budget accounting for only 1 percent of EU member states' gross domestic product (GDP), as compared with the average 45 percent accounted for by national government spending, the range of active policy tools at the national level far exceeds those at the disposal of the EU or the European Commission.

Among other functions, the EU will continue to provide common rules of the road for state behavior within and across their national borders, ensuring that markets remain open and promoting competition while challenging the use of national economic subsidies to avoid the pursuit of beggar-thy-neighbor policies as states turn their attention inward. The EU will continue to provide a formal context for peer review and pressure, as the European Commission does already on the Lisbon Agenda and in the area of fiscal performance. EU institutions such as the European Central Bank can help provide macroeconomic stability while individual governments focus their efforts on microeconomic reforms at the national level. If successful, EU governments and their electorates will start to appreciate that, in economics as in other areas, European integration is a force multiplier for its member states, not an alternative to national action.

A Growing International Presence

The EU has long been accused of being an economic giant but a political dwarf on the global stage. In the near term, however, even as EU nations turn inward economically, the pressure for them to develop more coordinated and even common foreign policies is likely to increase, irrespective of the failure to ratify the constitutional treaty. This trend has been apparent for many years, most recently during the process of EU enlargement to the east, which displayed what the EU had best to offer in terms of a "common" foreign policy. In coming years, this trend will continue to be driven by demand and context, pulling Europe out of the continent, rather than being pushed by a conscious and collective strategy of increased external activism from EU leaders and officials in Brussels. Again, as in the economic realm, a number of forces are at play.

The EU's New Neighborhood

The EU is being forced to invest increasing amounts of its time and resources in promoting modernization and stability around its eastern and southern periphery from Moldova to Morocco. In the past, these countries were ancillary to EU members' more immediate concerns. Today, the EU's eastward expansion has pushed its borders up against more unstable neighbors that have the potential to undermine the EU's internal security through migration, weapons proliferation, human and drug trafficking, crime, and other transnational movements of people and material.

From now on, however, the EU cannot rely on offers of membership to drive reform and stability in its near abroad. The union has pretty much hit the limits of its expansion. Bulgaria and Romania are due to join the EU by 2008, and the countries of the former Yugoslavia are on a membership track that will lead to their eventual accession. The withdrawal of that promise would run the unacceptable risk that those countries could become havens for organized crime and other transnational threats. During the coming years, Turkey will test the outer limits of membership and the meaning of partnership for the EU.

The challenge now for the EU is how to project stability to those countries on the edge of its hardening borders without the powerful political and institutional tool that the offer of eventual membership provided for Central and Eastern Europe during the 1990s. The EU has developed an alternative mechanism for engagement with these countries: the European Neighborhood Policy (ENP), which encompasses a diverse set of countries around the union's periphery. The goal of the ENP is to draw these governments into a structured set of negotiations on internal governance as well as political and economic reform in return for increased levels of political dialogue and access to EU markets. The ENP is evolving into a major undertaking, with a budget of €14.9 billion ($18 billion) for 2007–2013, as compared to approximately €8.5 billion ($10.4 billion) for 2000–2006.[13]

The scope of the ENP is a vivid reminder of the scale of demands and pressures that the EU faces from its periphery. The exploding demographics and pitiful economic performance of North Africa and the East Mediterranean countries is an extremely worrisome combination, made worse by growing political volatility in many of the countries involved. The success of the reform process in Ukraine and its eventual extension to its northern and southern neighbors is vital not only for its people but also for future EU relations with Russia, which supplies almost half of the EU's imports of gas and oil, 43 percent and 42 percent, respectively, in 2004.[14] Acting alone, EU governments cannot hope to have a positive impact on change in any of these countries. The imperatives for common policies and coordinated funding will be inescapable in the years ahead.

THE PULL OF AN EMERGING GLOBAL MULTIPOLARITY

The second driver of a more activist EU foreign policy goes beyond the EU's periphery and involves the realization by its member governments that they can no longer live with the simple ambition of being a regional security power and a global civilian power. On one hand, the EU is quite vulnerable to the dangers of today's transnational threats, such as illegal migration, international terrorism, the rapid spread of infectious diseases, and the trafficking of people and drugs. As noted above, the EU is now bordered on the east and south by underdeveloped neighbors incapable of serving as a buffer between it and the dangers beyond. Its integrated economic space means that any external threat that penetrates the EU's shell can spread within with ease.

On the other hand, the world is increasingly seeking out the EU, whether the EU thinks it is ready to assume an expanded role in the international community or not. Countries that lie well beyond the European neighborhood, such as China, India, and Russia, among others, are looking to the EU as a potential partner for their national and international priorities. The EU's strategic partnership with China is especially emblematic of this new global role. Their partnership has been driven to a large extent by the burgeoning economic relationship between the two sides; the EU is now China's leading trade partner. It is also driven by the EU's ability to engage well with a major rising power such as China, thanks to its incrementalist and consensus-seeking diplomatic approach, which is a natural reflection of the internal negotiating process that takes place daily among the EU's member states on their integration agenda. The practical results of the EU's approach remain to be proven, certainly in terms of influencing Chinese behavior on issues as diverse as human rights, intellectual property protection, and relations with Taiwan. Nevertheless, the sheer intensity and scope of the bilateral dialogues in which the two sides are engaged will, at most, make the EU the lead partner for China's gradual integration into the international system or, at the very least, complicate the conduct of diplomacy with China for other countries, such as the United States and Japan.[15]

AMBIVALENCE TOWARD U.S. LEADERSHIP

The third major driver in the EU's burgeoning international role arises from changing perceptions of the U.S. role in the world. The United States stands at a tipping point in terms of its international authority and influence. Early in its first term, the Bush administration sought to roll back much of the multilateral agenda that its predecessors had accepted or that remained from the bygone era of bipolar superpower competition. After the September 11 attacks, the Bush administration took the fight to the terrorists, wherever it believed that they or their supporters lay. In its second term, the administration has emphasized its mission to spread democracy and freedom to parts of the world where these values are suppressed. Both of these approaches make many allies and other countries nervous. The former are concerned about the unpredictable consequences of U.S. actions for regional or global stability, and the latter fear that they will be the targets of U.S. actions.

In this context, the emphasis placed by EU governments on diplomacy through multilateral consultation, institutions, and agreements as prerequisites for world peace often stands in contrast to the U.S. approach. This emphasis, coupled with its global economic leverage, can make the EU an increasingly attractive partner to other countries in their international relations. The United States was one of the key drivers as well as long-term enablers of European integration, providing the original economic impetus and subsequently the security guarantee under which the EU flourished for its first 50 years. It is ironic, then, that the desire of many EU members to differentiate themselves now from the United States may be an important internal driver of European cooperation and integration in the area of foreign policy. This differentiation may also serve as an important external driver toward that same end, as the world's rising powers try to build Europe up as an alternative pole to the United States.

SEIZING THE MOMENT?

Under such circumstances, the key question is, how will the EU respond to the demand that it play a more active international role? On one hand, the constraints on coherent EU action on the world stage will continue to be significant for the foreseeable future, whether because of a lack of strategic focus among the 25-plus EU member states, including the desire of some to keep in step with the United States and of others for the EU to branch out more explicitly; limited national military capabilities; or simply the paralytic effects of what is likely to remain largely an intergovernmental EU foreign and security policymaking process. Moreover, few EU countries have a real interest in foreign policy beyond Europe's periphery.

On the other hand, the outlines of a more active EU role on the world stage are becoming apparent. Two years ago, EU governments agreed on their first European Security Strategy (ESS), a document that laid out the principal global threats to EU security as well as the preferred means to tackle them.[16] The ESS served as a reminder that the split that occurred in 2002–2003 between the so-called old and new Europes over the U.S. invasion of Iraq represented more the exception than the rule in EU member states' perspectives on global challenges. Beyond an emerging consensus on the broad threats to European security, EU policies toward Iran, China, and Afghanistan, as well as toward the Middle East peace process, are areas in which there is policy agreement, not division, among EU members on broad strategy. Other areas where agreement is apparent are common and established EU positions on global issues such as combating climate change and promoting development in Africa, highlighted by the British EU presidency in the latter half of 2006.

Even in the case of EU policy toward Russia, an issue that is currently more controversial among EU members, one should not underestimate the power of EU internal socialization to elicit a more common strategy in the future. In other words, over time the habit of constant consultation and preference for consensus building—one of the hallmarks of the EU foreign policy process—could narrow the gap between new EU members' deep suspicion of the Putin government and the preference for more conciliatory approaches among some other EU member states located farther from Russia's borders. The EU's eventual support of the Orange Revolution in Ukraine in 2004 also demonstrated another aspect of an enlarged EU's growing flexibility in its foreign policy making:

the willingness of the majority to defer, after appropriate consultation, to the interests of the nations closest to or with the most direct interest in the foreign policy challenge at hand, even when, as in the case of Ukraine, these are some of its newest members.

Finally, EU governments are now making an effort to put enhanced capabilities at the disposal of their common foreign policies. These include the constitutional proposals that governments approved to create a new EU diplomatic corps and an EU foreign minister, which may be resurrected and adopted in some form on their own merits; discussions, in a series of recent position papers, on how the EU should approach the use of economic and diplomatic sanctions to uphold EU foreign policies;[17] and a renewed focus on acquiring some of the military capabilities needed to back up the EU's enhanced diplomatic ambitions. Although the EU cannot close the defense spending gap with the United States, its members are seeking to maximize the impact of their limited resources modestly through the creation of rapidly deployable multinational military forces such as the so-called EU Battlegroups, ambitiously through investment in the Galileo global positioning satellite system, and innovatively through the development of EU constabulary forces for conflict avoidance and postconflict stabilization.[18] The willingness of EU governments to put their collective capabilities to use can be seen in the noticeable expansion of EU military and other security deployments outside its borders during the last two years, from police training in Palestine to force deployments under EU command in Bosnia and Herzegovina, the Democractic Republic of Congo, Darfur, and Aceh. Overarching these nascent capabilities remains the EU power to dictate to other countries the terms of access to its commercial market.

Even though the structural constraints on the EU's ability to forge coherent common foreign policies are likely to persist, observers should not underestimate the extent to which the outside world is forcing EU governments to coordinate their foreign policies better or to which EU member states might choose to rise to the challenge. Both of these forces are likely to continue driving forward EU integration in the field of foreign and security policy despite the failure of the constitutional treaty.

The New Dimensions of European Security

Even as the governments of EU member states are forced to work more closely together to meet the demands of an encroaching world, they face more urgent internal pressures to open new avenues of integration to confront the changing threats to their domestic security. The EU's third pillar, focusing on justice and home affairs, has traditionally been the poor cousin in the EU's integration triumvirate. Now, in the context of the fight against terrorism in Europe, these roles might be temporarily reversed.

IMMIGRATION

The creation of the third pillar of European integration in the Maastricht Treaty reflected the growing need, after they removed the barriers to the free movement of people throughout the EU, for member states' governments to coordinate the sensitive issue of their national immigration and asylum policies. Since Maastricht, there has been a surge in immigration into Europe from North Africa and southeastern Europe. Recently, for example, the European Citizen Action Service reported that, since the EU's last enlargement in May 2004, 175,000 workers from the eight central European accession countries have registered to work in the United Kingdom, with 56 percent coming from Poland. According to the same report, the Irish government, which along with the United Kingdom is one of the only western European EU countries not to have imposed limits on the entry of workers from the new accession countries, issued 85,000 Social Security numbers to immigrants from these countries—a figure that may seem marginal but represents a 2 percent increase in the Irish population.[19] France, Spain, and Italy, on the other hand, have also faced large migrations from North Africa. This trend was highlighted dramatically in October by the attempted invasions of Ceuta and Melilla, the Spanish protectorates in Morocco, by migrants looking to enter Spain through these North African gateways.

Given the ease with which migrants can move across borders within the EU once they have gained entry, governments are being forced to respond to this precipitate rise in immigration at the national and the EU levels. Since the 1999 meeting of the European Council in Tampere, Finland, building common approaches and policies toward immigration and the granting of asylum to third-country nationals has become a priority on the EU agenda. The EU Council of Ministers has reached a series of agreements in this area, covering not only immigrant workers but also third-country students, vocational trainees, and volunteers, which include the February 2003 directive on the right of third-country nationals legally established in an EU member state to family reunification and the January 2004 granting of "long-term resident status" to third-country nationals who legally reside for a period of five years in an EU member state.[20]

Yet, coordination of immigration and asylum policies captures at best only half of the policy challenge for EU governments. Perhaps the more critical challenge at this juncture is to tackle the historical animosity of their societies to immigration. Popular resentment toward immigrants has been fed by high levels of European unemployment and fears over job security. This hostility has its roots, however, in the commonly held European assumption that immigrant workers crossed their borders only for a temporary period, that they were literally guest workers, an assumption that has been disproved as the great majority of migrants have settled across the EU and have served as a magnet for further immigrant flows.

In the coming years, EU governments and citizens will need to foster a culture of integration that no longer tolerates or feeds the native desire to exclude foreigners or panders to the immigrant's desire to stand apart. The urgency of meeting this challenge is twofold, not only to improve Europe's social stability and internal security but also to ensure Europe's economic well-being. Although modernized and coordinated immigration policies are no panacea for the continent's broader demographic and economic challenges, such policies must form a central plank in EU governments' coordinated response to the impending population crises in their countries.

THE THREAT WITHIN

Unfortunately, in the wake of the September 11 attacks and, more recently, the terrorist attacks in Madrid and London, what had begun principally under the EU's third pillar as a functional need to improve the coordination of national immigration and asylum policies has evolved into a far more pressing priority. The possibility that European countries would be targets of Al Qaeda–inspired terrorism after the September 11 attacks had been well accepted, especially following European governments' pledge of political and military support to defeat Al Qaeda in Afghanistan in the late fall of 2001. The terrorist attacks in Madrid in March 2004 and in London in July 2005, however, as well as the discovery of local terrorist cells in Italy, France, Germany, and the Netherlands over the past four years have opened the eyes of EU governments to the seminally different nature of today's security threats compared to those posed by the Soviet empire during the Cold War or by the nationalist or anarchist terrorist movements during the 1970s and 1980s.

The new European terrorism has exposed a long-standing societal fault line that had largely escaped the attention of intelligence and law enforcement agencies. It is now clear to most government and academic analysts that EU countries have alarmingly large numbers of citizens, primarily first-, second-, or third-generation Muslim immigrants, who are suffering from or are vulnerable to a deep identity crisis.[21] In many cases, these individuals work as nationals and citizens within their adopted European home but live in closed communities that relate more closely to their members' countries of origin. Significantly, these individuals feel that they are foreigners in both countries and, as such, are especially susceptible to the narrative of persecution, victimhood, and redemption offered by extreme Islamist groups. Especially worrisome is the conclusion that potential terrorists emerging from this background do not need to travel to a country such as Pakistan or to return from a fighting tour in Iraq to be motivated or sufficiently capable to mount a devastating attack.

The violent, economically disruptive, and potentially catastrophic effects of terrorism, combined with the perpetrators' ability to take advantage of porous EU borders and uncoordinated national intelligence and law enforcement agencies in launching their attacks, makes this a natural and in fact urgent area for deepening intra-European cooperation. It is also becoming a new test of the EU's relevance and ambition, as revealed in the series of high-level meetings of EU interior ministers over the past year and a half since the March 2004 Madrid attacks. The actual and potential agenda for cooperation revealed by these meetings is enormous: coordinating the protection and surveillance of EU borders, sharing information on terrorist threats and intentions, ensuring the effectiveness of the common EU arrest warrant and mutual extradition treaties, aligning judicial approaches with the admissibility of evidence in trials of terrorists, retaining data and maintaining privacy, and coordinating plans for emergency response and reconstitution after possible attacks.

As in the area of foreign policy, the obstacles to effective EU coordination are pervasive and significant throughout the field of justice and home affairs, an area in which member countries have, for example, different judicial systems, disjointed national law enforcement and intelligence agencies, and serious shortages of funding for technology and trained personnel. Yet, the recent agreements on combating terrorism in Europe reached on July 13, 2005, at the meeting of the interior ministers of EU member states confirm that all EU governments are aware that, despite the failure of the constitutional referenda, they can use both informal coordination and formal rulemaking under EU auspices to respond to this shared danger more effectively through collective action than they ever could nationally.[22]

Europe's Next Phase

Despite the turmoil caused by the rejection of the EU's constitutional treaty, the three principal drivers of European coordination and integration remain the same as they have been since the end of the Cold War and the signing of the Maastricht Treaty: economic integration, foreign policy coordination, and improved internal security. Europe is now entering a period, however, that will witness an important change in the balance of emphasis among these three drivers. EU governments' ability to squeeze real gains in economic performance from deeper economic integration at the EU level is reaching its practical and political limit. Although broadly implementing the Single Market program in the area of financial and professional services could offer gains to EU member states, governments must still prepare their economies at the national level first to meet the pressures of a more competitive internal European economy following enlargement, as well as an ever-expanding and more competitive global economy. As a result, a majority of EU governments must now focus individually on the difficult domestic process of reforming their welfare states and social compacts. During this period, the EU will appropriately serve more as a facilitator and arbiter than as an agenda-setter.

With the EU's first pillar entering a phase of consolidation, whether temporarily or not, the EU's third pillar will be a central focus of European integration in the near future. A great deal remains to be accomplished in this area, but the need to act collectively to meet the new demands of internal security is not a controversial proposition. It has the advantage of involving all EU member states around a common purpose, even as it spills into all sorts of cherished national competencies. The search for new modes of cooperation and integration in this area promises to be a vital new driver of European integration and also has the potential to open new avenues for transatlantic coordination.

Even as EU governments develop their third pillar of integration and turn inward economically, the pressure to be more engaged internationally is likely to increase. The sheer size of the EU economy, the instability of its periphery, the rise of new global powers, the proliferation of external threats to its security, and the growing European and global ambivalence toward U.S. leadership together are thrusting the EU, ready or not, into the role of a leading actor on the world stage. This development will pose serious challenges for the union. Not all member states will be interested in or capable of meeting, much less willing to meet, the demand for greater international engagement. Informal contact groups of the type formed by the EU-3 (France, Germany, and the United Kingdom) to deal with the Iranian nuclear issue may be a near-term solution, but it will be vital for the rest of the EU to buy into this approach if Europe is to deliver results from its more active diplomacy.

Member states will also find it difficult to devote the political attention and resources necessary to pursue a more active, joint foreign policy when they are concentrating simultaneously on pushing through contentious domestic reform programs. It could take up to a decade for the EU to translate sustained growth in its key national economies into the sorts of political and economic capabilities required to enable it to act on the world stage more proactively than reactively.

Nevertheless, an EU that is asked to be, and feels it needs to be, more assertive will inevitably have a growing impact on international relations. As slow and reactive as its intergovernmental decisionmaking may continue to be, the mere weight of its presence, representing 25 percent of the world's GDP and 30 percent of foreign assistance and with a growing diplomatic and security reach, inevitably presages the emergence of a more complex world order. Even if a majority of its members try to sustain the linkages of a transatlantic partnership, the fact is that the EU itself and other world powers will have alternatives to U.S. leadership. As the recent imbroglio over the EU's desire to lift its arms embargo on China revealed, U.S. policymakers can no longer assume that their global alliances, treaty commitments, and troop deployments will give them the space to define the diplomatic agenda in key regions of the world, from East Asia to the Middle East.

Despite the EU's loss of strategic direction precipitated by the failure to ratify the constitutional treaty, member states appear to be embarking on a new phase in their process of integration. They are looking inward for new models of economic organization that will meet their individual social and economic needs, while looking out at the wider world with a growing awareness that being economically engaged but politically detached is no longer a viable option. At the same time, member states are turning to each other with increased levels of intensity to deal with new threats to their internal security. The EU may lack its constitution and be destined to be a less than perfect union, but its members and institutions have a good chance to emerge strengthened from the difficult period that lies ahead. The key test for such an outcome lies in the ability of EU member states to unlock the economic potential that their stable, skilled, and well-developed national economies contain. Without each member taking the necessary steps to improve its national competitiveness and economic dynamism, the strains on its social fabric will intensify, and the EU will possess neither the self-confidence nor the resources to live up to its global potential. The opportunity to change course lies in the hands of Europe's citizens and leaders, not in the words and institutional arrangements of its constitutional treaty.

Notes

1. This goal was first proclaimed in the Treaty of Rome, http://www.hri.org/docs/Rome57/.

2. See Robin Niblett, "Shock Therapy," Euro-Focus 11, no. 2 (June 3, 2005), http://www.csis.org/europe/eurofocus/v11n2.pdf.

3. Eurobarometer, "The European Constitution: Post-Referendum Survey in France," June 2005, http://europa.eu.int/comm/public_opinion/flash/fl171_en.pdf.

4. Richard Jackson, "Germany and the Challenge of Global Aging," March 2003, http://www.csis.org/gai/germany_report.pdf.

5. For more detail on the reasons behind low European productivity, see Bart van Ark, Robert Inklaar, and Robert H. Guckin, "ICT and Productivity in Europe and the United States: Where Do the Differences Come From?" (working paper, The Conference Board, Centre for Economic Research, Groningen, the Netherlands, October 2003).

6. For more on the Lisbon Agenda, see http://europa.eu.int/growthandjobs/index_en.htm.

7. "Facing the Challenge: The Lisbon Strategy for Growth and Employment," November 2004, http://europa.eu.int/growthandjobs/pdf/kok_report_en.pdf (report from the High Level Group chaired by Wim Kok).

8. Tony Blair, speech to the European Parliament, Brussels, June 23, 2005, http://www.number-10.gov.uk/output/Page7714.asp.

9. Dominique de Villepin, speech to the French National Assembly, Paris, June 8, 2005, http://www.premier-ministre.gouv.fr/en/information/latest_news_97/declaration_of_general_policy_53247.html.

10. "EU Moves to Cut Knot of Red Tape," BBC News, September 27, 2005, http://news.bbc.co.uk/1/hi/world/europe/4285512.stm.

11. For more on this idea, see André Sapir, "Globalization and the Reform of European Social Models" (paper, Ecofin Informal Meeting, Bruegel, Manchester, September 9, 2005), http://www.bruegel.org/Repositories/Documents/publications/working_papers/EN_SapirPaper080905.pdf.

12. Angela Merkel, interview by Bertrand Benoit, *Financial Times*, July 21, 2005, p. 15.

13. For more information on the ENP, see http://europa.eu.int/comm/world/enp/index_en.htm.

14. For more information, see Fiona Hill, "Beyond Co-Dependency: European Reliance on Russian Energy." *U.S.-Europe Analysis Series*, July 2005, http://www.brookings.edu/fp/cuse/analysis/hill20050727.pdf.

15. For more on the EU relationship with China, see David Shambaugh, "China and Europe: The Emerging Axis," *Current History* 103, no. 675 (September 2004): 243–248; David Shambaugh, "The New Strategic Triangle: U.S. and European Reactions to China's Rise," *The Washington Quarterly* 28, no. 3 (Summer 2003): 7–25.

16. For the complete European Security Strategy, see http://ue.eu.int/uedocs/cmsUpload/78367.pdf.

17. For more on the EU and sanctions, see http://europa.eu.int/comm/external_relations/cfsp/sanctions/index.htm.

18. For more on European Defense Integration, see Michèle Flournoy and Julianne Smith, eds., "European Defense Integration: Bridging the Gap Between Strategy and Capabilities," October 2005, http://www.csis.org/isp/0510_eurodefensereport.pdf.

19. Julianna Traser, Monika Byrska, and Bartosz Napieralski, "Report on the Free Movement of Workers in EU-25: Who's Afraid of EU Enlargement?" September 2005, http://www.ecas.org/file_uploads/810.pdf.

20. For more on EU-wide immigration policies, see http://europa.eu.int/comm/justice_home/fsj/immigration/fsj_immigration_intro_en.htm.

21. For more on the Muslim identity crisis in Europe, see Shireen T. Hunter, ed., *Islam: Europe's Second Religion* (Washington, D.C.: Praeger/CSIS Press, 2002); Timothy M. Savage, "Europe and Islam: Crescent Waxing, Cultures Clashing," *The Washington Quarterly* 27, no. 3 (Summer 2004): 25–50.

22. For more on the July 13 Extraordinary Council Meeting of Justice and Home Affairs ministers, see http://ue.eu.int/ueDocs/cms_Data/docs/pressData/en/jha/85703.pdf.

Franco Algieri

A Weakened EU's Prospects for Global Leadership

The European Union has developed a significant presence as a regional and world actor, but its goals at times exceed its capacity to act as a supranational entity. With roots as an economic bloc, the EU has over the years attempted to correct the imbalance between its global economic and political presences, developing the Common Foreign and Security Policy (CFSP) and later the European Security and Defense Policy (ESDP) to allow for a more effective external profile. It has also increased the number and significance of its diplomatic and politico-military initiatives with other states and regional organizations. Since the Treaty of Maastricht creating the EU and CFSP took effect in 1992, however, the deepening process has proceeded rather slowly, puttering ahead with various treaty reforms but improving the operational capabilities rather incrementally.

EU widening, on the other hand, has surged ahead. On May 1, 2004, 10 new member states, eight of which are eastern European countries, joined the EU in the union's most significant expansion since the signing of the Rome treaties in 1957. Further enlargement rounds are being sketched out with the confirmed addition of Bulgaria and Romania in

Franco Algieri is a senior research fellow at the Center for Applied Policy Research (CAP) at Ludwig-Maximilians University in Munich. He is also a guest professor at Renmin University in Beijing.

Copyright © 2006 by The Center for Strategic and International Studies and the Massachusetts Institute of Technology
The Washington Quarterly • 30:1 pp. 107–115.

2007, and talks on Turkey and Croatia having already begun. The waiting list is growing: the Balkan states, Ukraine, Belarus, and Moldova in the east and Morocco and others in the south.

The EU's major strategic objective is to secure its expanding neighborhood, which now stretches from the eastern parts of Europe over the Balkans to the Mediterranean and the Middle East, against global threats such as terrorism, proliferation of weapons of mass destruction, regional conflict, failed states, and organized crime. If the EU were to admit Turkey, it would share borders with Iran, Iraq, and Syria, among others. With its expanding radius, the EU will have to improve further a variety of tasks, including humanitarian aid, rescue missions, peacekeeping, disarmament, and counterterrorism.[1]

The clamor for EU membership evident in enlargement has sparked high hopes for the EU project. In 2005, however, the integration project skidded to a halt when France and the Netherlands rejected the EU Constitution. EU member states' governments, publics, and EU institutions themselves have shown an increasing and critical hesitance toward further enlargement. As of late, debate revolves around whether the enlarged EU has the capacity to absorb even more members.

Consequently, the European integration project has reached a crucial stage. EU members clearly struggle with the conflict between their desire to exert power on the world stage as a larger entity and hesitance to surrender national sovereignty. Where do the failed referenda leave the EU as a global actor? With an expanding neighborhood comes greater responsibility and risks, as the EU's territory and mandate edges closer to potentially high-risk regions and problems. With pressures increasing out of area and member populations unwilling to "deepen," how can the EU adjust to address its changing political environment? How can it remain relevant in world affairs given its internal stalemate?

Small Steps toward Consensus

The idea that the EU should speak with one voice in world affairs has become more prominent over the course of the European integration process, but history reveals that merging national policies is a most difficult task. The global changes of the early 1990s, including the disintegration of the Soviet Union and the transformation of Eastern Europe, the reunification of Germany, the Persian Gulf War, and conflicts in the Balkans, demonstrated the need for a broad legal and institutional base for a common European foreign policy. Provisions for the CFSP were integrated into the Maastricht treaty, which formally created the EU as it exists today. Yet, despite the new legislation, the minimum consensus reached by EU member states for the CFSP, or rather their hesitance to bind national foreign policies more closely together, did not sufficiently increase the efficiency of the EU's foreign policy mandate. The CFSP framework regularly and systematically coordinated EU member states' national foreign policies on the supranational level. It soon turned out that further improvements for the CFSP were needed.

The 1997 Treaty of Amsterdam brought additional institutional developments and instruments, allowing the possibility of common strategies. The most outstanding innovation was the creation of the position of high representative for the CFSP, later filled by former NATO secretary general Javier Solana, and the creation of the policy unit inside the secretariat general of the council to be his strategic and planning unit. Moreover, the wording of the Amsterdam treaty clarified security and defense guidelines, giving member states the option to move in the direction of a common defense if they so desired. Again, however, international responsibilities took precedence when challenges arose in the Balkans and in places not in the immediate vicinity of the EU, such as the Caucasus and northern Africa.

Internal and external expectations grew that the union should take primary responsibility for conflict management and resolution of the former Yugoslavia to assert its authority in its "backyard" and assume a greater share of the global security burden. In December 1998, France and the United Kingdom released a joint declaration at St. Malo calling for the EU to possess the power of autonomous action and the appropriate military resources, a groundbreaking step forward.[2] At that time, however, the EU lacked a common structure for defense policy, so the Kosovo mission had to be conducted within the NATO framework and with U.S. support. In June 1999, building on the experiences of the Kosovo conflict and the St. Malo "spirit," EU member states agreed at the European Council in Cologne to develop and strengthen the ESDP as part of the CFSP. Subsequently, provisions for the ESDP were fine-tuned and integrated into the Treaty of Nice, which became the current treaty of reference for the CFSP/EDSP when it came into effect in 2003. The ESDP was a qualitative leap forward, paving the way for civilian, police, and military missions as parts of the EU's foreign policy.

Over time, EU member states have gradually strengthened the ESDP to put the union in a position to assume more responsibility for international security. Although the ESDP still has major shortcomings, especially in the military domain, 16 civilian, police, and military operations have been conducted throughout the world within the ESDP framework as of July 2006. These operations have mainly been concentrated in the EU's neighborhood and in Africa, but there also are ongoing missions in the Palestinian territories and Aceh, Indonesia.[3] The EU has shown proficiency in lower-end crisis management operations in these missions.

Its member states do not, however, show a uniform readiness for a far-reaching military integration on the European level, most having reduced their defense expenditures following the Cold War. Since 1994, the level of support for the CFSP within the EU-15 has been consistently higher than 60 percent.[4] In the spring of 2003, 74 percent expressed support for a common security and defense policy, and 50 percent stated that decisions relating to defense issues should be made at the European level. Yet, although European publics do recognize the need for the CFSP and ESDP, they express limited interest when the idea of increasing defense budgets comes up, and many governments avoid this unpopular topic. Consequently, even though the EU has an impressive catalogue of declarations and institutional agreements expressing the intention to become a comprehensive security political actor, they must take U.S. interests into account when considering major military operations. They are in need of U.S. assets in the NATO framework, 19 of whose members are also EU member states.

The overlap of EU-NATO members and missions is another thorny issue among the EU member states and between the EU and the United

States. The United States has historically been skeptical of any project that would decouple the EU from the larger NATO decisionmaking framework; duplicate military planning, command structures, and supply decisions; or discriminate against non-NATO EU members. The United Kingdom and most eastern European members want to maintain close links with Washington and to coordinate European and U.S. interests. They see NATO as the primary guarantor of defense policy and as a direct connection to the United States. On the other hand, France and some other EU member states would prefer to see a Europe that is more independent from United States, particularly in terms of decisionmaking procedure and capabilities. Such incoherence among EU member states damages the deepening of a real European security and defense policy. Moreover, the image of the EU as a single actor is compromised when member states accuse each other of not being committed or willing to develop the ESDP.

Iraq Reveals the EU's Fissures

A strengthened ESDP cannot prevent basic policy conflicts among EU members, especially with their recently expanded ranks. As European governments dissented over the U.S. plan to invade Iraq in 2003, for example, a debate over a CFSP collapse abounded. Although many EU members shared the goal of restraining the United States from taking extreme action, the EU as such did not appear as a singular entity. This episode revealed that the CFSP reflected an ambitious integrationist goal but not the true condition of European foreign and security policy.

While France, Germany, and Belgium led the way in protesting President George W. Bush's planned invasion of Iraq, the Czech Republic, Denmark, Hungary, Italy, Poland, Portugal, Spain, and the United Kingdom declared their transatlantic solidarity in the January 2003 "Letter of the Eight."[5] In reaction to this western European initiative, the 10 countries of the Vilnius Group—Albania, Bulgaria, Croatia, Estonia, Latvia, Lithuania, Macedonia, Romania, Slovakia, and Slovenia—also wrote a letter declaring their solidarity with the United States. To these young democracies, the United States was the principal guarantor of stability and success. Alarmed by the possible ramifications of alienating the United States, these eastern European countries assured Washington of their undiluted loyalty.

These different approaches of countries of western and eastern Europe revealed splits on several levels: among the EU member states, between the old and new EU members, and between the member states and the supranational level. Although President of the Commission Romano Prodi and High Representative Javier Solana were working intensely on a European position, the member states' counterproductive behavior damaged the overall performance of the EU. At this stage, enlargement would clearly prove to be a severe test for further development of the CFSP and ESDP.

Can and Should the Constitution Be Saved?

EU member states have chosen strikingly comprehensive and muscular defense-related political provisions and instruments in the ESDP and deliberately have not set geographical limitations on its area of operation. Although this indicates a highly ambitious project, the extent of EU action in any given conflict remains a highly intricate political decision. The EU has quickly developed an ambitious foreign and security policy agenda but cannot expand respective operational capabilities and coherence at the same speed, an obstacle that has become even more serious in the current internal reform crisis.

The helplessness of political elites in the aftermath of the negative French and Dutch referenda on the constitution left them no alternative other than rethinking their priorities and goals and hopefully "enabl[ing] a broad debate to take place in each of our countries, involving citizens, civil society, social partners, national parliaments and political parties."[6] The member states agreed to revisit the issue, but one year later, the assessment was rather sobering. The European Council's decision in June 2006 to now "focus on delivery of concrete results and implementation of projects"[7] indicates that EU member states want to delay an answer to the constitutional question. In political and academic circles, the analysis of the European Constitution as a dead project is gaining ground.

The negative votes in the French and Dutch referenda on the constitution were a political shock for EU governments. More and more European voters are concerned that European integration is a runaway train that is too complex and that has been disregarding democratic control. In France, the Netherlands, and other member states, people worry about issues such as immigration, crime, an out-of-touch bureaucracy, and loss of sovereignty and national identity. Accordingly, most analyses assert that the "no" votes had little to do with the constitution itself and more with frustration with the way that Europe is being built and with the political class. Nonetheless, the French and Dutch rejections of the European constitution reveal that Europe lacks an integrative will that no legislation or policy initiative can create. The old integration pattern of the twentieth century has lost its appeal and function, and a new vision and form of European integration does not yet exist.

Yet, this does not mean that the EU should abandon its project altogether. Europeans should not wait for a final conclusion on the fate of the European constitution but should move forward on improving the institutional and procedural framework for the CFSP/ESDP. Developing the governance of European foreign policy will make it easier to bring national interests together and to avoid overstretching the efficiency and effectiveness of the CFSP/ESDP. Currently, it is rather difficult to expect a major breakthrough, considering the centrality of the Big Three—France, Germany, and the United Kingdom—who rarely see eye to eye on the details of integration. Moreover, as of late, the topic of European integration is used rather hesitantly in national political debates. France is waiting for its next presidential elections in April 2007, the United Kingdom is facing the end of the leadership of Tony Blair probably in 2007, and the German grand coalition government is concentrating on surviving a full term.

This is where reviving parts of the constitution could prove useful. One of its more valuable features is a new central actor in European foreign policy, the EU minister for foreign affairs. This position would help to consolidate foreign policy competencies at a supranational level, enhancing the EU's policy coherence and its representation on the international stage. In contrast to the high representative for the CFSP, this new actor would have more competencies to act and a more powerful position inside the European Council and the European Commission, allowing it to create more coherence in the EU's foreign policy. Linked to this is the creation of a European External Action Service (EEAS) and the European Defense Agency. The EEAS would serve as an important and necessary support function for the foreign minister. The European Defense Agency, in effect since late 2004, works to improve the efficiency of the European armaments sector, thus helping to develop Europe's military capabilities.

Also, the constitution's allowance for "permanent structured cooperation" would allow those member states whose military capabilities fulfill higher criteria and who make binding commitments to each other regarding the implementation of highly demanding missions to move forward with integration while allowing others to be less involved. As such, the European integration process would become more differentiated and allow the EU to maintain its power to act.

Considering the current state of European affairs, it is more necessary than ever to ensure that forms of flexible integration permit smaller groups of interested members to go further than others. Otherwise, if EU member states choose to arrange their foreign, security, and defense policy activities outside the EU framework by building ad hoc coalitions, the EU's role as a global actor will come into question.

Looking at today's EU, its member states have to accept that only through cooperation and by pooling power will they be able to have a lasting global impact. If the member states do not come to terms on how best to organize supranationality in foreign policy, then they as individual states and the EU as a whole run the danger of rendering themselves inconsequential in world affairs. The United States, Russia, China, India, and other powerful actors are not patiently waiting for Europeans to have their self-awareness debate concluded.

The EU as an Indecisive Actor

The EU faces an external-internal divergence dilemma. The union is working to develop its role as an international actor. At the same time, it is confronted internally with a stalled reform process and an existential debate about its governance structures and future shape. This dichotomy has lasting consequences for the future of the EU as a global actor. In the short term, or until about 2009, the EU will remain an indecisive actor. If member states succeed in ratifying something like a European constitution by then, it will be much easier to describe the union as a global actor. If this project fails, the whole concept of the EU must be reconsidered.

The EU has a patchwork of policies rather than a common global vision and strategy. European foreign security and defense policy can be expected to be guided by multilateralism as expressed in the 2003 European Security Strategy (ESS).[8] The member states' agreement on the ESS was largely a reaction to the terrorist attacks of September 11, 2001, and their repercussions, including the Iraq conflict, all of which made it impossible for the EU to be inactive. Some observers in Europe interpreted the ESS in part as a response to the 2002 "National Security Strategy of the United States." Such a comparison seems problematic, not least because the ESS remains vague on the questions of when and how to use military means in defense of European interests. Rather, this document can be considered a reference for the broad orientation of the EU as a global actor. It regards cooperation with other powers, such as the United States and Russia, to be essential and defines the transatlantic relationship as irreplaceable. Furthermore, it declares Canada, Japan, China, and India to be strategic partners of the union. The ESS reveals the great importance the EU attaches to the United Nations, the World Trade Organization, and NATO as well as regional organizations, for example, in Asia or South America.

Will this be sufficient to meet the global challenges of the twenty-first century and to shape international relations powerfully? An internal dilemma is no novelty for the European integration process, but in view of the current enlargement debate, it has a new significance. The old pattern of deepening and widening does not work any more, if it ever worked efficiently. The number of actors involved and the heterogeneity of interests of 27-plus member states is overstretching the current EU governance system. Consequently, further and substantial extension of the union's presence in the outside world cannot be expected; in this case, bigger does not mean more powerful. On the contrary, as long as there is no substantial internal reform, enlargement might turn out to be the beginning of the end for Europe's global aspirations.

This would have major consequences for the EU's influence in the Middle East and other trouble spots. Moreover, its internal divisions allow external actors to play EU member states against each other or, as China does so well, to manipulate single European states for its own purposes. In the case of Asia-Pacific security, for example, China and the United States will not carve out a role for the EU in that region. As power politics are on the rise, the EU needs more than a basket full of carrots and only some incrementally developed sticks to compete.

Even though the EU is still a world champion in trade policy and development aid, it is in danger of becoming an irrelevant power. There is still hope for Europe if the respective provisions foreseen in the European constitution can be saved, not necessarily as a constitutional treaty. If this goal does not come to fruition, the concept of the EU as a global actor will have reached its end, and the reemergence of single European powers will be unavoidable.

Notes

1. On the EU's civilian crisis management and coordination of civil-military operations, see Catriona Gurlay et al., "Civilian Crisis Management: The EU Way," *Challiot Paper*, no. 90 (June 2006), http://www.iss-eu.org/chaillot/chai90.pdf.

2. See "Joint Declaration on European Defence," December 4, 1998, http://www.fco.gov.uk/servlet/Front?pagename=OpenMarket/Xcelerate/ShowPage&c=Page&cid=1007029391629&aid=1013618395073.

3. For an overview on ESDP missions, see "European Security and Defence Policy (ESDP) Operations," http://www.consilium.europa.eu/showPage.asp?id=268&lang=en.

4. See European Commission, *Eurobarometer*, no. 59 (Spring 2003), http://ec.europa.eu/public_opinion/archives/eb/eb59/eb59_rapport_final_en.pdf; Ger-

man Marshall Fund of the United States and Compagnia di San Paolo, "Transatlantic Trends Overview: 2003," http://www.transatlantictrends.org/index.cfm?year=2003.

5. See José María Aznar et al., "Europe and America Must Stand United," *London Times*, January 30, 2003, http://www.globalpolicy.org/security/issues/iraq/media/2003/0130useur.htm.

6. "Declaration by the Heads of State or Government of the Member States of the EU on the Ratification of the Treaty Establishing a Constitution for Europe," SN 117/05, June 18, 2005, http://www.consilium.europa.eu./ueDocs/cms_Data/docs/pressData/en/ec/85325.pdf.

7. "Brussels European Council, 15/16 June 2006: Presidency Conclusions," 10633/1/06 Rev. 1, July 17, 2006, p. 16, http://www.consilium.europa.eu/ueDocs/cms_Data/docs/pressdata/en/ec/90111.pdf.

8. See "A Secure Europe in a Better World: European Security Strategy," December 12, 2003, http://www.consilium.europa.eu/uedocs/cmsUpload/78367.pdf.

Part V:
Japan's Quest for Normalcy

Edward J. Lincoln

Japan: Using Power Narrowly

Fifteen years ago, Japan appeared to be an emerging new center of regional and global power. Although constrained from exercising military force by its constitution, various aspects of Japan's economic strength positioned the country to play a major role in important regional and global affairs. Today, that opportunity appears to remain bypassed. The notion that economic strength conveyed an ability to influence international affairs was not misguided; rather, the Japanese government retreated from the prospect. Despite new, unwelcome economic constraints that emerged as the Japanese economy sputtered in the 1990s, Japan remains the world's second-largest economic power. It nevertheless seems to lag behind comparable European nations considerably as a world power.

Although Japan has not contributed much to reshaping the global agenda, at least it has exercised an ability to modify or manipulate its external environment to advance its own national interests. It has not changed or even significantly influenced world institutions and systems, yet has successfully maintained access to foreign raw material sources, kept foreign markets open to Japanese goods as well as investment, and remained at peace with the world while keeping the United States at its side should conflict occur. Any fair analysis of Japanese power, therefore, and the coun-

Edward J. Lincoln is a senior fellow at the Council on Foreign Relations.

Copyright © 2003 by The Center for Strategic and International Studies and the Massachusetts Institute of Technology
The Washington Quarterly • 27:1 pp. 111–127.

try's global role must take this narrower agenda into account. In this sense, the economic and other nonmilitary levers at Japan's disposal have allowed it to meet Japan's immediate needs.

Great Expectations

Since the late 1980s, the world has recognized Japan as a major economic nation and has expected that it would play—and would want to play—a more influential role in global affairs. By that time, with an economy almost half the size of that of the United States and a level of affluence close to the U.S. level, Japan stood well ahead of any single European country in economic size. This characteristic alone conferred on Japan a high degree of recognition, with grudging respect or apprehension, among other industrial nations about the new kid on the block as well as admiration among developing nations desiring to replicate Japan's successful development process. Furthermore, with an average annual real gross domestic product (GDP) growth rate of almost 5 percent from 1987 to 1991, Japan was outperforming all other industrialized nations. Speculation that this pattern would continue was yet another reason why other governments might pay attention to what the Japanese government had to say.

TRADE

As Japan industrialized, it developed a successful export sector. Whereas Japan had primarily been an exporter of textiles and labor-intensive goods in the 1950s, Japan by the 1980s was a major player abroad in automobiles and electronics—two symbols of industrial success. For the United States, the rapid increase in U.S. imports of technologically sophisticated Japanese products implied that the United States had become dependent on Japan for some important products such as semiconductor memory chips. Some Americans fretted that Japan's export success, combined with the continued lack of openness of Japanese markets to foreign products, would be detrimental to the U.S. economy. James Fallows exemplified this view, writing in 1989 that Japan was engaged in a "one-sided and destructive expansion of its economic power."[1] Economists did not agree with such extreme views, but such expressions typify the belief that Japan was in a position to use its trade policies to benefit itself at the expense of the rest of the world.

FOREIGN AID

Concurrent with its economic boom, Japan emerged as the largest provider of foreign aid among major industrial nations, with its foreign aid budget reaching $9 billion by 1990, almost triple what it had been just a decade earlier.[2] Over the past half century, many governments have viewed foreign aid as a potential means to buy friends and influence among developing nations. Whereas Americans saw this means of influence through the Cold War lens of keeping developing countries out of the clutches of communism, the Japanese appeared to be playing the game for mercantilist economic reasons, or commercial advantage, by providing grants and loans for large infrastructure projects to developing countries tied to purchases from the Japanese. Since the late 1980s, Japan has been the largest supplier of foreign aid to developing countries in East and Southeast Asia; for example, in 1990, 54 percent of aid to the member countries of the Association of Southeast Asian Nations (ASEAN) was from Japan.[3] At the time, some outside observers saw this aid to Asia as one element in a Japanese effort to create an economic bloc in Asia, within which Japanese firms would have preferential access to neighboring markets at the expense of U.S. and European firms.[4]

CAPITAL SURPLUS

Since the beginning of the 1980s, Japan has had a current-account surplus, meaning that Japan exported more goods and services than it imported. Because the Japanese did not use all of their export earnings to import goods and services, they bought something else: foreign assets, including everything from U.S. Treasury bonds to Rockefeller Center and other real estate abroad. At the same time, government controls on the movement of investment money into and out of Japan were dismantled, so investments in each direction increased. Both Japanese net assets (what Japanese own abroad minus what foreigners own in Japan) and gross assets (what Japanese own abroad) rose dramatically. In just one decade, from 1980 to 1990, Japanese net assets held abroad exploded from $11 billion to $383 billion. Meanwhile, gross assets went from only $159 billion to $2.0 trillion, a twelve-fold increase.[5]

Outside observers felt that Japan's position as a major gross and net creditor conveyed it some form of power over debtors. For example, if Japanese investors were to dump their large holdings of U.S. Treasury bonds, then perhaps U.S. interest rates would rise to the detriment of U.S. economic growth. Threats by the Japanese government to do so, therefore, might be used as a form of leverage. In other words, U.S. officials would need to pay attention to demands on various bilateral issues made by their Japanese counterparts or risk facing the deliberate, punitive sale of U.S. Treasury bonds, according to this view. In reality, any very large owner of these bonds would be reluctant to dump their holdings on a massive scale because large sales would depress the price of the bonds further as each sale occurs, causing losses for the seller. As a result, there is no evidence that the Japanese government ever seriously threatened or carried out such a policy. Nevertheless, the worry among some U.S. officials during the past two decades that the Japanese could conceivably pursue such a tactic arguably affected U.S. bilateral policy in some cases. Furthermore, Japan's creditor role made it increasingly necessary for small, developing countries to think in terms of what would attract and keep Japanese money.

FOREIGN DIRECT INVESTMENT

A subset of capital outflow is foreign direct investment (FDI)—investments in corporations yielding a controlling interest in the firm. Until the mid-1980s, Japanese firms had preferred to stay at home; investment abroad remained largely in the form of general trading companies (handling the overseas sales and purchases of many companies), raw material supply, and labor-intensive industries such as textiles. In 1985, however, the yen rose strongly against the U.S. dollar, roughly doubling its value in less than two years. Japanese firms that had preferred to produce at home found themselves unable to export profitably because the rise in the yen meant that their products were much more expensive abroad, and they were driven to investing abroad to maintain their global market shares. At the same time, Japanese firms became increasingly alarmed at what they perceived to be protectionist trends in their largest market, the United States. Temporary protectionist measures that the U.S. Congress had taken against color televisions, automobiles, and several other products caused Japanese firms to relocate production to the United States to circumvent restrictions or to prevent them from being tightened or proliferating. From 1980 to 1990, the cumulative value of global Japanese FDI rose from $20 billion to $200 billion—a ten-fold increase.[6]

FDI provided Japanese firms and the Japanese government with a strong, new motivation to become actively involved in global affairs. Large sums of Japanese money invested in fixed assets in the United States and elsewhere were at risk if the host countries introduced rules and restrictions disadvantageous to Japanese firms. In addition to the fear of nationalization, as has occurred in some developing countries in the past century, labor laws, environmental laws, and other aspects of other countries' domestic political actions were suddenly important to Japanese firms and the Japanese government. Japanese operation of businesses abroad thus more intimately intertwined the nation with the rest of the world and gave it a greater stake in global operations.

This new, large FDI flow also gave Japanese firms another possible power lever to use internationally. In the United States, for example, Japanese firms made no secret of the fact that they intentionally located some of their factories within the states and districts of senators and representatives considered protectionist toward their particular industry. Having sizable numbers of constituents drawing paychecks from Japanese firms can have a moderating influence on politicians who might otherwise be inclined to support protectionism. Whether these actions were purely the choices of individual firms or whether the Japanese government played a role in encouraging or coordinating such location decisions is unclear, but a government role behind the scenes is certainly conceivable because combating U.S. protectionism has been a key policy priority in the past half century.

Exercising Power?

The international influence afforded to Japan by its economic stature is particularly significant because Japan's constitution constrains the nation's military posture. Drafted by Americans during the post–World War II occupation to prevent a resurgence of Japanese militarism, Article 9 of the constitution contains a prohibition on the use of military force. This provision stripped from Japan the ability to use "hard" international power—the threat or actual use of military action as part of resolving disputes. Although the constitution has not prevented Japan from assembling a large military force and interpretation of the constitution has shifted sufficiently to enable the government to send soldiers abroad for United Nations peacekeeping missions, sending soldiers abroad to engage in combat even as part of UN- or U.S.-led coalitions remains politically unacceptable, as evidenced by the raging domestic debate over the possible deployment of a small number of soldiers to postwar Iraq.

In broad strategic terms, without the ability to use its military muscle as a means to influence other countries but with its economic power as a viable alternative by the late 1980s, Japan was positioned to establish itself as a civilian power in contrast to the United States. Much like a conscientious objector under the U.S. draft system, Japan could have trumpeted its role as an appealing builder and healer in contrast to the destructive threats implicit in U.S. or Soviet military power. Nation building, buttressed with generous foreign aid, commercial bank loans, and FDI could have given the Japanese government the moral high ground in international affairs. Enhancing this possibility was Japan's own record of successful economic development and its highly visible, internationally successful manufacturing firms. Had the government demanded attention, Japan's ability to throw money at countries around the world would have at the very least forced the United States and other powers to listen seriously to the Japanese government's policy ideas. Imagine just for a moment a Japan prepared to offer Iraq several tens of billions of dollars in foreign aid and inducements for Japanese firms to locate factories there. Had such a Japan demanded a say in decisionmaking prior to the recent war against Iraq, the U.S. government likely would have listened because the potential financial flows from Japan to a postwar Iraq are much larger than what the Germans or French might have offered.[7]

The Japanese government in the 1980s took a few tentative steps in the direction of exercising soft power in the arena of global policymaking. In the late 1980s, some Japanese government officials became dissatisfied with the doctrinaire neoclassical economic approach that the U.S. government was pushing heavily at the World Bank and the International Monetary Fund (IMF), as Japan's own successful economic development had occurred through a very interventionist government that was not beholden to letting free markets determine all outcomes. In an attempt to change the IMF approach, therefore, the Japanese government first lobbied hard for larger voting rights in the IMF commensurate with Japan's share in the global economy, a change that occurred finally in 1990.[8] The Japanese government then pursued a campaign at the World Bank to gain the bank's acceptance of Japan's development model, funding a major study of the development experiences of East Asian countries. Meanwhile, the government successfully placed Japanese nationals as the heads of the World Health Organization (WHO) and the UN High Commission for Refugees (UNHCR) at the end of the 1980s.

In the end, however, these steps produced few changes in global policies. The World Bank's report, *The East Asian Miracle*, did not endorse the Japanese development model to the extent that the Japanese government wanted.[9] Nor did increased voting power at the IMF discernibly increase the Japanese government's voice in IMF policymaking. The Japanese head of the WHO, Hiroshi Nakajima, proved to be an ineffective leader unpopular with developed-country members of the organization, and the Japanese government damaged its own international reputation with overt efforts to buy votes from developing-country members for his successful reelection in the mid-1990s.[10] Sadako Ogata was an effective leader at UNHCR but often appeared to be in conflict with her own government and certainly had no impact on the Japanese government's own ungenerous policies on refugees, so Japan has not become a leading voice on international refugee policies.

Much the same proved true of Japan's foreign aid program throughout the 1980s. Rather than fostering the cause of economic development, Japan's aid program appeared closely tied to Japanese commercial interests—subsidizing construction of logging roads in Indonesia or providing infrastructure for industrial parks where Japanese firms would locate. This is not to say that the United States and other aid donors have been innocent of commercial motives, but by not concealing its commercial interests behind the façade of helping developing countries more effectively, the Japanese government lost an opportunity to create a positive image for itself.[11]

To a large extent, the Japanese government appeared more interested in the image of influence and power than its reality. Having Japanese nationals at the top of the WHO and UNHCR was more important symbolically (as a pleasing indication back home that the rest of the world regarded Japan as important enough to let a Japanese national serve in such a capacity) than was actually shaping the organizations' agendas. Arguably, Japanese power advanced an international agenda that consisted of selling the Japanese economic development model to the World Bank and the developing world. Unlike broad themes such as democracy or human rights, however, this was a very specific ideal, and even the Japanese had difficulty defining just what the model was or how important it had been in producing successful economic development in their own country. Thus, the government never reached agreement on a set of ideals that it could push with unified determination in the global arena through its soft power.

One major factor working against Japan taking a more activist stance has been its unwillingness to become more open to the outside world. In many ways, allowing the rest of the world into one's country through imports, investment, immigrants, and students buttresses a country's reputation as a global leader. Japanese society, however, has always behaved in a very insular manner. Markets for imported goods have opened but only slowly and grudgingly. Government policy long restricted inward direct investment, and even now, capital inflow remains much lower than that in any other industrial nation (despite an increase in recent years). Foreign workers or immigrants comprise a much smaller share of the population (less than 1 percent) than they do in other industrial nations. Political refugees admitted from abroad number only a few thousand. Finally, although the government has championed the idea of increasing the number of foreign students, their numbers remain significantly lower than those in other industrial nations. All of these policy decisions are deliberate, indicating that the Japanese government and society prefer to keep the world at bay than to act like a global leader.

Deteriorating Conditions

The economic factors that appeared to provide Japan with an opportunity to influence international affairs in the 1980s have undergone major—and largely negative—changes in the past decade. Japan remains the world's second-largest economy, but its image, among outside observers and the Japanese themselves, has undergone a profound change for the worse.

STAGNATION

Collapse of an enormous speculative bubble in the Japanese stock and real estate markets at the beginning of the 1990s, compounded by bad policymaking since then, has virtually stagnated Japan's economy since 1992. Between 1992 and 2002, Japan's GDP grew at a real annual rate of only 1.1 percent, well below the 5 percent rate of the late 1980s. Meanwhile, the collapse of asset prices spawned a huge number of nonperforming loans in the banking sector, complete with numerous scandals of imprudent, unethical, or illegal behavior by bankers and their corporate borrowers. Since 1998, Japan has been going through a period of deflation—a general decline in the level of prices—making it the first industrial nation to undergo this experience since the 1930s. So far, Japan has muddled through its economic ills, although a more serious crisis in the financial sector is a distinct possibility and a fiscal crisis (as the government's debt mounts to extremely high levels) in the next decade is conceivable as well.

Japan's international reputation as an admirable economic model for developing countries to emulate is in tatters. Among the major developed nations, a rising sense of amazement has emerged at the Japanese government's decade-long inability to fashion better solutions for its economic problems, and officials of these nations now wonder why they should listen to the proposals of Japanese government officials who cannot even put their own economy back on a path of solid recovery.

CONTINUED CREDITOR STATUS

Overall, gross and net assets held abroad by the Japanese have continued to rise. By 2002, gross assets had expanded to $3 trillion and net assets to $1.5 trillion.[12] Much of the increase has come in the form of foreign bond holdings, such as U.S. Treasury bonds, and foreign exchange reserves (now equaling more than $500 billion). Although its rising foreign asset position appears to provide Japan with stronger levers of soft power, specific aspects of capital outflow from Japan suggest otherwise.

DOMESTIC FINANCIAL WEAKNESS

In the 1980s, the threat of the Japanese government dumping U.S. Treasury bonds as a policy tactic seemed plausible to some Americans. Today, the issue is whether collapsing Japanese banks and other financial institutions would dump their Treasury bonds and other foreign assets to pay their depositors and other creditors back home. U.S. policymakers, therefore, still need to worry about Japan but because of financial weakness in Japan, not because of possible antagonistic Japanese government behavior.

FALLING FOREIGN AID

Japanese foreign aid peaked at $16 billion in 1997. Since then, it has fallen 40 percent to $10 billion (not much higher than in 1990), and this trend appears set to continue. By 2001, Japan had slipped behind the United States as the world's largest aid donor. For many years, Japanese foreign aid was immune to the domestic debate about the alternative value of helping foreigners to helping citizens at home that had been standard in the United States, but this is no longer the case.

To the extent that foreign aid provides a means of buying friends and influencing governments, the falling foreign aid budget has diminished the Japanese government's clout in the developing world. The one counterexample to this was the temporary surge in aid given to East Asian countries in the wake of the 1997 Asian financial crisis. The United States initially dithered over whether the crisis was important enough to intervene, and the IMF made some initial mistakes in its policy prescriptions to the crisis countries. The Japanese government stepped into this breach, first with a half-baked idea for an Asian Monetary Fund that would insulate the region from IMF interference and then with a unilateral offer of aid to help tide over the countries in crisis.

The New Miyazawa Plan, as this unilateral effort was dubbed, created some positive imagery, with the Japanese government claiming to have provided a very sizable $30 billion in assistance of various forms. A more careful accounting, however, reveals that Japan provided only about $16 billion in new aid for the region, most in the form of hard loans made at interest rates close to market rates. More importantly, the effort was a very short-term one, a temporary blip in the longer-term trend of shrinking foreign aid.[13]

FALLING COMMERCIAL BANK LOANS

The amount of commercial bank loans, another kind of capital flow from Japan to other countries, has also fallen greatly. The total dollar value of outstanding Japanese international bank loans fell 36 percent from its peak in 1997 to the end of 2002. Loan amounts to developing countries in East Asia have fallen much more, down almost 70 percent, while loan numbers to Hong Kong and Singapore, the two developed money centers in the region, fell an even larger 81 percent.[14] To the extent that Asian countries perceived the availability of commercial bank credit from Japan as an element of Japan's international reach, the nation's image has faded badly in comparison to other developed countries whose banks cut back on loans temporarily but not by as much and not for as long.

Falling FDI

Even though the yen has remained much stronger than it was through 1985, the pace of direct investment abroad by Japanese firms has dropped. In fiscal year 2002, the total outflow was 4.4 trillion yen (or roughly $35 billion), down 47 percent from a peak of 8.4 trillion yen back in 1990.[15] Regional perceptions of Japan's relative importance have fallen apace.

In one sense, FDI has nevertheless served its purpose even though the flows have diminished. For example, few would doubt that the extensive investment by Japanese companies in the United States has altered U.S. perceptions of Japan. For a brief period of time in the late 1980s, U.S. perceptions shifted against the Japanese when Americans felt they had sold their nation out to a bunch of dubious foreigners with their ostentatious purchases of trophy buildings and golf courses. Yet, the longer-lasting impact of Japanese investment in the United States has been the experience of Americans working for Japanese manufacturing firms. In a number of midwestern and southern states, Japanese firms, the expats that come with them, and the U.S. employees that work for them have become a regular part of the landscape. To the extent that the Japanese government hoped that these investments would generate more positive feelings about Japan on the part of their large economic and strategic partner, it was correct. This influence clearly was not an exercise of global power on a grand scale but certainly helped meet the modest goal of maintaining the goodwill of voters in the United States, Japan's key trading partner and indispensable security ally.

Shrinking Trade Importance

Economic stagnation has limited the rise of Japanese imports, while the strengthened yen has slowed the growth of Japanese exports. Although the value of Japanese exports and imports has risen in the past decade, in relative terms Japan's importance as a trading partner has shrunk for many nations. Back in 1982, for example, Japan supplied a very large 22 percent of all U.S. imports, a level that slipped by half to 11 percent by 2001. The same kind of reduction is true for other trade partners. Whereas Japan supplied 25 percent of other East Asian countries' imports at its peak in 1985, it only supplied 15 percent in 2001.[16]

To some extent, rising imports from developing countries offset this declining relative role in trade. Especially when the yen underwent a temporary strong rise against the dollar in the early 1990s, Japanese markets finally began to open up to imports of low-value-added imports from developing countries. Textiles and a few other low-value-added products that had moved only partially offshore prior to the 1990s shifted more quickly. Yet, Japan has certainly not shed its reputation as a stingy importer. Great Britain in the nineteenth century embraced free trade (for a time) and the United States led the post–World War II effort to lower global trade barriers through the General Agreement on Tariffs and Trade (GATT), but Japan has not used its newfound economic preeminence to behave as a leader in the global trading system. Instead, it has continued to be a laggard in trade liberalization, evidenced most recently perhaps in its stance at the current Doha round of negotiations in the World Trade Organization (WTO). Although protectionist behavior is unremarkable, acting as the leader on trade as a means of enhancing its reputation and influencing the world in a positive manner has been an opportunity for the Japanese government that it has chosen not to pursue.

Success through Subordination

Clearly, Japan's economic stature has afforded it numerous opportunities over the last two decades to secure a more influential role in global affairs than it has actually managed to obtain. Some might consider this development unsettling or even a reflection of a particular Japanese inability to use Japan's economic assets to affect much positive change beyond the country's borders. After all, is it not natural for a nation that has achieved great economic size and success to want to throw its weight around more in the world, as the United States did as it emerged economically in the first half of the twentieth century?

We should not write off Japan as a country that failed to capitalize on its economic power. The Japanese appear to be relatively content to have accomplished important goals concerning Japan's external environment. On the security side, Japan has remained subordinate to the United States, but that posture has met its security needs. On the economic side, Japan has managed to keep foreign markets open to its goods and investment. Beyond those immediate needs of the nation, the Japanese have had little interest in altering global policies.

Despite the economic setbacks of the past decade, Japan remains the second-largest economy in the world, is an even larger net and gross creditor than a decade earlier, has extensive direct investments despite the smaller annual flow, and has the world's second-largest foreign aid program. It also appears on the surface to be more of a player today in regional and global affairs than it was a decade ago. Yet, in areas of major global policy action such as trade negotiations or the response to terrorism, Japan's role has been small and cautious at best. Japan has in fact retreated from its earlier modest forays at being a major power.

At the regional level, the Japanese government has indeed been a participant in the ASEAN Plus Three (Japan, China, and South Korea) dialogue—a purely East Asian grouping that discusses regional economic cooperation—and has begun a program of negotiating bilateral free-trade areas (FTAs). Within ASEAN Plus Three, however, Japan does not appear to be much of an independent leader. The one real cooperative policy this group has established has been a set of expanded, bilateral swap agreements among central banks to help small Asian countries facing attacks on their fixed or quasi-fixed currencies fend them off without relying as much on help from the IMF. The Japanese government insisted though that activation of all but 10 percent of the money in these agreements be tied to explicit approval from the IMF itself, negating the original purpose of the concept. Rather than joining with its regional neighbors to achieve some independence from the IMF, therefore, the Japanese government's behavior proved more mindful of U.S. concerns.

Japan's new policy of forming FTAs has also been quite limited. At one time, pundits worried that competing European, U.S., and Asian trade blocs would emerge.[17] That vision seemed more plausible when the Japanese government finally embraced the idea of FTAs at the end of the 1990s. So far, however, Japan has successfully completed only one such agreement, with Singapore. In addition, even though Singapore has virtually no agricultural products to export, the Japanese government was unable to include agriculture in its agreement with Singapore, putting a damper on its ability to negotiate with countries such as Thailand where agriculture matters. The United States remains preeminent in the minds of Japanese government officials and politicians as a strategic ally and economic partner. FTAs to create an Asian bloc that would trade within itself and be less reliant on U.S. markets are not consistent with Japanese strategic thinking. This fact, along with the purely domestic politics of agriculture, explains why the Japanese government has not pursued bilateral or regional FTAs more vigorously.

The Japanese government's behavior regarding the war on terrorism and the war in Iraq even more clearly illustrates Japan's role as U.S. subordinate. During the Persian Gulf War, the Japanese government was badly embarrassed by the drawn-out process of acquiescing to Washington's demands for financial support for a war whose importance the Japanese simply did not support in principle or understand. Although the Japanese government eventually voted to provide $13 billion in assistance, the money came after the war had ended and in response to months of arm-twisting by U.S. officials. Not wanting to repeat that experience, Japanese prime minister Junichiro Koizumi and other Japanese government officials made a show of verbally supporting the United States quickly and strongly in the wake of the September 11 attacks. Similarly, Koizumi backed President George W. Bush often in the run-up to war with Iraq. Koizumi's only demand was a mild request in September 2002 for the U.S. president to go to the UN Security Council before invading Iraq; the Japanese did not join other European nations in demanding a second vote by the Security Council.

On one hand, Koizumi's boldness in supporting the United States in the face of opposition to the war from some 70 percent of the Japanese public appears an exercise of leadership. On the other hand, a closer examination suggests that Koizumi's behavior reflected a familiar pattern in Japanese foreign policy. The Japanese had three reasons to support Bush, none of which had anything to do with fighting outrageous dictators or bringing a better future to the Middle East. First, the Japanese government wanted to avoid aggravating the U.S. government the way it had during the Gulf War through its slow and grudging support. Second, the real strategic issue for the Japanese government was North Korea, and it expected that support for the war against Iraq would translate into influence with Washington on policy toward North Korea. Whether or not that assumption was correct, it factored into Japanese thinking. Third, Iraq became the most recent opportunity for conservatives in Japan to press to alter or reinterpret the constitution to permit dispatching soldiers abroad for combat.

Thus, in East Asia and on a broader global scale, the Japanese government has continued to act very much as it has ever since the end of the U.S. occupation, as a subordinate power tied to the United States. The U.S. government consults the Japanese government, but the reality remains that Japan does not have its own seat at the table of international policymaking. Although Japan criticized the U.S. government and the IMF during the Asian financial crisis, it has not acted on these sentiments to lead its neighbors toward a more independent stance on either international finance or trade. Neither in the Middle East nor in Afghanistan has the Japanese government moved to claim expertise in nation or economy building. Instead, it has ridden the coattails of the U.S. government, avoiding criticism and advancing the causes of domestic conservatives concerning the use of military force unrelated to the Middle East.

The notion that Japan would want to act as a leader in international trade and security issues rather than play second fiddle, furthermore, may be much more of an American conception than a reality for the Japanese. Instead, Japan has concentrated on manipulating its international environment in a much narrower fashion to suit its own needs. The Japanese want peace, exports, and investment abroad, as well as secure access to oil and other raw materials. Beyond these immediate needs, the Japanese government and most of the Japanese public regard issues such as human rights or the convoluted and violent politics of the Middle East as none of their business.

This aversion to interfering in human rights battles within other nations or conflict among other nations stems from Japan's own disastrous path of violent adventurism in the first half of the twentieth century. The forced annexation of Korea (1910), creation of a puppet state in Manchuria (1932), unjustified initiation of a grinding war against China (1937), and then initiation of war against the United States and Great Britain (1941) ended in 1945 with a cataclysm of death and destruction for the Japanese. That devastating experience has left many in society feeling that noninterference in issues that do not directly threaten Japanese territory is the best policy, either because they fear sliding down a slippery slope toward militarism again or because they feel use of military violence to solve problems is simply wrong.

Peace and security, even regarding cases in Japan's immediate vicinity, such as with North Korea, have come through reliance on the bilateral security alliance with the United States. Economic access has come through the GATT/WTO, of which Japan has been a member since the 1950s. Japan has been able to secure access to raw materials by relying on the GATT/WTO and its own efforts, such as providing generous foreign aid to raw material–producing countries. Although particular aspects may have been based on relying on others or adopting a low-key position in a multilateral setting, the government has pursued an active and deliberate agenda to maintain Japan's national interests.

For interests in security and economic access, the key has been to keep the United States and other major players sufficiently satisfied with Japan that they would not end existing relationships. Toward this end, Japan has agreed to pay part of the costs to maintain U.S. bases in Japan and has taken a series of small steps during the past two decades to play a larger role in security matters, such as increasing defense spending and dispatching soldiers for UN peacekeeping operations.

On economic access, Japan has offered just enough concessions on access to Japanese markets to prevent its major trading partners from closing their markets. It has also invested heavily in lobbying in Washington, supported academic programs around the United States, and created additional programs designed to foster more positive images of Japan among Americans (e.g., annual groups of businesspeople and academics to give speeches around the United States, support for local Japan-America societies, and funding for various bilateral conferences at which Americans could be exposed to Japanese views). The effectiveness of such policies might be debatable, but the Japanese government clearly seeks to ensure that its primary benefactor in the security and economic world will not forsake Japan. Bilateral relations have endured some periods of tension over problems of access to the Japanese market or allegedly unfair tactics (such as dumping) by Japanese firms selling to the U.S. market, but the bilateral relationship itself— security or economic—has never been in real jeopardy. The Japanese have, therefore, been quite successful in meeting Japanese needs.

Similarly, Japan has kept its Asian neighbors sufficiently satisfied to accept imports from Japan, not complain too much about access to Japanese markets, and accept direct investments from Japan. Japanese efforts to buy good will with foreign aid, direct investment, and commercial bank loans never evolved into a Japan-led economic bloc and are unlikely to do so in the foreseeable future, but Japan has used its power to maintain its economic relationships. Foolish actions such as Koizumi's repeated visits to the Yasukuni Shrine—dedicated to Japanese war dead, including war criminals from World War II—occasionally jar those relationships, but the government has made sure that they never spin out of control.

In securing the supply of raw materials, the government has used a number of tools, including diversifying supply sources, stockpiling, offering large amounts of foreign aid, encouraging Japanese firms to invest in countries supplying raw materials, and supporting supplier governments diplomatically. Japan's interest in maintaining close relations with the United States has not kept it out of negotiations concerning raw material supply with governments considered totalitarian and dangerous by the U.S. government—an engagement that led to Japan's initial miscalculation of the importance of Iraq's invasion of Kuwait. Japan's desire to obtain stable raw material supplies, especially oil, has often conflicted with the country's need to maintain close relations with the United States. When such conflicts arise, the Japanese government has tried to minimize offense to all sides, ultimately supporting the United States but remaining sufficiently on the sidelines so that Middle East suppliers would view Japan more favorably.

Soft Power Is Real

Because the Japanese government has not pressed for a stronger voice in regional and global affairs, the soft power arising from its economic strength might appear to be illusory. Such a conclusion would be a mistake. The Japanese government has indeed been able to use nonmilitary means to influence its external environment and has done so quite successfully. Elements of this soft power have come from Japan's economic size and affluence, ownership of a massive amount of assets abroad, substantial direct investments abroad, and large amounts of foreign aid. These elements provided the government with financial resources to spend (or withhold) abroad to influence foreign governments.

Had the Japanese government chosen to make a splash on the global scene, it could have done so. The timidity of the government's forays at the World Bank and other multilateral institutions a decade ago was not caused by the lack of leverage. The real cause was a lack of interest. The Japanese government has been relatively satisfied with the international status quo; the multilateral economic institutions (the World Bank and the IMF) have worked reasonably well for Japan, so why rock the boat? Therefore, the government was content to focus on the more immediate needs of the nation in ensuring peace and economic stability for the Japanese. That strategy has involved a deliberate choice to subordinate the nation to the United States on security policy and a major effort to keep Americans sufficiently satisfied with Japanese behavior as to eschew policies that would harm Japan's economic or security interests. Toward the rest of the world, the government has also pursued a policy of containing protectionist urges or other behavior damaging to Japanese economic interests, but always with an eye to U.S. reactions.

World economic stability and peace certainly need some governments to play a leading role in establishing international institutions or pressing others to join in collective action to resolve international problems. Japan has done little to exercise its soft power in that sense, but not all countries aspire to dominate others or change how the world works. Japan's effort to ensure its immediate needs of security and economic stability has worked rather well. Perhaps the world should be glad that Japan has chosen to exercise its power in this limited fashion.

Notes

1. James Fallows, "Containing Japan," *Atlantic Monthly*, May 1989, p. 41.

2. Japanese Ministry of Foreign Affairs, *Japan's ODA Annual Report 1992*, p. 80.

3. Edward J. Lincoln, *Japan's New Global Role* (Washington, D.C.: Brookings Institution, 1993), p. 182.

4. See Walter Hatch and Kozo Yamamura, *Asia in Japan's Embrace* (New York: Cambridge University Press, 1996).

5. Bank of Japan, *Balance of Payments Monthly*, April 1991, pp. 83–84.

6. Ibid.

7. For an extended discussion of what Japan could have done but did not, see Lincoln, *Japan's New Global Role*, pp. 241–267.

8. International Monetary Fund (IMF), *Directory: Members, Quotas, Governors, Voting Power, Executive Board, Officers* (Washington, D.C.: November 2, 1990), p. 9; IMF, *IMF Survey Supplement on the Fund* 19 (August 1990): 1–4.

9. World Bank, *The East Asian Miracle: Economic Growth and Public Policy* (New York: Oxford University Press, 1993).

10. See BBC, "WHO Director General—The Candidates," January 26, 1998, http://news.bbc.co.uk/1/hi/special_report/1998/health/47205.stm (accessed August 20, 2003).

11. For a critical review of Japanese aid policies in the 1980s, see Lincoln, *Japan's New Global Role*, pp. 111–133; Margee Ensign, *Doing Good or Doing Well: Japan's Foreign Aid Program* (New York: Columbia University Press, 1992).

12. Japanese Ministry of Finance, "International Investment Position of Japan," www.mof.go.jp/english/houkoku/e2002.htm (accessed August 20, 2003).

13. Edward J. Lincoln, *East Asian Economic Regionalism* (Washington, D.C.: Brookings Institution, forthcoming), pp. 258–262 (rev. manuscript).

14. Ibid., pp. 89–91.

15. Japanese Ministry of Finance, "Outward Direct Investment by Country & Region," www.mof.go.jp/english/fdi/2002b_2.htm (accessed August 20, 2003).

16. Lincoln, *East Asian Economic Regionalism*, pp. 64–65.

17. See Lester Thurow, *Head to Head: The Coming Economic Battle among Japan, Europe, and America* (New York: William Morrow, 1992).

Richard J. Samuels

Japan's Goldilocks Strategy

Many Japanese analysts do not believe that Japan has a realistic grand strategy, and more than a few insist that it never did. Sadako Ogata, one of Japan's most distinguished diplomats, declared that Japanese foreign policy has long been marked by "a conspicuous absence of strategic thinking."[1] Former ambassador Hisahiko Okazaki maintains that, apart from an "exceptional decade" between 1895 and 1905, Japanese strategy has been "naïve" and, since 1945, "sterile."[2] These eminent practitioners are hardly alone. The historian Saburo Ienaga dedicated a chapter in his influential book to the irrationality of the prewar military.[3] Political scientist Shin'ichi Kitaoka argues that one of the great misfortunes of Japanese history has been the extent to which idealism has dominated realism.[4] Historian Chihiro Hosoya associated this with General Hideki's famous argument for war to Prince Fumimaro Konoye in 1941: "Sometimes a man has to jump, with his eyes closed, from the veranda of Kiyomizu Temple."[5]

Most Japanese assessments of its postwar strategy have been a little different. Japan is often depicted as "groping" (*mosaku*) for strategy.[6] For some, postwar strategy has been incoherent for the same reason prewar

Richard J. Samuels is the Ford International Professor of Political Science and director of the Center for International Studies at the Massachusetts Institute of Technology. In 2005–2006, he was a visiting scholar at the Keizai Koho Center in Tokyo. This essay is derived from his forthcoming book *Securing Japan*, supported by the Smith Richardson Foundation.

Copyright © 2006 by The Center for Strategic and International Studies and the Massachusetts Institute of Technology
The Washington Quarterly • 29:4 pp. 111–127.

Global Powers in the 21st Century: Strategies and Relations

strategy was: Japan is chasing too many hares at once. By trying to pursue a policy that is simultaneously UN-centered, Asia-oriented, autonomous, and consistent with the goals of the bilateral alliance with the United States, Japan's foreign policy ends up confused and ineffective. The junior partnership with Washington is blamed most frequently for Tokyo's strategic deficit. Having little reason to build a military during the Cold War and having a limited sense of external threat, Japan could avoid strategic thinking and remain in its "cocoon."[7] The consensus is that Japanese leaders practice mere "karaoke diplomacy": background music and lyrics are set by the United States and Japanese diplomats are left only to decide what to wear and how to sing the songs.[8]

Japanese strategists deserve more credit. Not surprisingly, they receive it from Korean and Chinese analyses, which often posit a Japan once again preparing for regional domination. Many of Japan's neighbors are convinced that Japanese militarism, supported by an ever recrudescent, nationalist right wing, lurks just beneath the surface.[9] North American and European analysts seldom go that far, concluding instead that postwar Japanese planners have made a strategic choice to consistently punch below their weight in international politics. The outstanding question is whether they will continue to do so.

Fourth Time's a Charm

This is a particularly auspicious time to explore this question. Japanese security is once again the object of considerable debate, the fourth such moment in a 150-year-long historical arc of alternating debates and consensuses. A widespread belief in the efficacy of "catching up and surpassing" the West helped elites in the late nineteenth century forge the Meiji consensus on borrowing foreign institutions, learning Western rules, and mastering Western practice. This "Rich Nation, Strong Army" model was a great success, but by the end of World War I, when it was clear that the West viewed Japanese ambitions with suspicion, the consensus had become tattered. After a period of domestic violence and intimidation, a new consensus was forged on finding a less-conciliatory response to world affairs. Prince Konoye's 1937 "New Asian Order" attracted support from a wide swath of Japan's ideological spectrum. The new Japan would be a great power, Asia's leader. The disaster that resulted is well known, and from its ashes, again, after considerable debate, creative reinvention, and consolidation of power, Prime Minister Shigeru Yoshida conjured a pragmatic path to provide security cheaply as the Cold War began. This security, however, would not be free. The Yoshida Doctrine, which called for Japan to adopt the U.S. stance on international politics in exchange for military protection, would cost Japan its autonomy, an expenditure increasingly seen as more than Japan should pay. Thus, the strategy that has joined Japan and the United States at the hip is being questioned, both by those who support the alliance and by those who oppose it. The fourth consensus has yet to reveal itself, although its contending political and intellectual constituents are clearly identifiable.

Institutionalizing the Yoshida Doctrine required the political skills of two generations of mainstream conservative politicians, as well as a viable strategic model. At home, it required political management of nationalists on the right and the left. The former, fellow conservatives, were embraced within the ruling Liberal Democratic Party (LDP), while the latter, the leftist opposition, received periodic guarantees that Article IX of the constitution, revoking Japan's right to use force as a means of settling international disputes, would be preserved. Both were kept at arms length, while Yoshida and his political successors deepened their alliance with bureaucrats and downsized Japanese foreign and security policy. They restyled the recently imperial power as an island trading nation. Mercantilism replaced militarism. Yoshida embraced Article IX as his own, both to deflect U.S. demands and to mobilize popular support. By layering pacifist interpretations of the constitution with self-imposed constraints on the expansion of the military and the defense industry, "defensive defense" became the central tenet of Japanese security policy.

Shaping the New Security Discourse

A great deal has changed since the late 1980s, when Japan was known as an economic giant and political pygmy. Japan is still an economic giant, of course, but its willingness to play a political role in world affairs is no longer pygmy-like. Its defense budget, at more than $41 billion in fiscal year 2006, is one of the five largest in the world, while its Self-Defense Forces (SDF) have been dispatched as part of UN peacekeeping operations to Cambodia, Mozambique, and the Golan Heights, among other places. In 1996, in a joint declaration on the U.S.-Japanese security alliance, later passed by the Diet as law in the revised U.S.-Japan Defense Guidelines of 1999, Tokyo agreed to expand its security role from the homeland to "areas surrounding Japan." Then, after September 11, 2001, Japan joined President George W. Bush's "coalition of the willing," dispatching forces to the Indian Ocean and later to Iraq. Tokyo had begun to openly embrace a global security role. Influential LDP leaders now publicly advocate collective self-defense and the acquisition of greater offensive military capabilities. Japan may still be punching below its weight in world affairs, but it has been bulking up in preparation for new bouts.

After the Soviet Union disappeared, the most serious threat to Japanese security went with it. Indeed, by any conventional measure of military capabilities, the USSR was a far graver threat to Japan than China is today. The Soviet Union's Far Eastern fleet and its air and ground units in the region were better equipped and better trained than China's People's Liberation Army, which, after all, still depends on a lesser complement of Soviet-era equipment today. Yet, the Japanese government did not begin its sustained program of military modernization until after the USSR was gone. Something else was also at work.

Rather, four other factors were shaping Japan's security outlook: (1) a rising China, (2) a miscreant regime in North Korea, (3) the possibility of abandonment by the United States, and (4) the relative decline of the Japanese economy. Japan responded to each of these four with strategic agility. It responded to China by first embracing it economically and then by calling attention to a "China threat." It responded to North Korea by alternating between warm and cold diplomatic initiatives. It responded to the possibility of abandonment by the United States by "hugging it close," thereby enhancing the threat of entanglement. It responded to the specter of economic decline by readjusting familiar techno-national ideas to the complex dynamics of a globalizing world economy.[10] Importantly, each of these threats has been used to justify the modernization of Japan's military. Japanese strategists have determined that they must confront China and North Korea, reassure the United States, and reinvigorate Japan's industrial vitality, not least of all its defense-industrial base.

A second part of an explanation for Japan's force modernization lies in the security dilemma that grips Northeast Asia today.[11] North Korea, China, and Japan all have legitimate security concerns. Pyongyang's is existential; the regime fears for its survival in a world in which the lone remaining superpower has identified it as a cancer. China borders more states than any other and perceives, no doubt correctly, that the United States and Japan share designs on containing its rise. The response to these concerns in each country has been predictably excessive: each state is overinsuring against perceived risk. North Korea acquires nuclear weapons; China compensates for a decade of relative military decline by funding a rapid and opaque force modernization; and, with the United States cheerleading, Japan acquires missile defense and force-projection capabilities that it long had denied itself. As each country acts to increase its own security, it makes the others less secure.

This suggests a third, critically important element of Japanese decision-making. Each threat, each response, and each political calculation has been filtered through domestic institutions and debate. A new security discourse with identifiable historical predicates has taken shape in the context of a new national leadership. Revisionists led by Junichiro Koizumi and Shinzo Abe consolidated power during the early 2000s. They combined the four new threats—fabricating none but amplifying all—with the old ambitions of their forebears, the once "antimainstream" conservatives whose greatest battles were fought against Yoshida himself. Once in power, they seized the opportunity to reform the domestic institutions of national security and to marginalize pragmatists and pacifists.

Meanwhile, Washington's exhortations that Tokyo expand its security footprint have never been so grandiose. The Department of Defense promises to maintain its pledged defense of Japan but now openly expects Japan to cooperate in contingencies far from East Asia. It is Washington's "clear intent" to use its Japanese bases and the alliance overall as instruments in its global security strategy, and it expects Japan to underwrite the costs to a greater extent than ever before.[12] In late April

2006, U.S. deputy undersecretary of defense Richard Lawless announced that Japan would pay $26 billion to support U.S. force realignment in Japan, a sum that shocked even Chief Cabinet Secretary Abe and which Director General Fukushiro Nukaga subsequently denied. Regardless of the precise amount, the raison d'etre of the alliance has de facto already been transformed. What was once a highly asymmetric arrangement, in which the United States was pledged to defend Japan but received no reciprocal commitment, is now one in which Japan has pledged lucre but not yet blood to support the U.S. global strategy. Japanese leaders have long referred to the archipelago as "America's unsinkable aircraft carrier," but the shared ambitions for this expeditionary platform are bolder and more transparent than ever now that Japan's revisionist leaders have signed on to a global partnership.

Like many historical changes, the current reinstitutionalization of Japanese security policy is overdetermined. It has been catalyzed by international events beyond Japan's control; by domestic political struggles, societal change, and institutional reform; and by the transformation of the U.S. defense establishment. The Diet enacted 15 new security-related laws between 1991 and 2003, the most important ones on the revisionists' watch after 2001. The Japanese Defense Agency (JDA) became a policy agency, rather than one merely of procurement. More changes are on the way, including the possibility of Japan acquiring its first democratically crafted constitution that recognizes a fully legitimate military that will assume new roles and missions, including the use of force in collective self-defense.

No single "big bang" forced this transformation, although the end of the Cold War comes closest. Instead, the confluence of shifts in global, regional, and domestic balances of power enabled Japanese security strategists to whittle away at Yoshida's pacifist consensus. This strategy has not been decimated entirely, as suggested both by the delicate placement of lightly armed SDF troops in Samawah, as far from the violence in Iraq as possible, and by the Koizumi cabinet's unwillingness to increase defense spending even to the average relative level of advanced industrial democracies. Still, the facts that the United Nations never fully blessed the wartime presence of Japanese troops in Iraq, that Tokyo agreed to participate in ballistic missile defense and to relax arms export restrictions, and that Japan acquired new weapons systems that extend its reach all suggest how much has changed.

"Japan [has] become [both] more active operationally and better prepared legally" to act in its own defense than at any time since the alliance was established.[13] Japan has achieved this incrementally, in a series of discrete steps, which has given Japanese strategists new confidence and increased comfort in assuming additional roles and missions within the alliance. Some U.S. government officials have called this a process of "maturation," while other analysts have welcomed the "erosion of anti-militarism" and "strategic tinkering."[14] The most decorously indirect expression of this process is from a report by the JDA's National Institute for Defense Studies that refers to the "lateral expansion [and] greater depth" of Japan's defense capabilities since the end of the Cold War.[15] Whether this has been a process of erosion, tinkering, expansion, or slicing, change has been aplenty. However it is expressed, Japan has modernized its military and begun to shift its doctrine, and it is poised to continue.

The Battle to Redefine Japan's Security Identity Begins

What the next step will entail is currently under active debate in Tokyo, where there are strong disagreements about how Japan should provide for its security. These differences are not simple matters of left versus right. Nor do they strictly reflect party or other institutional affiliations. For example, the ruling LDP supports the U.S. alliance unconditionally but is divided on how to deal with Asia, while the opposition Democratic Party of Japan is unified on regional integration but divided on the alliance.[16] Moreover, the contemporary discourse about Japanese grand strategy is filled with strange and shifting bedfellows. Heirs to prewar nativism share antipathetic views of the U.S. alliance with heirs of the old Left. Today's small Japanists and big Japanists agree that the alliance matters but disagree fundamentally on how much Japan should pay for its maintenance and whether part of that cost should include Japan becoming "normal." The deck is reshuffled yet again on the issue of accommodation with China.

The security policy preferences of contemporary Japanese scholars, commentators, politicians, and bureaucrats can be sorted along two axes. The first is a measure of the value placed on the alliance with the United States. At one extreme, there is the view that the United States is Japan's most important source of security and must be embraced. On this account, the extent of U.S. power and the limits of Japanese capabilities are central to their calculations. U.S. bases in Japan are critical elements of any coherent national security strategy. At the other extreme is the view that, in a unipolar world, the United States is a dangerous bully that must be kept at a distance for fear that Japan would otherwise become entangled in its adventures. This entanglement is made all the more likely by the presence of U.S. bases. Located in the middle of this axis are those who call on Japan to rebalance its Asian and U.S. relationships more effectively. They are attracted to the idea of regional institution building but are not yet prepared to walk away from U.S. security guarantees. This first axis, then, is a measure of the relative value placed on the dangers of abandonment and entanglement. Those with a high tolerance for the former are willing to keep a greater distance from the United States than are those with a higher tolerance for the latter.

Those with a high tolerance for entanglement are not all status quo oriented. They are divided along a second axis, the willingness to use force in international affairs. Whether an individual supports revision of Article IX, wants Japan to assume a more proactive and global defense posture, desires the integration of Japanese forces with the U.S. military, or seeks the dispatch of SDF abroad are all measures of where Japanese stand on this second dimension. Some who support the U.S. alliance, then, are more willing to deploy the SDF to share alliance burdens than are others who prefer that Japan continue to limit itself to rear-area support. The former wish Japan to become a great power again and are associated with the idea that Japan should become normal. In the view of these "normal nationalists," the statute of limitations for Japan's mid–twentieth-century aggression expired long ago; it is time for Japan to step onto the international stage as an equal of the United States. The latter, "middle-power internationalists," believe that Japan must remain a small power with self-imposed limits on its right to belligerency. Japan's contributions to world affairs should remain nonmilitary. Among those who prefer Japan to keep a greater distance from the United States are "neo-autonomists," who would build an independent, full-spectrum Japanese military that could use force, and "pacifists," who eschew the military institution altogether (see table 1).

STRUGGLING TOWARD A POST-YOSHIDA CONSENSUS

These four classifications suggest four nominal strategic choices, each consistent with expressed national values. First, Japan can achieve prestige by increasing national strength. Of course, this is the path on which Japan has already embarked, led by the normal nationalists, who would further bulk up what is already the most modern indigenous military in the Far East. The normal nationalists seek to equalize the alliance to build an even better military shield. They are aware of the risk of entrapment but discount it. Over time, the "unsinkable aircraft carrier" would be configured to launch Japanese war fighters alongside those of the United States. Joint military operations far afield, formal commitments to policing sea lines of communication out to the Arabian Sea, collective self-defense, and the joint use of force would all be fully legitimated. Japan would acquire even more modern military capabilities, many of which would be interoperable with U.S. systems. It would cease pretending to follow the Yoshida script.

A second alternative would be to achieve autonomy by increasing national strength, the preferred path of Japan's neo-autonomists. They too would build a better military shield, but theirs would be nuclear and operationally independent of the United States.[17] In addition to a credible, independent nuclear deterrent, Japan would acquire a full-spectrum military configured not merely to support and supply U.S. forces or to defend against terrorists and missile attacks, but one that could actually reach out and touch adversaries. Armed with a stronger shield and sharpened sword, Japan would seek to maintain a military advantage over peer competitors. Japan would then truly be normal, engaged, like other great powers, in a permanent struggle to maximize national strength and influence. Such a program would certainly generate pressure for the elimination of U.S. bases in Japan and would enhance the prospect of abandonment by

Table I. Japan's Strategic Options

	Embrace U.S.	Distance from U.S.
More active military	Normal nationalists	Neo-autonomists
Less active military	Middle-power internationalists	Pacifists

Washington. It would also significantly accelerate the security dilemma already underway in Northeast Asia.

A third choice, the one preferred by the middle-power international-ists, would be to achieve prestige by increasing prosperity.[18] Japan's ex-posure to some of the more difficult vicissitudes of world politics would be reduced but only if some of the more ambitious assaults on the Yoshi-da Doctrine were reversed. Japan would once again eschew the military shield in favor of the mercantile sword. It would bulk up the country's considerable soft power in a concerted effort to knit East Asia together without generating new threats or becoming excessively vulnerable. The Asianists in this group would aggressively embrace exclusive regional economic institutions to reduce Japan's reliance on the U.S. market. They would not abrogate the military alliance but would resist U.S. exhortations for Japan to expand its roles and missions. The mercantile realists in this group would support the establishment of more open, regional economic institutions as a means to reduce the likelihood of abandonment by the United States and would seek to maintain the United States' protective embrace as cheaply and for as long as possible.

The final, least likely choice would be to achieve autonomy through prosperity. This is the choice of pacifists, many of whom today are ac-tive in civil society through nongovernmental organizations that are not affiliated with traditional political parties. Like the mercantile realists, they would reduce Japan's military posture, possibly even eliminate it. Un-like the mercantile realists, they would reject the alliance as dangerously entangling. They would eschew hard power for soft power, campaign to establish Northeast Asia as a nuclear-free zone, expand the defensive-de-fense concept to the region as a whole, negotiate a regional missile-con-trol regime, and rely on the Asian Regional Forum of the Association of

Southeast Asian Nations (ASEAN) for security.[19] Their manifest problem is that the Japanese public is unmoved by their prescriptions. In March 2003, when millions took to the streets in Rome, London, and New York City to protest the U.S. invasion of Iraq, only several thousand rallied in Tokyo's Hibiya Park.[20] Pacifist ideas about prosperity and autonomy seem relics of an earlier, more idealistic time when Japan could not imagine, much less openly plan for, military contingencies.

Although one of these four views will possibly prevail over the others, none alone seems fully plausible as the basis for the post-Yoshida consensus. One reason is that the Yoshida Doctrine has been institutionalized in ways that make sharp discontinuity less likely than continued incremental change. This is why we have observed "salami slicing" rather than wholesale revision of past practice. Budgeting is one example. As noted previously, despite the expanding roles and missions, cheap-riding realism remains a stubborn fact of life for the JDA. Defense budgets have been effectively flat since 1994. "Deteriorating fiscal conditions" were repeatedly mentioned in the 2004 National Defense Program Guidelines, which insisted that Japan could build a "state-of-the-art" military "without expanding its size ... with the limited resources that are available."[21] Japan continues to enjoy its cheap ride, an arrangement even the revisionists have not seemed eager to change.

No one should expect the preferences of any single group to prevail for long for several additional reasons. First, Japan is a robust democracy, and democracies tend to self-correct for policy excesses. The Japanese political process is much maligned by analysts and participants alike, but it has never been more transparent on the defense issue. Although Yoshida designed the JDA to be dominated by bureaucrats from other ministries, politicians today understand strategic issues better than at any other time in Japanese history.[22] Japanese voters may not be more engaged in the minutiae of security policy than U.S. voters, but they certainly are no less so. They are not likely to reward excessive tilts by their leaders in one direction or another for long.

Second, as befits a complex security discourse in a free nation, each of the quadrants in this notional discourse is internally divided. Among the normal nationalists are globalists, such as Ichiro Ozawa, who believe that Japanese forces should be placed under UN auspices, as well as neo-conservatives such as Abe and realists such as Yasuhiro Nakasone, who would continue to embrace the United States as tightly as possible. Likewise, there are those such as Yohei Kono and Koichi Kato among the middle-power internationalists who would be inclined to reposition Japan closer to Asia than some of their more U.S.-oriented brethren.

JAPAN'S STRATEGIC CONTEXT

Of course, any repositioning of Japan's national security strategy and formation of a post-Yoshida consensus will also depend on strategists' perceptions of the regional and world order. In this regard, three recent, related developments will be prominent. The first is the relative decline of the United States. Although the United States will undoubtedly remain the world's preeminent military power for decades more and possibly longer, Tokyo already sees U.S. diplomatic vigor, moral authority, and economic allure waning.[23] It has not gone unnoticed that Washington needed to share leadership of the six-party talks with Beijing. Nor did Japanese analysts fail to observe that Washington needed but could not coerce cooperation from China and Russia to pressure Iran to abandon its nuclear program. It was also a matter of some discussion that the United States was unable to conclude a regional free-trade agreement with Latin America and that it had exhausted its moral authority after its intervention in Iraq. A widespread Japanese perception that comprehensive U.S. power is declining will likely engender reconsideration of the extent to which Tokyo wishes to continue risking entanglement.

The second development is the rise of a China with soft-power resources and economic opportunities that rival those of the United States. Beijing's economic allure—China is already Japan's largest trading partner—could further blunt the threat that Beijing's military development might continue to present, especially if the Japanese military consolidates its gains. The extent to which China displaces the United States as a target for investment and as a market for goods and services will determine whether the China threat gives way to a China opportunity and, possibly, to progress toward a regional economic bloc. Although the majority of those surveyed in a poll by the *Yomiuri Shimbun* in December 2003 thought the United States was Japan's most important political partner, an equal number (53 percent) already believed that China was Japan's most important economic partner.[24]

Finally, any overt sign of Japanese ambitions for great-power status and for a fully autonomous security posture is bound to stimulate balancing behavior by Japan's neighbors and undoubtedly opposition from the United States as well. Japan suffers from what Professor Tadafumi Ohtomo has aptly identified as the "wolf in sheep's clothing" problem, one that is endemic to states with a bad reputation. As he notes, it takes a very long period of good behavior to overcome the distrust of other states, and Japan has not gone nearly far enough to merit the trust of its neighbors. It still has a very poor reputation in East Asia.[25] Although the Chinese and the Koreans have reached a common agreement on the language of history textbooks, a mutually acceptable Pacific War narrative between Japan and its neighbors has been impossible. Japan's unwillingness or inability to confront its history squarely is undoubtedly the largest single constraint on its diplomacy.

These several elements of Japan's strategic context—institutional inertia, the dynamics of democratic competition, pragmatism, concern about the future of U.S. power, and shifting regional balances of power—converge to make the discontinuation of Japan's revisionist course seem likely. If Japan does not proceed down a straight path toward muscularity, then what? There remains the possibility of a "Goldilocks consensus" that positions Japan not too close and not too far from the current hegemon and protector, makes Japan stronger but not threatening, and also affords new comprehensive security options. In short, we should expect Japan to hedge.

THE HEDGE

Given its centrality to Japan's strategic discourse, it is ironic that the Japanese language has no indigenous word that captures the concept of hedging. The closest approximation has perhaps been offered by one of Japan's leading security policy intellectuals, Tanaka Akihiko. Japan, he said in testimony before the Diet, needs "a strategy to prevent the worst (*saiaku*) while trying to construct the best (*saizen*)."[26] As Tanaka explains it, preventing the worst requires a strong alliance with the United States and for Japan to play a more active role in international security affairs. Meanwhile, building an East Asian Community that resembles the stable, prosperous, economically integrated western Europe and that is built on a Japanese commitment to the values of democracy and freedom would, in his view, go a long way toward constructing the best.

This particular framing of the balance between Japan's security insurance and economic optimization strikes at a defining characteristic of Japan's grand strategy: the analytic separation of military and mercantile components.[27] Japan not only hedges against U.S. abandonment by courting entrapment, but it simultaneously hedges against predation by courting protectionism. The analogue of the U.S. relationship with western Europe where a U.S.-led security community coexists with a regional trade regime is often invoked. The advantages for Japanese security that would accrue from such a parallel construction in Asia are easily grasped. As long as Japan properly attends to its security relationship with the United States, it could balance against U.S. and European economic power while simultaneously balancing against Chinese military power.[28]

This suggests a two-track strategy for Japan to escape the alliance dilemma of abandonment and entanglement. First, Japan would continue to indulge Washington by building a bigger military shield—the preference of the normal nationalists, who would transform the alliance to reempower Japan by prioritizing globalization of the alliance. They would continue with their salami slicing as opportunities present themselves. Japan would acquire more offensive weapons, allow its defense firms to participate in international weapons systems development projects, lift the cap on defense spending, enlarge Japan's defense perimeter to include patrols of the Persian Gulf, and abandon the doctrine of defensive defense by formally embracing collective self-defense. Following this path, Tokyo could even establish battlefield legitimacy by placing troops in harm's way for the first time.

Second, Japan would move to ameliorate the concerns of its neighbors by honing a sharper mercantile sword. Japan would use regional and bilateral preferential-trade agreements to reduce the risk of U.S. and European predation, to protect against the possibility of Chinese economic dominance, and to enhance the chance for China's smooth integration into the regional system, while gaining trade benefits for itself. The challenge for Japanese diplomats and strategists is to make this dual hedge, what is sometimes called "strategic convergence," acceptable to the United States and to neighbors who might fear its "soft expansion."[29] Their hope is that the United States will respond positively as long as the new economic architecture is open and built on a liberal vision. They would have to showcase universal principles of human rights and democracy and suppress "Asian values."

Such are the dreams of some strategic thinkers in Tokyo. Before the possibilities for such a strategic convergence can even be tested, however, Japan has to repair its relationships with Korea and China, the other two of the three in the ASEAN Plus Three core of the new East Asia Council (EAC). Revisionists have stumbled on the history and textbook issues, exacerbating mistrust and undermining the prospects for an effective EAC in the near term. Such problems reinforce Japan's need to rebalance its recently acquired hard-power resources and security doctrines with renewed attention to building its soft-power attractions in the region.

Even the most enthusiastic supporters of the alliance insist that Japan must leave room for independent action on matters of vital national interest, such as access to Middle Eastern oil.[30] Not surprisingly, the Japanese government has retained a number of opt-out clauses in its tilt toward globalizing the alliance. Its missions, all to "noncombat zones," have been authorized through temporary "special measures" laws with sunset clauses, limiting the precedent set by these actions and providing an opt-out option, if desired.[31] Japan may have lost some of its fear of entrapment, but it has not abandoned its pragmatism altogether. Its close hug of the United States, rather than being debilitating, generates options for Japanese national security that can potentially render Japan stronger and more independent. Just as the end of the Cold War and the subsequent reconfiguration of the U.S. alliance created space for the realignment of Japanese domestic politics, it also has created new possibilities for Japan's security strategy.[32]

These new possibilities are normally couched in terms of the additional muscle Japan must provide for the United States, even if the alliance is replaced by a more flexible security arrangement.[33] Yet, there are many others as well. If Tokyo is diplomatically competent, its newly acquired strength and confidence could make it more attractive to other potential security partners in the region, such as India and the ASEAN states.[34] Former JDA director general Shigeru Ishiba made this point by deftly shifting the conventional argument for collective self-defense. In addition to making Japan a more attractive alliance partner for the United States, he insisted that collective self-defense would also enable Japan to offer assistance to ASEAN states if they are threatened by China.[35] In his view and in the view of other realists, a stronger Japan would create new possibilities for regional security.[36] Of course, Tokyo would first need to reassure its neighbors and avoid isolation, which is why a continued tether to the United States makes sense. Some have even suggested that, by enhancing its role in the alliance, Japan could become the cork in the American bottle.[37]

The Goldilocks Approach

These shifts await a skilled consensus builder who will see new possibilities for Japanese security and can soften the harder edges of the contemporary discourse. Potential leaders who can move their faction toward the middle to build a wider national strategic consensus reside in each corner of Japan's strategic discourse. For example, on becoming head of the Democratic Party of Japan in early 2006, Ozawa, the godfather of normal nationalism, lost no time in criticizing Koizumi for visiting Yasukuni Shrine, dedicated to Japan's war dead, including 14 Class A war criminals, and for tilting too far in favor of the United States. In so doing, Ozawa was articulating an increasingly popular position in Japan. Ozawa insisted that Japan needs to mend its relationships with Asia and that it must distance itself from the hegemonic tendencies both of China and the United States. Abe, for his part, could begin to deemphasize Japan's military power and stress Japan's soft-power advantages over China, including its democratic political system and its protection of human rights and political liberty, as a way to soften his hawkish image, an approach Taro Aso, a competitor for party leadership, already advanced in a policy speech in Washington, D.C., in May 2006.[38] Even neo-autonomists such as Terumasa Nakanishi have voiced limited support for the U.S.-Japanese alliance, while Terashima considered "how to be pro-American and part of Asia at the same time."[39] Mercantile realists who already argue for improved ties with China, such as Kato, would have to accede to the idea that a stronger Japan is here to stay. Yet, if the 2001 conversion of his mentor, Kiichi Miyazawa, is any indication, this should not be too far a distance to travel. Moreover, once-confirmed pacifists, such as Naoto Kan, have already migrated to a more central position in the discourse.

Thus, although we cannot identify with full certainty the Japanese leader with whom the new security consensus will be identified, we can expect him to be a (small c) conservative and a (small d) democrat possessed of an independent, full-throated voice on security issues and a keen eye for economic advantage. He will neither lead Japan too far toward great-power status and abandonment, nor will he allow it to remain so dependent on the United States as to risk further entanglement. He will abandon cheap-riding realism and consolidate the military gains of the revisionists' tight embrace of the United States, without allowing Japan to be dragged into undesirable territory. In short, he will appreciate that the costs of remaining a U.S. ally—still Japan's most attractive option—are escalating but will avoid allowing them to become too great to bear.

As in the past, Japan's repositioning will not be linear. A new consensus will depend on the selection and construction of a national identity, whether Japan comes to see itself as a great or middle power and whether it will define its role in regional or global terms. It will depend also on shifting balances of power, particularly between China and the United States. Above all, it will depend on the way Tokyo opts to balance its need to hedge risk against its chance to optimize for gain. Japan may never again be as central to world affairs as it was in the 1930s nor as marginal to world affairs as it was during the Cold War, but once revisionism has run its course and once the necessary accommodations are made in its economic diplomacy, Japan will have constructed for itself a post-Yoshida policy space in which it can be selectively pivotal. In getting there, Japan will reduce associated risks by being cautious. It will be normal. It will hedge. The security strategy and institutions abetting this hedge will be neither too hard nor too soft. Japan will be neither too close to China nor too far from the United States. We await the appearance of Japan's Goldilocks, the pragmatic leader who will get security just right.

Notes

1. Sadako Ogata, *Normalization With China: A Comparative Study of the U.S. and Japanese Processes* (Berkeley: University of California Institute of East Asian Studies, 1988), p. 99.

2. Hisahiko Okazaki, *A Grand Strategy for Japanese Defense* (Lanham, Md.: University Press of America, 1986), pp. 75–76, 129.

3. Saburo Ienaga, *The Pacific War, 1931–1945: A Critical Perspective on Japan's Role in World War II* (New York: Pantheon, 1978), pp. 33–54.

4. Shinichi Kitaoka, "Sengo Nihon no Gaiko Shiso [The concept of postwar Japanese diplomacy]," in *Sengo Nihon Gaiko Ronshu* [Collected essays on postwar Japanese diplomacy], ed. Shinichi Kitaoka (Tokyo: Chuo Koronsha, 1995), pp. 11–12.

5. Chihiro Hosoya, "Retrogression in Japan's Foreign Policy Decision-Making Process," in *Dilemmas of Growth in Prewar Japan*, ed. J. W. Morley (Princeton: Princeton University Press, 1971), p. 92.

6. See "Shinsenryaku o Motomete [Searching for a new strategy]," *Asahi Shimbun*, April 2006 (year-long series).

7. Okazaki, *A Grand Strategy for Japanese Defense*, pp. 75–76, 129.

8. Jain Purendra and Takashi Inoguchi, *Japanese Politics Today* (London: St. Martin's Press, 1996), p. xv.

9. Chinese officials, interviews with author, Seoul, December 2005; Chinese officials, interviews with author, Tokyo, May 2006; Cheol Hee Park, "Japanese Conservatives' Conception of Japan as a Normal Country: Comparing Ozawa, Nakasone, and Ishihara" (unpublished paper, "Japan as a Normal Country" project, Shibusawa Foundation, Tokyo, 2005) Park makes this point but does not share this view.

10. For an evaluation of contemporary Japanese techno-nationalism, see Richard J. Samuels, "Give and Take: The Outlook for U.S.-Japan Industrial Cooperation," *Armed Forces Journal* (February 2006): 24–29.

11. Robert Jervis, "Cooperation Under the Security Dilemma," *World Politics* 30, no. 2 (January 1978): 167–214.

12. Christopher W. Hughes, "Japanese Military Modernization: In Search of a 'Normal' Security Role," in *Strategic Asia 2005–2006: Military Modernization in an Era of Uncertainty*, eds. Ashley J. Tellis and Michael Wills (Seattle: National Bureau of Asian Research, 2005), p. 124.

13. Narushige Michishita, "The Changing Faces of Defense Policy: Past and Future," in *Global Economic Review* 32, no. 4 (2002): 91–93.

14. "United States–Japan Strategic Dialogue: Beyond the Defense Guidelines," *Issues & Insights* 1, no. 1 (May 2001): 1–2 ("Agenda for the U.S.-Japan Alliance: Rethinking Roles and Missions" by Michael J. Green and Robin "Sak" Sa-

koda referring to a "maturing alliance"); Paul R. Daniels, "Beyond 'Better than Ever': Japanese Independence and the Future of the U.S.-Japan Relationship," *IIPS Policy Paper*, no. 308E (July 2004), p. 11 (speaking of "erosion"); James L. Schoff, Tools for Trilateralism: referring to "tinkering").

15. National Institute for Defense Studies, ed., *2001–2002 Report on Defense and Strategic Studies: Council of Defense-Strategic Studies* (Tokyo: National Institute for Defense Studies, 2003), p. 17.

16. For an incisive analysis of these differences, see Takashi Shiraishi, "Toajia Kyodotaino Kochiku wa Kanno Ka? [Is it possible to create an East Asian community?]," *Chuo Koron* (January 2006): 118–127. See also Bungei Shinju, ed., *Nihon no Ronten: 2006* [Issues for Japan: 2006] (Tokyo: Bungei Shinju, 2005), p. 197.

17. See Terumasa Nakanishi, "Nihonkoku Kakubuso e no Ketsudan [Japan's decision to go nuclear]," *Shokun* (August 2003): 22–37. Nakanishi is a sometimes supporter of the alliance. For less ambiguity, see Susumu Nishibe, "Kakubuso-ron ga Jishu Boei e no Michi o Kirihiraku [The debate over nuclear armament will pave the way for autonomous defense]," *Seiron* (September 2003): 86–98; Susumu Nishibe, "Amerika Senryaku ni Haramareru Kyoki [The madness inherent in American strategy]," *Seiron* (April 2003): 64–77.

18. See Yoshihide Soeya, *Nihon no "Midoru Pawaa"* [Japan's "middle power" diplomacy: Postwar Japan's choices and conceptions] (Tokyo: Chikuma Shinsho, 2005).

19. These plans are laid out by one such group, Peace Depot, on their home page and in associated reports. See http://www.peacedepot.org/e-news/frame.html.

20. For links to reports on activities of these groups, see http://www.worldpeacenow.jp.

21. Government of Japan, *National Defense Program Guidelines* (provisional translation), 2004, pp. 5–6.

22. For a good example, see Shigeru Ishiba, *Kokubo* [National defense] (Tokyo: Shinchosha, 2005).

23. For a prominent example, see Kenichi Ito, *Japan's Identity: Neither East nor West* (Tokyo: Japan Forum on International Relations, 2000), p. 1. See also Japan Forum on International Relations, ed., *New World Order of No-War Community and Future of Japan-U.S. Alliance* (Tokyo: Japan Forum on International Relations, 2004).

24. James J. Przystup, "Dialogue of the Almost Deaf," *Comparative Connections* 6, no. 1 (First quarter 2004), http://www.ciaonet.org.

25. Takafumi Ohtomo, "Bandwagoning to Dampen Suspicion: NATO and the U.S.-Japan Alliance After the Cold War," *International Relations of the Asia-Pacific*, no. 3 (2003): 29–55.

26. Akihiko Tanaka, "Yosan Iinkai Kochokai Giroku: Dai Ichi Go [Budget committee public hearings: Number one]," February 23, 2005, p. 18 (testimony before the House of Representatives Budget Committee).

27. For the introduction of the concept of a "dual hedge," see Eric Heginbotham and Richard J. Samuels, "Japan's Dual Hedge," *Foreign Affairs* 81, no. 5 (September/October 2002): 110–121. See also Hughes, "Japanese Military Modernization," pp. 105–134.

28. See Soeya, *Nihon no "Midoru Pawaa"*; Takashi Shiraishi, *Teikoku to Sono Genkai* [Empire and its limits] (Tokyo: NTT, 2004).

29. National Institute for Defense Studies, ed., *East Asia Strategic Review*, 2005 (Tokyo: Japan Times, 2005), pp. 8, 35–36.

30. For a particularly clear example, see Fumio Ota, *"Joho" to Kokka Senryaku* ["Intelligence" and national strategy] (Tokyo: Fuyoshobo, 2005), p. 174.

31. Christopher W. Hughes, *Japan's Security Agenda: Military, Economic, and Environmental Dimensions* (Boulder, Colo.: Lynne Rienner, 2004), p. 181.

32. See Mike M. Mochizuki, "Japan: Between Alliance and Autonomy," in *Confronting Terrorism in the Pursuit of Power: Strategic Asia, 2004–2005*, eds. Ashley J. Tellis and Michael Wills (Seattle: National Bureau of Asian Research, 2004), p. 104. For the impact of the end of the Cold War on domestic Japanese politics, see Richard J. Samuels, *Machiavelli's Children: Leaders and Their Legacies in Italy and Japan* (Ithaca, N.Y.: Cornell University Press, 2003).

33. Rajan Menon, *The End of Alliances* (New York: Oxford University Press, 2006).

34. See Hughes "Japanese Military Modernization"; Daniels, "Beyond 'Better than Ever.'"

35. Shigeru Ishiba, "Nitchu Arasowaba Katsu no wa Dotchi Da [If Japan and China were to fight, which one would win?]," *Bungei Shunju*, May 1, 2006, p. 141.

36. For the weighing of Japanese strategic options from the perspective of a former Ground Self-Defense Forces general, see Hiroaki Yokochi, "Chugoku no Tainichi Senryaku no Akumu: Nihon wa Chugaku to Do Mukaiaubeki Ka [The nightmare of China's Japan strategy: How should Japan confront China?]," *Anzen Hosho o Kangaeru*, no. 604 (September 2005).

37. Yukio Okamoto, "Japan and the United States: The Essential Alliance," *The Washington Quarterly* 25, no. 2 (Spring 2002): 61.

38. A senior U.S. alliance manager has already made this suggestion to Abe. U.S. official, interview with author, Tokyo, April 25, 2006. For Aso's speech, see "Statesmen's Forum With Taro Aso, Japan's Minister of Foreign Affairs," Center for Strategic and International Studies, May 3, 2006, http://www.csis.org/component/option,com_csis_events/task,view/id,975.

39. Terashima, "'Shinbei Nyuo' no Sogo Senryaku o Motomete [Seeking an integrated strategy for being both 'pro-American' and 'part of Asia']," *Chuo Koron* (March 1996): 20–38.

Akio Watanabe

A Continuum of Change

Beyond the direct effects on the United States itself, among the most significant global effects of the September 11 terrorist attacks are the realignment of today's major powers and the transformed military posture of Japan. The changed perception of threat, from Soviet-led international communism to vaguely defined transnational terrorism, precipitated the realignment of powers on the stage of global and regional politics. Archenemies during the Cold War, Russia and China have moved closer to the United States because antiterrorism also tops their own domestic agendas. The impact on the Indo-Pakistani rivalry and the two countries' respective relations with the United States have been more complex in view of their geographical proximity to formerly Taliban-controlled Afghanistan. Nevertheless, both countries have succeeded in promoting their usefulness for the international coalition to fight terrorism.

Ironically, it was Europe, the center stage of Cold War strategy, that was most dramatically affected by the structural transformation after the September 11 attacks. NATO's rationale was altered substantially when the Soviet empire collapsed and was delivered an additional blow by the

Akio Watanabe is president of the Research Institute for Peace and Security (RIPS) in Tokyo.

Copyright © 2004 by The Center for Strategic and International Studies and the Massachusetts Institute of Technology
The Washington Quarterly • 27:4 pp. 137–146.

emergence of a new type of transnational threat. The transatlantic alliance is not dead but clearly is severely strained and groping to find relevancy for the new security agenda.

Although nations in Asia and the Pacific region were affected, they were structurally changed less dramatically than the transatlantic region after September 11. The fact that the Soviet Union occupied a less prominent place in Asia and the Pacific region during the Cold War, coupled with most Asian nations' preoccupation with a long-term agenda of modernization, helped maintain a sense of continuity even after the demise of the Soviet threat. Al Qaeda's attacks did not cause as drastic a blow to the rationale of the transpacific alliance as compared to the transatlantic alliance. The continued presence of such regional issues as the uncertain futures of the Korean peninsula and the Taiwan Strait continues to justify the U.S.-Japanese alliance. Robust solidarity between the two largest economies in the world, the United States and Japan, is still required for the peaceful entrance of Asian nations into a modernized world. China's ascent as an important player in Asian diplomacy, demonstrated by its role at the six-party talks on Korean issues, and its improved relations with the United States does not threaten the U.S.-Japanese alliance.

In the post-9/11 security environment, as an important member of the advanced nations, exemplified by its participation in the Group of Eight (G-8) summit, Japan is now obliged to play a larger global role, even in the military or paramilitary field. Perhaps even more important in the long term, the United States will need Japan as an indispensable partner for the historic project of creating peace and stability in Asia and the Pacific region. The September 11 attacks and their aftermath have increased, not reduced, the importance of the development missions of the United States and Japan in regions where Islamic extremism might fester.

Major Powers Realignment

The world's major powers have realigned themselves in the post–September 11 international era. The archenemies of the United States during the Cold War—Russia and China—each cleverly seized the opportunity presented by new threats to breach remaining differences with the United States by offering assistance, even if sometimes symbolic, for U.S. efforts to combat Osama bin Laden and Taliban-controlled Afghanistan. Although President George W. Bush had already recognized Russia as a friend in his speech at the National Defense University in early May 2001, Russia became a virtual ally in Operation Enduring Freedom by allowing the U.S. Air Force to use bases in countries such as Uzbekistan and Kazakhstan, over which Moscow was believed to have some influence. President Vladimir Putin was the first among the major power leaders to call Bush to promise wholehearted support in antiterrorism efforts. In his televised speech, he went so far as to state that "we are with you and we will support you."

The People's Republic of China also chose to support U.S. efforts in the fight against terrorism in its representative's speech at the United Nations, although the Chinese representative carefully avoided mentioning the possibly questionable issue of the right to self-defense. China's relations with the United States had been poor, particularly since the advent of the Republican administration in early 2001 and the collision of the two countries' military planes off China's Hainan Island in April of that year. After September 11, both the United States and China found reason to shift their attention away from bilateral issues and redirect their efforts toward the issue of international terrorism. It was convenient for China to define its problems of ungovernable forces in provinces such as Xinjiang in terms of antiterrorism. Whatever its real motivations might have been, Beijing could now justify its tightened control over "rogue" forces (which some Chinese leaders argue includes Taiwan's separatism) as an example of international cooperation for antiterrorist efforts.

India and Pakistan also joined the international coalition against terrorism in their respective ways. Relations between India and the United States had improved prior to 2001, at the expense of U.S.-Pakistani relations. After the 9/11 attacks, the United States suddenly rediscovered the strategic importance of Pakistan in an anticipated war against Afghanistan. Gen. Mahmoud Ahmad, head of Pakistan's Inter-Service Intelligence (ISI), who happened to be in Washington, D.C., at the time of the attacks, was immediately called on by Deputy Secretary of State Richard Armitage, who showed the top ISI official a list of seven specific demands including the right to fly military missions over Pakistani territory. On receipt of the U.S. requests in Islamabad, President Gen. Pervez Musharraf had no choice but to accept. Under the new circumstances, it was necessary for Washington to alienate neither New Delhi nor Islamabad, even though severe tension existed between India and Pakistan over the issues of Kashmir (for which India accused Pakistan's acquiescence in, if not overt assistance of, cross-border terrorism) and Pakistani missile tests.

Although each of these countries' cooperation soon proved diplomatically contingent on U.S. adherence to the UN's multilateral principles (demonstrated by their strong reservations or objections to the U.S. decision to go to war in Iraq), the realignment of major powers after September 11, 2001, nevertheless signifies an important structural change in international relations. The structural change reflects a more fundamental reassessment of U.S. threat perception. Major powers no longer pose an imminent threat to the United States because none of them can match U.S. military strength. Ironically, the world's mightiest nation now feels vulnerable to asymmetric threats emanating from minor but defiant states and from unlawful nonstate actors, not from great powers. U.S. self-confidence coexists with hypersensitive wariness.

This fundamental threat reassessment has had two seemingly contradictory effects. As discussed above, it has helped cooperation among major powers, including those that had been traditionally regarded as adversaries rather than as allies. It also weakened Western alliances. The decline of the Soviet threat forced Western nations to reevaluate the role of alliances in general and NATO in particular. European NATO members have found new tasks for the alliance in the field of soft security, including humanitarian intervention and postconflict peace building in areas such as the former Yugoslavia and to a lesser extent Africa. The United States, although sharing similar concerns as indicated by its participation in peacekeeping efforts in Kosovo and Somalia with its European partners, tended to be interested in the Middle East and Asia. Even during the Cold War, various differences between the

United States and Western Europe continuously had plagued NATO, but transatlantic disparity grew deeper and wider without the common Soviet threat to hold it together.

Although the immediate impact of the September 11 attacks on transatlantic relations was positive, European misgivings and reservations remained just beneath the surface. After the catastrophic attacks initially seemed to restore transatlantic unity (hence the unprecedented invocation of the collective self-defense clause, or Article 5, of the NATO Charter), European disagreement with the U.S. tendency toward unilateral and overly militaristic solutions as well as disregard for international agreements or organizations emerged over the invasion of Iraq and its aftermath. Europeans seem ambivalent, however, about the leadership role of the United States in the post–Cold War, or more precisely post-9/11, world, demonstrated by the recent efforts at the D-Day commemoration and the Sea Island G-8 summit to reemphasize the transatlantic partnership. They are clearly interested in preserving their voice on Iraq, and the Bush administration's domestic struggles prior to the U.S. election has provided them with a chance to elicit a relatively compromising stance from Washington. Thus, one should not conclude hastily that the transatlantic alliance is destined to wither but, at the same time, recognize that it is certainly facing severe tensions.

Regional Impact

In contrast, a U.S.-centered alliance network in Asia and the Pacific region fares well. The impact of September 11 and the two wars in Afghanistan and Iraq have surely affected Asia-Pacific international relations. Most of the regional states, especially the Islamic nations in Southeast Asia, were strongly pressured by the United States to enforce effective control over transnational terrorism and other criminal activities. Reactions to U.S. unilateralism have been much more subdued here, however, than in Europe. Various factors help explain this difference. First, international relations in Asia and the Pacific region were not as clearly transformed by the end of the Cold War as they were in Europe. The Soviet presence in Asia was less prominent and less contiguous than in Europe, even if it was not insignificant and invisible. Instead, China had always been a conspicuous factor in the power configuration in Asian international relations somewhat, if not completely, independent of the U.S.-Soviet competition, even before China's remarkable economic and diplomatic ascent in recent years.

Accordingly, the demise of the Soviet Union did not hasten any dramatic and drastic changes in Asia comparable to the collapse of Communist regimes in Eastern Europe. Communist-led Vietnam not only survived but also seems on its way to modernization as China was. Even the ailing Communist regime in North Korea still clings to its last breath. For China, Taiwan's international status remains an unsettled issue, while some Southeast Asian countries, especially Indonesia and the Philippines, are still struggling with the problem of nation building. Insurgencies in Aceh, Indonesia, and Mindanao, the Philippines, are graphic examples of domestic insecurity in the region. These challenges all signify an unfinished task of modernization rather than the continuation of the Cold War, and Asian governments recognize, for the most part, that the presence of a strong and reliable United States is a prerequisite to accomplish this historic task successfully. A U.S. presence, however, is a mixed blessing for Southeast Asians. Practical wisdom welcomes the Americans; the Muslim ethos repels them. The U.S.-led antiterrorist efforts in the aftermath of the September 11 attacks helped elevate rather than lessen an inherent tension in their psyche.

In light of Indonesia's huge Islamic population, which exceeds that of Egypt, Turkey, and Iran (the three largest Muslim populations in the Middle East) combined, as well as Malaysia, it is quite understandable for the United States and the international community to pay special attention to Southeast Asia, a second front in the war on terrorism. Under pressure from the United States as well as from Australia since the Bali attacks on October 12, 2002, states in the region made individual and collective efforts to strengthen control over terrorist and other transnational criminal activities. At the same time, the danger posed by terrorist groups has also increased, partly due to heightened hostility against the United States and the West after September 11 and the war in Iraq. More importantly, a longer term and comprehensive approach is essential for addressing the root causes of the problem, such as poverty, social discrimination, and political oppression, for eventual success in the war on terrorism. In this sense, domestic insecurity in these Southeast Asian states is the product of a longer historical process, though certainly exasperated by September 11. Depending on the future direction of the United States and the international community's renewed interest in the local conditions of Southeast Asia, anti-American (and anti-Western) feeling may well prevail over the cooperative attitude of the moment.

In Northeast Asia, traditional issues other than terrorism still linger as concerns for the region's states, including Japan. Improved Sino-U.S. relations after the 9/11 attacks have been met calmly by Japan, which also succeeded, more than China, in cementing its friendship with its traditional ally the United States. Yet, the United States needs support both from Japan and China in respective ways. Japan is assisting the United States in the Indian Ocean and in Iraq, whereas China is making efforts in the six-party talks to resolve the North Korean nuclear issue. Taiwan finds itself in an awkward situation, concerned about diplomatic isolation in the midst of a semblance of a big-power consortium.

This is not to say that post–September 11 developments have not had any effect on the way that Northeast Asian states are handling these traditional issues. Both the Republic of Korea and Japan, especially the former, decided to send troops to Iraq despite considerable opposition at home, in hopes of acquiring sympathy from the U.S. government over the question of North Korea. Nevertheless, Washington does not always hide its disapproval of the Roh administration's appeasing attitude toward Pyongyang. From the U.S. perspective, North Korea is definitely a target of the antiterrorism campaign in light of North Korea's suspicious relations with some Islamic countries.

As for Japan, it is more concerned about other aspects of the North Korean threat, such as abduction issues, medium-range missiles, and spy ships. Despite a similar experience of terrorist attacks by Aum Shinrikyo at a Tokyo subway station in the spring of 1995, with 12 casualties and 5,500 injured from sarin gas, few Japanese people associated this experience with the terrorist attacks on the World Trade Center in New York.

In the minds of the ordinary Japanese, Islamic extremism is a clash-of-civilizations phenomenon between the Judeo-Christian and Islamic religions—something remote to the Japanese imagination. The Japanese abhor any type of clash of civilizations and are therefore inclined to define the issue of terrorism primarily in terms of economic and social disparity rather than religious strife.

The Pivotal Role of Japan

Japan's role as a reliable U.S. ally accounts to a great degree for the relative stability of the alliance network in Asia and the Pacific region. It has played a unique and important role in the historical transformation of Asia-Pacific international relations. As a model and critical provider of financial resources and industrial technology, Japan has made a valuable contribution to modernizing underdeveloped economies in Asia, notwithstanding faults here and there. This nonmilitary aspect was and remains an indispensable ingredient of Japan's role as an ally to the United States because that was what many Asian countries needed most. One cannot fully explain the success of many Asian economies, including those in Southeast Asia and in China and Taiwan (and probably a united Korea in the future), relative to other, more unfortunate parts of the Third World, without taking into account Japan's presence.

Since the mid-1970s, Japan has been with few exceptions a leading donor for developing nations in the Asia-Pacific region. It was Prime Minister Masayoshi Ohira that inaugurated pan-Pacific cooperation schemes, whose outgrowth is today's Pacific Economic Cooperation Council (PECC) and Asia Pacific Economic Cooperation (APEC) forum. Apart from money and technology, Japan served as a non-Western modernization model.

The historic task of modernization remains unfinished in Asia. This task involves not only domestic issues such as economic development, nourishing constitutional democracy, and spreading the rule of law into every corner of social life, but also external challenges such as settling territorial disputes, creating a sense of community among nations, and constructing regional organizations for international cooperation. A robust alliance between the two largest economies in the world—the United States and Japan—will continue to be an essential condition for the successful achievement of that great task. This task is so huge that, notwithstanding temporary aberrations due to the pressing needs of the time, the core agenda remains unchanged, and the mission of developing Asian states gives the U.S.-Japanese alliance more of a sense of purpose than U.S.-European alliances.

Japan's behavior in the post–September 11 world is best understood as a continuation of the country's adjustment to the changing international security environment that started after the bitter experience of an ill-prepared and clumsy response to the Persian Gulf crisis of 1990–1991. With the Persian Gulf War, Japan began to realize that it could no longer afford to evade responsibility beyond its national borders under the pretext of its constitution's prohibition of the use of force. The Japanese, like many others in the world, became aware of the fact that the issue of international security is not gone with the Cold War. The Gulf War aroused anger among Japanese taxpayers because Japan contributed a total of $12 billion in various forms for the multinational forces and war-stricken nations in the Gulf area and received little appreciation from them.

Nevertheless, it took several more months for Japan to adapt its security policy and thinking to the new reality. It was only after nervous discussions that the Japanese Diet passed the 1992 International Peace Cooperation Law, which authorized the government to send Self-Defense Forces (SDF) to Cambodia on postconflict missions. The 1947 constitution, which was essentially a product of Gen. Douglas MacArthur's occupation policy after Japan's surrender but still remains valid, prohibits the use of force as a means to settle international disputes. Nothing in the constitution specifically prohibits the dispatch of troops abroad, but domestic debates in subsequent years firmly entrenched a belief that the spirit of that document prohibited the use of force except for territorial defense (namely, as a last resort only after enemy forces actually attack Japanese territory).

Extremely cautious about provoking likely negative reactions from neighboring countries were it to use force, the Japanese government stubbornly adhered to that belief and was thus reluctant to make any military contribution at the time of the Gulf War. SDF participation in Cambodia was justified in the 1992 law as a noncombatant mission that did not contradict the spirit of the constitution. In 1998 the Japanese Diet broadened that law to allow the SDF to participate in UN-sponsored peace operations, most notably in East Timor alongside troops from Australia and South Korea, among other countries. The fact that SDF troops have been engaged in noncombatant missions and in places geographically far from Northeast Asia, the area most sensitive to Japan's military resurgence, helped ease anxiety both at home and abroad as long as those activities were conducted under the UN umbrella.

One other series of events also pushed Japan to improve its preparedness for military contingencies: North Korea's suspected development of nuclear weapons, launching its missiles over the Japanese archipelagoes, and unidentified ships engaging in dubious operations off of Japanese shores. Unlike during the Cold War era, the Korean peninsula is not likely to become a stage of armed conflict among Russia, China, and the United States. One cannot entirely rule out, however, risks of military contingencies sparked by desperate North Korean actions. Japan should not dismiss such a contingency as someone else's concern; it would endanger Japan itself, and U.S. forces in Japan would be mobilized to meet the threat.

The U.S. and Japanese governments have improved, therefore, the modus operandi of U.S.-Japanese security cooperation by various measures newly introduced to make Japan's contribution to the alliance surer and swifter in the case of contingencies in the Far East. The United States and Japan concluded in 1996 an acquisition and cross-servicing agreement so that the SDF and U.S. armed forces can provide each other with goods and services necessary for joint exercises. They also agreed in 1997 to amend guidelines for Japanese-U.S. defense cooperation to provide a general framework and policy direction for the roles and missions of the two countries' armed forces in case of armed attacks against Japan or in contingencies in areas surrounding Japan. This marked the first time that Japan indicated its intention to commit troops beyond its national borders. A new law in 1999 addressed the question of the

SDF's role in case of war in "areas surrounding Japan," the phrase commonly interpreted as contingencies in Korea. North Korea's development of medium-range missiles, whether equipped with nuclear warheads or not, certainly created a sense of urgency among the Japanese, resulting in the enactment of additional emergency laws in 2003.

By September 11, Japan had become better prepared to undertake its responsibilities as a U.S. ally and as a UN member. On account of the country's domestic debate on constitutional constraints on international military undertakings and also because of a characteristic deference for the UN, the Japanese tend to find legal justification for overseas military (or quasi-military) missions in the UN Charter. For example, the Antiterrorism Special Measures Law, enacted in the aftermath of the September 11 attacks, officially enables the Japanese government to engage the SDF in overseas duties to provide "support to military forces of the United States and other foreign countries working to achieve the goals" of the UN to eliminate the "threat to international peace and security" posed by international terrorists.

Two points deserve mention regarding the significance of this post–September 11 law. First, unlike Japan's slow and inadequate response to the Gulf crisis in 1990, the country reacted rather quickly this time, thanks to the significant transformation of public attitudes during the previous 10 years or so. The Japanese have become more accustomed to the concept of international security and the role of armed forces in it. Second, none of the stipulations of the U.S.-Japanese security treaty were invoked to justify Japan's participation in the U.S.-led war against Taliban-controlled Afghanistan, in contrast to NATO, which invoked Article 5 of their treaty. Instead, the Antiterrorism Special Measures Law was hastily legislated to respond immediately. This type of ad hoc approach was repeated on the occasion of the war in Iraq. These developments still leave Japan uncertain about its international obligations. The existing treaty with the United States is unusable as a legal instrument to justify overseas SDF missions in situations such as Afghanistan and Iraq. As conveyed by the Antiterrorism Special Measures Law quoted above, Japan adheres to UN Security Council resolutions as the legal justification for its participation in multinational efforts for peace and security.

Ultimately, the impact of September 11 and its aftermath stimulated Japan into a larger, global, international security role. This change did not occur overnight but rather is a new stage of gradual adaptation that started about 10 years ago. Nor is it a complete turnaround for Japan as far as the country's strong reservations about the use of force. Despite the qualified acceptance of military obligations, its traditional emphasis on "civilian power" is very likely to be maintained in relation to international efforts to fight terrorism. Should the SDF's role in Iraq prove to be successful in assisting reconstruction and rehabilitation of that country, this experience would reinforce the Japanese ethos about the SDF as an instrument of "civilian power."

As for Asia and the Pacific region, Japan is very likely to continue to play its role as a catalyst for the historic task of modernizing developing nations. The immediate task of punishing unlawful terrorists needs to be followed by the more sober but painstaking task of getting at the roots of the issue. From a long-term perspective, it is in this realm that continued cooperation between the United States and Japan can play a decisive role to shape the future world. The U.S.-Japanese alliance will serve as the bedrock for endurable cooperation between the two nations. That type of U.S.-Japanese cooperation is essential to transform the Asia-Pacific region in an orderly manner by absorbing the inevitable effects stemming from the rise of China, peaceful or not.

Michael J. Green

U.S.-Japanese Relations after Koizumi: Convergence or Cooling?

"Thank you, American people ... for 'Love Me Tender.'" Thus spoke an ecstatic Japanese prime minister Junichiro Koizumi on June 29, 2006, after meeting with President George W. Bush and before heading off to a lavish White House dinner and an unprecedented presidential tour of Graceland, the home of Koizumi's beloved Elvis Presley. By any account, Koizumi steps down in September 2006 having built the strongest personal ties ever seen between Japanese and U.S. leaders, as well as the tightest security cooperation of the Washington-Tokyo alliance's five-decade history.

Yet, was the Bush-Koizumi connection too close? Did it mask underlying areas of divergence between the United States and Japan that will surface with less committed or skilled leadership in Tokyo? Some analysts voiced such concerns on the margins of the Koizumi visit to Washington. Dan Okimoto of Stanford University, a longtime Japan expert, warned in the *Christian Science Monitor* that, "after Koizumi steps down,

Michael J. Green holds the Japan Chair and is a senior adviser at CSIS, as well as an associate professor of international relations at Georgetown University. He previously served as director for Asian affairs (2001–2003) and special assistant to the president and senior director for Asian affairs at the National Security Council during 2004–2005. He would like to thank Shinjiro Koizumi, Yuko Nakano, Koki Nishimura, and Kiyoto Tsuji for their comments on this manuscript.

Copyright © 2006 by The Center for Strategic and International Studies and the Massachusetts Institute of Technology
The Washington Quarterly • 29:4 pp. 101–110.

we'll see an adjustment back to something that is not so one-sided and pro-American."[1] Ivo Daalder, a senior fellow at the Brookings Institution, told the *New York Times* that "Mr. Bush, for instance, is unlikely to challenge Mr. Koizumi on his much-criticized visits to the Yasukuni shrine, which honors the Japanese war dead of World War II, including the wartime prime minister who ordered the attack on Pearl Harbor."[2] Critics of Koizumi in Japan echoed these observations, arguing as Socialist parliamentarian Mizuho Fukushima did, that "Japan is the 51st state in the union. Koizumi's attitude is just to obey ... the [United States]. To show his friendship, he sent troops to Iraq even though it is against our pacifist constitution."[3]

It is not surprising that political opponents of Bush or Koizumi might criticize the leaders' close personal relationship, but even supporters have expressed some concern about whether the tightening of U.S.-Japanese relations over the past five years is an aberration based on personal chemistry rather than a long-term trend and whether the post-Koizumi period will see continued strategic convergence or a cooling of relations. This question is important because even if the convergence trend will continue, both governments will have to make an effort and recognize the soft spots in their relationship.

For their part, Bush and Koizumi have pointed to what they see as the enduring qualities of a converging U.S.-Japanese security relationship. In their joint statement for the summit, entitled "The Japan-U.S. Alliance of the New Century," the leaders "celebrated their close personal friendship and the deep and increasing ties between the American and Japanese people" and noted that "the United States and Japan stand together not only against mutual threats, but also for the advancement of core universal values."[4] They also pointed to the importance of "deepening bilateral economic cooperation." On the whole, they "shared the expectation that the U.S.-Japan friendship and global cooperation shall continue to grow stronger." In other words, the two leaders spotlighted exactly what has contributed to the strong U.S.-Japanese alliance under their tenure and what they believe will likely keep it strong: relationships between their leaders, the external threat environment, common values, and economic relations.

Personal Synergy

Although another sighting of an Elvis-singing leader like Koizumi may not emerge for some time, the odds are good that the president and next prime minister will have reason to continue good personal ties and to keep their countries aligned. For the critics who say Bush became too close to Koizumi to be correct, one would have to assume that the next leader of Japan will resent that relationship and push away from the United States or simply be unwilling to attempt the same kind of close relationship. Judging from the race to succeed Koizumi as president of the Liberal Democratic Party and prime minister of Japan, however, the next prime minister will likely come into office with an affinity to collaborate with U.S. leadership.

The two strongest contenders in that race are Koizumi's first chief cabinet secretary, Yasuo Fukuda, and current chief cabinet secretary, Shinzo Abe. Although these men are rivals, both are members of Koizumi's faction and have served as his lieutenants during the most significant developments in U.S.-Japanese security relations over the past five years. With then–Foreign Minister Makiko Tanaka embroiled in scandal, Fukuda acted as de facto national security adviser in the challenging months after the September 11 terrorist attacks. He orchestrated Japan's seven-point counterterrorism strategy, including the dispatch of oilers and destroyers to the Indian Ocean to support Operation Enduring Freedom in Afghanistan. Fukuda also formed a project team to pave the way for permanent legislation that would allow Japan's Self-Defense Forces (SDF) to participate in coalition operations without having to pass a separate bill each time, an initiative that will be a key agenda item for the next prime minister.

Abe served as Fukuda's deputy throughout the post–September 11 period and did much of the heavy lifting required to pass the legislation allowing the SDF to be deployed to Iraq. He appeared on television regularly and made passionate appeals for standing with the United States in its time of need to ensure that the United States will support Japan in future Asian crises. Abe continues to be more hawkish on China and North Korea. In contrast, since stepping down, Fukuda has grown critical of Koizumi's controversial visits to the Yakusuni shrine and has called for improved relations with China. Both Fukuda and Abe have a proven track record on the U.S.-Japanese alliance, however, and have made it clear they will continue to strengthen alliance ties. (Fukuda dropped out of the race on July 21, but others quickly stepped in to try to fill the void with a similar policy line.)

Criticism of the Bush-Koizumi relationship is understandably more pronounced in the opposition Democratic Party of Japan (DPJ), and it is theoretically possible that Abe could stumble as prime minister in upper-house elections next summer, opening the way eventually for a DPJ-led coalition. The current leader of the opposition, Ichiro Ozawa, has decided to make China one of his first foreign visits to highlight Koizumi's inability to improve relations with Beijing because of the shrine visits. Ozawa has also criticized the troop dispatch to Iraq, arguing that Japan should have had a UN Security Council mandate before dispatching troops abroad. Ozawa's DPJ is a badly divided party, however, with as many pro-U.S. alliance hawks as former Socialist doves, and his UN mandate argument is at best a placeholder to keep his party from splitting on security issues. Moreover, Ozawa played a key role in managing U.S.-Japanese economic and security relations when he served as deputy chief cabinet secretary of the LDP administration of Prime Minister Noboru Takeshita in the late 1980s. If the DPJ comes into power, it will be at the helm of a coalition that includes parts of the LDP and therefore a majority inclined to maintain strong security ties with Washington. In short, Japan has come to look like the United Kingdom, with a "loyal opposition," in which both major parties support alliance relations with the United States.

On the U.S. side of the equation, Bush will undoubtedly attempt to build a strong relationship with Abe or Ozawa and to maintain a focus on Japan as the linchpin of U.S. strategy in Asia. This forecast applies through 2008, but one must read the tea leaves of U.S. politics to anticipate how the next president might handle Japan. Within the Republican Party, potential frontrunner candidates such as Senator John McCain (R-Ariz.) have already demonstrated an interest in the U.S.-Japanese alliance, and conservatives would likely sustain a Japan-centered Asia policy regardless of the chosen candidate. The Democratic Party has focused relatively little on Japan in its national security debate, but there are some indications that the party could be divided on Asia policy just as it has on Iraq. In their forthcoming book *Hard Power*, Kurt Campbell and Mike O'Hanlon advanced the view that the balance of power matters in Asia and the U.S.-Japanese alliance is central to the U.S. position in the region.[5] Some potential candidates have already picked up on that theme, as former Virginia governor Mark Warner (D) did in a speech to the Japan Society of New York in June 2006.[6] Further to the left of the Democratic Party, some may be drawn to the *New York Times* editorial of May 2005, which argued that the United States has become too close to Japan and had failed to accommodate the rise of China.[7] Time, as well as the midterm congressional elections and the Democratic primary race, will tell.

The Asian Threat Environment

Toward the end of the Cold War, a scholarly consensus began to emerge in Japan and the United States that the relationship would come apart without the unifying threat of the Soviet Union and with the new complications of techno-economic competition.[8] That consensus rapidly evaporated as the collapse of the Japanese economic bubble, Chinese and North Korean nuclear and missile development in the mid-1990s, and revelations that Pyongyang had been abducting innocent Japanese civilians pushed Japan back toward the United States. Rather than letting the alliance drift, Prime Minister Ryutarô Hashimoto and President Bill Clinton signed a joint declaration in April 1996 reaffirming the security relationship and opening new areas of cooperation both in missile defense and in response to "situations in the area surrounding Japan."[9]

Following North Korea's ballistic missile tests in July 2006 and the Japanese public's subsequent increased sense of insecurity and closeness to the United States, this trend is unlikely to change significantly in the years ahead. North Korea will test the alliance in new ways, however, primarily because the Japanese side will eventually want to know how the United States plans to dismantle, deter, and defeat a North Korean nuclear weapons program that continues to grow in spite of intensive diplomatic efforts.

For the first few decades of the U.S.-Japanese alliance, Tokyo was extremely careful to avoid becoming entrapped (*makikomareru*) in the U.S. competition with China. Now the U.S. side must, for the first time, make decisions about how it positions itself as an ally of Japan in the growing competition between Tokyo and Beijing. This is particularly important as Japanese and Chinese warships and aircraft have been maneuvering at close ranges around the contested Senkaku/Diaoyutai island chain in response to Chinese unilateral, exploratory oil drilling and the subsequent dispatch of Japanese military and coast guard patrols. Japan does trade more with China now than with the United States, but this fact has done little to improve Japanese public opinion about China or to soften the Japanese Defense Agency's warnings about China's military buildup, given the increase of People's Liberation Army (PLA) Navy submarines and surface combatants in disputed territorial waters around Japan. On the diplomatic front, the Chinese-Japanese rivalry has heated up, with Beijing organizing international efforts to block Japan's UN Security Council bid and Tokyo pulling other democracies such as India, Australia, and New Zealand into the new East Asian Summit to balance Chinese influence. Japan and China have never been powerful in Asia at the same time, and these two giants will struggle to find a stable equilibrium for years to come.

If there is a possibility for divergence between Tokyo and Washington regarding Northeast Asia in the years ahead, it will not be because Japan takes the Asian threat environment less seriously than the United States, which was always the U.S. concern during the Cold War. Instead, the challenges may come in areas where Japan reacts to regional threats with greater sensitivity than the United States. In short, to keep the alliance strong, the United States will have to demonstrate continually that the U.S.-Japanese alliance remains Japan's most credible line of defense against regional threats. The North Korean nuclear and missile programs and the PLA military buildup will continue to preoccupy the United States and will almost certainly lead future administrations to continue strengthening U.S.-Japanese defense cooperation.

For the United States, the key question may be whether future governments in Japan can live up to Koizumi's standards. After the successful dispatch of Japanese forces to the Indian Ocean and Iraq, U.S. military planners and senior officials have come to see the dispatch of the SDF as the rule rather than as the exception. In Japan, however, future dispatches of forces could become prisoner to other priorities or crises in the Diet if a separate bill is required for each mission. Moreover, polling evidence suggests that although the Japanese public was impressed with the efforts of the SDF in Iraq, they still see the dispatch of Japanese forces as the exception rather than the rule and remain averse to casualties. U.S. confidence in Japan could also be shaken by a failure to implement the May 2006 "Two-Plus-Two" agreement on the realignment of bases in Okinawa. Bush and Koizumi lauded the agreement during their June 2006 summit, but there is opposition in Okinawa and from members of the Diet unhappy about the price tag, which is estimated at up to $6 billion.

On the whole, the international threat environment is likely to continue pushing the United States and Japan closer together as alliance partners. Already, the depth of coordination in areas ranging from development assistance to missile defense and export controls is unprecedented and reflects a shared assessment of the challenges both nations face. Yet, the nature of the threats will continue to test traditional ways of managing the alliance, and each side has high expectations for mutual security cooperation. It will take continued high-level attention in both governments to ensure that the U.S.-Japanese alliance lives up to those expectations in the next major crises to come.

Common Universal Values

What is most striking about the new U.S.-Japanese alliance relationship, after the closeness of the president and prime minister, is the degree to which both governments have highlighted the bond provided by their shared values. As Bush and Koizumi noted in their joint statement on June 29,

[t]he United States and Japan share interests in: winning the war on terrorism; maintaining regional stability and prosperity; promoting free market ideals and institutions; upholding human rights; securing freedom of navigation and commerce, including sea lanes; and enhancing global energy security. It is these common values and common interests that form the basis for U.S.-Japan regional and global cooperation.[10]

This is a far cry from the frequent ideational confrontation that characterized U.S.-Japanese relations a decade or so ago. At that time, Japan's leading strategic thinkers tended to highlight the ideological differences with the United States as often as the commonalities. Typical was Eisuke Sakakibara's "A Japanese Economy That Has Surpassed Capitalism"[11] or writings praising Japan's adherence to Asian values rather than global values or the Washington consensus.

So, is Koizumi just signing on to the Bush administration's freedom agenda, or does Japan really share these values? After all, there are still differences between Washington and Tokyo on Burma's troubled democratic transition, and Japanese bookstores still sell millions of books such as Kokka no Hinkaku (The Nation's Qualities),[12] which decry the loss of "Japaneseness" to American culture. The evidence is strong, however, that common values are not just a talking point in a summit joint statement. There is a fundamental convergence on universal norms between Washington and Tokyo that did not exist a decade ago.

In 2001 the Japanese government proposed the Initiative for Development of Economies of Asia with the Association of Southeast Asian Nations, designed to focus on good governance, rule of law, and economic transparency—hardly uniquely Asian norms. In the Asia-Africa summit in April 2005 at Bandung and numerous other occasions at which there were no Americans present at all, Koizumi and other senior Japanese ministers called for other states to join Japan in "disseminating universal values such as the rule of law, freedom, and democracy."[13] In 2006 the Office of the Prime Minister commissioned a panel on overseas economic cooperation, which argued that, "for the first time it is possible in today's international system to center international relations on a collection of countries with shared values and ideals."[14] Based on the panel's recommendation, the prime minister's office created the equivalent of a National Security Council to oversee overseas development strategy and to ensure that "democracy, freedom and rule of law" become central priorities.[15] Even on Burma, which has been a perennial symbol of Japan's independence from the U.S. agenda in Asia, Foreign Minister Taro Aso and Secretary of State Condoleezza Rice agreed that the international community should apply stronger pressure on Myanmar to prompt the country's democratization.

The concept of universal democracy promotion, however, does not now dominate Japanese foreign policy decisionmaking. Yet, the convergence of Japanese and U.S. interests in universal norms is pronounced, as a response to the rise of Chinese influence and as an instinctive spotlight on what separates Japan from China. It is also partly the result of Koizumi's destruction of the old Japanese political economy and a recognition that an Asian-values buffer against globalization and U.S. pressure for reform is no longer necessary, but it is also based on Japan's increased realization that the promotion of democracy, good governance, and rule of law provide stability across Asia in ways that directly contribute to Japan's national interest.

This trend really began in the mid-1990s, when Tokyo found that economic tools of aid and investment were almost completely ineffective in dissuading China from testing nuclear weapons, bracketing the Taiwan Strait with missiles, and sending PLA Navy submarines and destroyers into contested waters. Japan's identity in Asia also came under pressure from China's use of the history card and by China's growing assertiveness in forming regional multilateral groupings favorable to Beijing, such as the Shanghai Cooperation Organization. Leading politicians and strategic thinkers in Tokyo seized on one undeniable truth in their search for a response to the China conundrum: Japan is a democracy, and China is not. Born from a combination of internal political and economic reform and growing concern about China, values have become increasingly central to Japan's own identity.

The future of Japan's focus on values and the bond it provides to U.S.-Japanese relations will depend to a significant degree on whether the freedom agenda survives beyond the Bush administration. For some

Americans, on the right and the left, democracy promotion has been discredited by the election of Hamas in the Palestinian Authority and the difficult situation in Iraq. In Asia, however, democracy is clearly on the march, and compelling reasons exist for a continued regional focus on the consolidation of democracy. The only question is whether future U.S. leadership will focus on it.

Economic Relations: From Threat to Asset

Economic issues once represented the greatest threat to the U.S.-Japanese security relationship. In 1988, Representative Richard Gephardt (D-Mo.) quipped that the United States and the Soviets fought the Cold War and Japan won, while polls that same year showed that more Americans feared the Japanese economy than the Soviet threat.[16] Today, the only major bilateral economic irritant was Tokyo's decision to close its market to U.S. beef after the outbreak of mad cow disease, and even that issue was resolved at the 2006 Bush-Koizumi summit. The Bush administration's problem with the Japanese economy was never the threat it posed to U.S. companies but rather the protracted slump that lowered Japan's strategic weight and denied opportunities for U.S. firms. After five years of reforms, as well as changes in business practices that go back five years prior to that, Japanese firms have largely corrected their bad balance sheets and are once again competitive. With the reform process opening new opportunities and the Japanese economy growing again, U.S. firms made more than $11 billion in profit in Japan in 2005, compared with only about $3 billion in China.[17]

Clearly, the "threat" of Japanese economic strength is no longer a problem in the alliance, and the danger of nongrowth in the Japanese economy seems to have been largely overcome as well. The problem to watch, therefore, is whether the Koizumi reforms slow down, given that only 16 percent of Japanese recently polled said they should continue unchanged, and whether U.S. companies start losing interest in Japan as a result. As it is, there are now five U.S. chambers of commerce in China and only one in Japan, even though Japan's gross domestic product is four times China's, as are U.S. profits in Japan.

Recognizing this possibility, the U.S.-Japan Business Roundtable and other groups have called for formal economic integration agreements or even full free-trade agreements (FTAs).[18] An FTA would require Japan to liberalize its agricultural market, however, something the ruling LDP is still unwilling to do even though it now relies on agricultural support much less than in the past. In their joint statement, Bush and Koizumi called for further steps to "deepen economic cooperation," which will help sustain broader strategic and ideational convergence and set a high standard for broader Asian economic integration.

Elvis Has Left the Building

The strategic convergence of the United States and Japan began before the famous Bush-Koizumi relationship and will very likely continue for years after it. Undoubtedly, the deep trust and friendship between the president and prime minister compelled both governments to step up cooperation and captured the attention of the press in an unprecedented way. Yet, the leaders' relationship was as much a reflection of the closer strategic, ideational, and economic convergence of the United States and Japan in the twenty-first century as it was the cause. At the same time, the closer Washington-Tokyo relationship in recent years also suggests that alliance management cannot be done on autopilot. It requires leadership, proactive dialogue, and close strategic coordination. The alliance can easily drift without attention from the top.

Notes

1. Howard LaFranchi, "Is Japan's Support for U.S. on the Wane?" *Christian Science Monitor*, June 29, 2006, p. 2.

2. Sheryl Gay Stolberg, "Bush's Farewell to Koizumi Is Also a Reward," *New York Times*, June 29, 2006, p. A6.

3. Louisa Lim, "U.S.-Japan Relationship Questioned as Koizumi Exits," *Morning Edition*, NPR, June 29, 2006, http://www.npr.org/templates/story/story.php?storyId=5520395.

4. Office of the Press Secretary, The White House, "Fact Sheet: The Japan-U.S. Alliance of the New Century," June 29, 2006, http://www.state.gov/p/eap/rls/68464.htm.

5. Kurt Campbell and Mike O'Hanlon, *Hard Power: The New Politics of National Security* (New York: Basic Books, 2006).

6. Mark Warner, keynote speech to the Japan Society of New York, New York City, June 7, 2006, http://info.japansociety.org/site/DocServer/060607_annualdinner_warner.pdf?docID=381.

7. "A Rising China," *New York Times*, May 6, 2005, p. A26.

8. James Fallows, *Looking at the Sun* (New York: Pantheon, 1994); Wayne Sandholtz et al., *The Highest Stakes: The Economic Foundations of the Next Security System* (New York: Oxford University Press, 1992).

9. "Japan-U.S. Joint Declaration on Security," April 17, 1996, Tokyo, http://tokyo.usembassy.gov/pdfs/wwwf-mdao-joint-declaration1996.pdf.

10. Ministry of Foreign Affairs of Japan, "Japan-U.S. Summit Meeting: The Japan-U.S. Alliance of the New Century," Washington, D.C., June 29, 2006, http://www.mofa.go.jp/region/n-america/us/summit0606.html.

11. Eisuke Sakakibara, *Shihon Shugi Wo Koeta Nippon* (Tokyo: Toyo Keizai Shinpohsa, 1990).

12. Fujiwara Masahiko, *Kokka No Hinkaku* (Tokyo: Shinchosha, 2005).

13. Junichiro Koizumi, address at the Tokyo Plenary Meeting of the Trilateral Commission, April 22, 2006, p. 3, http://www.kantei.go.jp/foreign/koizumispeech/2006/04/060422.pdf.

14. Office of the Prime Minister, Government of Japan, "Kaigai Keizai Kyoryoku ni kan suru Kento Kai: Hokokusho [Study group on overseas economic cooperation: A report]," February 28, 2006, pp. 3, 7.

15. Ibid.

16. Norman J. Ornstein and Mark Schmitt, "The 1988 Election," *Foreign Affairs* 68, no. 1 (America and the World 1988/89): 44.

17. Paul Wiseman, "Profit Makes Japan 'America's No. 1 Cash Cow in Asia,'" *USA Today*, May 17, 2006, p. 1B.

18. The U.S.-Japan Business Council, "2006 Policy Statement," May 22, 2006, http://www.usjbc.org/2006PolicyStatementFinal5-5-06.pdf.